Under the Influence

Alyssa, Brent, Casey & Jake

Thank you for loving your family and leading by example.
Best Wishes.

Previous Books Authored/Edited by

Patty Jo Sawvel

Winston-Salem: Bright Star of the Future

Drugs and Controlled Substances: Information for Students
(Contributed two chapters)

Introducing Issues with Opposing Viewpoints: Water Resource Management

Introducing Issues with Opposing Viewpoints: Cheating

Issues That Concern YOU: Student Drug Testing

www.UnderTheInfluence.org

Under the Influence

The Town That Listened to Its Kids
<u>Completely Revised 2nd Edition</u>

Patty Jo Sawvel

Bailey Press
Kernersville, North Carolina

Published by Bailey Press
931-B South Main Street #215
Kernersville, NC 27284

Patty Jo Sawvel is a member of the National Speakers Association. Contact her directly to inquire about seminars, presentations, or interviews at www.UnderTheInfluence.Org or call 1-336-906-7238.

All rights reserved. No part of this book may be reproduced or transmitted in any form or by any means, electronic or mechanical, including photocopying, recording or by any information storage and retrieval system, without written permission from the author, except for the inclusion of brief quotations in a review.

Copyright © Patty Jo Sawvel, 2011, 2013
All rights reserved.

ISBN- 13: 978-0-9886354-0-1 (hardcover)
978-0-9886354-1-8 (softcover)
978-0-9886354-2-5 (eBook)
978-0-9886354-3-2 (audio book)

Copies of this book are available at:
UnderTheInfluence.org
Amazon.com
Kindle
Kernersville Chamber of Commerce

LIBRARY OF CONGRESS CATALOGING-IN-PUBLICATIONS DATA

Sawvel, Patty Jo
Under the Influence: The Town That Listened to Its Kids

978-0-9886354-0-1
1. Drugs in schools—US. 2. Youth Leadership—US. 3. Drug testing—US.
4. Investigative reporting—US. 5. Community Journalism—US.
6. Autobiography Sawvel, Patty Jo.
LCCN: 2011939114

Printed in the United States of America

Cover design - Amanda Weiss

Dedication

To all the students of Kernersville
who changed their community
by letting their voices be heard
and
to the community
that listened and created
Kernersville Cares for Kids
and
to my high school principal
Dorothy Lugar Baker
and all principals like her, who can see us
(the students) before we can see ourselves.

*10% of the net profits from the sale of this book
will be donated to a Kernersville Cares for Kids Fund
in appreciation for the education and uplifting
bestowed upon the author since 1996.*

Upon reading this book, if you find its message valuable,
please *pass it forward*. Help give kids a national voice.

www.UnderTheInfluence.org

Contents

Preface	i
Prologue	ii
Introduction	iii
Acknowledgements	iv

Book I: Under the Influence: The Town That Listened to Its Kids

1.	An Unexpected Opportunity *Lesson 1: I have a lot to learn*	1
2.	Getting Started *Lesson 2: Know your audience*	7
3.	Survey *Lesson 3: Talk to the man*	15
4.	Getting Results *Lesson 4: Accept personal responsibility*	27
5.	Community Response *Lesson 5: Let everyone be heard*	37
6.	Gathering the Facts *Lesson 6: Do your own homework*	45
7.	Publicity *Lesson 7: Take publicity personally*	57
8.	Voluntary Drug Testing *Lesson 8: Ask everyone*	61
9.	Community Meeting *Lesson 9: Know your facts*	73
10.	Meetings at Glenn and East *Lesson 10: Expect to do some things for free*	81
11.	Losing Momentum *Lesson 11: People make their own choices*	89

12.	The Press Conference *Lesson 12: No one wins alone*	93
13.	Four Teens From Two Families *Lesson 13: Dig beneath the surface*	99
14.	School Board Policy Change *Lesson 14: Look for a natural fit*	125
15.	Police Accept the Challenge *Lesson 15: Share your vision*	133
16.	Kicking Off the Project *Lesson 16: Leadership makes a difference*	139
17.	Victory *Lesson 17: Keep questioning*	145
18.	We Can't Do It *Lesson 18: Know your people*	151
19.	Finding a Better Way *Lesson 19: Find the real leaders*	155
20.	A REAL Community Organization *Lesson 20: Give real leaders real authority and real recognition*	163
21.	Kernersville Kids Lead the U.S. *Lesson 21: Good news is not always popular*	171
22.	Middle Schools Come Aboard *Lesson 22: Applaud others*	177
23.	Thirty Days of Madness *Lesson 23: Ask for help*	183
24.	KCK Gets a New President *Lesson 24: Focus on the positive*	191
25.	Letting Go *Lesson 25: Be open to new ideas*	203

| 26. | Getting a Better Grip | 209 |

Lesson 26: Positive actions plant seeds for future opportunities

| 27. | New Voices | 215 |

Lesson 27: Truth is powerful

| 28. | A Study of the Test | 225 |

Lesson 28: Test the test

| 29. | Retreat | 229 |

Lesson 29: Brainstorming builds momentum

| 30. | 10th Anniversary | 237 |

Lesson 30: Ask someone who knows

| 31. | Selling the Tickets | 245 |

Lesson 31: Keep it fun

| 32. | Community Hug | 253 |

Lesson 32: Recognize success

| 33. | The Final Lesson | 261 |

Lesson 33: There is no final lesson

| 34. | A Mountain Top Experience | 267 |

Lesson 34: Keep chasing the question

| 35. | Grand Central Station | 277 |

Lesson 35: The joy is in the journey

| 36. | Passing the Baton | 291 |

Lesson 36: Transitions take time

| 37. | The Handoff is Complete | 297 |

Lesson 37: It is okay to let go

2012 KCK Update   307

The National Picture   314

Epilogue   317

Mini-book I: A Call for Compassion—10 Tips   319
    Please read this Mini-Book first. It briefly outlines the forces that are driving the rise in teenage drug abuse. This is followed by 10 proven tips to help drug-proof young people. Key links give readers quick access to additional online help. Understanding the forces that shape today's young people give readers the power to help and not hurt an already fragile situation

Mini-book II: Parent Handbook   329
    *Misguided wisdom prevents well-intentioned parents from nurturing and protecting their young people effectively. Scientific studies in this section reveal the truth, and return to parents their place of authority in the family. Key links give readers quick access to additional online help. (**Please read Mini-book I: A Call for Compassion before beginning this section.**)*

Mini-book III: Teen Handbook   338
    *Times have changed and so has the road to adulthood. Real life stories and scientific studies help teens identify issues confronting youth and solutions that work. (**Please read Mini-book I: A Call for Compassion before beginning this section.**)*

Mini-book IV: Lessons Learned—Three Recovered Addicts   362
    Three vivid first-person accounts let readers "see for themselves" how and why some teens become addicted to drugs while still in high school. Walk the path of recovery and embrace the healing as these recovered addicts dedicate their lives to helping others. Ask: What if they'd received help earlier—maybe through a random drug testing program in their school?

Mini-book V: EVERYONE Can Help   378
    Whether you are child, adult, neighbor, single, married, leader, follower, business entity, media, higher or lower education, employer, employee—if you are alive—there is something simple and meaningful that you can do to help keep yourself, your family, your neighborhood, and your community free of drugs and underage drinking.

About the Author	385
The Book Team	386
A Reading Group Guide to *Under the Influence*	388
Online Resources/ Websites	390
Author Contact	391
Index	392

Preface

Parents want to raise children in healthy communities, and healthy communities want to bond with *all* their citizens. But, somewhere along the line, teenagers and adults often get disconnected. This happens in both the family and the community. When it happens, the likelihood of teenage drug abuse or underage drinking rises dramatically.

This real-life story, spanning 1996-2013, takes place in the pleasant town of Kernersville, North Carolina—a town proud of its award-winning parks, community festivals, and small town traditions. In 1996, the town is shocked to discover that its teenage drug problem mirrors the national average.

The hometown paper, the *Kernersville News,* becomes the forum for teens, principals, police, parents, and others to grapple with the truth. Finally, a solution is found that the teens support in record numbers.

Here is a chance to view the complex social issue of teen substance abuse through the lens of a small community. Best of all, it's an opportunity to share in its success—the success of reconnecting with our youth.

Prologue

I always thought the goal in American life was to be number one—the biggest, the fastest, the strongest, and the smartest. This certainly seemed to be important at public school because everyone is measured to the 10th, 100th, or 1000th decimal place, especially, in grade point and athletic averages.

Even in my own family—a step-family—there was intense competition and a push to "be special." These two centers of education—my family and public school—didn't do a very good job of teaching me the truth about healthy human relationships. I only learned the truth when I got involved in community journalism.

Working at the Kernersville News*—I came face-to-face with hundreds of ordinary people. They were all "e pluribus unum"—one of many. These people taught me that they were big enough, fast enough, strong enough, and smart enough to live their lives in a meaningful way and have enough left over to share with others. I had no choice but to draw the conclusion that not only is there room for everyone, there is a need for everyone.*

And yet, as powerful as this life lesson was, the community taught me an even more potent concept.

Profound change often hangs by the thread of one committed person. Though different people fill that role as time marches on, that person is always someone who cares deeply, connects with others, and is convinced that change is imminent. This book retraces the events that taught me some of the most valuable lessons of my life.

www.UnderTheInfluence.org

Introduction

Young people and adults may not see eye to eye on many issues, but according to two separate studies, both groups rate adolescent drug abuse as their number one concern.[1] One study[2] found that teens who daily spend time on social media—Facebook, Myspace, and others—are twice as likely to use marijuana as teens who don't typically spend time on such sites.

Teens who have seen pictures of kids drunk, using drugs, or passed out on these sites are four times likelier to use marijuana and three times likelier to use alcohol. Interestingly, 90 percent of polled parents do not think that teens visiting these sites will increase the likelihood of drug or alcohol abuse.

Another factor driving the rise of teenage drug abuse is the breakdown of the family unit. Studies indicate that *most* children in the U.S. are now being raised in homes with only one biological parent. This makes them ten times as likely to abuse drugs as teens living with both biological parents.[3] Add to this the easy access to unwholesome Internet sites and suggestive television, and it becomes apparent that society is creating a corrupting culture that is endangering our youth.

But let's do some possibility thinking. What if a community decided to strengthen its support net to keep youth on the drug free path? What if there was a random *voluntary* drug testing program . . . maybe in the schools because that is where young people hang out. What if the community found a way to get 80-90% of the 12-18 year olds *voluntarily* in the program? Now here is the best part: If a teen has gotten off track and fails the test, the youth receives,

- Free help
- Nothing is recorded on the teen's permanent school record
- Police are never called
- Classmates never find out—student continues sports and extracurricular

Best of all—what if this program was paid for by money confiscated from illegal drug sales! Guess what? This is not wishful thinking. This program actually exists in North Carolina. It has been operating successfully in the Winston-Salem Forsyth County Schools for 15 years. Read this book and find out why teens love it, why it really works, and how it might help your teens. And don't forget to read the mini-books at the end of the story. These are a fast track to directly helping your teen or a child you care about, today.

---

[1] 2011 National Survey of American Attitudes on Substance Abuse XVI: Teens and Parents. 2011 University of Michigan C. S. Mott Children's Hospital National Poll on Children's Health.
[2] ibid
[3] Mini-Book II: Understanding Today's Student in the back of this book.

Acknowledgements

I am greatly indebted to *The Arts Council of Winston-Salem and Forsyth County* and the *North Carolina Arts Council*. Writing a book is intimidating and many times the compelling difference between my ceasing or continuing with this project was the fact that I'd accepted grant money and given my word to the Council.

Additionally, the grant made it possible for me to work with Ed Friedenberg, formerly of the *Winston-Salem Journal*. Friedenberg, in his 70's, proved to be a seasoned writer and a gentle teacher. Like "The Horse Whisperer" for writers, Friedenberg used nearly imperceptible means to help me maintain my balance through the highs and lows of our five-year endeavor. Most admirably, when the money ran out half-way through the project, Friedenberg worked for free. More than an editor, he became my friend and my mentor.

Sadly, Friedenberg passed away on July 17, 2006, and did not live to see the completion of this book. Thankfully, his good and able friend, Carl Clarke—a retired English teacher, actor, and coach—stepped up to see me through the next five years and all the way through the final chapters! As the years passed, Clarke became so enthralled with the *Kernersville Cares for Kids* phenomena that he actually became part of the story. In 2010, Clarke coached the students in public speaking— catapulting the youth to new heights in personal growth and community leadership.

A special thanks also to my friend and editor, John Staples. He took a chance on an unpublished and unschooled writer and printed my first story in the *Kernersville News*. Under his mentorship, I was given the opportunity of a lifetime—a chance to understand how a community works.

Publisher John Owensby was immeasurably helpful. True to the proverb, "Iron sharpens iron," though we sometimes grated on each other's nerves— it was his oversight and foresight that made the community initiative and the resulting *Kernersville Cares for Kids* sustainable.

Without the trust and the blessing of Superintendent Don Martin, Principal Adolphus Coplin, and Principal Dan Piggott of the Winston-Salem/Forsyth County Schools, this project never would have gotten off the ground. They not only opened the door for me, they opened up a whole new topic of conversation in the local schools: Most students don't use illegal drugs, and they are proud to admit it.

Of course, all of this conversation was nothing but talk until Kernersville Police Chief Neal Stockton decided to pilot the *Kernersville Cares for Kids (KCK)* initiative. As the program blossomed, especially when student representatives joined the board, the Police Department remained a cornerstone to KCK's existence. Moreover, when Stockton recently retired, Chief Ken Gamble stepped right up and continued the KPD's outstanding involvement.

I'm deeply indebted to the principals at the five high and middle schools in Kernersville from 1996 and forward, to the students who were leaders on the *Kernersville Cares for Kids* Board, and to all the students they represented.

At a Kernersville Chamber of Commerce, Jim King heard about my 10-year book project and took it upon himself to help me transition from writer to publisher. In six short months, King kept me focused on the outcome by taking one step at a time—all the way to the printers! Thank you, Jim.

Additionally, my brother Roger M. Bailey stood by me through all the ups and downs of this endeavor becoming whatever he needed to be, which included editor, innovator, comforter, comrade, and friend.

I owe a special thank you to all my readers who insured that this story was accurate, complete, and helpful. These readers include, but are not limited to, Dorothy Baker, Mike Brown, Stephanie Cordick, Ann & Cliff Bridges, Dr. Don Martin, Mr. John Owensby, Chief Neal Stockton, Chief Ken Gamble, Mayor Dawn Morgan, John Staples, Bruce Boyer, Captain Doug Kiger, David Fitzpatrick, Mina Cook, Ginger Amos, Jim Hood, Dr. Wallace Baird, Bill and Barbara Moran, Heather Camp, Henrietta Barrett, Bobbie Wolfe, Porter Halyburton, Dr. Lane Anderson, Altina Layman, Bob Higgins, Linda Rozelle, Amanda Weiss, John Friedenberg, Candice Pryor, Doris Caruso, Kelly Hall, Aja Holguin, Deborah Jarrett, Cathy Rickman, Chuck and Jeanie Amboy, Dayna Fondersmith, Rebecca Hiatt, Don Sawvel, Forrest and Joyce Bailey (Thanks, Mom, for giving the manuscript one final red pencil edit. Amazingly, but not surprisingly, you caught mistakes that had slipped by everyone else.)

And finally, I'm so grateful for my husband Don and our three children for their patience, support, and sometimes thinly-veiled tolerance during this 15-year obsession.

2013 Revised Edition Acknowledgements

I am so grateful for the honest feedback from literally hundreds of people who invited me to their clubs, watched televised interviews, or attended book seminars in the 12 months since the first edition was released. Two things became clear. First, people of all ages really do care about young people and the problem of drugs and underage drinking. Secondly, readers want more *actionable tips* to help families, young people, and communities. Due to this response, readers will now find a greatly-expanded *Parent Handbook*, a new *Teen Handbook*, and *A Call For Compassion—10 Tips to Drug-proof Kids*, included as mini-books. Each mini-book contains clearly **bolded** actionable TIPS.

A special thanks to media professionals who continue to honor young people by giving them a broader voice, including television stations High Point Fox 8, Greensboro Cable 8, abcTV 45, Winston-Salem Cable 2, and Austin, Texas KXAN, and printed media including the *Kernersville News, Greensboro News & Record, Sanford Herald, Kernersville Magazine, and Charlotte Woman and more.*

I'm deeply indebted to writer and editor Bill Cissna and quilter Julie Bodford for their wonderful eyes for detail in editing the manuscript. Thanks to my son, Clif, who once again formatted this book. Lastly, I'm grateful to my family for their continued support as I travel and speak— sometimes twice a week — to tell this story.

Main Street — Kernersville, North Carolina

Though not officially designated as a Main Street USA community, Kernersville, North Carolina has all the charm of a restored and historic downtown, making it a true destination.

In 1817, Joseph Kerner, the town's namesake, purchased 1032 acres, which included an inn and store at the crossroads of downtown. The town was incorporated in 1871 and has been growing ever since. Currently the 17.4 square mile city limits has a population of 23,000. The 81.4 square mile zipcode area has a population of 53,000.

www.toknc.com

Photo taken February 2, 2013 by Patty Jo Sawvel

1

An Unexpected Opportunity

Lesson 1: I have a lot to learn

The first time I read the *Kernersville News*, I laughed—not because it was funny, but because it was deficient. Our exhausted family had just driven 2,000 miles to move from Dewey, Arizona, to Kernersville, North Carolina, and we wanted something fun to do. Unfortunately, this newspaper, in the heart of three big cities—Greensboro, High Point, and Winston-Salem—offered few options besides church activities or bowling.

I ended up spending another 50 cents to buy a "real" newspaper. It was either the *Greensboro News & Record*, or the *Winston-Salem Journal*—I can't remember. Both had plenty of local arts and entertainment and did a respectable job reporting the news.

As I read the *Kernersville News* over the coming weeks—mainly the Tuesday edition because it was free—I wondered how this little newspaper survived. Front page news featured newly appointed ministers, community volunteers, or cute little children. This is the stuff that real newspapers bury.

And it wasn't as though the real news was hidden elsewhere in the paper. The deeper I dug, the softer it got. The inside was stuffed with pictures of children playing school sports or people preparing church socials or "do-gooders" doing good. All of this was woven around local weddings, obituaries, politics, business, and church news.

There was one good page of the paper though—the Police Reports. This actually contributed to our family bonding. One of our children would grab the paper and read the terrible crime reports out loud. We giggled when we learned that two flower pots were stolen. A similar thing happened to us when we lived in our home state in Michigan, but it never made the news.

Other serious offenses included a man charged with damaging a cash register with a pool stick, a drunken man arrested while sleeping in a parked car, a woman charged with possession of two marijuana cigarettes, and a dog that bit a boy on a bike. These reports, in 1995, gave our family a sense of security.

After weeks of reading the paper, I finally figured out that the *Kernersville News* wasn't a newspaper at all. Instead, it was a "glorified" family newsletter—a sort of grandma's scrapbook. To get the real news, I'd have to buy a real newspaper.

Little did I know that a few months later, I would be working for this journal. That having been said, I must admit that just as the *Kernersville News* was not a real newspaper, I was not a real journalist. I was an unpublished college drop-out Yankee who obviously did not understand Southern culture or community journalism.

For as much as I mocked the *Kernersville News* in the confines of my own home, the thought of asking them to publish one of my stories was overwhelmingly intimidating. And yet, it was a commitment I'd made to myself, my family, and John McCollister.

McCollister, a published writer, led a two-hour seminar in Winston-Salem on "How to Get Published." It was a lifelong dream of mine, so, shortly after our arrival, my husband, Don, paid the $20 fee and I went to class.

At the end of the day, McCollister gave us a homework assignment. Write a story about something you know about and submit it to your local paper. Tip: The smaller the paper the better! Probably the newspaper will print it and then you will be published. Once you have a byline, the sky is the limit!

For my story, I wrote about a polymer science project that I presented to my son's fifth-grade class. I kept myself out of the story and simply highlighted the teacher, the children, and the stringy goo they made.

The very next day—before my enthusiasm cooled—I took the story to Editor John Staples. Thankfully, Staples is one of the least intimidating people I've ever met. He's pudgy, balding, bespectacled, and distracted. All my fears evaporated when he smiled, shook my hand, and immediately accepted the story. Then he asked if I had a picture to go with copy.

"People like to see what they are reading about," Staples said.

I told him that I didn't have a picture, but I was willing to get one. He told me to wait a minute. He ran upstairs, got a camera, and lent it to me.

Driving to school, I pondered his sense of trust. He had just given me a camera, knowing full well by my Michigan accent that I wasn't from around here. Equally important, he gave me a generous serving of his time. My only negative reaction was that he didn't seem to care about how "good" my story was—this first baby story that I spent hours perfecting. But all things considered, he was about to give me the best gift of all—my first byline.

By the time I arrived back at the office with the pictures, Staples had read the story more carefully. He said he really enjoyed it. On the spot, he offered me a part-time job. The pay was pathetic, only $7 per hour. I don't think I'd worked for such meager wages since I was a teenager and now I was 37. But, I accepted because the opportunity was much more valuable than the money.

Something else happened. I suddenly found myself intrigued by this newspaper. What was its secret? Why did people read this newspaper? Did everybody buy two different newspapers? And, how did the *Kernersville News* survive for 57 years?

As those questions simmered on the backburner, Staples secretly enrolled me in Journalism 101. My first assignment was to interview a retired school teacher. My story took up half-a-page in the newspaper and included some of the minutest details of her 89 years of life.

Staples—a gentle teacher—ignored the excessive length and the flaws and merely said, "Good story. Next time you might try to use a couple quotes."

With each successive story, he focused on the positives and offered just one or two tips. So when he called me into the office in April of 1996—a mere four months after we met—I was eager to go. Little did I know that he would offer me the assignment of a lifetime!

He and Publisher John Owensby wanted to win the Community Service Award, and they wanted me to tackle the project.

The Community Service Award is the highest award of the North Carolina Press Association (NCPA). To win the award, the journalist has to know the community, which obviously I did not, and to know which issues are of local importance. Then, stories are written to move the readers to resolve the issue. In this way, the newspaper *serves its community.*

Obviously, I didn't have the best qualifications for the job, but Staples said that I wrote with *heart,* and heart is the one thing that can't be taught. The rest I could learn as I went.

In reality, the *News* really didn't have much of a choice. The best writers on staff were needed to write the daily news and they didn't have time for extra projects. I, on the other hand, wasn't even a staff member. I was a stringer—a call me when you need me, part-time journalist. I was chosen because I was there.

Large daily papers, on the other hand, use their best reporters or team of reporters. So, the Press Association levels the playing field by creating several divisions. The *Kernersville News* competes in the non-daily division as it publishes three days a week.

Initially, I was more interested in winning a prize and proving that I could write than I was in solving a problem for a community that I didn't really know.

But then, Staples gave me a handwritten list that he and Owensby had brainstormed. It was titled <u>Guns, Drugs & Crime—How Safe is Kernersville?</u> They isolated six possible problems that were susceptible to a sense of urgency: concealed weapons, violent crime review, drugs in general, drugs in the schools, domestic violence as it relates to drugs and guns, and general arms.

Only one topic caught my attention—drugs in the schools. I immediately knew that researching this would be my singular chance to answer questions that had gnawed at me for years.

I cared about this problem because it affected my life. Even though I never experimented with drugs, half of my eight siblings used drugs. It wasn't a matter of teens goofing off and having a good time. It was a real problem that for most of them started in high school, but persisted into adulthood. Two of them, a sister and a stepbrother, broke free fairly early in their lives. However, for two others the problem persists. What hurt me most was watching them hurt their children.

Probably saddest of all was my sister, Diane. She continued to abuse drugs and alcohol even after she became the mother of three children. I was especially close to her oldest child Sara because I lived with them right after high school. Years later, it broke my heart when Sara—an extremely bright 12-year-old—was going to fail sixth grade because of the instability of her home life. So I decided to rescue her.

4   UNDER THE INFLUENCE

(photo reprinted with permission from *Kernersville News*)

John Ed Staples, editor of the *Kernersville News,* (1972-2002) gave Patty Jo Sawvel her start as a "stringer" newspaper reporter in 1995. Known as a man who organized his work by "piles" not "files", Staples was amazingly adept at finding what he needed.

Staples soon became Sawvel's first mentor in Kernersville and he continues to guide this Michigander in Southern social protocol and community journalism.

http://www.kernersvillenews.com

After much persuasion, Diane agreed to let Sara live with our family. My husband and I paid all of Sara's expenses, and our family expanded from three children, ages five, three, and one—to four children.

Sara wanted to come because she always wanted to have a father, and she thought that moving in with us would make her life better. It did get better for a while. Her new school in Genesee, Michigan—the school I graduated from—reversed the failing and allowed her to start 7th grade.

Sara followed our family routine and enjoyed regular homework time, meals, recreation and worship. She helped around the house and played well with the other children. She even became an honor roll student.

But she missed her mom, her brothers, and her life. She wanted to go home and didn't know how to ask. So, she broke some rules that carried the consequence of being sent home.

Before she left, I asked, "Sara, why do you want to go home? We gave you everything. We cared for you. We showed you that you could do better. We tried to help you."

She said, "I know. But I didn't want you to do it. I want my mom to do it."

It was a humbling lesson. I realized that the people and the problem of substance abuse are extremely complex. Families aren't like Legos. A child can't be snapped off from an unhealthy family and connected to a new one. Breaking connections—especially with parents—is extremely painful and causes a whole new set of problems.

Reviewing my own childhood, I also realized that setting a good example was not enough to prevent substance abuse. My father and step-mother didn't use drugs and I never ever saw them drunk. They even went a step further and let us know that substance abuse of any kind—even tobacco—was not allowed in our family. And yet, about half the children ended up abusing drugs and alcohol.

So now, as the mother of three children, ages 11, 13, and 15, I desperately wanted to know: *Why* do some teenagers use drugs when others—even their siblings—choose to stay drug free? Finding the answer to that question became more valuable to me than prizes or paycheck.

"Happiness is the net result of making yourself useful."

— The late Dot Stone, beloved and extremely useful Kernersville resident.

Route 66 – Kernersville, N.C. in 2013

Less than three miles from downtown Kernersville, cows grace a roadside farm that borders Route 66. Scattered around town are working farms that grow tobacco, corn, soybeans, and other crops.

Proceeding north of this farm towards downtown, Route 66 crosses over I-40 and Business-40 which can quickly transport travelers east to Greensboro and the Piedmont Triad Airport or west to downtown Winston-Salem.

Moving in the opposite direction on Route 66, a quick hop onto Highway 311 lands visitors in High Point, home to the largest furniture market trade show in the world.

All of these destinations are less than 15 minutes from the homestead of these docile cows.

www.discoverKernersville.com

2
Getting Started

Lesson 2: Know your audience

To move the community to action, I would have to talk their language. But as I've already confessed, I didn't know their language. The only thing I knew was that this community saw itself as caring, wholesome, and values-oriented.

Based on these observations, one thing was certain: People in Kernersville were not going to be *moved* by national statistics. Like any small town with a healthy self-esteem, Kernersville feels it is *better than average* in things that count. Therefore, national averages do not apply.

But children—Kernersville would listen to the voices of its children. If the community could see drugs and schools the way their children saw them, that could make a difference. Using the children's voices would also solve the problem of the language barrier.

I chose four boys attending Kernersville's two high schools, East Forsyth and Robert B. Glenn High School, to start the conversation with the community. These students lived with both biological parents and appeared to be comfortably nestled in middle-income families. Each family seemed to approximate the standard of the local community.

On June 8, 1996, the new "Drugs in Schools" series was kicked off with one student interview and a survey of over 1,700 high school students in Kernersville. As the survey process became a story in itself, the student interviews will be considered first.

The first boy to be featured on the front-page was named "Mike." He was a freshman at East Forsyth, 14 years old, and eager to share his insights.

I'd known Mike's family for about a year. His parents and I talked often. And while we were friendly with each other, Mike and I never talked at length.

I did watch him. Mike was smart. Around his friends, he spoke a little faster and laughed a little louder than the others—until all the attention was on him. Mike wooed his peers with flashing smiles and full-body gestures. But he could cut it off as easily as he could turn it on. Sometimes this happened when his parents walked into the room. He would dry up. Suddenly, Mike could become as inanimate and immovable as a block of ice.

Mike knew what he wanted. His goals centered on freedom. His three dominant desires were to get his driver's license and car as soon as he turned 16, graduate from high school with his class, and move out of his parents' house.

One question I did not ask was if Mike ever experimented with drugs. Years later, Mike told me that he had tried marijuana once, prior to the interview. At the bus stop, a younger boy offered him a joint. He was curious, smoked it, felt no effect, and left drugs alone.

Mike said he saw drugs at school about twice a week in spite of the sheriff department's regular drug-dog searches. He believed that students could outsmart the law by keeping drugs out of their cars and lockers. Teens who knew what they were doing kept their drugs close to their bodies. If necessary, the students could put their drugs in their underwear. The police would not search a student there.

He said, "They only search certain places, like your cars and lockers. And if they search a kid . . . well, there's certain places they won't search you."

Mike thought it was pretty easy for students to buy drugs at his school. The most common drug, he said, was pot. It sold in "nickel bags," $5 for a plastic pouch. He even said that some kids were passing fake drugs, selling parsley for pot, and plain paper squares for acid.

Asked how many students he believed were doing drugs at his school, Mike said, "In my school, 80% of the kids, even kids who don't look like it. A lot of the students (users) dress neatly, tuck in their shirts and have money. Kids at my school aren't poor, but as soon as their parents drop them off . . . well, they change. Little preppy girls tell me they've been busted several times. And then there's the wiggers."

Now, I had never heard the term "wigger" and neither had anyone back at the office, but Mike, a proud African-American, was happy to tell me. "A wigger is a white nigger. You know, a white guy trying to act black with baggy clothes and the way he talks. A lot of those guys use drugs."

The students that sell drugs, he said, fit no stereotypes. All kinds of kids sell them: white, black, Mexican, rich, poor, and smart.

In fact, a local judge had snagged a smart kid who was on his way to college with a full paid scholarship. Before graduation, he was caught selling drugs. He hollowed out a large book to hide his drugs. When asked why he did it, he gave two reasons—for the money and the excitement.

For all the drugs supposedly floating around in this school, Mike had only seen kids smoking pot at school three times. To me, this didn't add up. However, Mike had a believable explanation: "Students talk about drugs a lot. It's normal to use drugs. Students think it is cool, but most of them use drugs at home or at parties. If they do use drugs at school, they don't broadcast it because that would draw attention. So they just do it and get it done with . . . not in crowds."

Mike claims he can tell when students are "high" at school. He believes that everyone can tell. He recounted how the very day of our interview a girl came into class so high she could barely stand up.

When I asked how the teacher responded, he said, "They can't do anything to you, unless you have drugs on you. She just says she is sick and they can't bother her. And she had on sunglasses. Most of our teachers allow us to wear hats and sunglasses to class. So as long as you are quiet, the teacher doesn't bother you. Most of the kids know the routine."

I wondered if, for some kids, this sacred institution of high school has been reduced to a simple game of cat and mouse.

I ran into Mike a few years later, just days before he turned 19. I was embarrassed that he recognized me first. Of course, he had the advantage. I hadn't changed much in crossing the line from 30's to 40's. But Mike had spent the last five years in that magical age of transformation. His scrawny frame was now strapped with muscle. His shoulders were broad and his thighs were sturdy. Gone was the round-faced lad. This boy had become a man.

That realization sparked a question. What kind of man was he? Had the boy so impatient to grow up met his goals? Did he like his car? Was high school graduation fun? Where was he living? What was he doing?

Mike and I had lunch. It was delightful to find that he had not outgrown his open and honest nature. Mike was quick to admit that life had not gone according to his plan. As a matter of fact, he had met *none* of his goals. At age 19, he had yet to have his first driver's license. He didn't own a car. He ran away from home and dropped out of school when he was 16. And at the moment, he was back living with his parents.

What went wrong? When Mike was 15, his family moved 20 miles away to a rural subdivision. Although he was still in the Winston-Salem/Forsyth County school district, as a non-driver he had to ride the bus to the neighborhood high school. He hated changing schools. "That affected me big time. It was the worst time of my life. It was a snap decision by my dad. When he says something, that's it, no discussion."

In his new neighborhood, Mike met a boy his age and they became fast friends. He and his "friend" shared their troubles and found a common solution—zoning out on pot. A couple of times they tried some other drugs such as cocaine and acid.

Mike explained why he felt the family move caused his life to spin out of control: "I was with the kids at East Forsyth my whole time I was growing up," he lamented. "At East Forsyth, I hung out with kids that didn't do drugs. So I didn't do drugs. I hated my new school and I wanted to go back to my old school. So when I was 16, I ran away from home."

Mike's life began to take on a predictable pattern—a strange loop. For months at a time, he would run away, "party," decide to make a change, go back home, enroll in school, get mad at his dad and run away. It was like the Monopoly game, except this was Mike's life. He kept getting a card that says "Return home. Do not pass Go. Do not collect any graduation credits."

Whether at home or on the run, Mike smoked marijuana nearly every day. To him, it seemed to be the only way he could "cope" with life. During the "party" phase, he would smoke several blunts a day with each cigar-like blunt being the equivalent of six marijuana cigarettes. While he was at home, he did better. He secretly smoked one blunt a day.

As I listened to Mike talk for over an hour, two issues began to surface. Foremost was his anger with his dad. Secondly, he didn't seem to know what he wanted from his life.

> *"My dad sees me as a bad kid always causing problems. But I'm a kid trying to make a little money and stay out of trouble, and I have to listen to his mouth. The only thing I hear from him is what I'm doing wrong."*
> —Mike, teenage drug abuser

According to Mike, his dad bullied him with abusive threats like, "Do you want me to come over there and put your face through the wall?" "You get smart with me and I'll go outside and get the baseball bat."

Mike shook his head and said, "Maybe it makes him feel good to have fear from his son. I can't stand him."

Mike called his mom an "object hitter." She picked up nearby items, such as a hairbrush, or shoe and whacked her kids across the arm or back. However, Mike does not hate his mother. He smiles and speaks fondly of her. "She cares about me and I can sweet talk my mom."

Earlier in his life, Mike fantasized about killing his father and getting him out of the way. Another favorite daydream was that his parents would get a divorce. "Then I would live with my mother and he would have to pay child support. He would hate that."

As much as Mike hated his dad, it was difficult to keep his dad out of the conversation. I wanted to hear about Mike, yet it seemed that in Mike's mind, every problem he had was directly linked to his father.

For example: Mike would decide to return home to enroll in school. Everything would go fine for a while as Mike attended school and followed the family rules.

"Then," Mike exploded, "something would happen. My dad does it every time! He'll do something so that I can't go to school because I can't stand being around him. And if I'm not at home, then I'm not going to keep going to school."

Next to "my dad," the most common phrase Mike used was "I dunno." In our brief time together, he "didn't know" anything about himself or his future.

Then I asked, "What did you do to manage your anger when you were 10, 11 or 12 years old, before you started smoking pot?"

"I dunno. I just did what my dad said and mumbled under my breath. You can't do anything when you are that young. My dad is big. Just about anything I said I could get hit for."

"Mike, right now you're 19. In four or five years you'll probably settle down, get married and have children. What are you going to tell your kids about drugs?"

"I dunno. It depends on who I marry. If I marry the girl I'd like to marry, I'd have to straighten up my life. I'd have to quit doing drugs and do a 180-degree turnaround. But, if I don't marry her, I'm going to let my kids smoke pot. I'll sit down and talk with them about it."

"What do you want out of life for yourself?"

"I dunno. I don't want to be broke. I want to live in my own home. I want to have my own things. I don't want to have to depend on other people for everything."

"Do you ever think that you might be dependent on pot?"

"I dunno. No. That would really bother me to think that I was dependent. Pot is the least addictive drug. It is just a little voice in your head that tells you, you need it. But that is just your weakness. It is just your own willpower. I have gone without smoking and I did fine."

*   *   *

Three days later, the second boy's interview was printed. The *Tuesday News,* as this edition of the *Kernersville News* is called, is free and home delivered. It is the preferred edition for advertisers and writers because 19,000 people have to pick it up just to get it out of their driveway. Again taking the headline, the second student story alerted the community that a "Drugs in Schools" series had begun.

"Steve" was 16 years old and attended Glenn High School. He was an affable young man. With his blonde hair, blue eyes, and handsome build, he reminded me of a living Ken doll. But unlike a lifeless toy, Steve was always on the go—mentally and physically. Like many teens, Steve stayed busy. He went to school, worked part-time, toyed with computers, and rode his bike.

Perhaps his bicycle riding best illustrates his tenacity. One mid-summer day, I saw Steve after he'd ridden about 20 miles under a cloudless sky. It must have been 90-95 degrees outside. After accepting some water, he told me about the tough street terrain he had just conquered. I was impressed. He just smiled really big and said, "I'm a natural." He wasn't bragging. He just had a great sense of self-esteem and loved riding up and down the hills and curves. After our chat, he was off to do another 20 miles before reaching home.

Steve's family was very supportive. When he began bike riding, the whole family took up the hobby. Though he enjoyed riding more than the rest of his family, it was not unusual for family vacations to include a day or two of bike riding. When I saw Steve with his family at home or in public, there were always plenty of hugs, laughing, and affection among them. Also, Steve and his older brother were very close.

Mentally, Steve was equally tenacious. He had scored very well on the PSAT and had hopes of going to a four-year college to study computers or marine biology.

The *Tuesday News* story began with Steve's response to certain adults in the community. He was addressing those who refused to believe there were drugs in the schools in Kernersville. "*They* must be smoking something," he said.

Steve claimed that he saw classmates smoking pot in the bathrooms during class time and in their cars on school property at Glenn High School. He saw loose marijuana in clear plastic bags and blunts. He explained, "A blunt is a hollowed out cigar filled with pot."

He also saw marijuana in gym class. That was surprising. How could a student see pot in gym class when a teacher was present?

"Easy," said Steve, "there are a lot of kids in class and the teacher can only be in one group at a time. As a matter of fact, the first time I was ever offered drugs was in gym class. A kid showed me it and asked me if I wanted any."

He believed there were mainly two different types of teenagers that used drugs. He said, "The A-type is the burnout. They look like they take drugs. The B-type is the preppy, rich kid. These kids are good-looking and smart. And I know some athletes that use drugs."

> Is it easier to get drugs at work or at school? As absurd as it sounds, Steve said, *"At school. Drugs aren't allowed at work!"*
>
> "Well drugs aren't allowed at school either!"
>
> *"Yeah, but it's different at work. There aren't any drugs there. At work you have to take a drug test (urinalysis) just to get hired and then I hear they give random tests after that."*
>
> —Steve, age 16

Like Mike, Steve did not think the drug-dogs were very effective.

"The way I see it," he explained, "dogs and drugs are like cops and speeding. When the kids see the dogs, they have a brief "heart attack" so they may slow down. But when the dogs are gone they speed up again."

Steve believed that about 50% of the students at his school used drugs. Those who used drugs mainly used them some place other than school. Then he added this insight, "Personally, I think alcohol is even a bigger problem because a lot of families have it around so it's easy to get and it's free."

In a hit-or-miss fashion, I kept up with Steve and his family over the next five years. About a year before he graduated from high school, his family began to break apart. His mother was feeling trapped. About 20 years earlier, she became pregnant when she and Steve's dad were using drugs and dating. Wanting to do "the right thing," they married quickly.

They stopped using drugs, became religious, and by most accounts had become a model family. But she kept looking back, wondering what she'd missed, and what was left for her now. So at Steve's graduation, though both parents attended, they did not sit together. Shortly after graduation, "when the kids were raised," his mom divorced his dad. His dad moved out of state, and his mom moved on to a new relationship.

Steve was hurt terribly. The final blow, though, was when Steve's older brother married Steve's girlfriend.

Steve never did complete the application for a four-year college. Over the years, he has been in and out of the community college. I don't believe he ever completed a full semester. After that, his work life took on an erratic pattern. I have no reason to believe he got involved in drugs. He just got lost.

*   *   *

Two days later, the Thursday newspaper featured the final two student interviews. Both of these boys attended East Forsyth High School. Neither of them volunteered anything extra about drugs, but each answered my questions. "Tommy" is a skater. He loves to take his skateboard over curbs, down stairs and up giant half-pipes. He and his dad built a huge ramp in his backyard. He does very well at keeping his balance. His father is a business owner and Tommy works in his father's store to earn spending money.

He said he saw drugs "about two or three times a week . . . mainly marijuana . . . a nickel bag." He believed that about 40% of the students were using drugs. He based this on "pro-drug" conversations at school. He said it was common to hear kids say, "I'm going to go home and smoke some weed."

What kind of kids was he talking about?

"Most are people with money. They are good kids . . . well dressed . . . preps."

What about buying and selling drugs at school? Tommy had seen this often.

How do students feel about drug users? "If the kids use weed, it is no big deal. But if a kid uses crack, the others really think they're cool."

> *"They pass it quickly. They do it on the bus and I see them do it a lot in front of the lockers. We have these places where there are lockers on both sides of the walls and they pass each other and exchange the money and the drugs."* —Tommy

Finally, I asked Tommy my favorite question. I explained that in an informal survey of a few civic leaders and law enforcement officers, one official was adamant that the kids would not "dare" to bring drugs to school. He admitted there were teens with drugs, but *not* at school. So I asked Tommy how he would respond to this guy.

He smiled and said, "I would say, 'Yeah there is!'"

Tommy graduated though he never particularly liked school. Nonetheless, he realized the value of getting occupational training and commuted to the community college for two years while living at home. At age 20, he got married and, as far as I know, he has never used drugs.

"Mark" was a friend of Tommy's. I had only seen him a few times. School came very easily for him. He also did skateboarding for a hobby. Like Tommy, he was tall and thin and wore a conventional over-the-ears haircut.

To Mark, I asked the last question first, but broadened it a bit. "What would your response be if the adult community said that there was *not* a drug problem in Kernersville's high schools?"

"I would laugh."

Mark claimed he saw marijuana at school about three times a week. "I've seen kids smoking joints in the bathroom. And once I walked in and it was all smoky in there and there were a bunch of ashes in the soap dispenser. And then, in my French class, a student brought in his bong pipe (a water pipe often used to smoke marijuana).

And right during class he had it inside his desk and he cleaned it and filled it with herb and then asked to go to the bathroom. He came back smelling like pot."

"Aren't students at school afraid of getting caught?"

"I think when they get caught, they just get written up."

"What kind of teenagers do you believe take drugs?"

> *"All kinds of kids use drugs. They consider it normal. They say, 'why not?' It is not just the unhappy kids. Normal kids do drugs."* —Mark

Mark said it was easy to buy drugs at his high school. He told about a new pupil who came into orchestra class. "He just said to the class, 'Does anyone in here do drugs?' Then he made arrangements with a girl for him to get some."

Mark graduated from high school with a scholarship to a local university. He chose to live at home while going to school. The last time I checked, Mark had completed his second year and was on track to complete his degree. Mark plans to marry his high school sweetheart shortly after graduation.

> *How does a community grapple with the fact that in a randomly selected American classroom with 36 students, an average of 13 students use drugs and one student is or will become an addict?*

> **The number one reason** people move beyond experimentation and into patterns of substance abuse is that people are struggling with *relationships*. They are having problems making *positive connections* with family and friends and they have *unresolved conflicts*.

www.UnderTheInfluence.org

3

Survey

Lesson 3: Talk to the man

Three months before interviewing the four boys, I was searching for a way to capture the student body's perception on drugs, without interviewing 2000-plus individuals.

I remembered taking a written survey on dreams when I was in high school. I still remember some of the questions. Do you mainly dream in color or black and white? Do you ever dream that you are falling? What about flying? Do you ever feel like you are floating just before you wake up?

The process was over in less than 15 minutes. But the students talked about it for weeks. We did our own "research" and quizzed our friends. Some of us went home and surveyed our families. We never did find out the "answers" to the survey, but we surely had fun with the questions.

Therefore, a student survey seemed like the method of choice to gather drug-use statistics at the two high schools in Kernersville. Unfortunately, the high school principals did not think so.

First, I called Adolphus Coplin, the principal at Glenn High School. Our telephone conversation went something like this:

"Mr. Coplin. Hi. I'm Patty Jo Sawvel with the *Kernersville News*. I'm doing a series of stories on drugs in the schools, and I would like to survey your students. We will pay for the surveys and it should take only about 10 or 15 minutes for your students to complete the 10 questions. I was wondering . . ."

"How many of my students did you want to survey?"

"Well, all of them if I could."

"Ms. Sawvel, it is difficult to get all the students together for something like that. Is this something you want to do just at Glenn, or is this something you are planning to do at all the high schools?" he asked.

"Well, you know the *Kernersville News* is a Kernersville paper, so we are really only interested in the two high schools in Kernersville."

"Uh huh. And if we did the survey, what would you do with the results?"

"We want to print the students' responses in the newspaper," I explained, "so that parents and other people in the community can hear what the students are saying and then they will be moved to take action."

"You want to do what? (pause) You're going to move the community to take action? Uh-huh. Well, Ms. Sawvel, that is not what has happened in the past. Whenever we have a gun on campus or a student arrested for selling drugs, the newspaper comes in here for one day, writes a big headline and then we never see them again. Newspapers are interested in selling newspapers, not in solving the problems at school."

"Well, I can't speak for what has happened in the past, but I know for a fact that that won't happen this time, because I'm personally writing the stories."

"Ms. Sawvel, I've been the principal of this school for 10 years, and I am familiar with how newspapers operate," Coplin countered.

"I'm sure you're right that sometimes newspapers are only interested in selling a story. But in this case, we are trying to do something bigger. The *Kernersville News* is trying to win the Community Service Award. To do that, we *have* to stick with this problem until the community decides what to do about it. So I can assure you that we are not just looking for a headline. We are in it for the long haul."

He chuckled at my persistence. Principal Coplin said, "Ms. Sawvel, I'm not interested in you winning the Community Service Award. I have got a school to run. And I can tell you right now what the community wants to do about the drug problem. They want the schools to solve the problem."

"You're probably right, but that is because they don't really understand the problem. No one wants drugs in the schools."

"Who says drugs are only in the schools? Why are you picking on the schools?"

"We're not trying to pick on the schools. We are trying to help the schools by helping the community to see what the schools are dealing with. We are trying to understand clearly the drug problem from the students' point of view. If we can do that, then we can help the community solve the problem."

"But why do you want to write on something negative? We have a lot of good things happening here at Glenn. Why don't you try writing about the good things our kids are doing?"

"Actually, Mr. Coplin, I am known as a 'good news' writer. If you've read my stories you will see that I always try to look for the positives. I really think we can make a difference here."

"Well, Ms. Sawvel, even if I wanted to, I could not allow you to survey my students without the superintendent's permission."

"As principal, you can't authorize a 15-minute survey?"

"No. We can't just go doing surveys. Our time here is supposed to be spent teaching these students."

"That's true... Well, if the superintendent says it's ok, can we do the survey?"

"He's the superintendent. If he says to do it, we'll do it."

Coplin's casual agreement to participate in the survey, with the superintendent's blessing, led me to believe that the blessing would be elusive. Instead of calling the superintendent, I hoped for a more favorable response by calling the other high school principal.

The second conversation was much shorter. East Forsyth's Principal Judy Grissom was not interested in allowing the *Kernersville News* to survey her students.

period. She gave me little explanation. She raised few questions. Unlike Mr. Coplin, she gave me no clues on how to proceed.

Undeterred, I went to see Superintendent Don Martin. As I entered the room, he left his desk and joined me on the upholstered furniture where we faced each other. He gave me his full attention.

He was familiar with the *Kernersville News*, perhaps more so than I.

"How long have you lived in Kernersville?" he asked.

"Almost a year now," I replied. "I love it. We're originally from Michigan and spent a couple years in Arizona, but this feels like home. The friendly, small town atmosphere is just what we were looking for."

We talked a few more minutes.

Then he asked, "How long have you worked for the *Kernersville News*?"

"Several months. I mainly write about the schools. I don't know if you saw my story on Mr. VanDerWerken's fifth-grade class at Union Cross Elementary. They made a polymer for science class, and I did a story on that. (I did not tell him that this was my very first newspaper story, that I brought the polymer project to the class, and that I contributed the story to the paper.) A couple months ago, I did a story on Emma Orr Nelson. She spent over 44 years in elementary school education and now she is 89 years old and still going strong. (That was my first assigned story as a free-lance reporter.) And I have always been very involved in the schools as a volunteer."

"Newspapers can do a lot to support the schools. The *Kernersville News* does an especially good job with covering sports and special events at the school. What was it you wanted to see me about today?"

"Well, Dr. Martin, I believe that drugs create a real challenge for students today and a lot of people don't really understand the pressure kids are under. I want to let the community know about drugs in the local schools so people can help. Probably the most powerful way to do that is to let the community hear what the students have to say. So, I would like to do a drug survey at Glenn and East. It would only have about 10 questions, and we would pay for the survey."

"We get a lot of requests for surveys."

"You do?"

"Oh, yes. Researchers want to survey students on all types of things. And just as a matter of time, we can't let everyone who asks do a survey. You know, Bowman Gray Medical School does a scientific survey of our students and their perceptions of drug use. Would it be possible for you to use that data?"

"Can I get the results for just the two high schools in Kernersville?"

"No. We never break the data out for individual schools."

"Well, the problem is this. Kernersville prides itself on being a nice little town. And the people of Kernersville don't believe that their kids have the same problems as the inner city kids of Winston-Salem. So if I printed statistics with all ten high schools lumped together it would probably have no impact. But if I could survey their kids at their schools, it could wake them up."

"What are you hoping for by doing all of this?"

"Well, we're hoping that by hearing the voices of their own children, the community will realize that drugs are a problem everywhere—even in Kernersville. We are hoping that the community of Kernersville will decide to accept some responsibility in trying to solve the problem."

"Well, I do believe that this is a problem the schools cannot solve by themselves," agreed Martin. "To really solve the drug problem, parents, businesses, and the schools will all have to cooperate. Have you talked with the principals at the high schools?"

"I talked to Mr. Coplin at Glenn and he was a little hesitant, but he did say that if I had your permission, he would do it."

"Did he say why he was hesitant?"

"He said that in his experience, newspapers aren't interested in helping the schools, they are interested in sensationalizing bad news stories and selling newspapers. But I told him this was different. We are interested in staying with this topic until we have moved the community to action."

Supporting Mr. Coplin, Martin said, "Well, I can understand his concerns. I've been misquoted and even misrepresented in the newspaper myself. It does seem like newspapers have a tendency to go after the negative stories, and sometimes they don't get the facts right. They may expose a problem and actually make it worse, and they usually don't help to find a solution. It can end up just creating more of a mess for the principals to clean up."

"Well, I explained to Mr. Coplin that our goal is to stay with this until the community decides what to do about the problem."

"Patty, the problem is that you are just one reporter. You might have good intentions and then get called off this story and asked to do something else. Even if you intend to stick with this, the newspaper may not."

"That's a good point," I conceded, "but actually, we are doing this whole project so that we can win the Community Service Award. To win the award, we have no choice but to stick with the problem. If you have ever been in Mr. Owensby's office and have seen all his medals and trophies for running, then you know that when he decides to win something, he doesn't give up."

Martin leaned back, took a deep breath and thought for a moment. Perhaps he was recalling the publisher's office. As you walk through the doorway of Owensby's office, immediately to the right is a five-shelf glass trophy case. It contains no less than 30 medals. Most of them are First Place running awards. Around the office are six trophies, along with other plaques and posters. Directly on the back wall is a large print of his alma mater, Guilford College. Not far from that is a portrait of Owensby, his wife and three children. Just to one side of that is his master's degree from the University of North Carolina at Greensboro.

"Well," said Martin, "I think the Kernersville community needs to know the truth about students and drugs. I think the principal's main concern is having the problem exposed and then dropped."

"And I can understand that. It is like getting a physical. Most of us don't like to get undressed in front of an audience, but we will get undressed for a doctor, because we know he wants to help us. If the schools will allow us to expose the drug problem so the community can really see it, then we will commit to staying with this problem until the community decides what to do about it."

"Ok. We'll do the surveys."

"Great! Can you make that decision? Don't you have to ask the school board or something?"

"I'll take care of it. Just let me read over the survey before it is printed. By the way, who is going to tabulate all the data?"

"I guess the *Kernersville News* staff will do that."

"We have over 2000 students in Kernersville at the two high schools. That would be a huge undertaking. You might suggest to Mr. Owensby that we do that for you here at the central office. We are equipped to do it, and it would save you a lot of time."

"Ok. I'll talk with him and we'll get you a copy of the survey as soon as it is ready. Thanks."

Though I was ecstatic that he approved the survey idea, I was suspicious of his offer to tally up the survey results. Would the Winston-Salem Forsyth County School system really be unbiased when reporting the results?

I discussed my concerns with Owensby. He was delighted that the school system would save him the expense of processing the surveys. He believed that as long as we ended up with the surveys, we could always double-check them. He seemed to have full faith and confidence in Martin.

Years later, I learned that my fears were unfounded. As a physics major, Martin has an innate appetite for problem solving. For instance, when he found out the job prospects were lousy for his major in the 1970s, he enrolled in Duke University's Master of Art and Teaching program. Duke found him a teaching job at Wilkes Central High School. At this school, he realized that science, math and English needed to be more integrated. A little ahead of his time, he integrated these subjects in his math and science classes.

Glenn High School after renovation. http://www.wsfcs.k12.nc.us/ghs

Dr. Don Martin, Jr., Superintendent Winston-Salem Forsyth County Schools

(1994-2013) Named 2011 Superintendent of the year for N.C. Martin oversees 53,000 students and 7,800 employees.

Dr. Martin allowed the *Kernersville News* to survey 1,707 local high school students even though the principals were hesitant to comply.

"I think the Kernersville community needs to know the truth about students and drugs. I think the principal's main concern is having the problem exposed and then dropped . . . We'll do the surveys." Dr. Don Martin, Jr.

www.http://wsfcs.k12.nc.us

In 1974-75, there was an energy shortage. He initiated a classroom project to compare the current 300-watt silver-bottomed-bulbs with energy efficient fluorescent bulbs. The students discovered that fluorescent lights were 75 percent cheaper to burn and delivered more candlepower. Martin shared the results of the students' analysis with his principal who agreed that the upgrade was needed. Over a period of time, the school upgraded the lighting.

Martin said that he discussed several other school problems with his principal. The principal suggested that while Martin meant well, he did not understand institutions. This same principal wrote recommendations and encouraged Martin to go to graduate school to study school administration. Martin enrolled in a doctoral program in education administration at the University of Kentucky and found out the principal was right.

His first administrative job was with the smallest school district in Kentucky. He was superintendent of a one-school district with 180 students. Actually, it was five jobs in one: superintendent, principal, assistant principal, cafeteria manager, and part-time music teacher.

When he arrived, the district's finances were a mess. The district was spending more money than it was taking in. The district's savings were shrinking. To Martin, it was a simple mathematical problem. He gave the board three choices: 1) Go out of business, 2) Reduce staff, or 3) Raise taxes.

The school board opted to raise taxes but the citizens voted the plan down. Not wanting to go out of business, they followed his suggestion to reduce staff. Six months later, the tax increase passed and all the cuts were restored.

His next job was in Nicholasville, Kentucky, where he was superintendent of 5,200 students. He was immediately faced with difficult problems. The district voters defeated a school bond issue just four days before he started.

The school board had outlined a list of the consequences if the bond failed, but they were reluctant to implement the penalties. Martin insisted that the board keep its word. The critical issue was transportation. Students who lived less than one mile from school would no longer be allowed to ride the bus. That would save the district $50,000. It was that or reduce staff, and the board was trying to protect the education of the students.

The next board meeting was packed. Over 300 people crowded into the room. An attorney stood up and said he intended to take the school to court and force busing. He did. He lost. The school won, but Martin lost favor with the public. A year later, the people who wanted busing filled the seats on the school board and busing was reinstated. Martin barely got his contract renewed. He stayed six years and credits his education in public opinion and leadership to this experience.

His next move was to North Carolina. Two school districts—Salisbury and Rowan Counties—were merging. Both superintendents retired. There were 15,000 students involved. Once again, he made tough decisions in redistricting, new curriculum standards, new policy, reducing the central office staff by one-third, and helping a $44,000,000 bond issue pass after being defeated once. He was also instrumental in starting a new building program.

His final move, in 1994, was to the 110th largest school district in America, the Winston-Salem/Forsyth County Schools. With 39,334 students, this district was also looking at redistricting, building and bond issues. He again looked at increasing efficiency and reducing the central office.

This was the man, with a heartfelt desire to make things better, who authorized my student surveys. Had I known this, I never would have questioned his intentions about tallying the results. He is a practical man. He probably calculated that a staff of less than a dozen people at the *Kernersville News*, who were already over-committed, might take weeks or months to process 20,000 questions (2000 surveys x 10 questions each). In the interest of time and accuracy, he offered to help, and help he did.

He also took the issue of drug abuse personally. Like me, he never experimented with drugs, but he saw it ruin the lives of those around him. Three years after our first meeting he told me: "I knew a guy at Duke University. I was his orientation leader. He got a 1550 on his SAT and he smoked pot daily. He got into a daily habit. In his sophomore year, he flunked out. He was brilliant, but he was high all the time and didn't do any work. He liked to smoke marijuana."

Martin said pot was prevalent in college in the 1970's. He knew the smell and saw it often. He said, "One guy I went to school with had bags of it and a scale on his desk. He didn't even try to hide it. But I had no desire to experiment. I was not a 1550 coming into college. I worked hard, and I could not afford to take any substance that might impair my ability."

When Martin went to high school in the late 1960's, marijuana was talked about but he never saw it or knew anyone who used it. Today, he realizes things have changed.

"I don't think the drug problem in the high schools is now like the level at my college. But drugs are much more prevalent today. Clearly, even in middle school there is exposure and opportunity. Almost every student knows someone who has used marijuana," said Martin.

In the Winston-Salem/Forsyth County (WS/FC) Schools, the average age of students caught using drugs is 15 years old. They have been "using" for an average of two years. This is not surprising, as this is the national average.

"The younger the students are," said Martin, "when they are faced with this kind of a decision, the less prepared they are to make a good decision. Peer pressure is a very big factor."

I wrote up an 11-question survey. Owensby looked it over and added three questions. He also suggested that the explanation at the top of the survey be clarified so the students did not confuse prescription medication, alcohol or tobacco with illegal drug use. The superintendent read over the survey and made a few minor suggestions on the spot. He suggested that I call the two principals and let them decide how to administer the surveys so that the bulk of their students could participate.

Following is the survey, which was delivered to East Forsyth and Glenn High Schools:

Newspaper Questionnaire

The *Kernersville News* is interested in finding out what students in the Winston-Salem/Forsyth County Schools believe about illegal drug use. For the purpose of the survey, the term "drug" refers to illegal drugs, street drugs and drugs not prescribed to you by a doctor. (It *does not* include over-the-counter medications, alcohol or tobacco.)

Important note: This is an anonymous survey. Please **do not** put your name on your paper. Thank you for sharing your viewpoint with us.

1) Do you believe most high school students have experimented with drugs at least once?
   _____Yes   _____No   _____No opinion

2) Students who use drugs:
   _____Keep it a secret   _____Brag about it   _____Neither, it's not a big deal

3) It is OK to use drugs as long as it is only pot (marijuana).
   _____Yes   _____No   _____No opinion

4) I believe most students who use drugs use:
   _____Marijuana only   _____Marijuana and other drugs   ____Mostly other drugs

5) At which place are drugs easiest to get?
   _____My neighborhood   ____My school   ____My workplace

6) Have *you* ever taken drugs? If "yes" how many times this school year (95-96)?
   ____Yes ____No ___1-5 times ____Weekends only ____Monthly ___Weekly

7) Students that use drugs, use them:
   ____Mostly at school   ____Rarely at school

8) Have you ever seen drugs at school?
   ____Never   ____Once   ____Monthly   ____Weekly   ____Daily

9) In my school, most students:
   ____Use no drugs   ____Use drugs once in a while   ____Use drugs regularly

10) How difficult or easy is it to get drugs at school?
____Easy ____Very easy ____Difficult ____Very Difficult ____Impossible

11) My view of students using drugs is:
____It's their business ____They are stupid ____It's OK with me

12) In my school this many students use drugs daily: ____None ____Very few ____About 1 out of 10 ____About 3 out of 10 ____About 5 out of 10 ____About 7 out of 10

13) In my school about this many students use drugs weekly: ____None ____Very few ____About 1 out of 10 ____About 3 out of 10 ____About 5 out of 10 ____About 7 out of 10

14) In my school about this many of the students use drugs monthly: ____None ____Very few ____About 1 out of 10 ____About 3 out of 10 ____About 5 out of 10 ____About 7 out of 10

15) Fill in the blank. Drug users in my school tend to be
_____
_____

    The principals, of course, were less than pleased that their schools had been selected to participate in a public investigation of "drugs in schools." After some delay, the principals determined that I could deliver the surveys on April 15. It was my first time on either high school campus. I took my 14-year-old son, Joe, along to help carry the surveys. He had been homeschooled since middle school and had never been to a high school during class hours.
    First, we went to East Forsyth. Classes were in session. We could find no clear directions to the office. We were in no hurry. We stopped and looked at a doorway and through a window. The paint was faded and peeling. Inside, the students moved slowly. They were slumped in their seats and looked disinterested.
    My son said, "Mom, I bet in other countries like Russia, they would never believe that American students look like this or that their schools look like this. I bet they think schools here are really nice and kids have exciting classes."
    "I never really thought about it," I said.
    "This looks like a prison. I'm glad I don't go here," he said.
    I thought back to my old high school. Actually, I went to two high schools. The first, in Swartz Creek, Michigan, was so overcrowded that it threatened to go on split sessions just before we moved. This school was beautiful to look at, but it felt cold and like an institution to me.

The other high school was about 30 miles northeast of Swartz Creek in Genesee. Genesee High School was so small that in 1976 there were less than 50 students in my senior class. The building was so old that sometimes the windows did not open and occasionally sections of the ceiling fell down. As expected, the books, lab supplies, and technology left much to be desired.

Yet, Genesee felt warm and caring. I thrived—just as splendidly as a transplanted seedling that is moved from an overcrowded pot to its own place in the garden. Also, I received more nurturing –as teachers only had 15-20 pupils. I, like all the other students, was really known at this school—not just my name, but the real person behind the name.

Best of all, this school had a wonderful principal, Dorothy Lugar Baker. She loved her job and she loved "her kids." She knew all the students by name, and it seemed that she spent more time in the halls enjoying our company than she did in her office. In short, this school became part of my extended family and filled some very real needs of mine for acceptance, recognition, and connectedness.

Instead of sharing all this with my son though, I quickly said, "Oh, school is like anything else. You get out of it what you put into it. You would get used to it, but I'm glad you get to do school your way."

Finally, a couple of students came and directed us to the office. Once there, we plopped the surveys on the counter and inquired as to *when* the surveys might be given. The staff was less than cooperative and gave no clear indication. I reminded them what the "superintendent said" and told them I would call later.

At Glenn, Principal Coplin accepted the surveys and said he would look at the schedule and try to do the surveys in the next couple weeks. I could call him. He was professional but not overly enthusiastic.

> *"Whenever we have a gun on campus or a student arrested for selling drugs, the newspaper comes in here for one day, writes a big headline and then we never see them again. Newspapers are interested in selling newspapers, not in solving the problems at school."*
> —Principal Adolphus Coplin (1996)

Best of Both Worlds

A single mile connects Historic Downtown Kernersville – with restored turn-of-the-century homes and owner operated shops – to the most modern shopping experience offered by Walmart, Target, Kohls, Staples, Starbucks, Harris Teeter, Petco, and more.

www.discoverKernersville.com

4

Getting Results

Lesson 4: Accept personal responsibility

Arrangements were made for 2000-plus completed surveys to be picked up on the 25th of April. This was about seven weeks prior to the start of the "Drugs in Schools" series in June. However, when the day arrived, the schools refused to give them back.

After numerous calls to East which Principal Grissom did not return, an office worker finally told me *why* I could not have the surveys. Evidently, one of the teachers "read" the surveys completed in her class before taking them to the office. She was shocked by her students' responses and did not feel that the results should be printed in the newspaper. Principal Grissom reviewed the surveys and agreed.

At Glenn, Principal Coplin was keeping his surveys until this was resolved. He did not mind being part of a group survey in Kernersville, but he did not want his school singled out.

On a follow-up phone call, the East office worker asked me, "Why are you doing this witch hunt? Why are you trying to get our principal in trouble?"

It never dawned on me that a principal could believe that her job was at risk based on a student opinion survey. Whereas I knew the true motivation behind the student surveys, she did not. The goal was to give the students' voices an audience—the community. Ultimately, this would lead to a broader understanding of the teenage drug problem. A better understanding could lead to a possible solution. But, because this principal refused to talk with me, she was not convinced of my true intentions. Principal Grissom was assuming that this survey was a ploy to single her out so she would not budge.

Over the next several weeks, I periodically called Owensby and explained that the project had stalled. It was the middle of May and school would be out for the summer shortly. Might we miss our window of opportunity if something didn't happen soon? Finally, he called me into the office. He was furious. He threatened to call the superintendent and tell him that we were going to run the student interviews with or without the surveys. We would tell the readers that we did the surveys and the schools refused to let the community see the results. He called it "a pregnant situation." Aborting the baby would not work. The surveys had already been completed. The public would demand to know "what happened to the baby."

I was taken aback by his caustic reaction. My illusion—that with his authority as owner of the newspaper this problem could be painlessly resolved—was quickly replaced by the reality that forcing the schools' hand could create more problems. Suddenly, handling the problem myself didn't seem like such a bad idea. I quickly explained that Martin had not been notified of the problem. I asked permission to make the call.

When Martin learned of the schools' reluctance and the newspaper's timeline, he willingly offered to get involved. He negated much of the tension by having the surveys retrieved directly by school personnel. Finally, on June 6, two days before we ran the first student story, I was given the results and the completed surveys.

*   *   *

When the June 8, 1996, Saturday newspaper rolled off the presses, it was loaded with "drugs in school" information. My interview with Mike took the top headline. The survey was received too late to be printed with the compiled results, but John Staples wrote a summary headlined "Students: Drug use is common in area schools." He wrote that 1,707 students at East Forsyth and Glenn High Schools took the survey and "92 percent of the respondents believed that 'most students in my school use drugs'". Both our stories continued on page three where readers could see a copy of the survey questions.

The "Vox Populi" or "Voice of the People," which regularly appears in the top right corner of page two, also highlighted teens and drugs. This feature allows random residents to speak out on a topic of the week. It is a chance to hear from the general population instead of the experts and authorities. Perhaps, most importantly, it is a way for readers to see themselves and their neighbors in the newspaper— because respondents are photographed. In this issue, five randomly selected residents were asked, "Do you think there is a serious drug and alcohol problem among local teenagers, and if so, what should be done about it?"

One middle-aged resident, Louise Fulton, expressed a sentiment I had heard often. She said, "I think young people locally don't have anywhere near the problem with drugs and alcohol that kids in larger metropolitan areas have."

Three of the five interviewed believed the problem and the solution rested with the parents. Respondents also blamed world culture, calling our times an "era of drugs and alcohol," and they blamed the court systems for being so lenient with young drug offenders.

To the left of the Vox Populi was the editorial opinion box. This box is generally reserved for the opinions of editor John Staples. But on this day, it was mine. It was headlined, "The drug survey."

It happened quite by accident. In my inexperience, I thought I was writing another story, but I went beyond stating the facts. I was drawing conclusions and trying to persuade my audience. Staples gently explained that this crossed the line of reporting and what I had was a very good editorial.

The purpose of my editorial was to convince the community that we were doing the right thing. It is necessary to do a *local* survey to solve a *local* problem. I also wanted the community to know that doing a survey was only one of several steps necessary for bringing about positive change. Sitting at home and reading about the problem in the local paper was not going to be good enough. The community would have to participate.

My editorial was based on information published by the U.S. Department of Education. The report was entitled "Success Stories '94: A Guide to Safe, Disciplined, & Drug Free Schools." It not only confirmed that we did the right thing, but it also gave us five additional steps to follow that had worked for 70 other schools across the country. Suddenly, the foggy vagueness of this assignment—of moving the community to action—lifted. I received a clear vision of how this could be done. This government report became my roadmap.

The six steps are as follows: access the drug problem and publicize it; set drug policy; develop drug education and prevention programs; educate and train school staff; promote parent education and training; get the community involved.

Incidentally, in addition to including the *expert backing* of a government report, I also included a quote from the superintendent. Don Martin said he supported the surveys of the *Kernersville News* because he "saw someone wanting to help, and the newspaper has the ability to reach the community."

In the next issue of the *News*, Staples wrote his own editorial. His editorials have considerable clout. He grew up in Kernersville and has worked for the *Kernersville News* since 1972. He is well liked and trusted. On more than one occasion people have told me that the only reason they buy the paper is to read Staples' editorials.

In this editorial, Staples directed attention to the survey that was now printed with student responses. In part he said, "Drugs are seen as easy to obtain both at school and on the street. Fifty percent of the students believe 70 percent of their peers use drugs at least monthly. Ninety-two percent believe most students in their schools use drugs at some time during the school year. National surveys indicate drug use has risen among teenagers in the last few years. Many suggest the *actual use* increases with the *perception of increased use*, i.e. that if 'Everybody does it, it must be okay.' If true, it is a frightening scenario."

Staples prefaced that quote by saying, "The survey, though not scientifically valid, indicates that drug use is believed by the students themselves to be widespread and pervasive." He addressed this lack of scientific basis because Principal Coplin, in particular, felt that if a survey was to be done it should be scientific. I, on the other hand, believe that ordinary people can do much to solve extraordinary problems. Too many people are inclined to wait for the government to solve a problem or wait for the experts. In reality, reasonable people can do their own research and draw logical conclusions.

Also, to appease the schools, Staples put the following disclaimer on the bottom of the published survey, "In conjunction with school officials, the *News* wishes to point out that the above survey is not necessarily meant to be scientifically accurate, merely a reflection of student opinion. School officials and the *News* agree that several questions may be somewhat misleading in that the language of the questions may imply certain information that is not based on factual information. These include questions No. 4, No. 7 and No. 8."

So what did the non-scientific survey reveal? Here are the results as seen in the June 11, 1996, *Kernersville News,* page 4.

Newspaper questionnaire

Below is a preview of the 15-question drug survey given to the students and faculty of Glenn and East Forsyth high schools. The survey was prepared by the *Kernersville News* and administered by the schools. The surveys were completed the week of April 25, 1996, and the results released by school officials on June 7. In addition to the survey of 1,707 students, the *Kernersville News* interviewed four students from the schools directly before the 1995-96 school year concluded. Each student was interviewed privately and with the permission of the parents. The students' names were changed to protect their privacy. The survey reads as follows:

******

The *Kernersville News* is interested in finding out what students in the Winston-Salem/Forsyth County Schools believe about illegal drug use. For the purpose of the survey, the term "drug" refers to illegal drugs, street drugs and drugs not prescribed to you by a doctor. (It *does not* include over-the-counter medications, alcohol or tobacco.)

Important note: This is an anonymous survey. Please **do not** put your name on your paper. Thank you for sharing your viewpoint with us.

1) Do you believe most high school students have experimented with drugs at least once?
   _1502_Yes　　_____No　_205_No opinion

2) Students who use drugs:
   _202__Keep it a secret　__717__Brag about it　_788__Neither, it's not a big deal

3) It is OK to use drugs as long as it is only pot (marijuana)?
   _273_Yes　__956_No　__461_No opinion

4) I believe most students who use drugs use
   _717_Marijuana only　_922_Marijuana and other drugs　____Mostly other drugs

5) At which place are drugs easiest to get?
   _597_My neighborhood　_973_My school　_110_My workplace

6) Have *you* ever taken drugs? If "yes" how many times this school year (95-96)?
   _615_Yes _956_No　___1-5 times ___Weekends only ___Monthly ___Weekly

7) Students that use drugs, use them:
   _256_Mostly at school   _1400_Rarely at school

8) Have you ever seen drugs at school?
   _256_Never   _461_Once   _129_Monthly   _143_Weekly   _1

9) In my school, most students:
   _137_Use no drugs   _737_Use drugs once in a while   _706_U
   regularly

10) How difficult or easy is it to get drugs at school?
    _802_Easy _580_Very easy   _188_Difficult _34_Very Difficu
    _34_Impossible

11) My view of students using drugs is:
    _1024_It's their business   _478_They are stupid   _188_It's OK with me

12) In my school this many students use drugs daily: ____None   ____Very few _22%_About 1 out of 10   _24%_About 3 out of 10   _20%_About 5 out of 10   _23%_About 7 out of 10

13) In my school about this many students use drugs weekly: ____None ____Very few _13%_About 1 out of 10   _19%About 3 out of 10 _27%_About 5 out of 10   _31%_About 7 out of 10

14) In my school about this many of the students use drugs monthly: ____None   ____Very few
    _12%_About 1 out of 10 _13%_About 3 out of 10   _19%_About 5 out of 10   _50%_About 7 out of 10

15) Fill in the blank. Drug users in my school tend to be
    _____
    _____

The apparent contradictions were most intriguing. For instance, on the first question, 88 percent of respondents believed that "most high school students have experimented with drugs." This strong belief is confirmed in question nine where 92 percent of respondents believed that "in my school most students" use drugs. Again in questions 12, 13 and 14, 50 percent of the respondents believed that 70 percent of the students in their school were using drugs monthly. And yet in question six, when asked, "Have you ever taken drugs?" 61 percent said no.

So there is an apparent gap between perception and reality. At first glance one might assume that most students did not tell the truth. However, when this survey

32   UNDER THE INFLUENCE

question is compared with like questions on the scientific surveys such as the "Monitoring the Future Survey" by the University of Michigan, Kernersville's student responses fall in line with the national averages. According to the scientific surveys, 36 percent of high school students nationally were self-reporting drug use.

Another possibility is that there was so much pro-drug talk among the youth that students believed the drug use was much more widespread than it actually was. If this is the case, this creates two problems for a community wishing to eradicate drug use by its students. First, as perception usually foreshadows reality, this could be an indicator of increased drug use among high school students as a whole, in the future. Second, as individuals, many teens succumb, at least temporarily, to the herd approach in decision-making. Believing that "*Everyone* is doing it" can compel *individuals* to use illegal substances.

Question two seemed to support this. Using drugs was not seen as something to be ashamed of, such as, perhaps wetting the bed. Only 12 percent of the respondents said, "students who use drugs keep it a secret." About 46 percent of the students thought users were ambivalent about drug use and marked "It's not a big deal." Still, 42 percent of respondents believed that student drug users "brag about it." Combining these two figures, 88 percent of the respondents felt that students who use drugs either normalize (neutralize) it or promote it. This raises a valid question. What are all non-using students saying when this bragging is going on? Are they presenting a convincing counter-argument?

Question 11 gives some insight. 61 percent of the respondents said, "My view of students using drugs is it's their business." Only 28 percent of the respondents felt a strong negative feeling and said, "They are stupid." 11 percent actually gave their approval and said, "It's ok with me." In later interviews, students explained why they did not speak up at school and share their anti-drug beliefs.

It is interesting to note that the reason for anti-drug silence was not based on beliefs that taking drugs was ok. In question three, 58 percent answered "no" to the statement, "It is ok to use drugs as long as it is only pot (marijuana)." Only 17 percent answered "yes." The rest had "no opinion."

Another contradiction was in the prevalence or availability of drugs at school. According to question 10, 84 percent of respondents believed that it is "easy" or "very easy" to get drugs at school. And in question five, when given a choice between their neighborhood, school or work as the easiest place to get drugs, 58 percent said school was easiest. Another 36 percent answered, "My neighborhood." And only seven percent marked "Work." But in question eight, when asked, "Have you ever seen drugs at school?" 64 percent of respondents claimed to see drugs at school only once or never. So how were they drawing the conclusion that drugs are easy to get at school? Could it be the pro-drug talk again?

Question four was meant to give some insight into the drug of choice. It was thought that in the small town of Kernersville that marijuana would be the most common drug used by students. However, most respondents (56 percent) believed students who were using drugs were using "Marijuana and other drugs." 44 percent believed students were using "Marijuana only."

With question seven, we tried to find out if drug use was a "school" problem. 85 percent of respondents felt students who use drugs use them "Rarely at school." The answer to this question was crucial for community support. This showed that drug use among students was not just a school problem. In fact, the schools were doing a pretty good job in keeping actual drug use off school property. So more would be necessary than just more drug policing at school.

One of my favorite questions on the survey was question 15. This was a fill-in-the-blank. Here students were asked to complete: "Drug users in my school tend to be . . ." This question was at the end of a 14-question check-the-box survey and it required writing words on a paper. So I was overjoyed when approximately 1,100 students took the time to complete this. It told me that they had an opinion and cared to share it. Their words were authentic and refreshing. And some of them were downright poetic.

The *News* printed excerpts from this question on the third day of the series. It began: Drug users in my school tend to be:

"a lost child covering their pain."

"the ones who seem to have the most going for them."

"cool as h—l because I use them too."

"low life punks who think they are cool; or nice calm people who experience sad events in their little lives."

"the same as everyone else, because most people do them. There's nothing wrong with them."

"the people who sit beside you with the best grades and the nicest clothes and are happy with themselves."

"people who try too hard to be cool. They think drugs make them look cool."

"practically everyone."

"regular students who like to party on the weekends and when out of school."

"no general stereotype. Anyone could be using them."

*   *   *

Five years later, while writing this chapter, I divided the 1,108 student comments into two groups. Group "A" respondents completed the sentence "drug users in my school tend to be . . ." with negative descriptions—one that people generally would *not* be proud of. There were 490 comments in group "A". A sampling of the disapproving comments are:

"the ones with low self-esteem."

"they need to mature and grow up."

"uncaring about themselves."

"the drop outs."

"act like losers."

"trouble makers."

"lazy or inactive."

"the ones who have given up."

"morons desperate for their next high because they are too #*#* stupid to face reality."

"having problems at home or are having an inner conflict, and they don't know where to turn so they turn to drugs."

*   *   *

Almost an equal amount of respondents fell into group "B". This group of 462 either used the word "normal" or "average," or described drug users in a way that most people would find flattering. A sampling of these comments are as follows:

"They can not be categorized. People of every race, background and social status are using drugs."

"most popular and sometimes athletic. Also the ones who are smart and have the most going for them."

"just about everyone i.e. preps (well dressed and behaved), freaks (favor black and gothic dress), wiggers (whites that try to act black), nerds (highly intelligent and bookish), rednecks (loud and favor country music)."

"the majority of the people."

"the people you would least expect, sneaky preps that their parents wouldn't think would, the real popular people."

"their own person. They do what they want to do. Nobody can change that."

"9 out of 10 students who eat and sleep daily."

*   *   *

The remaining comments were apathetic and included phrases such as:
"it's their #*#* business what they do."
"I don't get involved."
"no opinion."

A few went into the "other" category with comments such as:
Drug users tend to be:
"drug users."
"high a lot."
"Indebted to me. Ha! Ha! Ha!"

*   *   *

We were running front-page stories on "Drugs in School" every issue, Tuesday, Thursday and Saturday. One week from the first story, or on Saturday, June 15, I wrote a cover story called, "School System Responds to Drug Survey."

I wanted to show the community early on that the schools and the readers were on the same side. While the Kernersville high schools did have a higher student drug use problem than generally believed—the same as the national average—the school system was doing a stellar job in implementing popular anti-drug programs.

The six-step drug-free model explained below was used as a backbone for this story to show the readers that the schools were doing their part. Per step one, the school administrators gave the students the survey and allowed the results to be published in the *Kernersville News*. A five-year scientific survey was also completed six months earlier in conjunction with the Department of Public Health Sciences of Bowman Gray School of Medicine, now known as Wake Forest University School of Medicine. This study confirmed our finding that about 36 percent of high school students system-wide were using drugs.

The next step involved setting, implementing and enforcing drug policy. The WS/FC schools had an attractive student handbook, which clearly explained the drug policy. It is given to each student. Some schools ask that both the students and the parents sign the policy.

Step three involved developing and implementing a drug education and prevention program. In 1987, the WS/FC schools took advantage of federal grant money and hired Angela McReynolds as a full-time "Program Manager of Alcohol and Drug Defense Program." Within a few years, she had videos, curriculums, and drug programs in place in all the schools K-12. This was no small task as there were 11 high schools, 14 middle schools and 33 elementary schools.

McReynolds was especially proud of the Drug Abuse Resistance Education (D.A.R.E.) program, which focuses on prevention. She said that ultimately, "A well-rounded program will not only address drugs, violence and alcohol abuse but also self-esteem, peer pressure and decision- making."

Under her supervision, the WS/FC schools pioneered a new intervention program for drug policy violations. It was the first of its kind in the state and entailed getting help for students and their parents as opposed to just suspending the student.

The next step was geared to staff education and training. Here again McReynolds had done a great job. She provided 20 free workshops a year for teachers and staff. One workshop was called, "The Student Assistance Program." It trained teachers to look for signs and symptoms of substance abuse, violence and pregnancy. Then teachers were encouraged to address the issues with professionals both inside and outside the school system.

Step five recommended promoting parent involvement and educating parents. The school system offered free seminars, such as the one offered the same month I interviewed McReynolds entitled, "Helping Parents Help Themselves," by Milton Creagh. In addition to this, every parent was invited to check out a video series entitled, "Successful Parenting Series," which was placed on each school campus. Parents were invited to help plan student activities such as Project Graduation. (This community-sponsored alternative party was drug and alcohol free and featured rock climbing walls, an electric bull, NASCAR simulators, music, food, and beverages for students to enjoy on the night of their graduation.)

Finally, step six, which was perhaps one of the school district's proudest achievements. This involved interacting and networking with community groups and agencies. Working with the Winston-Salem Forsyth County Sheriff's Department, the first program of its kind in the state was created.

According to Sheriff Ron Barker, "We pioneered this program in 1970 when we made available a School Resource Officer (SRO) at two high schools, East and West. Over the years, that number has increased to all the high schools and most of the middle schools. The SRO program is catching on statewide and one of our SROs is going across the state to assist other schools and sheriff departments to implement the program."

As this program grew, each high school was assigned a uniformed deputy on campus who could walk the halls, talk with the kids, and build a rapport with the students. Over the years, this has worked out amazingly well as some students quietly alert the officers of drug and weapon violations.

Besides all of this, some community groups had clubs in the high schools. These included the Coalition for Drug Prevention, Step One (a substance abuse and counseling program), SADD (Students Against Drunk Driving), IDAC (Identify, Disassociate And Convert with love) and some that were specific to each high school such as Carver's CADDY (Carver (High School) Against Drugs and Drinking in Youth).

The story ended with a galvanizing quote from McReynolds:

"We are not different," said McReynolds, "from any other small or large community. There are drugs and alcohol in all of them. The difference is how a community *addresses* the problem. The community decides whether drugs and alcohol will be accepted and at what level. And there is not just one answer. The solution goes beyond the school system's efforts and must include the parents, the judicial system, and ultimately every single citizen."

How would the community respond?

> *"All that is necessary for the triumph of evil is that good men do nothing."*
>
> *—Edmund Burke*

5

Community Response

Lesson 5: Let everyone be heard

After the sixth set of front-page stories, publisher John Owensby decided it was time to have a "community leaders" meeting. Before he invested any more time and money into the "drugs in schools" investigation, he wanted to meet with the local leadership. He wanted to know if they wanted to pursue a solution.

He reserved some neutral ground at Dudley Cosmetology University. Then Owensby gave me a list of people to invite. The meeting was to be limited to a few select leaders and would last only one hour. People were eager to accept.

On June 20, just 12 days after our first story, 15 community leaders sat around a conference table to discuss the teenage drug problem. Owensby opened by saying, "I just wanted to see if this is something we want to do something about or not."

I passed around copies of the pertinent newspaper stories and went over a few of the highlights. Then the conversation began.

Jim Wilhelm, assistant superintendent of the WS/FC Schools said, "One key to the solution is to get peer groups to say that drugs aren't cool, they aren't okay to use, and we won't tolerate drug use."

Wilhelm was familiar with teens and drugs as he was principal at East Forsyth for 14 years. He took the drug problem personally. In the 1970's, while he was at East, he allowed an undercover policeman on campus. Rumor has it that the "wrong" kids were arrested and he almost lost his job over the incident.

I couldn't believe what was said next. Kernersville resident and vice-chairman of the school board Rick Bagley said, "Our schools reflect society, and I don't think tougher drug laws are the answer. We, as a society, might look at decriminalizing certain drugs and putting the money into changing behavior."

I was shocked. Did I just hear a school board member say he was in favor of legalizing drugs? Some drugs? Any drugs?

When I wrote the story, I made sure Bagley's quote and position in the community was near the top of the story. Owensby called and wanted me to remove his quote. I felt that if this man could say this to 14 fellow leaders, it needed to be heard by the community. I offered to verify the quote with other sources. That was agreeable and the quote remained. I did add in another quote from Bagley that softened the blow a little and appeased my publisher. Bagley said, "It's not a politically popular stance to take. But I don't think we can establish laws strict enough to act as effective deterrents. . . If money wasn't there (in illegal drug sales) maybe we could get it (drugs) out of the schools."

Photo by Wendy Freeman Davis, *Kernersville News 2011*

John Owensby, Publisher
Kernersville News

Two weeks after printing a steady series of shocking stories on the "Drugs in Schools" investigation, Publisher John Owensby invited 15 community leaders, including school officials, law enforcement, a judge and a county commissioner to meet. Owensby opened the meeting by saying, **"I just wanted to see if this is something we want to do something about or not."**

http://www.kernersvillenews.com

Bagley's comment was the only pro-legalization statement in the forum.

Captain C.C. McGee of the sheriff's department suggested, "Consistency would help. There is a lot of difference between how each high school addresses the problem. Also, kids should be involved in the task force and, really, we should have some kids right now at this meeting."

This was an issue that would come up again and again over the next several years. If this is a problem of the youth, then how much good will it do for a bunch of adults to sit around and talk about it? Where are the students? Why aren't *they* invited to the meetings too?

Two (SRO's) from the sheriff's department were there. They walked the halls at Glenn and East daily. One said, "The students need help in the community and in their homes."

This officer believed that most drug use takes place off school property. This was exactly what the kids indicated in the survey. Eighty-five percent of the respondents felt that students who use drugs use them "rarely at school."

Kernersville Police Chief Neal Stockton, a graduate from East Forsyth High School, supported the sheriff's SRO and gave the group some insight on the local youth problem.

"Kids are hunting for something to do. The major time kids get into trouble with drugs and gangs is that crucial time between when school lets out and when their parents get home from work. The community needs to provide a positive environment."

County Commissioner Dave Plyler was quick to respond. "Money is being poured into numerous programs already. Now we need to open a new floor of the jail. It will cost one to one-and-a-half million dollars to operate that one floor. And there's not enough room to house all the juvenile delinquents. Spending more money on more programs isn't the whole solution."

As the discussion went around and around the table, I could see a pattern developing: Someone would lay the blame on the "schools" and the schools would say it was not just a school problem; then the blame would be passed to another element of the community and that representative would defend his position.

Glenn's Principal Coplin detected the fray in the cord of leadership and in one sentence spliced the voices together.

He said, "It must be the community, the schools, and the parents that work together to solve this problem."

Then Judge Ron Spivey made the best received comment of the day. ***The News*** put it in a box for the story:

> "We really need to activate the most powerful force in the community—the parents! I was surprised to read that of the four high school students interviewed that only one of them had parents that talked to them about drugs this whole school year."

Spivey was referring to the June 20 newspaper story. It reported that the four students interviewed reported seeing drugs at school about twice a week, while hearing pro-drug talk from their peers on a daily basis. But when asked how often their parents were talking with them about the dangers of drug abuse, only one in four students could recall a single conversation in the last 12 months. Noting the lack of parent/child communication in this small random sample, I sought to find out "why" this topic seemed to be taboo.

I found that many parents were not talking to their children about using drugs because they did not want their kids to ask, "Did you ever try drugs?" So, many parents avoided the topic. Some parents were also under the illusion that if they brought up the topic they might be planting the seeds of curiosity. Somehow, these parents were unaware that the children's peers were planting these seeds bountifully and regularly.

Instead of interviewing parents, I talked with two kids whose parents had talked to them about drugs. In both cases, the parent/child conversations were ongoing and the teens had never experimented with drugs. What differed was that one set of parents had used drugs as teens and the other set had not.

> *"I have never taken drugs because my parents told me what happened to them, and I've heard a lot of adults tell me about the bad effects of drugs, and it didn't seem worth it to me."* —Angie, 17 years old

I asked, "What did your parents tell you?"

She replied candidly, "Well basically that they lost control of themselves and they could not use good judgment, and they ended up doing stupid things."

"Did you feel that if drug use was good enough for them, then it was good enough for you?"

"No. They made a lot of stupid mistakes and worse could have happened, and I don't want those kinds of problems."

"Did you lose respect for your parents when they told you they used drugs?"

"No. They were just typical kids and they are respectable now. But they had to overcome a lot of problems from taking drugs, and I don't want to have to overcome all those problems."

This interview was followed immediately by an interview with 16-year-old Jason. His parents never took drugs. Jason, who is now 23, has never taken drugs.

"They say that just because everyone else might seem to be doing something," said Jason, "don't give in to peer pressure. What everyone else is doing is not always best. They told me about the results of their old school friends taking drugs. They have seen many of their friends with good career outlooks ruined by drugs. And I also don't use drugs because I respect my body."

The story then went on to quote the U.S. Department of Health and Human Services: *Research indicates that parents, grandparents, elders, foster parents, youth leaders, coaches, and others can play a major role in keeping young people from using alcohol, tobacco, or illicit drugs.*

Photo by Pam Corum Snyder Photography

NC Superior Court Judge Ron Spivey participated in Kernersville's first community meeting when the Town was deciding if it wanted to pursue a solution to the local student drug problem. Judge Spivey, who started the TEEN COURT in Forsyth County, was innately interested in helping Kernersville's youth.

> *"We need to activate the most powerful force in the community – the parents! I was surprised to read that of the four high school students interviewed that only one of them had parents that talked to them about drugs this whole school year."*
>
> –Judge Ron Spivey

http://historicalstate.lib.ncsu.edu/student-leaders/ronald-eugene-spivey

It also gave a script for parents who had used drugs in the past. In short, parents can begin a conversation by asking what the teen knows about illegal drug use. If the teen asks if the parents used drugs and the parents did, then the parents can explain the lack of factual information at the time and explain why they stopped using drugs. It is important that parents close the conversation by stating clearly that they do not want their child using drugs. The parents can also point out that the teen does not *need* drugs as he has many good things going for him.

Right below this was the story, *"Tests for Parents Who Want to Know If Their Child Is Drug Free."* After doing all this research, I realized that drug dependency in youth can become like a disease. It can keep a youth from growing and functioning properly. Just as we would want to know if our child had polio or sugar diabetes, parents need to know if their child has a drug problem.

The telephone numbers for two companies that do non-invasive drug testing were then listed. The first number would put parents in contact with Psychemedics Corporation of Cambridge. Parents could send in a small sample of their child's hair and have it analyzed for drug use. Each half-inch length of hair would have a 30-day history of drug use embedded in it. Interestingly enough, over 600 corporations in America, including Blockbuster, Sports Authority, and Steelcase, were using this method to test their employees.

According to Ray Kubacki, the president of Psychemedics, the only reason they started offering the test to parents is because "parents feel like their kids may have found a way to beat the urine test and believe this is more accurate."

The second number was for Drug Alert. Parents could order a special cloth to wipe across their child's computer keyboard, tennis shoes, or steering wheel of their car. It is similar to the swipe test done by the airlines on cameras and baggage to check for residue from explosives. Once the cloth is returned, Barringer Technologies uses an ion-mobility spectrometer to detect residues of marijuana, cocaine, heroin, or speed.

At the community leaders' meeting, the 15 participants discussed these stories. They decided that the newspaper stories alone were not going to be enough. It was agreed that if a Town Meeting could be held, these leaders would serve as a panel. Hopefully, the community would support the meeting and arrive at a plan of action.

> *"Last year we tried to have a Town Meeting in Kernersville and we advertised and put up flyers and only five people showed up!"* —Angela McReynolds (Program Manager of the Alcohol and Drug Defense Program of the WS/FC schools)

Angela McReynolds was pessimistic about a community meeting in Kernersville.

Other community leaders then joined in and noted a similar lack of interest. It wasn't just Kernersville, it was a trend in all the communities in Forsyth County. All nine high schools were having community meetings and yet the parental support was not there. Past experience showed that most parents did not want to invest the time needed to be part of the solution.

Wilhelm said, "It's so complex. Many people have the attitude that 'I'm just going to worry about my kid and my house and let the rest take care of themselves.' How do we reach these parents?"

> *"Many people have the attitude that I'm just going to worry about my kid and my house and let the rest take care of themselves. How do we reach these parents?"* —Jim Wilhelm, WSFC Schools

I was taken aback by all this negative talk. I interpreted it as a lack of leadership and vision. Wasn't the whole point to see if the community wanted to solve the problem? How could you tell, if you didn't invite them to get involved? The anticipation of complacency and failure on the part of the community made me doubly determined to do everything in my power to make the community meeting a success.

At the end of the hour, it was agreed that a Town Meeting would be held in July, with the exact date to be announced at a later date. Jim Wilhelm, assistant superintendent of the schools, would serve as chairman.

Beginning with the story of the "community leader's meeting" in the next paper, virtually every story in the series ended with the invitation for parents and members of the community to call Jim Wilhelm for more information about the Town Meeting.

East Forsyth High School After Renovation. http://www.wsfcs.k12.nc.us/efhs

A "Giving Back" Community

The Paul J. Ciener Botanical Garden is just one of many examples of local residents who give back to their community in a large way. The gardens are open free of charge 365 days a year.

The website says:

"The vision of Paul J. Ciener Botanical Garden is to create a dynamic public garden in Kernersville, North Carolina that surprises visitors from near and far by its scope, quality and benefits for tourism, community events and civic pride."

http://www.cienerbotanicalgarden.org

Civic Clubs – including Kiwanis, Rotary, Lion's, Civitan, Lady's Civitan, Newcomers, and more – are alive and well in Kernersville. Clubs support the students, the schools, the parks, the underprivileged and ultimately the hopes and dreams of the community.

6

Gathering the facts

Lesson 6: Do your own homework

The "community leaders meeting" raised several new questions. First, what about legalizing marijuana? As legalization was now part of the community conversation, the front page story June 25 was headed, "Warning: Marijuana is Different Today."

The story started out with six hard-hitting facts:
- Counterfeit marijuana is common with impurities ranging from harmless fillers to street drugs to outright poisons.
- There are stronger forms of marijuana available to teens today than in the 1960s.
- The average age of first use has dropped significantly to 13 years of age.
- Marijuana is harmful to your health.
- Marijuana can be a gateway drug.
- Marijuana can be addictive.

First, for proof of counterfeit marijuana in Forsyth County, I went to Nancy Dixon, a Certified Substance Abuse Counselor and Community Educational Director of STEP ONE, the drug intervention service.

"Today kids get anything from counterfeit pot (harmless cooking herbs such as parsley)," Dixon said, "to marijuana that's been laced with ether or PCP (phencyclidine, an illegal drug that causes hallucinations) or dry cleaning fluid that is actually poison."

Next, a *Family Circle* magazine story titled "Why 'Just Say No' Hasn't Worked" backed up the fact that stronger forms of marijuana are available today. It stated, "In the 1960's, when marijuana first became popular, its THC level (the mind-altering substance in marijuana) was around 0.2 percent. Today's pot contains THC levels as high as 5 percent, making it 25 times as strong."

Third, I went back to Dixon for the local statistics on the average age of first use and found it mirrored the national average.

> *"Not only is marijuana very different from the 1960's drug, a different person is using it. A 13-year-old (average age of first use in the local schools) and a 20-year-old (average age of first use in the 1960's) are two different people, both emotionally and physically. . . Kids are using at a younger age and it is doing more damage."* —Nancy Dixon, Certified Substance Abuse Counselor

Fourth, the National Institute on Drug Abuse (NIDA) confirmed marijuana's negative health effects. According to its research, "THC disrupts the nerve cells in the part of the brain where memories are formed. . . In laboratory research, some scientists found that high doses of THC given to young rats caused a loss of brain cells such as that seen with aging. At 11 or 12 months of age (about half the normal life span) the rats' brains looked like those of animals in old age. . . Studies show that someone who smokes five joints per week may be taking in as much cancer causing chemicals as someone who smokes a full pack of cigarettes every day . . . Driving while high leads to car accidents. Drug users also may become involved in risky sex. Students may find it hard to study and learn. Young athletes could find that their performance is off; both timing and coordination are affected by THC."

The fifth bullet point, the idea that marijuana can be a gateway drug, is borne out by tracking drug use patterns. "Long-term studies of high school students and their patterns of drug use show that very few people use other illegal drugs without first trying marijuana," according to NIDA. As a marketing technique, it is common for drug sellers to throw in a "free" rock of crack (a smokable form of cocaine) with the purchase of marijuana, further encouraging a progression to other drugs.

The final bullet claimed that marijuana can be addictive. Again turning to NIDA, funded research found: *"While not everyone who uses marijuana becomes addicted, when a user begins to feel that he or she needs to take the drug to feel well, that person is said to be dependent on or addicted to it. In 1993, over 100,000 people entering drug treatment programs reported marijuana as their primary drug of abuse, showing they need help to stop using."*

Without ever using the word legalization in the story, I hoped the facts would speak for themselves.

My thoughts now turned to the parents. What if they read this and are worried about their teenagers? How can parents tell if their child is using drugs? The next issue of the *News* told them, "What to Look for and Where to Turn For Help."

According to NIDA:
- Very red, bloodshot eyes
- Seem dizzy and have trouble walking
- Seem silly and giggly for no reason
- Difficulty remembering things that just happened
- Change in eating and sleeping habits
- Loss of interest in favorite activities
- Carelessness in grooming
- Hostility and depression
- Signs of drugs/pipes and rolling paper
- Odor on clothing or in room
- Use of incense and deodorizers
- Use of eye drops
- Clothing, jewelry, posters promoting drugs

Telling the difference between "normal" teenage behavior and changes due to drug use can be difficult. Parents were advised that if they noticed several changes in the above behavior list, it could indicate drug use or teenage depression. Both are problems that need attention, so we named two community resources which parents could call for help.

What about teens helping teens? When talking with young people, I found that while most parents seem to be in the dark about their child's drug habits, teens know what other teens are doing. So the natural question was: How can teens help their friends?

S.M. (Bert) Wood, Jr., CEO of Step One, answered the question on our next front page: "The earlier we intervene (by speaking up), the more effective it is. Even if your friend is just beginning to experiment, let him know how you feel. That is the definition of friendship, speaking out and being there when your friend has a problem."

Bert Wood, CEO of Partnership for a Drug-Free NC
formerly known as Step One
www.drugfreenc.org

We gave teens the 1-800-I-Do-Care number from a free booklet entitled, "Does your friend have an alcohol or other drug problem? A Guide for Teens."

Also, teens were told that Step One could help them with a drug or alcohol problem without parental permission and regardless of ability to pay.

This story appeared on June 29. It was amazing that back in February, when I was first assigned this project, I wasn't sure how to proceed. Now, the series had taken on a life of its own. There was no shortage of story ideas because I could barely keep up with the questions that presented themselves.

Why would a teenager choose to use drugs? I found a young man who recently quit the habit. He was willing to share his insights. On July 2, we ran "Confessions of a Former Teenage Drug User."

"How old were you when you began using drugs?"

"I had just turned 13."

"Why did you start?"

> *"It was a combination of things. I saw my brother doing it. And I was told by my best friend that it would help the pain of my broken ankle. And it puts you in a different state of mind ... you're all relaxed."*
> —Recovered teen drug abuser

"And so the first time I did it," he added, "I was all alone, but after that, I did it with people because it was there."

"What drugs did you use and where did you get them?"

"I got them through my brother and his friends. The first thing I did was a dime bag of pot or $10 worth. I did it in my room by myself."

"You said you did drugs because you were in physical pain. Could it also have been because you were in emotional pain?"

"Yeah. You weren't cool if you didn't do drugs. And then at home, there were rules, but we didn't obey them. My mom and dad were split-up—divorced—(at age seven) and I lived with my mom. My mom was strict and she would ground us, but two minutes later we would walk out of the house. She knew our standards. Whatever she said went in one ear and out the other. There were four of us kids and we lived in a low-income project house. About a year after we moved there, my mom found out she had cancer so we went on that welfare assistance thing. It had some effect. It hurt me that my mom was sick and that we lived in that place. But it didn't hurt me very much because I'm not the kind of person that cares what other people think about me."

"How long did you do drugs?"

"When I hit 15 ½, I realized that doing drugs was wrong and stupid. During that couple of years, I mostly did marijuana and acid."

"Why did you do acid?"

"Well, I wasn't very experienced in using drugs. And there was this movie called *Pink Floyd The Wall* that my friends said if you watch it while you're tripping (taking acid) you'll see all kinds of weird things. So I watched it right after work when I was straight—and I didn't see anything. So a couple of days later, I had $20 and acid is $5 a hit so I bought three hits for $15. Then I put all three on my tongue and then it usually takes about 30 minutes to get the full effect and then it hit me. I had a visual/body trip. Body means you feel like you're floating on air and visual means you see trails (after effect shadows of moving objects: they appear to leave a path). And then I saw the movie again, and I saw things I never saw when I was straight. Like I saw a guy shaving all the hair off his body and when I was tripping I could totally relate to the guy. But when I came down I got paranoid."

"That sounds uncomfortable. Did you ever do it again?"

"Yeah. It was a different state you're in. It's like people say, you can leave yourself."

"Why did you quit using drugs?"

"The money... and I knew it wasn't right. And I saw my friends going nowhere and I was almost 16. I was going to be getting my license and my friends that had their license were wrecking their cars and stuff like that. Also, my brother had some bad trips and I watched what he went through. And one of my best friends went insane."

"He literally went insane from using drugs?"

"Yeah. I had a friend that was in math class tripping on acid. He was just sitting there gazing at a brick on the wall and the teacher yelled at him or something and he went insane. He started kicking things and ran out of the class and they called the police and he started bashing in windshields and started running. He is still locked up today. That is one of the things that got me thinking."

"How did you quit using drugs?"

"I just stopped. I guess I was one of those lucky ones that could do that. Just the willpower of saving my money for a car and knowing I had to do it by myself because my mom couldn't help me."

"Did your mom ever talk to you about drugs?"

"My mom never really talked to me about drugs. We weren't that kind of a family. We didn't sit down and talk. But we were really street smart."

"What kind of family were you?"

"When my dad was home (before the split-up) he smoked and drank. He said he'd rather see me smoke and drink in front of him than behind his back. So when I was between five and eight years old, he gave me my first cigarette and beer. The cigarette wasn't that great... it was nasty! But the first beer was great! It was cold and everything a good beer should be. By the time I got in middle school, my beer drinking was endless. I used to steal beer from bars and stores. We became masterminds at stealing beer."

"After the split-up and you were living with your mom, what was the typical school day like?"

"I had my own alarm and got myself up about 5:30 and showered and dressed. I never had breakfast or saw my mom before school. She was gone to work. I'd run out to catch the bus. I'd visit with my friends at school and then in class I would either sleep or be rude or the class clown. After school, I went to friends' houses either to drink or to do drugs. Sometimes we went roller-skating on Friday nights. Our family all ate dinner at different times. We didn't eat together except on a rare good day. No bedtime. No curfews."

"What do you think would have prevented you from using drugs?"

"Having my dad around... and just the family thing... you know."

"How long have you been straight and what do you have to do to stay that way?"

"I haven't used any drugs for two-and-a-half years. Drugs are around. I go to East Forsyth, and they do it in the bathroom a lot during that five-minute break they give you to go to your lockers and stuff. Kids are smart. You've got to give them credit. To stay straight you have to drop your drug-using friends and keep it in your mind that you want to do it for yourself. I had to make a lot of changes, but when I want to do something, I can get it done."

"What would be your advice to a 13-year-old kid thinking about taking drugs?"

"What would I say? I'd say, 'Don't do it.' There's mainly two reasons kids take drugs—to be popular and there's nothing else to do. Don't do it because it tears you down and for health reasons. But 13 year olds, they just don't listen to authority at all!"

"Lastly, what do you think the solution is for the drug problem at school?"

"Drug testing! It is a violation of privacy, but you can't stop the drugs. Before, you could tell who was using drugs—the longhaired guys with an attitude; and the 'I don't care scene people' that were disrespectful and got kicked out of class. Nowadays, it's the people you highly respect. It's the good students with good grades, preppies, momma's kids, and rich kids living with their moms and dads with a good life. I don't see any other way than drug testing."

It was clear why this teen fell into a life with drugs. But why would young people who "had it all", caring biological parents, nice house, nice cars, the "good life." Why would they take drugs?

Step One set up a blind interview with a drug-using teen that fit this description. A time was set for "Janis" to call me at the *Kernersville News* office. She picked her pseudonym in honor of Janis Joplin, a rock singer who died of a drug overdose.

Janis was privileged. She got a $100 a month allowance, accompanied her parents on trips to Europe each summer, and lived in what she termed "a nice yuppie neighborhood." Aside from this, she was blessed with good looks, a mind that operated at honor-roll level, and the energy to be involved in several extracurricular activities. She even had some noteworthy accomplishments to her credit in the community and would have been easy to identify, had I had the inclination. Janis was 16 and used drugs daily.

"At what age did you begin using drugs and why?"

"I was 13. I don't know why I did it. I screamed out that I wanted to get high. I was with my friends and felt compelled to try something different. There's nothing to do in town! So my friends looked around and found someone and we bought a dime of hash (marijuana in brick form) at the mall. Then I went to my grandmother's to spend the night and me and my boyfriend and another friend smoked it in my grandmother's backyard. Now, I smoke pot almost every day!"

"What did you think?"

"We had a blast. Great! I was very . . . really, really happy. Everything was funny and interesting. Without drugs me and my friends would have been bored."

"Have you tried other drugs?"

"I smoke pot mostly. I've tried acid and I trip on acid whenever I can get it, but that's not very often because it is hard to get. And if the acid is 'dirty' your jaw and back start to hurt and you have to drink lots of orange juice. I like mushrooms (psilocybin) but I've only had them twice because the conditions have to be just right to get them. (It involves digging through cow manure on a full moon just before the sun comes up. According to Janis there is a lot of risk of getting poisoned if improperly done.) Mushrooms are a 'clean' high. It's natural, like pot is natural if it is not laced with something. Crack is different because it is manmade—it is not clean. You can overdose on it and it eats up your nose and messes with your brain."

"Why do you like acid?"

"Well, it's like you're sitting on a couch and first you feel 'crawling'—like things crawling on you. But it's a good crawling feeling unless you trip when you are upset. Never do that! And if you are staring at a painting, first you will see ripples and then you feel really drunk and see things. Everything around you is moving."

"Has using drugs caused you any problems?"

"Well, I got expelled from school, but I went to an alternative school. And I've had several car wrecks, but I'm just a really bad driver. I only got in one accident when I was high. I draw the line at driving drunk though! I never drive drunk, but I do drive when I'm high on pot or acid. I drive fine high. Really, I think the drugs have helped me. I used to be anorexic, but smoking pot makes you hungry and now I am recovering. And I never got good grades since second grade and now I'm an honor-roll student. All my friends smoke pot and so do most of my adult friends. I know more people that do than don't!"

"Do you plan on quitting at some point?"

"I don't plan on quitting, but I probably will at some point in my life. I'm not going to stop until I can stop for myself, and so far I don't have a good reason to quit."

"What do you feel is the solution to the drug problem in the schools?"

"There is no solution. It doesn't matter how many kids you bust—the drugs are going to be there. There's mad cash in drug dealing."

"What do you do after school?"

"I hang out in the parking lot for a while and then I take some of my friends home. And then I hang out with my friends until 10 or 11 o'clock at night and then I go home and chat with my parents for a few minutes and then go to bed."

"Last question, do your parents ever talk to you about drugs?"

"I get along well with my folks, but they never talk to me about drugs. When they found out I was using drugs, they told me I had to go to this program (Step One). But they never talked to me before because I guess they thought I would be perfect like my sister. And they still don't talk to me about drugs. Maybe they think I don't do them anymore!"

As I hung up the phone I realized, there can be pain in 'paradise' too. This girl's sister seemed to have the market cornered on positive attention so perhaps she was taking the opposite tack. The news story concluded with another invitation to call Jim Wilhelm about the Town Meeting.

Next, I focused on another question raised at the "community leaders meeting." Whose problem is the drug problem? If my kid is not doing drugs, why should I care what the rest of the kids are doing?

Detective Gerald Jacobs of the Kernersville Police Department recounted an incident that took place in Kernersville to illustrate how the drug problem eventually becomes everyone's problem.

"This past winter we got a call, and when we arrived, we found an 18-year-old male—in the dead of winter—freezing outside in a pair of sandals, a short sleeve shirt and blue jeans. He had a $10 rock of cocaine in his mouth and when he saw us he swallowed it. We called the EMS (Emergency Medical Service). Crack ruled his life.

"He said, 'I have a problem. I have to get off this stuff, but I don't know how.'"

"We asked him why he was outside without proper clothing on. He said, 'I can't afford any other shoes because of my crack habit.'

"Any money he got went to crack. In reality, his parents had tried to get him help and counseling. The reason we were called that day is because the apartment manager had evicted him from his parents' apartment and he was trespassing. He was evicted because of his stealing and other problems he had caused in the complex. This included the problems caused when his drug-using friends, many of who were in high school would hang around the apartment with him. In time, he ended up being arrested and going through the court system and now he is in jail."

Drug users steal in another way, according to Kernersville Police Officer Joe Walls. He said they have more accidents and more emergency room visits and this results in higher healthcare costs for everyone. He also believed that drug abusers in the workplace tend to be lazy, uncommitted, and disloyal. This causes the cost of goods to rise for consumers and is the very reason why so many companies have drug-testing policies.

Walls believed that drug use was rising in Kernersville. "Out of 100 cars pulled over (in Kernersville)," he said, "more than 50 percent of them have drugs or drug paraphernalia in them."

Now, he wasn't saying that half the cars in Kernersville have drugs in them. But he was saying that if a car is pulled over for any reason, including a broken tail light, or speeding, he finds evidence of drugs over half the time.

What if all these people were arrested? Would that solve the drug problem?

Walls explained that if an officer pulled over 12 cars and six of them had drugs/paraphernalia, it would take him all day (an average of one-and-a-half hours per offense) to write up all the paperwork. That would leave no time for domestic violence, emergency or other police work. Besides, more arrests would cause more court cases and the courts were already overloaded.

According to Forsyth County Judge Ron Spivey, "The majority of our cases are drug cases. And not only does the drug problem generate drug cases, it generates crime." Spivey said that the drug "explosion" which began in 1989 has caused a caseload "explosion" for judges.

"We have the same number of judges," said Spivey in this 1996 interview, "working more sessions with less time to prepare. Each judge is currently doing over 7,000 cases every year."

He went on to explain the related problem that comes from this overload.

"People complain that judges are not giving out harsh enough drug sentences . . . but the prisons are bursting at the seams! The same problem that caused the explosion of cases (drugs), caused the problem for prison admissions. So the prison system has had to start releasing people early and as a prison system, if you had to choose whom to release early, would you choose the person in for murder, rape or drugs?"

That pushes the solution up a step further to building more prisons. But bringing that back to the local scale, Forsyth County Commissioner Dave Plyler had already told the community, "It will cost one to one-and-a-half million dollars to operate that one (new) floor."

This story concluded by suggesting that instead of pushing the solution up higher and higher into society, perhaps the answer lay in bringing it down to the individual. Perhaps parents could make a difference.

Detective Gerald Jacobs said, "Parents need to get involved with their kids and know where their kids are and who their friends are. Parents should try to find other parents that share the same values and curfews and try to get their kids to associate together."

He also suggested that churches not compromise their values and morals and should embrace the youth.

"The community," said Jacobs, "should pull together and say, 'No, we don't want drugs here,' and have more positive programs for the kids to get involved in."

To help the parents, Jacobs suggested a change in the tax laws, which would allow married couples with children to have one stay-at-home full-time parent.

Again, all individuals in the community were invited to the Town Meeting to share their ideas and become part of the solution for the drug problem in Kernersville.

The more I learned about the insidious effects of drug abuse, the more passionate I became. This was readily apparent in my next editorial. It began:

> If parents were told that there was a one-out-of-three chance that their child had cancer, due to exposure to a deadly substance, and that the cure factor was directly related to early detection, no doubt there would be long lines at the testing centers.
>
> There would also be public outrage. The Kernersville community would demand to know . . . whose fault was it! How did a deadly substance permeate the community to such a degree that one in three children was involved before it was publicly exposed? And, most importantly, what will be done to eradicate it from every home and institution affected?
>
> To be sure, one out of every three Kernersville children does not have cancer. But, according to the *News* survey, slightly more than

one out of three high school teenagers was using drugs during the 1995-96 school year, according to their own admission.

In all fairness, can this drug epidemic among teenagers be compared with an insidious disease like cancer? Yes!

"Substance abuse, a major preventable cause of morbidity and mortality in most regions of the world, is thus ultimately a *health issue*," according to the WHO (World Health Organization). As far as early age detection, WHO goes on to state, "In many societies, habit-forming exposure to tobacco, alcohol and drugs can start at an early age, with grave consequences in later life."

Parents need to think seriously about their values and beliefs when it comes to marijuana and other illicit drugs. And they need to bear in mind two things: First, drug use may not just keep your children from being all that they can be . . . it may assist them in becoming someone they don't want to be; and second, marijuana and other drugs may not kill your child's body, but it certainly can kill his spirit.

Once parents decide how they feel about drug use they need to talk with their children. Ask viewpoint questions and listen carefully to discern how deeply the children have been exposed to this epidemic. And if parents feel impelled to reach out a little farther in solving the drug problem, they can make plans to attend the public meeting by calling Jim Wilhelm of the WS/FC Schools.

It was now July 12, a mere 36 days since the "Drugs in Schools" series began, with the intention of "moving the community." So far, the series was comprised of 25 stories. And yet, something was missing. The voices of the students, school officials, and community leaders had all been heard. Whom was left?

I remembered the galvanizing words of Judge Spivey. He said, "We need to activate the most powerful force in the community . . . the parents!" To activate the parents, I had to touch their hearts. I needed a way to help them feel the pain, the fear, and the sense of loss—when a beloved child gets entangled in drug abuse.

I called Step One, and in short order got a blind interview with a local mother who just realized three months earlier that her 17-year-old son was using drugs. She found out that he had been using drugs for the previous five years.

Q: What problems are caused in a family as a result of a child using drugs?

A: The biggest problem is that when a child uses drugs, you lose the trust you had in them. Every time he (her son) walks out that door, you don't know what he's going to do. I don't trust him because he lied to me so much.

Q: What kind of drugs was he using?

A: He was doing pot and speed and cocaine and glue. They do all kinds of things today. I had no idea because he seemed to be a person with a head on his shoulders. I talked to him about drugs since he was a little boy. When I talked to him he would always say, "Are you kidding mom? I would never do drugs!"

Q: How did you find out he was using drugs?

A: A long time before I found out, I saw things that didn't add up and I would talk to him. And I have always checked up on him and checked his room and his car. Sometimes he would come home and wouldn't be acting right or his eyes would be red or look different. But I guess I just didn't want to believe it. And he was good at hiding it. Then he started coming home late, or not coming home. Or he would say that he was working late and he wasn't there when I called his boss to check. But I still didn't think he was doing drugs. I talked to him so much about it. But one day he got careless and I checked the trunk of his car.

Q: What was in the trunk?

A: I found a pipe in the back of his car. He made it himself out of a Slurpee cup and some aluminum foil.

Q: What did he have to say about it?

A: He lied and said it belonged to a friend. I told him I was not going to stop until I found out whose it was. I told him the next day he was going to get a drug test.

Q: How did the test go?

A: On the way to the test (at PrimeCare), we drove around and around and I told him that I wished he would tell me before the test if it was going to be positive or negative. I told him that I really couldn't afford the test ($40). It ended up that I did not have to take him to get the test because he told me the truth. After that, I took him to Step One (a local drug treatment organization). The doctor suggested Step One.

Q: When you look back, were there any early indications that your son was using drugs?

A: Before he was using drugs, he was an A, B, C, student in school. But since he started using drugs, he's a C, D student. And the teachers tell me he's above average and could be a straight A student, but he puts forth no effort.

Q: Many times drug use and stealing go hand-in-hand. Was this also a problem with your son?

A: There was this jewelry missing. It was valuable and it was some diamond jewelry and some gold chains my mother gave me. I didn't even wear it because I was so afraid that I might lose it. I had it in a special place that only a few people knew about it. When I checked it one day and it was gone, he said that he didn't take it. And I should have known, because after it happened, a friend of mine told me that my son was over at his house selling gold chains and I told him it must be my "junk" ones. That was a long time before I checked and discovered my gold ones were missing. You don't want to believe bad things about your kids.

Q: Before you discovered his drug use, what was your son's life like?

A: He was working and going to school. He was in school sports and karate and he had plenty of freedom as to how he spent his leisure time.

Q: What measures have you taken to address his drug problem?

A: He's grounded. He had to quit his job and everything. I told him once you lose that trust you have to earn it back. And I'll be looking and I'll be on your back and right behind you. And we are both involved in Step One. All together we are helping him.

Q: Why don't you want your son to use drugs?

A: They are dangerous and they don't do anything good for him. And I know people who have done drugs and I don't like what it does to them. You can't concentrate on your schoolwork while you are doing drugs. And drugs cost money and if you don't have money what do you do? You steal! He told me a lot of stories about how drugs are passed around at school. (This mother believes her son picked up the drug habit at school.) They pass drugs to him and he passes the drugs to someone else and collects the money. He gets enough drugs for his use for free. I guess that makes him a drug dealer, doesn't it?

Q: How has all this affected you as a mother?

A: It really hurts because I think of him as my baby still, and I wish that I could help him out so bad. It hurts too bad because I talked to him so much and I really thought he was listening. And I found out that he was not listening at all. He was pulling my leg and acting like a sweet, innocent child. And whenever he went out that door, he was a different person. I'm glad he's out of school right now! (It's summer vacation.) And he always wanted to be an engineer. He talked about it since he was a little boy. But I don't think these things even go through his head anymore.

Q: What advice would you give to other parents?

A: I wish someone would have given me some advice. Don't trust so much. Check up on your children and see what they are doing. Sometimes parents give their children too much free time and let them do too much. If you have any suspicions—it's for a reason! Check up on it! So many people are doing drugs: professionals, family, friends, and it is hard for children to stay away from it. You have to understand that it is hard for your kids.

The mother concluded tearfully by saying, "When you hear that other kids are doing drugs, it doesn't bother you that much. But when it is your own kid, you hurt inside."

The research was done. The voices had been heard. Now it was up to the community.

> *"Substance abuse, a major preventable cause of morbidity and mortality in most regions of the world, is thus ultimately a **health issue**,"* according to the WHO. (World Health Organization)

www.UnderTheInfluence.org

7

Publicity

Lesson 7: Take publicity personally

The foreboding prediction by Angela McReynolds haunted me.

She said, "Last year we tried to have a town meeting in Kernersville and we advertised and we put up fliers and only five people showed up!"

That comment precipitated a flood of negative comments as one leader after another acknowledged that community involvement was weak and unpredictable. If it was predictable, it was predictably low.

I also thought about my first conversation with Glenn High School Principal Coplin. First, he questioned the integrity of the *Kernersville News* when he said, "Newspapers are interested in selling newspapers, not in solving the problems at school."

And we had sold lots of papers. Some people even came in and asked for parts of the series that they had missed.

Secondly, Coplin questioned the concern and involvement of the *community* when he said, "... I can tell you right now what the community wants to do about the drug problem. They want the schools to solve the problem."

On both counts, I felt I had defended the honor of the accused. And now, the day of reckoning had been set. Tuesday, July 30, at 12 o'clock noon, the public would have a chance to prove that they cared. Would they show up?

I took the problem on as a personal challenge and met with my mentor and editor, John Staples. Staples knew the people of Kernersville. These were his people. He attended high school with them, served them for decades as the editor of the town paper, and planned to retire with them. He would know what to do.

Staples and I came up with a three-fold plan: First, print up flyers and post them in public places such as the library, grocery stores, the YMCA, and the Kernersville Chamber of Commerce; secondly, send out a personal invitation signed by Owensby on *Kernersville News* letterhead; thirdly, make personal telephone calls to prominent residents, business leaders, and all my friends.

I got started immediately. We had just 10 days until the meeting. First, I composed Owensby's letter.

> *Your attendance is requested at a special leadership meeting to be held Tuesday, July 30, 1996, to discuss possible solutions to the teenage drug problem in Kernersville.*
>
> *This is the second meeting of its kind. The first meeting was held to determine the scope of the teenage drug problem in Kernersville.*
>
> *The first meeting included members of the community including County Commissioner David Plyler, District Court and Teen Court Judge Ron Spivey, School*

Board Vice Chairman Rick Bagley, East Forsyth and Glenn High School principals Judy Grissom and Adolphus Coplin, Captain C.C. McGee of the Forsyth County Sheriff's Department, Kernersville Police Chief Neal Stockton, and several Winston-Salem/Forsyth County Schools officials, including Jim Wilhelm, director of high schools, and Angela McReynolds, coordinator of the schools' anti-drug programs.

While the core group will be present again, it is hoped that others in the community will respond to the invitation to help decide the direction of the actions that will follow this meeting.

It is hoped that those in a position to contact concerned teens will make every effort to inform them of the meeting also. As they are in direct contact with the drug problem among their peers, their input is extremely valuable.

Parents are invited to attend the meeting and to offer suggestions as to practical solutions. (Printed material will also be available to those who attend.)

I posted dozens of flyers inviting the public to the meeting. The flyers were packed with information. Seven statistics were cited from the *News'* student surveys to substantiate the availability, acceptability, and actual use of drugs among the local high school students. Then eight possible solutions were listed. At the bottom of the flyer was an invitation to "bring your lunch" to the noon meeting.

Next, I made about 100 telephone calls. Some were to people who could contact other people. Ron Pannell of the WS/FC Schools agreed to send a public service fax to alert the media about the meeting. Ava Troxler, the executive director of The Coalition for Drug Abuse Prevention would do her best to notify her supporters. Bert Wood, CEO of Step One, said he would spread the word about the meeting. Next, I called local business leaders. Finally, I called personal friends. But was this enough? Were we really tapping all our resources? I went back to Staples.

"What about radio and television?" I asked. "Do you know any stations that would let us advertise this meeting for free? After all, this is a community cause."

"I don't think you'll have much luck with television stations," Staples said. "But Dave Plyler owns a radio station. Why don't you call him?"

Plyler, who was at the first meeting and planned to attend the second, was more than happy to help. As owner of WTOB AM 1380, he arranged for a live interview to be aired on Tuesday, July 23 at 3:30 in the afternoon. He would then air the program again on Wednesday, Saturday, and the day prior to the meeting.

As I drove to WTOB, I reminded myself that I had done this before. In the 1980s, I'd given daily closing stock quotes for a radio station in Houghton Lake, Michigan. And then in 1994, while living in Arizona, I took my son and a few of his classmates to the radio station to talk about their solar cooker project.

But today's radio interview was different. I wasn't just sharing information. Today, I was trying to move the community. Specifically, I was trying to move 50-100 people to come to the YMCA in Kernersville to show that they cared about kids and the drug problem.

I arrived at the studio 30 minutes early. My goal was well in mind and I had several pages of notes. I was dressed up and felt up tight.

The disc jockey, E. L. Burton, took an opposite approach. To him, this was all in a day's work. He was dressed casually, sported a ponytail, and had his sleeves unevenly rolled up. He didn't look at the papers that I brought him until about 15 minutes before live airtime. And even then, he seemed to scan them more than to read them.

After introductions, he asked me about the "astonishing" student drug surveys.

I said, "When the paper decided to do this program (the surveys), what we were looking at is, instead of drawing a conclusion based on hearsay, we decided to go right to the students to see what *their* perception of the (drug) problem was... One thing we were interested in was "belief"... The reason why belief is so important is because if kids believe it is pretty unpopular, . . . "

Burton finished my sentence: "Then they are not going to do it."

"You've got it," I said. "And, if teens *believe* that most kids are doing it, then even if they aren't at the moment, they may begin in the future, because studies show that *use* shadows perception. So it was amazing that 92 percent of those who responded to the survey . . . *believed* that most students in their school used drugs. And that was much higher than anyone really anticipated."

From there, we talked about the reality of 36 percent of the respondents self-reporting drug use. Bringing this into perspective I added, "It was shocking that more than one out of three Kernersville teens—which is exactly what the national average is— were using drugs. It is surprising because a lot of people think of Kernersville as a little bedroom community with some problems, but it's not as bad as the big cities."

"Yeah," said Burton, "that is what everybody seems to think. That it (drugs) is just a major city, urban area problem. While in reality, more and more today, it is becoming something that is happening all over."

Burton next focused on the availability of drugs in the schools. He asked me to read the "amazing" survey results.

"I was quite surprised also," I said, "because we all know that for several years now schools are supposed to be a drug-free zone. And what we found out . . . (is that) 81% of the students *believed* that drugs are either easy or very easy to get at school. They believe drugs are easy (to get), but have they ever seen them at school? This again, to us, was a crucial point in finding out how available drugs actually are. Eighty-three percent, of those taking the survey, indicated that they have seen drugs at school during this last school year . . . If this much drug availability is being seen at school, obviously something different has to be done here."

Burton added, "It seems as though the drug providers are doing a better job with their sales pitch than the anti-drug crusaders are doing."

"With these figures (perception of use and availability) in the 80 and 90 percents," I added, "that definitely shows it's not a matter of whom we *believe* is winning the war (on drugs). The *facts* are kind of here."

Burton next drew attention to the acceptability factor. He commented, "The kids seem to think it (drug use) is just a normal part of life. This is frightening, especially in a town like Kernersville."

> *"It seems as though the drug providers are doing a better job with their sales pitch than the anti-drug crusaders are doing."*
> —E. L. Burton, disc jockey for WTOB AM 1380 during a live interview with the Patty Jo Sawvel.

"Absolutely," I said. "What we've got as far as drug use acceptability is that 66% of those surveyed believe 'it's the users' business and no one else's,' if a student decides to use drugs. And that is kind of disheartening because what they are really saying is that drugs are a personal choice. It shouldn't matter to anyone. And what is missing there is the fact that drugs can either be an immediate danger or a long-term danger to a person's well-being. The other thing we had is an additional 11% (who) believed 'it was ok with them,' if students used drugs. We did have 28% of the students who believed that 'people who use drugs are stupid' . . ."

"Now there's something to take heart in there," said Burton. "At least 30% of them think that it is kind of not a great idea to do that."

"Of course," I replied, "we'd really like to see these numbers reversed."

Burton then introduced the upcoming meeting and invited the public. He concluded by listing some of the solutions that would be discussed on the 30th. He then asked me what I personally liked as a solution.

I favored a three-prong approach. Voluntary drug testing gives teens a reason to say "no" and creates positive peer pressure. Mandatory parenting classes, added into the high school curriculum, might activate the parents of tomorrow by giving them parenting tools today. And I liked having undercover police to reduce drug availability at school.

Burton concluded the generous 21-minute interview by once again announcing the details about the public meeting on July 30.

Just hours before the interview aired the first time, nearly 19,000 residents in Kernersville received the *Tuesday (Kernersville) News* in their driveway. A front-page story invited them to the meeting. The story began like the letter that Owensby had signed. But it also noted that "no solution has yet been decided upon." The story then went on to list some of the solutions that would be considered, such as, undercover police, more community-based after-school activities, voluntary drug testing, decriminalizing certain drugs, having tougher consequences for drug use and possession, having a mandatory parenting class for high school students, increasing drug dog searches, increasing the number of School Resource Officers, and expanding the DARE (Drug Abuse Resistance Education) program to all grade levels.

Sharing the front-page was a story on a voluntary drug-testing program. It was one of the most ingenious solutions I'd ever heard of, and yet I almost missed it.

8

Voluntary Drug Testing

Lesson 8: Ask everyone

I was searching for an appropriate solution to share with the community. Many of the proposed solutions—more lectures, more searches, more supervision—seemed negative and disempowering. The students needed something positive to rally around. They needed something that reached their hearts and that they could be a part of. The students needed something that would create positive peer pressure, convince them that "most kids" don't use drugs, and commend students who took the lead.

But what did this program look like? Where could I find it? I didn't know how to look for it, so I started asking virtually everyone I met.

One day I was housecleaning for Ginny Roberts to supplement my writing income. I asked Roberts the question. She suggested that I talk with her niece, Leslie Bradshaw. Bradshaw was a teacher in Illinois and was visiting Roberts.

Bradshaw immediately identified with Kernersville's concern. Her community, too, had become concerned with the drug use among their teens. It was a very faith-based community, so the residents met at a church and decided to give the students incentives to stay drug free.

As it worked out, the students were very accepting of the program. The students signed a pledge to stay drug free, and took a random drug test. In return, as an incentive, they received a discount card to be used with local merchants. A popular discount, according to Bradshaw, was a reduced rental rate for prom tuxedos.

Immediately, I called Angela McReynolds and told her about this great idea from another small town.

After listening patiently, McReynolds said, "We have that here."

"We do!" I exclaimed. "Why didn't you ever tell me about it?"

"You never asked," she said.

"Well, why didn't you tell me about it when you told me about all the other things the school system is doing?"

"This isn't a district-wide program," said McReynolds. "Some schools implement their own strategies in addition to what we do as a district. Carver High School came up with this idea a few years ago."

I met with Carver High School's principal, Dan Piggott, the following week. As we talked, he kept his desk between us and rolled his chair back.

"What can I do for you?" he asked.

"I want to hear about your voluntary drug-testing program."

Before he could speak, he got a telephone call. He excused himself by nodding and took the call. After hanging up, someone came in and he signed a paper. This gave me a chance to study him for a moment. Piggott is a big, beefy black man with a very full face. He accentuates this roundness with extended fuzzy sideburns, a mustache, large round glasses, and about a one-inch Afro. His eyes are serious but with a certain sense of playfulness or mischievousness behind them.

His door opened again and someone else came in. She appeared to be a teacher. In a stern manner, Piggott said that he decided against her idea. There was little conversation before the intruder departed.

He read my face like a book and said, "I make the decisions around here. We can't do everything, even if it seems like a good idea. Now, where were we?"

"I want to know about Carver's voluntary drug-testing program. Why did you start it?"

"I didn't. Rob Clemmer started it. You need to talk to him. And you need to talk to Ginger Amos. You see, the principal is just the cheerleader. Ginger is on point. She makes it happen. She knows the nuts and bolts of it."

"Well, while I'm here with you, what do you think about the program?"

"I fully support the program."

"How do the students like it?"

"Last year 90 percent of our students and staff signed up and this year 88 percent signed up. The name of the program is 'It's My Call', and if you are a member you agree to random drug testing."

"Why did Carver want a program like this?" I asked.

"We felt like we were perceived by others as the step-child of the schools. This is the only high school that is the traditional and original black high school in the WS/FC Schools. All the rest were closed or changed to middle schools. Carver has been here since 1951, and it has the highest black population (61 percent). People feel that Carver is not safe. But if they research it, they will find that Carver is equally, or more, safe than the other high schools. So, at Carver, we are building respect. The 'It's My Call' program shows the community that we are serious about learning at Carver and that most of the students don't use drugs. Our students aren't afraid to be tested to prove it. Respect has to be earned and this helps us to earn the respect of the community."

Respect! That is what Dan Piggott is all about. In an interview three years later, I found out that he has the reputation of Joe Clark, the tough-minded and determined principal depicted in the film, "Lean On Me." As a matter of fact, he is often called Joe Clark. The identity is so strong that when he was the assistant principal at North Forsyth in 1989, the students affectionately presented him a baseball bat bearing their signatures.

At that time, Piggott garnered considerable respect from both the white and black communities. He was an authentic role model for African-American students, or any students that start out disadvantaged and aspire to be leaders. He was the personification of respect.

He experienced the mountaintop reward of being named the 1999 North Carolina Principal of the Year award after starting out in life as a shoeless sharecropper's son. He knows what it was like to be at the bottom and he knows all the territory that lies in between. Piggott shared the highlights of that journey with me after he decided that I was "good people."

Piggott's father only completed the third grade and his mother stopped after the seventh grade. He claims they are two of the smartest people he ever met.

"There were two things my parents taught me," said Piggott. "You need to get as much education as you possibly can. And you have to establish a personal relationship with God for yourself. Get those two things and you can be successful in the world."

Piggott's teachers could see his determination to excel at school and they supported him emotionally and sometimes even physically.

"They let me spend the night with them so I could participate in the school plays, and often they bought me things that I needed. I didn't always know who bought me things, but they were there," said Piggott.

When Piggott wasn't at school, he was working on his other goal of building a personal relationship with God. Here again he received attention and encouragement.

"When I ran out of things to do as a kid," said Piggott, "I went to church. Anything I did not have, I prayed for."

In high school, Piggott realized that his family did not have the money to send him to college. It would be up to him. He worked hard, graduated as valedictorian of his class, and received a scholarship to attend a historically black college, A & T State University, in North Carolina.

With his bachelor of mathematics education in hand, he taught and coached at Winston-Salem's Atkins High School. According to Piggott, the principal, Don Golding, "pushed" him into school administration. Again, watching and listening, Piggott continued his education. He also adopted Golding's style of being the first to arrive and the last to leave the school.

Twelve years later, Piggott became assistant principal to Nash Hardy at Mount Tabor High School. "Nash was a very caring guy. There was no job that he would not do. So now, if I see a piece of paper on the floor at Carver, I pick it up. If there is water on the floor, I get a mop. If we don't have a bus driver, I'll drive the bus. That's what I learned from Nash."

His next mentor was Principal Ron Jessup at North Forsyth. "He was the first one that I saw who tried to run the school based on Christian principles. When he had to deal with someone, he would turn and ask me, 'If that was you, how would you want it to be done?' That was the Bible's way!"

The last principal he trained under was Kaye Shutt. She stressed the need to be fair and to make decisions based on principles—not on "who" someone was.

All of these lessons were put to the test, when years later he would have to make a tough decision regarding a good friend's son.

Here is the story as it appeared in his application for Principal of the Year award:

> *An administrative problem that I encountered recently involved my peer's son, a senior at Carver High School. My peer was a high school principal in the WS/FC school system and a neighbor for 24 years.*

The son was a gifted and popular student who served as president of the senior class. He was an excellent athlete who had been awarded several college scholarships including one to the Naval Academy. As this student was taking his senior group picture in the gymnasium, something happened that upset him. As a result, he lost his temper and became very belligerent and cursed several senior sponsors as he walked from the gym.

When the incident was reported to me, I met with the teachers to be certain as to what actually happened, and then I met with the assistant principals. It was determined that the student should be suspended from school for a total of five (5) days and that he not be allowed to be inducted into the Vocational Honor Society, where leadership and force of character are two attributes of the organization. (The student had recently been notified that he had met the criteria for the induction and was given the date for the induction ceremony.)

The parents objected to the prescribed punishment and demanded something much less. In addition, they contacted several elected officials to speak to me on their behalf. I didn't change my position. When I made no concessions, they obtained the services of a high profile lawyer to fight the decision. The parents and their lawyer appealed my decision to the superintendent. Dissatisfied with his decision, the matter came before the Board of Education. My decision was supported by the Board of Education.

As I reflect on this situation and upon my decision, I'm grateful to God that I was able to endure the stress and pressure exerted from the politicians and others to change my decision. I did the right thing. In the final analysis, respect and appreciation among staff, students, and parents soared because I did not compromise my principles. It is lonely at the top. I made the right decision.

The more I learned about Dan Piggott, the more I realized that regardless of who started the voluntary drug testing at Carver, once Dan Piggott was in charge, if he didn't believe in it—it wasn't going to stay. As it turned out, he was the biggest cheerleader. He nurtured one of the most innovative and successful drug-free campaigns in the U.S. The proof was in the student participation. In 1995, he had 90 percent of his students voluntarily taking a stand against drugs. Their words were backed up by their agreement to take random tests.

Piggott's first reaction to student drug testing was negative. This program was instituted in 1992, at Carver, while he was still the principal at Independence High School.

"I had two kids here (at Carver)," said Piggott, "and as a parent, I thought [voluntary drug testing] was intrusive. I thought it was none of the school's business. I didn't want to sign [the permission slip/pledge card] for my daughter, but she wanted me to. She said that if I signed, maybe kids who looked up to her as an athlete and a serious student might sign up for the program. She said, 'I'm not using drugs whether I sign or not, but maybe by signing I could make a difference in someone else's life.'"

She signed and he countersigned, but he wasn't fully convinced. He didn't like the idea of giving up rights, any rights, which blacks had fought so hard to win. Giving up this right to privacy—even voluntarily—seemed to be a step backwards.

The following year, he became the principal at Carver and examined the program and its impact on the students.

"After I got to understand the program," said Piggott, "I thought it might help. So I got on board. I thought, 'We'll go after this thing.' So we went after this. Our number one goal was to become the most respected high school in the WS/FC school district. This program could help us meet this goal."

Piggott explained that the "It's My Call" voluntary drug testing changed the public perception. It proved that at this traditionally black high school, most students do *not* use drugs.

"This random and voluntary drug testing," said Piggott, "is a way for our students to help dispel this myth."

Next I met with Ginger Amos. After 25 years of volunteering in schools, she was now on the payroll. Amos is an enthusiastic and generous Caucasian who continued to serve at Carver after her two sons graduated. She constantly refers to the students as "my kids."

"Mr. Piggott told me that you are the one that 'makes it happen'," I said, "and you are the one who knows the 'nuts and bolts' of the 'It's My Call' program."

"Mr. Piggott," said Amos, "does a lot more to support this program than he lets on. At every assembly he talks to the kids about the importance of staying drug-free and alcohol-free. They know that this is important to him. And he gives me everything that I ask for to help the kids. But really, it is the students that drive the program."

"How do you get the students involved?"

"Well, it starts with my CADDY (Carver Against Drugs and Drinking in Youth) kids. They are the leaders and they start by signing up themselves. We raise money for incentives and they promote this among their peers. CADDY students go two-by-two into the homerooms and ask the students to sign up. Another thing they do is invite students who aren't signed up to come to a special assembly. The assembly is designed by the students and that is important. It is peer-driven."

Amos went on to explain that school spirit and class spirit is also tapped. Seniors will compete with the freshmen, while juniors compete with the sophomores. The grade with the highest percentage of student pledges receives a party.

"A typical party," said Amos, "is given during lunch on the last Wednesday of the month. Usually we serve pizza or subs and have music. It is paid for by our business partner, Sara Lee Direct. Sometimes the competition is between classrooms. The freshmen class is usually the most difficult group to get on board. So the freshmen classrooms compete with each other and the one with the highest percentage of participation wins a pizza party."

"Do you think incentives are really a good idea?" I asked.

"Kids are incentive oriented. They love food, music, certificates, and T-shirts. Besides, we as adults like incentives too. Most businesses give incentives to you if you participate in United Way. They give out awards and time off work. The objective is to get the kids into the program. And incentives and recognition help tremendously."

"What happens if a student fails the drug test?"

"The school never gets called as long as the student agrees to drug counseling and accepts help. The school only gets called if the student refuses help. At that point, the student is taken out of the 'It's My Call' program."

"How does the drug testing actually happen?"

"We make an event out of it. Our students climb in a van and we go down to the testing center. The test is a urine test. And then, when they are done, we all go out for pizza."

"Obviously, you really believe in this program. Why do you like it so much?"

"We are dealing with a different clientele of kids than 10 years ago. Kids have more opportunity to utilize drugs and alcohol. These things are more accessible. So a program like 'It's My Call' helps kids to think twice. If they are at a party, they will think twice because these values have been instilled in them at Carver. Also, they know that they can be tested. I tell my kids that they need to be like the Scouts. Always be prepared. I believe this program really makes a difference with our kids."

Amos' experience with high school students goes far beyond the drug program. She was a stay-at-home mom who followed her children to school. She was not only a "grade mom," but for years was the PTA (Parent-Teacher Association) president. For 15 of the 25 years that she volunteered at school, she was at the school daily. Amos graded papers, prepared bulletin boards, listened to children read, helped with book fairs, supervised field trips and helped with parties. She was one of those rare parents who continued to volunteer at every school her children attended until they graduated.

"What I saw," said Amos, "is that by the time the kids got to high school, the parents were burned out and didn't want to participate."

Amos also noted that there is a myth that high school kids don't really need parental involvement. To the contrary, Amos believes that kids need *more* support as teenagers.

"Think about it," said Amos. "They are going through emotional growth and change. They are being faced with decisions that they didn't have earlier in life. Parents need to be there to remind them of the values that were set when they were younger regarding drugs, alcohol, sex, or whatever. My kids didn't mind my being at high school. I was real convenient when they needed money!"

"Didn't your family ever question you," I asked, "about giving all your time away? You mentioned that for years you were volunteering daily for four to six hours."

"I did it to benefit my family. We could have had a lot more materially, but money isn't everything. My husband and I showed our kids how important it is to give to the community, to be connected, to work together. And we got paid. We made lots of lasting friendships, we learned a lot, we grew and became stronger, and

It's MY Call

Principal Dan Piggott, at Carver H.S., reclaimed the KCK "Oscar of Recognition" Drug-free Trophy–recognizing the *Its My Call*– random voluntary drug testing program started at his school in 1992. To the left is CADDY President Laura Grubbs, who, along with her classmates, rallied the school to 93 % enrollment in the program in the 2002-03 school year. Ginger Amos, right, spearheads the program at Carver and received *KCK's Triple L Award* (Leaders Leading Leaders) in 2002. (photo reprinted with permission of *Kernersville News*)

Initially, Piggott was against drug testing.

"As a parent, I thought it (voluntary drug testing) was intrusive. I thought it was none of the school's business. I didn't want to sign for my daughter . . ."

Piggott did not like the idea of giving up rights–any rights–which blacks had fought so hard to win. Giving up this right to privacy– even voluntarily– seemed to be a step backwards. What changed?

http://www.wsfcs.k12.nc.us/chs

we became more compassionate of others. I would do it the same way if I had to do it over again."

Amos also said that volunteering helped her to be a part of her children's lives. Later, in 1995, when her son Stephen died in the line of duty as a police officer, she said that the years of volunteering brought her great comfort.

"One thing," said Amos, "that helped me deal with the loss of Stephen—one thing that has given me peace of mind—is that I was able to do so much for him."

Amos knows that not all parents can volunteer at school, but they can be actively involved in their children's lives.

"I have noticed," said Amos who spends some time as an ISS (In School Suspension) teacher, "that where there is strong family bonding and parents are actively involved in their kid's lives, the kids are less apt to be involved in making destructive decisions. Kids whose parents don't take time with them are the ones we often have discipline problems with at school."

Amos recommended that I talk with Chuck Chambers. Chambers was the CEO of Sara Lee Direct, the business partner of Carver High School. It was Chuck Chambers and former Carver Principal Rob Clemmer who originated the idea of voluntary drug testing for students.

"Just like a lot of people tithe to the church," explained Chambers, "Sara Lee executives are expected to give back to the community. In 1985-86, I participated in Leadership Winston-Salem because I was not involved. If I had to be involved, I wanted to do something fun. I wanted to help kids see their potential."

Leadership Winston-Salem is a private educational program, offered by its namesake non-profit organization. It allows citizens interested in assuming leadership roles to see how their community operates. About 40 applicants are admitted annually and, while costs can be as high as $2,500, most attendees are sponsored by their employers. Over a 10-month period, participants tour the jail, talk with the mayor, police chief, and other officials, tour neighborhoods and businesses, explore health and education, look at things as simple as garbage collection and as complex as economic development.

"Going out of that," said Chambers, "I saw the need for young people to have real-world role models to solve real problems. I was aware that Sara Lee had adopted a school in Chicago and I wanted to adopt a school in the WS/FC school district."

Chambers flew to Chicago to see for himself how a school-business partnership could work. Then he met with Zane Ergle, the then superintendent of the WS/FC schools.

"I went to him," said Chambers, "and said, 'this community needs an adopt-a-school program. I will personally participate. I want Sara Lee to adopt the first school.'"

The school officials were apprehensive. None of the 54 schools in the WS/FC district had ever had a business partner. What would they be giving up? Would the corporations use this as an opportunity to "sell" their products to the students? Would the businesses try to tell the principals how to run their schools? What price would the schools pay for accepting substantial financial support from one corporation?

According to Chambers, a community leader in East Winston named Louise Wilson wanted Carver to be the first school to be adopted. And so it was. Lily-white Chuck Chambers, a man organized, driven, and articulate, was going to serve personally as the liaison between Sara Lee Direct and the predominately black Carver High School.

"Our first meeting," said Chambers, "was awkward. A marketing person looks at cost per impression. Carver never had a business partner, and it looked like it was going to be too much work. But I was doing this out of principle—as a service. So I got involved and then I really fell in love with it."

Chambers really found a way to make a difference at Carver when Rob Clemmer became principal. Chambers invited Clemmer to attend a presentation at a local charity golf tournament, the Crosby Tournament. This celebrity golf tournament was named for the late Bing Crosby, and sponsored by his widow, Kathryn, who lived near Winston-Salem. Among other things, the money raised was used to fund scholarships for students in Forsyth County who couldn't afford to go to college. To be in the program, students pledged to be drug-free, take a random test, and attend academic workshops. At the 1992 event, Sara Lee was making a presentation on its use of drug testing in the workplace.

"Sara Lee," said Chambers, "was challenged about the constitutionality of mandatory drug testing of employees. Our ground for defense was that we are employers and that drug testing is one of our conditions for employment." Sara Lee won and other corporations followed.

So, in 1992, Chambers and Clemmer sat side-by-side with hundreds of other people from the community to hear about the rather new concept of employee drug testing.

"When Sara Lee mentioned voluntary drug testing," said Chambers, "we looked at each other. Our eyes met. The idea came to us at the same time. Sara Lee is the business partner of Carver. Our common goal is to prepare the students for work. When they go to work, they will likely be expected to pass a drug test. Let's try this at Carver."

Chambers was right. By the time a freshman in 1992 reached his graduation day in 1996, drug testing would become widespread in corporate America. According to American Management Association, more than 80 percent of the large firms surveyed in 1996 tested for drugs. That was up from a mere 22 percent in 1987.

"The real hero in getting voluntary drug testing in the schools," said Chambers, "is Rob Clemmer. We got the same idea at the same time, but he did all the leg work. He worked it through the bureaucracy. He worked with the school attorney Doug Punger, and he managed to get a front page interview with the *Winston-Salem Journal*."

Sara Lee declined to fund the cost of the drug testing. But Sara Lee would give the students incentives. As a leading producer of T-shirts, Sara Lee would, among other incentives, give a school T-shirt to every student that joined the new "It's My Call" program.

For funding, Chambers believed that "good ideas attract money." He had faith that somewhere the funds would be found.

According to Chambers, the day after the story ran in the *Winston-Salem Journal*, the man who invented the heat pump came in and wrote a check to cover the first year of testing. Then the ABC (Alcohol Beverage Control) board stepped forward and offered to pay for the testing for the following four years.

With the funding in place, Clemmer set about to promote this to his students. Clemmer decided to have an assembly and to have Chambers speak to the students.

"We had just created the concept of 'Carver Nation' at the school," said Chambers, "and our school goal was to be the most respected high school in the community. So we presented this as a primary way to earn the respect we wanted."

To build school pride, a "Vision of Carver Nation" was created, printed, and handed out. Here is the vision:

"We are a nation with no geographical boundaries, bound together through our beliefs. We are like-minded individuals sharing a common vision of what we want to be. We call our vision Carver Nation.

"Our common vision has the power to make Carver the most respected and admired high school in Winston-Salem. It has the power to lift us all.

"The source of our power is the unity and commitment of Carver citizens to constantly and forever improve in learning, teamwork, quality, imagination, leadership, and attitude.

"Vision without action is merely a dream. Action without vision just passes the time. Vision with action will change our world. This is the promise of a new day."

The students were given a printed copy of the seven guiding principles of the Carver Nation, which included those listed above along with learning and diversity. They were given an annual theme that was promoted for the entire year. In 1993-94, the theme was, "If it's to be . . . it's up to me." In 1994-95, it was "The power of one." In 1995-96, when I first visited Carver and interviewed Principal Piggott, the theme was "Expect to win."

The students who embraced the Carver Nation and joined the "It's My Call" program were given T-shirts they could be proud of. The shirts had an eye-catching cartoon of the school mascot, a blue and yellow yellow-jacket, hovering over the words *Carver Nation*.

Speaking at an assembly to kick-off the new school year became a tradition with Chambers. He got more and more involved. Though he had "groomed" an associate to take his place once the partnership was well established, Chambers never turned over the reins until he retired.

On September 4, 1996, I accepted Piggott's invitation to hear Chambers speak at Carver High School. This local business leader addressed an auditorium full of high school students at the start of a new school year.

Chambers stood on the stage and said, "Expect it. Expect what? . . . Expect to win. Our theme for this year at Carver High School is *Expect to Win*. Why? The idea was inspired by Dr. Maya Angelou's remarks last October in this auditorium when she referred to Carver High School as a "Rainbow in the Clouds."

He went on to explain that the rainbow—the vision—is "Carver Nation." "The goal of Carver Nation," said Chambers, "is to become the most respected high school in Winston-Salem."

He told the students that they had advanced one step farther toward that goal. That week, the Public Broadcasting System was going to air a 30-minute documentary entitled "Carver High School, A Rainbow in the Clouds."

When Chambers talked to the students, he talked to them like they were partners in a company. They had a job to do and together they could do it.

"One of life's most important lessons is this: It is impossible to advance properly in life without goals!"

While focusing on the goals and rainbows, Chambers encouraged the students to pay attention to the clouds. He said that the worst cloud was a negative attitude that "expects to lose."

Chambers shared some examples of negative thinking with his students.

"I come from a broken family. Nobody in my family ever amounted to anything. I'm not off to a very good start at school. Nobody believes in me. There's no way my family could afford to send me to college. People will laugh at me if I do what I dream of most."

Chambers said that the real problem is not outside us. It is *in* us. It is fear of failure. He next quoted Robert Schuller saying, "I'd rather attempt to do something great and fail than attempt to do nothing at all and succeed."

He next encouraged the students to forgo making excuses and to *choose* to make a commitment to overcome problems.

He quoted Napoleon Hill, who is often heard mentioned in corporate sales meetings, and said, "What the mind can conceive and believe, it can achieve."

Again he reaffirmed the 1996-97 school theme. "Expect to win. The world has a way of surrendering to those who expect to win. Expecting to win is what we call a "good" attitude. I think it is the best. I can tell you that in business it is *essential.* How would you like to work for a company that expected to lose? . . . You deserve the attitude advantage. . . Your attitude advantage is not a matter of luck. It is a decision."

Chambers closed with a powerful quote by Charles Swindoll. "The longer I live, the more I realize the impact of attitude on life. Attitude to me is more important than the facts. It is more important than the past, than education, than circumstances, than failures, than successes, than what other people say or do. It is more important than appearance, giftedness, or skill. It will make or break a company . . . a church. . . a home. The remarkable thing is we have a *choice* every day regarding the attitude we will embrace for that day. We cannot change our past . . . we cannot change the fact that people will act in a certain way. We cannot change the inevitable. The only thing we can do is play on the one string that we have, and that is our attitude . . . I'm convinced that life is 10 percent what happens to us and 90 percent how we react to it."

Chambers concluded the rally by saying, "Let's make this the best year at Carver yet! Let's *expect to win*."

The students clapped respectfully and seemed to be thinking about what Chambers had said. But when Piggott got up and unbuttoned his suit jacket to reveal the bright new Sara Lee T-shirt the students hooted and hollered and yelled out with pride. This was their leader. It would be up to him to reaffirm everything Chambers said at this opening meeting. And he would.

Chuck Chambers

"I'm convinced that life is 10 percent what happens to us and 90 percent how we react to it."
—Chuck Chambers, quoting Charles Swindoll during an assembly at Carver High School.

9

Community Meeting

Lesson 9: Know your facts

The day of reckoning arrived. Tuesday, July 30, 1996. I was out of bed before sunrise, fueled by the potent mixture of fear and anticipation. Had I done enough? Did the community really care? Had the community been "moved"? These questions—this entire "community service" project—would be judged by one measurable act. How many people would attend the noon meeting at the YMCA?

There wasn't much time to worry. There was still plenty of work to do. Each attendee was promised a packet of information. It would be up to me to create the packets. So I arrived at the *Kernersville News* office at eight o'clock sharp to make about 100 copies each of several newspaper stories. The copying and collating took much longer than anticipated. It was nearly 11 o'clock before I arrived at the YMCA.

Racing against the clock, I placed the packets on seats of about 75 metal chairs. Then, I waited. Doubt began to surface. Would we spend the next hour talking with five or ten people in a sea of empty chairs—or would the community show itself?

My anxiety faded as people filled the room. While a few people quietly perused the packets, most were busy greeting friends and neighbors. The people were cheerful and obviously connected. It began to remind me of a large family reunion. By noon, the excitement was almost palpable.

As people were finding their seats, Jim Wilhelm, the assistant superintendent and the facilitator for the meeting, centered himself at the head table. To his left was Glenn's Principal Coplin. Interestingly, I had misspelled Coplin's name in every story that cited him. He never brought it to my attention until this meeting. And then, he only did so by underlining his last name on the sign-in sheet.

Next to Coplin was Kernersville Police Chief Neal Stockton, followed by Judge Ron Spivey. Spivey arrived a few minutes late and brought a television crew with him. Just minutes before the meeting began, Owensby decided that I should be at the head table also, so I took the end seat next to Spivey. Ginger Amos, Captain C.C. McGee from the Sheriff's Department, County Commissioner Dave Plyler, and the two School Resource Officers (SROs), Larry Handy and Terry Gray, were also at the head table.

The meeting proceeded much differently than I expected, though I'm not sure where I acquired my expectations. I'd never been to a town meeting in any of the states where I lived—Michigan, Arizona, and North Carolina. But I envisioned the meeting as being highly organized, formal, and systematic. Instead, it unfolded like a neighborhood picnic. It had a "Hi. How are you doing? Hey, did you hear about what happened?" kind of a tone.

Wilhelm stood and introduced himself and briefly stated the purpose of the meeting. He then said, "There are enough people and enough energy in this room to make something happen."

County Commissioner Dave Plyler was the next to speak and said, "We can make it safer if we want to. What happens in the schools is a mirror of what is happening in our homes. The county needs to play a continuing part in this problem."

Captain C. C. McGee of the sheriff's department directed attention to the 85 citizens that were seated in the audience and said, "I've been to a lot of meetings and this is the first time I've looked out and really seen an audience. A lot of times there are only five to ten people."

Police Chief Stockton focused back on the problem and explained, "The drug problem is a big concern. It is sad to see 13-14 year olds committing suicide, beating their moms, and stealing their stuff. We're trying to save the kids at an early age."

Coplin then put the focus back on the community and said, "It is encouraging to see so many here. After 16 years in education, I'm encouraged to see the community pulling together."

Finally, Judge Spivey, who started the Teen Court in Forsyth County, chimed in. "I'm very excited about this meeting. To all of us, it means a great deal. I hope this meeting will make my job a little easier in the future."

After everyone else on the panel had a chance to speak, I encouraged the audience to look inside the packets on their chairs. Specifically, they were asked to take out their copy of the story, "Drugs in school . . . Discussing solutions." The three A's of drug use listed in this story could be used as a guide to measure the probable impact of solutions.

> Acceptability—the belief that drug use is OK, or that everyone is doing it.
>
> Availability—the belief, especially through sightings, that drugs are easy to get.
>
> Actual use—the real number of young people using drugs.

The audience started participating, but the comments were scattered and disconnected. Parents talked about "values," the "good old days," and the "horrors" of teenage drug use.

I was impatient and wondered when we would actually get to the point of "solving the problem." Meantime, I was taking notes as fast as I could, while trying to be a part of the panel.

Then, someone who introduced himself as a youth director brought the conversation back to the purpose of the meeting and said, "Through the articles, I got concerned and started questioning youths and found out that all kids are susceptible to drug use. Until we throw out the stereotypes, we can't solve this problem. Good kids are using drugs recreationally."

Brenda Moorefield, a nurse and PTA president, built on this. "I work in the Emergency Room. I spoke to the community 20 years ago, and people wanted to keep their head in the sand. I'm happy the community is finally ready to do something. Living here in Kernersville, we may feel we are protected. But that is just a smoke screen," she said.

Just when I thought we were going to get down to business, people started to pat the *Kernersville News* on the back.

"I applaud the *Kernersville News*," piped up Alderman Rene Plante, "for bringing this to the forefront."

Fellow Alderman, Jim Waddell chimed in, "This meeting is an excellent first step to solve the Kernersville drug problem."

Someone else added, "I hope we keep taking *all* the necessary steps to really reach the solution to this problem."

Angela McReynolds put the power back in the hands of the people and emphasized, "The community determines the acceptance or denial of an alcohol or drug problem. So it is great that this community cares and is here."

Winding the lengthy introduction to a finish, with everyone having had a chance to speak his mind, Chuck Chambers, CEO of Sara Lee Direct, concluded, "Drugs never helped us accomplish our goals."

And finally, Owensby cinched the opening by saying, "We have the opportunity here to solve this problem. We have the community and we have the public officials. Don't let this moment pass."

Wilhelm took his cue and centered the attention on the task at hand. He said, "When kids reach about 14, the peer group is incredible. The *peer* group will outweigh the parents' influence unless they are exceptionally well-connected."

He mentioned that one of the possible solutions was a peer-driven program currently being piloted at Carver High School. Wilhelm then gave Ginger Amos a chance to explain this option to the community.

"We're very excited about 'It's My Call,'" she said. "Students have the opportunity to sign up and stay drug-free during their lifetime and especially during their four years of high school. They are subject to a random test once or twice a month. Eighty-eight percent signed up this year and I think this shows that their peers made a *commitment*."

Wilhelm picked up on this and added, "This is the number one trait wanted in entry-level employees. Employers want people with positive attitudes, who can *keep commitments*, and work with a team. None of these are in our school curriculum."

Someone in the audience asked if Carver ever received complaints about the voluntary drug-testing program. Amos answered first.

"I've been part of the program," said Amos, "for three to four years and I've never been called. I tell the kids it's like being a Scout—you always must be prepared."

Carver Principal Piggott then answered from the audience, "We try to make sure there is no coercion. We let the positive peer pressure drive the program—that's what promotes it. We want the kids to really commit to not be fooling with the drugs."

A Carver student, Jason Berry, spoke up.

> *"There are advantages to being in our program. You get a free T-shirt. And if you get tested, you get free pizza."*
> —Jason Berry, Carver High School Student

Someone asked how many students at Carver were randomly tested in a year. Amos answered that 155 kids were tested.

A man in the back of the room changed the subject. He said, "When I was 15-16 years old, I was involved in drugs and arrested at my school. What helped in my school was the reward system. One thing people are afraid of is their peers—not the authority. If we put notices in the hallways at school offering a $200 reward for drugs and stolen goods, even if it doesn't produce turn-ins, it produces fear in the drug dealers. That is a tremendous intimidation factor for the drug dealers. The majority of the students know who is doing what."

Continuing in this new direction, Alderman Plante said, "My concern is that we've seen a number of news reports about sports figures and politicians who have done drugs and are found guilty—so it becomes a minimized thing. It's time you *put that person's picture in the hall* with an "X" on it and say 'you don't want to follow that person'."

From there, the meeting wandered farther from local control. Someone said, "Drugs are a problem. But perhaps it is a symptom of a bigger problem—like no values."

Someone else offered a solution. But again, it was outside the reach of Kernersville, which has no radio or television station, nor does it own a sports team.

> *"We need to use TV spots to show what recreational drugs support. We need to fine sports figures who use drugs 25 percent of their annual pay. We need to publicize. Have pop stars say, 'Drugs are wrong!'"*
> —Open comment at the meeting.

Closer to home, someone brought up the role of the parents. "Parents," said the attendee, "not only are *not* talking to their kids about drugs—but they are actually supplying alcohol to under-aged kids for parties."

Someone else chimed in, "We need to educate the parents and then hold them responsible. I've heard of parents giving kids their marijuana back because they don't feel like they are abusing it."

The Police Chief agreed. "We had parents rent a motel room for 30-40 kids who were using drugs and alcohol and having sex. The police made arrests and the number one complaint of the parents was that the police were harassing their kids. It took a month to get the parents off my back."

A parent spoke up and agreed with the Chief. "There are some very irresponsible parents. Some of my son's friends have gotten drugs from their parents. Our schools are a major source of drugs. Just like you get lumber at a lumberyard and clothes at a mall—kids know they can get drugs at school. It is so available that even kids that normally would not take drugs—do."

With the conversation on the parents' role winding down, I suggested that a mandatory parenting class prior to high school graduation might be part of the solution. I cited a statistic in the "Discussing Solutions" newspaper story from *Institute for American Values* which said, "90 percent of all American females eventually become parents." Maybe, if all high school students had a parenting class, they would be empowered to talk to their future children about drug use, violence, problem resolution, and individual family values. Also, the class might reduce acceptability of drug use as students envision themselves as the parents of the future.

Captain McGee said that part of the solution might be to have more uniformed officers in the schools as School Resource Officers (SROs).

He explained, "Our job is 50 percent law enforcement, 33 percent teaching, and 11 percent talking with the kids about their personal problems. I spent six and a half years in vice and narcotics, and I've had parents call and ask me what they can do about their kids being on drugs. One of several keys is—parents must get involved. You need to know where your kid is going and what he is doing. The gang influence is here too. The premise behind gangs is money. And, drugs equal money."

> *"We find that five to nine percent of the population causes 90 percent of the problems at school. More SROs would help."*
> —Captain McGee, Forsyth County Sheriff's Dept.

Evidently, McGee's words reminded another attendee of his own juvenile experience with the law. "I was sent to reform school for six months at age 16. I thought a dozen times a day, 'I will never do anything again that will allow others to take my freedom.' So I never broke another law."

Chuck Chambers then steered the meeting back toward the voluntary drug-testing program.

> *"Kids get mixed signals from society. The kids are poorly led. With 'It's My Call' we tell the kids—'you're poorly led, but you are still accountable for your choices and it's your call.' 'It's My Call' was a good idea that drew money and student support."*—Chuck Chambers

The meeting was running overtime and Wilhelm quickly threw out to the floor the remaining possible solutions that we listed in the information packets.

As I was at the end of the panel table, I was given the final opportunity to comment on each item before the next item was considered.

In a nutshell, when "more D.A.R.E." was considered, I suggested that more education was probably not the answer. It really wasn't getting to the root of peer pressure. When "more drug-dog searches" were suggested, I reminded the audience of what a local Glenn student said. He said, "The way I see it, dogs and drugs are like cops and speeding. When the kids see the dogs, they have a brief 'heart attack,' so they slow down, but when the dogs are gone, they speed up again."

When the idea of "undercover police" was addressed, Wilhelm assured the audience that this was a real possibility. He was principal at East Forsyth when he allowed undercover police in the school. At the time, it was a daring move that almost cost him his job. But it was decided at that time that if an individual school wants to implement undercover police, the school does *not* need school board permission.

I heartily agreed that this was effective. However, unlike the "It's My Call" program, which focuses on rehabilitation and positive peer pressure, the undercover police operation resulted in student arrest records and caused fear. Personally, I favored a combination of both these programs, along with a mandatory parenting class.

The ideas of legalizing certain drugs or creating more youth activities were barely mentioned, and then John Staples spoke up.

> *"You can't cure a problem, unless you admit you have one."*
> —John Staples, *News* editor

Staples then asked, "Do you think we should continue?"

"Yes," the group said unanimously.

At that point, a parent recommended that Glenn and East parents meet in separate groups, as she was anxious to get something in place at school before the school year began. As school started in August and this was July 30, that did not prove possible. But within two weeks, evening meetings were scheduled.

As soon as the meeting was dismissed, I went into the audience and asked people two questions. "Why are you here? How did you think the meeting went?"

One father, who insisted that he remain unnamed, said, "I have two teenage sons—one of which gave me plenty of problems, including drug use. I came to make sure that my ideas got stated, to tell people about the prevalence, to see what is going to be done, and to see if I can help. This meeting gave me the sense that we really can get something done."

The only student I saw, Jason Berry, said, "I was interested in seeing what the other schools were doing. And since Carver has the 'It's My Call,' I thought I could share something. Overall, the meeting was pretty good. We covered a lot of ground on a lot of different subjects, but we heard a lot of good ideas."

Jason's mom, Debra, said, "I want the drug testing and education at my son's school to continue. I'm really proud of the work his school is doing. Maybe other schools will at least give it a look or a try."

The mayor of Kernersville, Tom Prince, said, "I thought the meeting went great. I was surprised and pleased at the turnout. People were surprised by the surveys and interviews. It was great to see parents and elected officials and others coming together."

"I thought the meeting was very successful. I was impressed by the number of people, plus the thrust of the meeting was on finding a solution. I think it is wise for each school to address its own solution," said Ginger Amos.

East Forsyth parent Ann Crutchfield said, "Everyone needs to get together and decide something. It worries me that my daughter will be at school and the peer pressure is so great. I like the idea of voluntary drug testing. We do that at work."

Kim McClure, the Child Care Director at the YMCA with up to 300 elementary school students, said, "Maybe I can learn something to help with prevention in my age group. My question after the meeting was over was, 'What can I do now?'"

"I was shocked at the result of the surveys and that the drug problem could be so bad in such a pleasant little town like Kernersville," said resident Ronald Allison. "For a first meeting, it went quite well. A lot of times, you get that many people and nothing gets done. But here, the community leaders all got to speak."

Luther Conger, Jr. said that though his children were grown, he attended the town meeting because he lives here. Then he went on to reprimand the rest of the town.

"Jim Wilhelm," bristled Conger, "said he was pleased with the group. But based on all the information in the newspaper, I thought a whole lot more people should have been here. This meeting should have been held at the Benton Convention Center and had 2000-3000 people there. People who weren't here should be embarrassed. People that attended should go to their work and their churches and ask the other people, 'Why weren't you there?'"

Dee Dee Sullivan, who has a 15-year-old son at East Forsyth, was fired up.

> *"I'd like to see some solutions implemented. I'm going to the school tomorrow to tell them what I would like to see done. Especially, a program like at Carver and the undercover police."* —Dee Dee Sullivan, mother of a 15-year-old student

Judge Spivey noted, "My judgment of a good meeting is how quickly the time goes by and the time went by fast. Now we need to take one or two ideas and go full force."

2013 Town Government

Kernersville has a Council/Manager form of government. The Board of Aldermen are elected every two years and include a Mayor and five aldermen. Kernersville protects its citizens with its 82-member Kernersville Police Department, and 60-member Fire & Rescue Squad.

Front left, Dale Martin, town clerk, Dana Caudill Jones, ald., Mayor Dawn Morgan, Keith Hooker, ald., Irving Neal, ald. Back left, Tracey Shifflette, ald., Neal Stockton, ald., John Wolfe, town attorney, Curtis Swisher, town manager.

10

Meetings at Glenn and East

Lesson 10: Expect to do some things for free

Both schools had advised the *News* of their meeting dates. Glenn's meeting was set for Tuesday, August 27, and East's was scheduled for September 10.

As with the past meetings, I wanted to take some copies of the surveys and stories for the parents to keep and to read. I asked Owensby how many copies he thought I should make as the *News* was paying for the photocopies. He thought for a moment and then suggested that we do a special section in the newspaper. It would highlight five or six of the stories from the series and a copy of the survey. He would use the section as an insert in the Saturday and the Tuesday paper. Then he would print several hundred extra copies for the meetings at the schools.

"Really?" I excitedly asked. "That's a great idea. Maybe a recap will move more people to come to the meetings."

"Of course," he said, "we will have to sell enough ads to pay for it. Do you think you can sell some ads?"

"I don't know. I guess. I used to sell stocks and real estate. But who would I sell them to?"

We sat down and made a list. He suggested Sara Lee Direct, YMCA, Step One, the Coalition for Drug Abuse Prevention, the health department, the mayor of Kernersville, Kernersville Police Chief Neal Stockton, Sheriff Ron Barker, Kernersville Parks and Recreation, WS/FC Schools, and Judge Ron Spivey. Owensby said that it would take $600 in ads to pay for the special section. The charge for a full-page ad was $200. If I could garner $400 of the $600, he would take care of the rest.

I scanned my list for a sure "yes." I called Chuck Chambers at Sara Lee Direct. Chambers listened patiently to my pitch, declined to buy an ad, but said that he would sponsor a story on Carver's drug-testing program for $200. He agreed that I could use the story that ran in the newspaper on July 23. With two photos, the story took up a full page in the section.

Next, I called Judge Spivey. 1996 was an election year and Judge Spivey had supported the leadership and the community meeting in Kernersville. Would he buy an ad in our special section? He bought a full-page $200 ad that reminded people of the election on November 5 and his interest in Teen Court.

Though I had reached my required $400, I went ahead and made a few more calls. Sheriff Barker wanted a $50 ad showcasing the two SROs, Larry Handy at Glenn, and Terry Gray at East Forsyth. In their quotes, the officers explained that they were at school every day to help the students and to provide a safe environment. There was also a photo of the sheriff. He reminded the public that it was the Forsyth

County Sheriff's Department that pioneered the uniformed SRO program which was now catching on statewide.

The Coalition also bought a $50 ad, while the YMCA and Step One each opted for $100. At that point, I quit calling and took the list of $700 in sales to Owensby. He had the sales staff sell additional ads and told me to select the stories to be reprinted.

Owensby wrote a small story for the front page. It reminded parents that according to the National Household Survey on Drug Abuse, drug use among American teens has doubled from 1992 to 1996. He concisely correlated the national problem to Kernersville. He concluded: "We therefore urge all local residents to get involved and to become aware of this crisis."

Under this story was a 5" x 6" photo of Sheriff Barker in a bulletproof vest. Behind him, several of his Gang/Drug Taskforce officers were looking into the back of a truck that held confiscated marijuana. The caption beneath the photo was an alarm: "Is this unit looking for your child? Sheriff Ron Barker's department created this team to help stamp out drug dealing in Forsyth County."

In all, 11 stories were reprinted for this section. I didn't think the caption sent the right message. We weren't threatening to arrest someone's child for drug dealing. Our goal was to encourage, enlighten, and empower. But we were running over deadline, so I kept quiet.

On either side of this photo were reprints of student interviews from the two high schools, Mike Hill's story for East Forsyth and Steve Logan's story for Glenn. Boxed out on the front page were the meeting time, date, and place for each school.

The actual drug survey appeared on page two, along with the results and interpretations. An editorial by John Staples followed on page three. In part it stated:

> *"The most dangerous thing we hear from any generation is that ubiquity makes for morality. It is the ageless illogical conversation that says: 'Everybody does it, that makes it OK.' It is like the old joke: 'Manure tastes good; 50 billion flies can't be wrong.'"* John Staples

A few days prior to the meeting at Glenn, I received the findings from two drug studies and wrote a story on each one. The first was the National Household Survey on Drug Abuse. The other was local. It was prepared by William B. Hansen, Ph.D. of the Department of Public Health Sciences at Bowman Gray School of Medicine. The report was dated January 30, 1996, and was labeled *Report of Substance Abuse Behaviors in Winston-Salem/Forsyth County for the Years 1990 through 1995.* Hanson noted:

> "This report presents findings from a five-year study of adolescents conducted in Winston-Salem and Forsyth County. Between 1990-91 and 1994-95 academic years, 40,542 surveys were administered to students attending public schools in grades 6-12."

"Between 1991-92 and 1994-95 lifetime use of marijuana among 8th grade students nearly doubled and lifetime prevalence among 9th grade students rose from around 20% to nearly 35%."

"Two drugs, marijuana and inhalants, have increased in prevalence during the recent past. These findings indicate that efforts to prevent alcohol, tobacco, marijuana, and inhalants in particular need to be bolstered."

"These increases mirror national survey results, but are nonetheless disturbing in that the increase in use has been so dramatic and shows no signs of slowing . . . There appears to be no slowing in trend over time, suggesting that this trend will continue into the future unless effectively addressed."

I noted that the findings of this *scientific* study reflected the student responses from the *Kernersville News* survey at Glenn and East Forsyth earlier this year. At the end of the story, parents were invited to attend the meetings.

Three days later, I carried several hundred copies of the special section to the meeting at Glenn. Principal Coplin greeted me warmly and asked me to leave any extra copies for parents who were unable to attend.

Coplin enthusiastically welcomed the 65 people who came to help solve the drug problem. He let the group know that prior to the meeting much work had been done. A nine-member task force had been put in place which included Don Hancock, representing the school's business partner, Lee Apparel, Captain C.C. McGee of the Forsyth County Sheriff's Department, Jane Dietrich, a teacher at Glenn and the S.A.V.E. (Students Against Violence Everywhere) sponsor, Principal Coplin, Tab Hunter, Forsyth County District Attorney, Rick Bagley of the WS/FC School Board, Karen Culler, PTSA (Parent/Teacher/Student Association) representative, and two Glenn students, Destiny Gentle and Jerry Saunders.

After Coplin outlined the schedule for the meeting, the two student representatives spoke:

"I stand up for what I believe in," said Destiny Gentle. "By standing up for myself and my rights, people respect me more. I'm involved in sports and drama, and standing up doesn't make me less popular . . . If more kids would stand up, and say, 'I'm drug free and I'm proud of it,' it would help."

"I'm drug free, always been drug free, and plan on staying drug free," said Jerry Saunders. "You always have people that talk about drugs. But I love Glenn. It's a spirited school. I don't think drugs are a part of Glenn."

Next, Angela McReynolds said, "We have one of the strongest drug policies in the state. Each school chooses which drug program it will use, based on its populations and its success. We have to keep the best of what we've got, try new things, and let go of those that don't work as well."

"As parents, when our teens get older, we think we have little influence or control over them—but we do," said Nancy Harris of Step One. "We are the most influential ones in our child's life. We do have power here."

"There's no simple solution," Ava Troxler from the Coalition for Drug Abuse Prevention reminded the group, "It's a community problem. It's everyone's problem."

The group broke into six lively brainstorming groups. In all six groups, the findings seemed to center on two themes: People wanted to create a program at Glenn that would change the conversation at school to, "I don't use drugs and I'm proud of it." And secondly, people wanted the solution to be visible—something the students could see and focus on.

The "It's My Call" program from Carver was discussed because it accomplishes these two goals. But there was no decision to implement the program. Instead, the Glenn taskforce decided to look for ways to create a similar medium for its students.

Coplin was committed to reaching a solution in a timely manner. He scheduled a follow up meeting for October 1. At that time the PTSA would announce the new plan of action. In February, another meeting would be held to evaluate the performance of the new initiatives. And, finally, in May, a meeting was planned for further evaluation and to make recommendations for the next school year.

> *"Maybe we can make a difference not only here at Glenn, but maybe at other schools too!"* —Principal Adolphus Coplin

After the Glenn meeting, a concerned grandmother wrote a letter to the editor. She had attended the meeting at the YMCA and she urged the public to attend the next meetings at the schools.

"If a circus train came to Kernersville," she said, "and somehow a 15-foot python escaped, and word got out that there would be a meeting to see what could be done for our safety, no building would be large enough to hold the people. The python's danger could never, never be the danger of drugs to our children and families. This is a wake-up call. Please check the newspaper for the next meeting concerning drugs. We need parents, grandparents, and concerned friends to attend."

At East, two weeks later, Principal Judy Grissom opened the discussion by stating that the meeting was being held as a result of the survey and she felt a need to defend herself and her school.

"I'm beginning my second year as principal," she said, "and the drug problem is not greater here than at any other high school. Of course, the drug problem is here, but it is not any worse. It is just that we participated in the survey."

Senior Tiffany Spears followed her. Spears too defended her school.

"As a student," said Spears, "I see drugs as a problem in the community, school, and homes. I have never seen drugs being used and I've never been approached. Some students believe it is cool to downgrade their school. If the survey was retaken, I think we wouldn't find as many kids using drugs as the first survey said."

East had the same guest speakers as Glenn, but the speakers had new speeches.

"A lot of baby boomers have children," said McReynolds, "and two-thirds believe they couldn't do anything about their kids using marijuana. It's here. They are *our* kids in *our* homes. They look normal, and they are normal, but they need our support." McReynolds was citing a survey published in 1996 by Columbia University's Center on Addiction and Substance Abuse.

"One parent said to me," Nancy Dixon of Step One said, "I don't want to talk to my kids about drugs because I don't want to give them any ideas. I said, 'They already have ideas, honey. Talk to them!'"

"By the time a child reaches 18 years of age," said Ava Troxler from the Coalition of Drug Abuse Prevention, "he's seen 75,000 positive drinking messages through the media. How many of us have given our kids the message 75,000 times, 'Don't drink unless you are 21?'"

Like Glenn, the 60-plus attendees divided into brainstorming groups. Unlike Glenn, there was no discernable common thread in the solutions. Some suggestions were as follows: School uniforms or a stronger dress code, parent networking, parents patrolling the "hill" on campus, undercover police, voluntary random drug testing, more D.A.R.E. type programs, more teacher parent conferences, and a way to recognize and reward students who model positive behavior.

Grissom reminded parents that the solutions would be submitted to a taskforce. The taskforce would unveil its plan of action on Monday, October 14. All were invited to attend.

The story on the meeting at East Forsyth was the final entry in the portfolio of stories that was submitted for the Community Service Award in the 1996 NCPA contest.

* * *

All entries for the contest had to be postmarked by October 3. That was only two weeks away. Staples asked me to put the entry together for the Community Service Award.

"Will I be paid to do this?" I asked.

Money was an issue at the newspaper. There were always threats of cost cutting, reducing staff, and managing unauthorized overtime. When I wrote my first commissioned story on the 89-year-old retired schoolteacher, I'd turned in a bill for two hours of interviewing and four hours of writing. I received my check for $42 ($7 per hour), but Staples told me that Owensby was not accustomed to paying that much for one story.

"But it took me four hours to write it. The story took up nearly half a page of print. And it was a good story," I protested.

"That's not the point," Staples said. "In the newspaper business, we all end up doing a lot of things that we don't get paid for. I sometimes say that the more I write, the less I earn. So usually, your charge for writing a story should not be more than twice your time spent in the interviewing. And an interview shouldn't normally take more than an hour."

Money had proved to be a sore spot during the "Drugs in Schools" series too. I knew that Owensby wanted to win the award. But I also knew that he was always counting pennies. I'd given my word to the schools that the *Kernersville News* would stick with this series until the community decided whether or not to be a part of the solution. So I withheld my bill until the *News* had printed enough stories to keep my promise.

When I turned in my first bill, it was for $461.20. This was over five times larger than my typical bill, as it represented several weeks' work. Even at that, I only charged for about half the actual work that went into the project, because journalists "end up doing a lot of work they don't get paid for." Still, I got the reaction I anticipated. Once again, Owensby sent Staples to deal with me.

"Mr. Owensby was pretty upset by your bill."

"Why?"

"Well, he had no idea that the series was costing this much. It would have been better for you to turn in several smaller bills."

"I thought about turning in more bills, but I was afraid that he would cancel the series when he saw how much it was costing. And I gave my word that we would stick with this. I didn't want to take the chance that he would stop the series before all the questions were answered."

"Patty," said Staples, "this is the age-old battle between journalists and publishers. Journalists always want to write more and publishers are always interested in keeping the newspaper profitable. We journalists would give the paper away because we think stories *need* to be told. But the paper would go broke if journalists operated the newspaper. We need someone to make sure that the paper stays profitable or there would be no newspaper for us to write for."

"Well, I think he knew about how much it was costing because he saw all the stories. He approved of them before they ran. I don't think he thought I was writing them for free. And I still have some stories that need to be written in this series. Is he going to pay me?"

"He's going to pay you. But you need to turn your bills in every week," said Staples.

So when I asked if I was going to be paid to put together a 25-page submission for the press contest, it was for good reason. I didn't want to do four to eight hours of work for free so that the *Kernersville News* could win its first community service award. I'd already done a lot for free.

Staples agreed that I would be paid. I would also be fully responsible for the entry, which would include a cover letter that explained the origin of the project, the method used to "move the community," the obstacles, the timeline, the results, and the conclusion.

My first attempt was quite literary. It opened:

> *Historian H.G. Wells suggested that a man's greatness can be measured by "what he leaves to grow, and whether he started others to think along fresh lines with a vigor that persisted after him." In comparison, the Kernersville News believes that the greatest service a newspaper can render its community is to become a medium through which the community can focus and unite to*

solve a problem in a unique and sustained manner. **The Kernersville News** *was able to render such a service to its community by means of the "Drugs in School" series.*

The three-page cover letter ended with: *Over 200 years ago, philosopher Edmund Burke, stated, "Evil triumphs when good men do nothing." Kernersville News decided to be among the "good men" that took a firm and direct stand against teenage drug use in the community and to take the lead in giving it front page focus. The commitment to this decision proved to be the most outstanding community service rendered, as the community quickly followed suit and began initiating its active defense.*

Staples read it and said it was nicely done, but it was a bit more than the judges needed. After listening to him, I came up with, "The most outstanding service a newspaper can render its community is to present a problem so clearly and convincingly that the community itself unites to meet the challenge. The *Kernersville News* was able to render such a service to its community."

Along with this entry, I submitted an entry for Investigative Reporting at my own expense. This award goes to the individual journalist, as opposed to the entire newspaper. The entry required a one-statement introduction explaining the circumstances surrounding the extensive investigation. Judges would be looking for "evidence of probable impact." I wrote a summary, selected half-a-dozen stories and placed my entry in a box with the staff's entries.

Before the box was postmarked, I asked Staples, "Do you think we'll win the Community Service award? Do you think I have a chance at the Investigative Reporting award?"

He chose his words carefully. "In the past, I've entered the Community Service Award contest and felt sure that we would win. And we didn't. So you never know. But we do know that we really made a difference in Kernersville with this. As far as your award, there are plenty of very talented journalists who have never won a press association award. So you have to view it like Christmas. You never feel like you deserve a gift, but if you get one, that's great."

Just a couple weeks prior to submitting our entries, Ava Troxler told me the *Kernersville News* was receiving an honorable mention at the Coalition for Drug Abuse Prevention's 1996 awards banquet. She detected the disappointment in my brief response. Troxler explained that her organization only gave awards for community service if the service was rendered on a volunteer basis. The newspaper sold newspapers and was in the newspaper business, so it didn't qualify. But the Coalition did want to recognize the positive impact the *Kernersville News* had in raising drug awareness in the community.

I attended the banquet and accepted the award on behalf of the *News*. I couldn't help but feel that we were getting a consolation prize instead of real recognition. I certainly hoped for much more from the press contest and from the community at the future meetings.

Housing

Kernersville takes pride in its homes. Whether houses are in the Historic District, small neighborhoods, out in the country next to a well-preserved original homestead cabin, condominiums, farm houses, apartments, simple bungalows or gated community homes – maintaining clean and inviting homes is a community priority.

11

Losing Momentum

Lesson 11: People make their own choices

About 50 people met at Glenn for the follow-up meeting. Unfortunately, only about 20 of them were parents. The rest were officials of the Parent-Teacher-Student Association (PTSA), members of the Glenn taskforce, teachers, administrators from the WS/FC schools, and a few business people.

Principal Coplin reminded the attendees, "It's not just a school issue. All of us need to work collectively, together, the parents, students, school, and community." The plan included:

- Student focus—Voluntary Drug Testing
- School focus—Student Assistance Program (SAP)
- Parent focus—Parent Support Group
- Community focus—Widespread financial and educational support

> Glenn's voluntary drug testing program was patterned after Carver's *"It's My Call"* program. In 1995, 88 percent of Carver's students *voluntarily* signed a pledge to live a drug/alcohol-free life and to be tested randomly.

"It gives our students," said Coplin, "a way to measure their perception about drug use. It's not a cure-all."

The Student Assistance Program (SAP) supplements the voluntary drug-testing program because often, students who use drugs are trying to escape from long-term unresolved problems.

"SAP is a group of interested teachers," explained Angela McReynolds, "who are trained to recognize teen problems. These problems are not just alcohol and drugs, but also deal with absenteeism, teen pregnancy, and many others."

SAP reviews students' problems and assists them in finding real solutions. Sometimes they are assigned a case worker and are referred to an appropriate community agency. The idea is that if you solve the underlying problem—the issue causing the teen pain—the teen will no longer be inclined to numb the pain with drugs.

The third prong of the new program was the Parent Support Group (PSG). The PTSA made this group a standing committee. The PSG would provide parenting workshops and networking opportunities. The first meeting was set for Tuesday, November 5th.

"It's for parents," said Glenn High School Taskforce member Karen Culler, "and other interested people. It is a chance to share concerns and to see how other parents are addressing these issues."

The community, too, was given a job. The voluntary drug testing would cost $8,000 to $10,000 annually. It would be up to the community to raise the money. Also, the Glenn Taskforce wanted the community to stay alert and educated on teens and drugs.

The *Kernersville News* agreed to use its pages to keep the community informed. The Forsyth County Sheriff's Department made arrangements to educate parents, teens, and teachers in Gang Awareness. The North Carolina Highway Patrol offered to create a program on Vehicle Safety and Alcohol Prevention.

Near the end of the meeting, Captain C.C. McGee of the sheriff's office put everything into perspective. "The community is asking us to do our jobs. The school's staff is here, the teachers are here, and we are here. Where are the parents? Without the parents—and the 1,100 students who attend here—we can't solve this problem. Where are the parents?"

This time, no one commented on how encouraging the turnout was. But Coplin ended the meeting on a positive note. He commended the taskforce for doing what the community had commissioned it to do. He applauded the new four-prong program.

"At Glenn High School we have a favorite saying," said Coplin. "We are going to get on up. Get on up and meet the challenge. We can do it! Let's encourage as many people as possible to get on up to the success."

After the meeting, Coplin came up and shook my hand warmly. He thanked me for all that the *Kernersville News* had done. He also told me, "If we can find the money, we're committed to doing the drug-testing program."

East Forsyth unveiled its new plan at the October PTSA meeting. Since I was unable to attend, Reporter Wendy Freeman Davis covered the story. Principal Grissom asked the attendees for more parent volunteers to monitor the hallways and the campus. There was also talk of taking away driving privileges of students caught with drugs at school. Drug testing was not part of the recommended solution and, like Glenn, East Forsyth suffered a low parent turnout for the meeting.

"There was not a lot of outpouring of support," said PTSA vice president and Kernersville alderman Jim Waddell, "but they (those attending) did understand the issue."

* * *

October faded into November and sadly, the "drugs in school" project seemed to mimic the seasons. It was full of hope in the spring, blossomed with unprecedented support in the summer, and was quickly becoming dormant in the fall.

Less than 25 parents supported the first Parent Support Group (PSG) meeting on November 5th. And those attending were from three schools, Glenn, East Forsyth, and West Forsyth.

The West Forsyth parents came to share information on their parent support group, which was established in 1994. In a nutshell, the West Forsyth parents realized that students were better networked than parents. The students knew where the parties were, and who used drugs or alcohol. The parents wanted to develop a comparable resource of information. The West Forsyth parents passed on the following tips:

- Ask your kids where they are going—don't just tell them when to be home.
- Trade telephone numbers with other parents. Give them permission to call you if they hear anything of concern about your child.
- Call and confirm that your teens are where they say they will be.
- Call other parents to verify the level of supervision and the activities planned at parties or teen events.
- Make your supervised home a place for teen gatherings. Make sure it is an alcohol and drug-free environment.
- If there is an unruly party in your neighborhood, call the police. The next day, call the parents.
- When traveling and leaving the teens home alone, ask a neighbor to keep on eye on the house and to report any parties. Tell your teens that the neighbors are watching.

They also reported, "One shock through our support group is that some parents *allow* and some parents actually *supply* alcohol for these teens."

One parent talked about older teenage boys luring younger high school girls to parties in the woods. The girls desperately wanted to "fit in" and "feel accepted," so they would go. The boys would have beer there and encourage the girls to drink with them. Once impaired, the girls had little skill in maintaining boundaries for themselves. Many lost their virginity in the process. It was murder on their self-esteem when word got around school, and surely, word does get around!

> *"Marijuana was the cause of my son having lung surgery last year to the tune of $20,000."* —Concerned parent

"There are children out there whose parents really don't care," observed another. "How do I give my children the strength to stay away from these problems?"

Glenn's Parent Support Group set its next meeting for December. It was hoped that the group would grow as more parents learned about it and as people trusted that conversations at the meetings remained confidential and anonymous.

I found the low attendance very disheartening. Of course, it wasn't the school's fault. Glenn could not *make* the parents attend. But nonetheless, it was apparent that the sizzle of the community movement was beginning to fizzle.

The community was not taking charge of its prong in the program, either. It was not organizing fundraising for drug testing. Unlike the Carver success story, where a businessman got the ball rolling, no one came forward to fund the Glenn drug-testing program.

I began to wonder what I could do. I remembered John Staples' caveat. "It is a reporter's job to report the news, not to create the news." But where do I draw the line between being a reporter and being a concerned citizen? Was I banned from helping Glenn find the money just because I was the reporter?

I decided on a compromise. I would not sit around and do nothing, but also, I would not do it all. I would help get things started. I made a couple of telephone calls and in November sent a letter to Principal Coplin.

I told Coplin, "In doing my job as a reporter, I was able to make contact with two sources that have an interest in supporting the Glenn High School Random Voluntary Drug-Testing Program, and then I listed the two businesses.

The first was the Winston-Salem Chamber of Commerce. This organization has a "Make a Wish" program and the director thought drug testing would be a good match. Secondly, I found a company in Kernersville that was a drug-free workplace. It was looking for a way to reach out in the community. In a preliminary conversation, the director of quality assurance recommended that a request be submitted on Glenn letterhead. I gave this to Coplin and suggested that donations be solicited from a list of drug-free businesses in Kernersville. I said I would not be against helping out on this project personally.

About that same time, Mary Turner, a local columnist and a substitute teacher, wrote about athletes and drugs. She had overheard some students discussing drug use among athletes and decided to poll some students about mandatory drug testing of athletes.

She wrote:

Only a few felt that student athletes who use drugs should be kicked off the team, and only a very few thought they should be kicked out of school. Is it because our athletes are our heroes and our "role models"? So how do others feel?

"No, they should not be tested because it is nobody's business what athletes do." Most of the students felt it was an invasion of privacy and a person's rights. Many of them felt that "there would be no athletes left to play." Some felt that "as long as the students are not doing it in school, it's no one's business."

I did ask a couple of the coaches what they thought about it and most were afraid of the legal aspects of mandatory testing. One coach was 100 percent in favor of it because "athletes must be mentally and physically focused," and they can't do that if they are on drugs.

Near the end of her column, Turner talked about the cost of implementing a voluntary drug-testing program. She pleaded with the community of Kernersville to help the schools. She wrote: "Our high schools need help in funding these programs and are looking for corporations or businesses willing to help. Parental support is vital, as is student support."

Still, nothing happened. No one came forward with money. The two leads I'd given Coplin proved to be dead ends. As far as soliciting the public for donations, why should the schools do it? It was their job to teach, not to do fundraising. Worse yet, I kept remembering Coplin's words from our *first* conversation: "I can tell you right now what the community wants to do about the drug problem. They want the schools to solve the problem.

12

The Press Conference

Lesson 12: No one wins alone

"Christmas came early for you," said John Staples.

"What?"

"You won first place for investigative reporting. Congratulations! The awards ceremony will be in January. We also won the Community Service Award and second place for appearance and design."

"Great!"

Staples then took me into the back room for a private conversation. He said that some of the staff felt like I was getting all the credit for the "Drugs in Schools" series and it was causing some hard feelings.

"Well," I said, "I did do 95 percent of the writing and research."

"Yes, but if they weren't all doing their jobs, then you wouldn't have a newspaper to write in. The others had to report the news and they did that so that you could focus on this. In the end, we all worked together to make this happen. So you want to make sure they know that you appreciate their hard work too."

Staples suggested that he and I buy lunch for the office. With my newfound perspective, it turned out to be a memorable lunch. By the end of the afternoon, I understood that no one is flying solo when great things happen. It took immeasurable support from inside and outside the office to make my success, *our success*, possible.

The big day came quickly. Thursday, January 27, 1997. My husband, Don, and I drove to Chapel Hill for the 1996 NCPA Awards Ceremony. We arrived early and saved seats near the front. Then we looked for my entry.

Posted on a big board was a sampling of my stories with a royal blue ribbon attached. The gold print on the ribbon read "First Place." Don took some pictures of me standing by the exhibit. Then I studied other first and second place stories to try to understand what it takes to be a winner as a writer.

When John Staples arrived, he introduced me to dozens of reporters, editors, and officials of the NCPA. One question kept surfacing. Reporters kept asking, "How did you get into the schools, past the superintendent?"

I told them. "I just asked. I didn't know any better."

I was feeling like a million bucks. My husband and I drank some wine, had some cheese and fruit, and talked. There was such a buzz of excitement.

At 5 o'clock, we were asked to take our seats and at 5:30 the ceremony began. Then, one by one, writers from all over the state of North Carolina were recognized. North Carolina Governor Jim Hunt personally presented the awards.

Finally, it was my turn. I was lined up along the wall with dozens of writers. It reminded me of high school graduation. While it is a landmark event, the presentation of the individual awards takes only moments.

The governor read from the blurb in the NCPA half-sized keepsake newspaper. Under the category of Investigative Reporting for non-daily newspapers with circulation of more than 10,000 it states: First Place: Patty Jo Sawvel, *Kernersville News*, "Drugs in schools"—A comprehensive inquiry into a national problem. Good writing, series well-organized. Congrats on getting through the school door.

When it came time to receive the Community Service Award, Staples, associate editor Paul Grantham, and I all went up. This time the governor went into much more detail about the impact of the work and the stories. He commended the *News* for bringing to the forefront something that was very important to him.

In the NCPA keepsake newspaper, Caesar Andrews of the Gannett Regional Newspapers, who judged the Community Service Award entries, wrote:

> *The* Kernersville News' *ongoing coverage of illegal drug use exhibited an impressive commitment to exploring the extent of the problems among local youths. The newspaper's leadership and its authoritative reports had to have made the issues nearly impossible for local readers to ignore. Stories were saturated with the voices of teens offering a wide range of perspectives some resisting pressure to experiment with drugs, others already consumed by regular use. Importantly, coverage ventured beyond merely chronicling concerns about illegal drugs. The newspaper worked closely with schools and others to build community-generated solutions.*

After the presentation, I quickly grabbed John and the governor. My husband snapped some pictures of the three of us. The governor then asked us to mail him the entire Community Service Award entry.

That night, I wrote in my day planner:

Well, it happened! Tonight I went to the North Carolina Press Association Awards, shook hands with Governor James Hunt, Jr., and received the First Place investigative award for the drug series. The newspaper—Kernersville News—received the highest award for the series: the Community Service Award. The Governor of NC requested that he be personally forwarded the entire entry, as his chief goal is to improve the schools in NC. (NC public schools rank #45 (bottom) out of 50 states.) The award was important to me because it should help me to accomplish my real goal—which is not to be a newspaper reporter—but a free-lance writer. I view this award as my contracting license. It's great to be licensed and pass the test—but it doesn't make you any richer unless you go out and practice your trade. I hope this year, 1997, I get published someplace, anyplace, other than just the newspaper.

Also, the NCPA asked all first place winners to be judges for the Alabama Press Association's "Better Newspaper Contest." I felt unqualified to be a judge, but John Staples suggested that I accept. So I did.

The next day, Staples called me into the office for a photo of the *Kernersville News* writing staff to commemorate the Community Service Award.

We all filed into the back room. Staples arranged everyone, including Owensby. I was the only one not yet in the picture. Owensby looked at me and asked Staples, "Where are we going to put the girl?"

I didn't say anything at the time and after I was shuffled into two or three different places, the picture taking was finally done.

As soon as it was over, I took Staples to the side and said, "Why did he call me "the girl"? I just accomplished what he asked me to do—to win this award—and he can't even call me by my name? Why would he do that?"

"Don't take it personally. You're a woman and you didn't graduate from college. He doesn't respect that. That's just the way he is. If I got upset every time he offended me, I would quit. Actually, I did quit before. But I came back because I love the community. Forget about it," advised Staples.

A few days later, Staples told me that I was grounded. I'd taken the series into my own hands and not turned in my bills properly. Owensby did not want me to be used as a stringer for a while. Staples recommended that I lay low and let the storm blow over. And I did.

About the only thing I was allowed to write was the "Voice of the People" twice a week. It wasn't really writing. It was more like taking dictation. I would approach people at the park or the supermarket and ask them the question of the day and take their pictures.

At the end of February, I asked Staples if I could write my own question for the "Vox." I wanted to resurrect the "drugs in schools" discussion. Every time I looked up at my official red and black NCPA certificate, instead of feeling satisfied, I felt unsettled. Would this whole "move the community" project end with a piece of paper in a frame? Or, would the community support the schools in resolving the problem? Staples and I wrote the question. It was longer than usual.

> *Last year, by means of high school surveys and interviews, the* Kernersville News *brought to light the extent of the teenage drug problem. Community leaders, members of the community, and school officials all agreed that positive action was needed. In reality, little progress has been made since the initiative started. Do you feel it is the responsibility of the schools to tackle yet another community problem, such as drug use among teenagers? What solution would you recommend?*

The answers showed that people wanted the leadership to come from outside the schools.

Terry Rothwell said, "Definitely, the schools should not be asked to solve this problem. The solution is to provide positive options that the kids prefer. I witnessed this when I was in Utah. The Mormon Church funded family-oriented community activities for the youth and were tremendously successful in avoiding the drug problem. Here's what I would do: Kernersville needs to organize a program where kids can go and have fun while being in a supervised and controlled environment. Drugs are a free-time problem. Generally, if kids are occupied, they won't use drugs because they have something else to do . . . As far as financing the programs, the Mormons simply used existing facilities such as schools, parks, and community centers and used volunteers to operate and promote the activities."

And from Joy Dalton, "Children should be required to attend drug workshops outside the school setting. Of course, the students would need incentives. We would have to consider WIIFM or What's In It For Me. They could be required to obtain a certain number of credits as a condition for getting their driver's license at age 16. Drug testing could also be linked with the privilege of driving. As far as manpower for conducting the numerous drug-free workshops, I believe every business and civic group and church in the community should be required to volunteer some time to the community action of eliminating the drug problem."

Lisa Stefani offered her solution, "The Kernersville town government should spearhead an effort to unite the businesses and the teenagers to work together on solving the problem. . .You need to get the kids involved. It seems like the current resources of S.A.V.E. and S.A.D.D. and D.A.R.E. could target the healthy kids in the schools. These kids could be visible role models with T-shirts or buttons or something visible and they could distribute literature to the other students and set up crisis hot lines. That would supply the manpower and the organizational structure. Money for the shirts and booklets and other things would need to come from local businesses. . . But it all needs to start with the town government."

Vince Rizzo suggested, "Find the central activities important to young people, whether it's music, sports, drama, etc. Make these activities available and start with the healthy kids. Then go to the malls where kids hang out and to other areas and recruit other kids to the programs. These activities will keep the kids busy and involved and will provide a basis for consistently introducing the concept of healthy bodies and healthy minds free of drugs. . . The clergy, the police, the funeral director and the other town authorities need to take the lead in activating the parents and the kids in getting these programs established and maintained. It's also critical that local businesses get involved."

Kim Shore concluded with this: "The schools are doing too much already so it is not fair for them to handle this problem. I think the solution needs to start from the top down. The town government needs to get involved. . . I would set in place a teenage curfew up to the age of 18. The curfew should be 10:00 p.m. in Kernersville, unless you are with your parents. Back when I was a teenager, we could run the streets of Kernersville anytime we liked and I think that needs to change . . .

> "I don't believe the community is going to pull together to solve this problem. Too many parents believe, "not my kid" and see no reason to get involved. Personally, I would be a part of a community action."—Kim Shore

Staples used his editorial space the following Tuesday to write a column titled, "Not a School Problem." A teenage drug problem in Kernersville, he explained, had been identified. Implementing the solutions seemed to be difficult. He recommended that people "recognize the difficulty and commit to solving the problem anyway." He concluded the column: "Schools are a good place to start trying to solve the teen drug problems; but schools can't do it alone. It takes parents, government officials, and everybody who has a stake in a sane and safe society to convince young people that using drugs does not produce a sane and safe society."

Still, nothing happened! The *Kernersville News* was doing its job of keeping the issue alive for the public. The schools were doing their job. But the community had yet to organize and find a way to pay for the drug testing, or to volunteer in large numbers at the high schools.

By April, my ban from writing for the *News* was lifted, but my assignments were sporadic. I only wrote about a dozen stories for the *Kernersville News* for the entire year of 1997.

Over the course of that year I had a lot of time to think. My thoughts often turned to the "Drugs in Schools" initiative. I wondered what went wrong. One year earlier, we had community leaders and parents joining together in unprecedented numbers to solve the problem. Now we had nothing. There was no joining and there was no movement. What happened?

The process seemed to break down when it was decided that each school would have its own meetings and devise its own solutions. Maybe it was too early in the process to split the core group in half. Or, maybe support dried up when the meeting location was changed to the schools. Perhaps, as Coplin suggested, parents figured that once the meetings were at the schools, the schools would take care of it. Or, maybe people detected the lack of high level leadership, since the police chief, sheriff, county commissioner, and judge were not at these meetings. It could even have been something as simple as the fact that school started and people were getting back to their daily lives.

I didn't know how to find the answers to these questions. And I no longer had the use of the newspaper as a forum to present the questions to the public. So, I decided to let it go and to get on with my life.

*   *   *

The *High Point Enterprise* advertised for columnists. I sent in three "Above and Beyond" sample columns and was amazed when the series was accepted.

It was both exciting and fear-inspiring to write a regular column. Sometimes, stories were plucked fully formed from my mind. But most times, I worried, searched, wrote, rewrote, and ultimately hoped for the best.

Oddly, this wrestling with fear and the unknown was very satisfying. And yet, it could not still the restlessness inside my head and heart. I could not quiet the voices of all the teens, parents, and people of the community who told their stories about drugs. Without realizing it, I went from just caring about my own family, to caring about their families.

Religion in Kernersville

Over 60 churches and religious learning centers — dating from the mid-1800s — find their homes in Kernersville. Religious services are regularly offered in Spanish, Chinese, and American Sign Language. Kernersville prides itself as being a faith-based community.

Kernersville's New Hospital

In 2011, Kernersville Medical Center opened — Kernersville style! This 50-bed hospital has friendly greeters who meet you at the door and escort you to your destination. Visitors are allowed in 24 hours a day, seven days a week, and all rooms are private. The hospital is equipped with two 1250 KW generators and 20,000 gallons of fuel in case of an emergency. Additionally, Kerner Café, the onsite restaurant, is becoming a favorite meeting place for friends.

13

Four Teens from Two Families

Lesson 13: Dig beneath the surface

The most valuable lesson I learned as a reporter is that young people will eagerly talk to the press. They are open and honest, want to be heard, and are honored when their viewpoint is sought.

The "Drugs in Schools" series gave me the courage to keep asking teens questions, even when there was no place to publish my findings. One question haunted me: Why would two teens from the same family make opposite choices about illegal drug use? In other words, we all know why children of poverty and abuse often turn to drugs—to numb the pain, but why do "good" teenagers from "good" families take drugs?

Four young adults agreed to share their experiences if I would keep their identities hidden. Their families are very active in the community. While they wished to help answer the question, they did not wish to hurt their families by honestly sharing some of their problems.

The four children grew up in Kernersville. Two were the offspring of an African-American couple, while the other two were Caucasian.

These two families were chosen because they exemplified the values of the community. They were honorable representatives of middle America. The parents had stable marriages, were college educated, and they provided well materially without being excessive.

These were model families, but real families. They were not "Leave it to Beaver" or "Cosby Show" creations. Problems did not get resolved in the hour or half-hour. And some problems never got resolved. This was real life.

The parents were not interviewed or aware of the interviews. Therefore, the names and some superficial details have been changed so that we can hear the voices of the children without sharing their identity. Here are their stories:

CASE STUDY ONE

Bobby and Jill were born three years apart. Placed into a group of 100 peers, neither Bobby nor Jill would stand out. They are not noticeably attractive or unattractive, heavy or thin, tall or short.

They were born to Caucasian parents in the latter half of the 1970s. Both parents are employed in public education and are active in the community. Neither parent experimented with drugs.

Bobby, the eldest, remembers the "Just Say No" campaign. Jill participated in the DARE program in school. Both had plenty of friends. Bobby never experimented with drugs. Jill started smoking pot at age 16. She was still using marijuana at age 21. Why?

Jill first experimented with marijuana with two of her friends, Melinda and Michelle. Melinda was Jill's best friend since the age of 10 and they lived in the same neighborhood. Jill often hung out at her house. One boring day, the topic of marijuana came up.

"I was with some of my freaks from school," Jill explained. "The other girls had heard about it and they said, 'Let's try it.' We got the pot from a neighbor boy. He got it and rolled it up for us. We smoked it and none of us got high—because it takes about three times before you get high. I did feel dizzy and we got the munchies. I felt something—but it was not high."

It seemed incongruent to hear mild-mannered Jill refer to her friends as freaks, but she said this was a generally accepted way of describing her peer group.

> *"At high school, students were separated. Freaks, mostly drama students, wore 1970s stuff. Preppies were cheerleaders and football students. Rednecks wore cowboy hats and rode around in trucks with Rebel flags."*
> —Jill experienced "culture shock" when she started high school

Jill felt she fit in best with the freaks and joined the drama club. She attended their events and handed out programs. She adopted their dress code, thereafter filling her wardrobe with tie-dye. Their music became her music: Led Zeppelin, CCR, Santana, and Jimi Hendrix.

Jill said freaks were not to be confused with gothic-freaks. Gothic-freaks wore red and black. They painted black lipstick on whitened faces. And their music tended toward Nine Inch Nails and Marilyn Manson.

This clearly-delineated social culture at high school was overwhelming to Jill. She left middle school with high hopes. She'd won the DARE championship and was sure she would remain drug-free. She had decided to get involved in extracurricular activities, but once she got to high school, she found herself shrinking back.

"I was really excited and had all these plans. I was going to join SADD and join a sports team. But I didn't try as much as I thought I would."

Instead, Jill invested more time in her existing friendships. These were friends she'd had since elementary school. When asked to describe them, she focused on their loss and their pain.

Melinda, Jill's friend since the age of ten, came from a broken home. Her mom and dad divorced when she was five years old and her dad moved out-of-state. Her mom had trouble keeping a job and so they were always living with relatives. Finally, at the tail end of middle school, Melinda's dad moved to North Carolina and she was able to see him on alternate weekends.

Jill wasn't as close to Michelle. While she came from an intact family, Michelle complained that her mother wasn't there for her. Her mom worked at night and slept during the day.

In this melancholy mix, Jill amplified her own pain, which centered on her relationship with her mother.

"My dad and I can talk for hours and hours. We talk about 'what if'. What if you had only 24 hours to live? What if aliens invaded the world? Those conversations got my mind working. But my mom, she doesn't know how to talk to me. My mom's only conversations are like this: 'Jill, clean your room. Do this. Do that.' She maybe talks to me about her soap operas or her school kids. But we don't have heart-to-heart talks."

Almost as an afterthought, Jill added, "Probably part of the reason I was smoking pot was out of rebellion because she couldn't talk to me and I was mad at her."

About this time, Jill also made some new friends at school. Brandy was popular, outgoing, and seemed to be accepted by all the peer groups. Margaret, Brandy's younger cousin, seemed to enjoy life in Brandy's shadow. Jill fit right in between them.

They introduced Jill to "cruising." In an ongoing tradition, on Friday and Saturday nights, hundreds of teenagers wash their cars, don their coolest clothes, and go to a neighboring town. From eight o'clock until midnight, they cruise up and down Main Street, smiling, styling, and profiling.

Jill and her group drove around in Brandy's mom's car. It was a boxy black Buick LeSabre, a family car. Later, Brandy got a well-worn white Honda. According to Jill, it was "a lot more cool." The girls called it "the foxhole" because it operated as if it had been through a war. One door and two windows did not open. And sometimes they would squeeze seven people into the little machine to wage war on the world.

"It was exciting to be away from our parents. It was fun—meeting people—hollering—acting stupid. I would wear my tie-dye."

Part of the fun was exchanging passengers. "We would ride around and yell at cars of guys. When you meet someone, then you hop into his car. Then you go to McDonalds or to the pool hall. One time, we played hopscotch behind the cinema. Then you meet up with your friends later."

Of course, there was room to get into trouble if you weren't careful, or if you were looking for trouble. It was during a cruising night out that Jill got drunk for the first time.

"I was 15. We were cruising and met some guys having a party in Thomasville (a nearby town). It turned out the party was just us and them. We were at someone's house. One guy handed me a 40 (40 ounces of beer). I was the only girl that drank. I drank three-quarters of it. I had fun. I started dancing. I tried to get on a bike and I couldn't ride it. My friends looked out for me. Brandy and Margaret took me home with them and I spent the night. The next day I had a hangover. Brandy's mom called my dad so he wouldn't be worried. He had been out looking for me."

Jill's friends always kept track of each other while they were cruising. They would never leave one of their friends behind.

"What we were doing was pretty harmless. But now (since 1996), there are so many crazy people out there that I would be afraid to get into someone else's car."

By the time Jill was 17, Brandy and Margaret had lost interest in cruising and were hanging out at ICU. ICU had a double meaning and stood for "I see you" as in "I see you for who you really are" and Icon Creek University. Jill was accepted there and said that ICU was where she got her real education about what matters most in life. What matters most is loyal friends.

ICU was no university. It was a hang out. It was made possible by an insurance settlement. A young man involved in an unfortunate work-related accident used the money to buy a house for himself and his friends to hang out in. Unfortunately, he wasn't always able to maintain the basic necessities.

"They did not have jobs and there was only one car. For a while they were out of water. For about a month and a half, there was no power. The nearest gas station was several miles away so you either went to the bathroom outside or you drove to the gas station. I learned that I did not want to live that way. That encouraged me to stay in school."

Dropping out of high school was a real temptation for Jill, especially after Brandy and Margaret quit. Brandy dropped out because she went into a deep depression. She didn't want to eat and she didn't want to see anyone. Margaret followed suit. The two girls intended to home school but they didn't stick to it. In all, of the nine young people that frequented ICU, seven of them were high school dropouts. There were five guys and four girls and most of them were two or three years older than Jill.

Jill began to care less about her school friends and more about her ICU friends. Melinda and Michelle were fading into the background. When she looked back on it, she said, "We became basically just friends to get high with."

But Jill found real soul mates at ICU. These people understood her. They filled a need that her family was not filling.

"I feel like they (ICU) are my real family. My (biological) family sees a part of me and what they want to see. But my friends see the real me. I feel restrained around my parents. With my friends I do crazy stuff. With my friends I am not afraid to do stupid stuff because no matter what I do, they will be there. My friends would not judge me, but my mom and dad would."

Jill's parents objected to her new friends and she was often grounded. So she found a way to avoid their intervention. She started sneaking out of her house at two o'clock in the morning and sneaking back in at six o'clock before school.

At ICU, drugs and alcohol flowed abundantly. "They didn't care. Their main focus was to get high and stay high all day. They were musicians and they wanted to get a band started. They still have that dream today."

> For Jill, the main draw of marijuana was its ability to relax her and to let her see the world the way she *wanted* it to be.

"When you are high, it looks like everything is in a box. Some people get real paranoid, but it is not uncomfortable for me. I liked to be by myself at ICU. We would get on the roof and look at the clouds. It would be like meditation. You would feel the wind on your body more. If everyone is laughing—you will be laughing a lot and having a good time. But if you are alone or on the roof, it is totally relaxing."

And relax is just what Jill did. With two college-educated parents and a brother in college, she too, initially, planned to go to college. But once pot became commonplace in her life, she began to ratchet down her expectations.

"I was high a lot at school my senior year. Probably if I would not have started smoking pot in high school, I probably would have done better and went on to college. I noticed that I lost my motivation when I smoked pot. I didn't care. I said, 'I'm going to GTCC (Guilford Technical Community College). Anyone can get in there. I'll go there two years and then transfer.'"

While noting what she gave up, Jill was quick to defend what she had gained.

"Probably if I had not started smoking pot, I would not have had the friends that I have and they are my real friends. Also, I think that pot, acid, and alcohol helped me to see things in a different perspective. It has been a benefit. It helped me to be more open-minded."

Jill first used acid when she was 18 and still in school. Her friends had all tried acid and she hadn't, so they got her some. She went alone to her bedroom on a Sunday night, chewed up the acid-impregnated paper, and waited. About 45 minutes later, her black-light wall poster began to come alive.

"The branches on the trees were bleeding. It was extremely intriguing. My other poster, with a person walking up a mountain—it became three-dimensional. I couldn't sleep at all. The next morning I was still feeling it as I drove to school. My teacher asked me to run a simple errand and I spent 30 minutes wandering around the school. I was so freaked out. By second period I was coming off—but I had a headache for the rest of the day and I was tired."

Jill can't remember why she did acid a second time. But she does know why she hasn't used acid since. It is hard to get.

Jill not only drove when she was still high on acid, she also drove when she was high on marijuana.

"When I first started driving home high, I would wait one hour. As the months went by, I got braver about driving high. You have to be really focused. I would have to tell myself, 'Ok, only five more streets.' Each street would be like a big journey. And I remember one time I had to keep telling myself to brake around this big curve. Driving high is like driving through an obstacle course just to get to the end."

As with driving, Jill was at first cautious about interacting with her mother when she was high. Later, she was braver and would actually seek her out.

"My mom didn't know that I was high. She was totally clueless. She was naive a lot. I got to the point where I would look for my mom on purpose when I was high. Part of the fun was that my mom didn't know. She was totally clueless."

Jill also used to laugh secretly at the DARE trophy that sat in the family room next to her brother's sports trophies. She won that trophy in fifth grade and even gave a speech about how she would stay drug-free. And at the time, she believed it.

What happened between fifth grade and that day in Melinda's driveway?

"At the time, I really believed that I would never use drugs. But when I was in that driveway at age 16, what I learned in fifth grade never came to mind. When I was 16, I was going along with everybody. I started smoking pot so that I could fit in and go with the crowd. I kept doing it because it was fun and something to do."

At the age of 21, Jill was still smoking pot regularly, though not daily. She had been in and out of community college and even tried a university, but had yet to complete a semester. She still viewed marijuana as a viable recreational choice.

"I pay $5 for a joint. It is a fair cost. If I go to a two-hour movie, it is $6 plus popcorn. Pot is a recreational experience."

The day following this interview, Jill was going 100 miles to a Tom Petty concert at the Pavilion in Raleigh with some friends. She was planning to take her pot with her. She was planning to smoke this illegal substance on public property with policemen in view. She'd done it plenty of times before and she knew that the police winked at marijuana use at concerts.

"People smoke pot right out in the open. You can smell it all over. The police check and make you open your handbag—but they don't check your pockets. I'll roll mine up before the concert and take two or three joints."

I asked Jill a few more questions. At age 21, she has yet to reconcile her differences with her mother. Why?

"I think my mom still carries this conversation in the back of her head: 'Jill is the bad child and she just wants to get attention. We can't trust her.' My dad has gotten over that, but she is still stuck."

"Did any adults know you were high?"

"My mom was clueless. I think my dad knew but he never said a word. I think the teachers knew I was high—but they could never prove it. We probably annoyed them because our attention span was shorter, and a boy from school told my manager that he thought I was coming to work high. She said that she didn't care as long as I could do my job."

What is the truth about marijuana?

"I don't think marijuana is bad. I believe alcohol is a lot worse. It depends on whose hands it falls into. I'm against legalization because I am afraid how people will start using other drugs. My friends, some of them are the wrong people because they take it too far. They don't know how to be responsible users—even though they are now in their 20s."

What will you tell your kids about pot?

"I thought about that many times and I don't know yet. I might tell them that I'd rather they do that than drink. I just think it is safer. You never hear about a high driver killing someone—it almost always is a drunk driver."

Jill still smokes pot occasionally and believes she can stop at any time.

* * *

Bobby is Jill's older brother. At age 24, he had still never experimented with drugs.

Bobby was in middle school in the late 1980s, when the "Just Say No" national anti-drug campaign was reaching a peak. School discussions about drugs began about the same time Bobby and his skateboard buddies saw some drugs.

"One of my friends, Brandon, had an older brother that was kind of wild and more into that stuff. I remember being at his house one day when a kid pulled up. He was one of his brother's older friends. He got out what was like a brick of marijuana. I mean it was packaged and everything. It was big and solid packed."

That prompted a discussion about drugs. As a group they decided they would not get into drugs. It was not a pact, it was just a consensus.

Like his sister, Bobby was jolted by the abrupt change in social culture upon reaching high school. "When I got to high school, it was different. Suddenly, a lot of kids that I used to hang out with in middle school saw me as this little skateboard guy. I wasn't cool anymore. Some of my older friends that were already in high school gave me the cold shoulder when I got to high school."

As it worked out, the peer pressure that worked so well to lure many kids into experimenting was a total turn off to Bobby.

> *"The thing that really bothered me—the kids would come to school and say, 'Oh, I got so drunk this weekend' or 'I did this' or 'I did that'. I thought, 'Why do you need to do that to have a good time? Why does your life revolve around that? And why do you have to come to school and tell me about that?'"*
>
> —Bobby, never experimented with drugs

"Now you're bragging about it," he added. "It is almost like now that you did this you are cooler than everyone else.' I never bought into that."

But some of his friends did. One friend, Eddie, is still trying to work his way out of the web of drug use. "Eddie really got into drugs. I think he was really susceptible to peer pressure. He wanted to be cool."

According to Bobby, Eddie came from a middle class family similar to his own. Eddie was the last of four very bright children. His older brother graduated cum laude from UNC-Chapel Hill. His two older sisters graduated from Wake Forest and Guilford College, respectively. And then there was Eddie.

"He was a really smart kid. He just got sucked into it (drugs) and I really saw him change in high school. He forgot about school and became all about drugs. He went though a period where he couldn't control his life. He was selling the stuff."

According to Bobby, Eddie attended the University of North Carolina at Wilmington at the coast "for about a year and failed out. A couple years ago, I ran into him after I got out of college. I asked him if he was still messing around with drugs. He said, 'I don't know. I'm still smoking a bit here and there, but I'm not selling or anything like that.' Then we went to the driving range and he pulled out a wad of $20s. I asked him, 'Why do you have to lie to me like that?' He said, 'I'm keeping it under cover. I don't do it as bad as I used to, but I still make a little money on the side with it. At this point, he is so stereotypical. He talks like a burn-out. And he used to be this really bright, funny, energetic kid."

Brandon, from the original crew of four skateboarders, also used drugs in high school. "Brandon did it, but he was not controlled by it. He was part of the party scene. Whenever I was with him and my other friends, they never put pressure on me whatsoever. If I was there, it was cool. If I wasn't there, it was cool. Most of them knew that I didn't use drugs."

Why wasn't Bobby overcome by the desire to fit in and be cool like some of his friends? "I cared about being cool. But I still had plenty of friends and I didn't need that. I liked my life. I loved high school."

But he had to pay a price for not going along with some of his friends.

"There were times when I would get mad because these people that I used to hang out with before high school were now in a different group. We didn't have the same kind of friendship. It was different because they knew I didn't do drugs or drink. Even though I could still hang out with them and I still went to parties and stuff, I didn't do what they were doing. I don't know if it was on their end—but I felt uneasiness. I didn't like the uneasiness of them doing something that I was not doing."

Bobby estimated that he saw drugs at high school in Kernersville about 10 to 15 times during his four-year stay in the early 1990s. He saw drugs by the tennis courts, in the student parking lots, or behind the school. He saw kids actually smoking marijuana in their cars, on the hoods of their cars, in the woods by the big hill, and at the school amphitheater. But much more than seeing drugs, Bobby heard seemingly endless pro-drug talk by students.

"I was never asked to use drugs by anyone that I gave a shit about. If they would have asked me, I would have stopped giving a shit about them. That could have ended our friendship—if they were trying to pressure me."

What kind of anti-drug support was Bobby getting at home?

"I don't remember a single conversation about drugs. We just never went there. I don't think my parents really knew how to deal with it. They were from a different generation. Not sex, not drugs. They just never went there. I do remember a couple of conversations about alcohol and 'why would you need it?'"

Alcohol was another area where Bobby drew a hard line. Unlike his sister, Jill, who started experimenting with the neighbor girls, one shot glass at time, at age 13, Bobby never had a drop of alcohol until his senior week in high school.

"I had a lot of fun that week and I will admit that. That week was just to let go and to have fun. The biggest difference between drugs and alcohol was that drugs are illegal. Of course, alcohol was illegal at that point too. But I guess it all goes back to middle school and that campaign that we were raised with. The 'Just Say No,' drugs are bad, and marijuana is a starter drug that could lead to so many bad things that you really don't want."

Through college and up to the point of our interview when he was 24, Bobby still did not use alcohol to be cool or deal with stress.

"I could count on two hands the number of times that I've been drunk. That is pretty good for a guy my age who's been to college."

So what did Bobby use to cope with stress?

"I would either jump on my bike, or my skateboard, or go shoot basketball. It was one of those three, depending on how old that I was. In high school, basketball was my hobby. I went and played basketball with my friends. I played every day with my friends. We went to the YMCA. Even today, I play three times a week. It still helps me deal with stress."

How does basketball relieve stress?

> *"If I have something that is really stressing me out, I'll go to the gym and stay for three hours. When I'm doing that I can just forget everything. If I'm there by myself, it gives me a chance to think the problem out. I can think it out in a relaxing, pressure-free kind of way."* —Bobby used exercise to reduce stress instead of drugs

"If there are a bunch of people there and I actually get to play a game," he added, "then I forget about it while I'm playing. Both ways work just as well for me because I have a couple of hours where it is not stressing me out."

Bobby's success in avoiding drug use and alcohol abuse is not the result of a stress-free childhood.

"Our family life still drives me crazy to this day. My parents would not take any of my advice. They didn't really listen to me. Like on the decision to move when I was in eighth-grade. I was extremely against it."

Just before becoming a teenager, Bobby got into the habit of losing his temper regularly. Prior to that, he'd had few social problems at home or at school. But now, he was out of control.

"I just hadn't learned how to control my anger. I was old enough to get mad and to understand why I was mad. But I just couldn't control my temper. I got into fights with my friends. I would hit the walls, scream, hit my friends."

It was ordinary things that caused this shocking reaction—a difference of opinion, a misunderstanding, a restriction. At home, it was his father's inability or lack of desire to make decisions. All the decisions were left up to Bobby's mom. Bobby used to sit around and stew about how his father was not really the man of his house. But he focused most of his anger on his mother. Like many teens, Bobby interpreted her communication as nagging. And he felt that she was not listening to him.

"I remember one time I got so mad at my mom that I grabbed her and just started shaking her. I felt bad, but I just couldn't keep myself from doing it."

After that incident, Bobby's mom scheduled a visit with the psychiatrist.

"She had to drag me in there because I did not want to go. I was kicking and screaming because I didn't want to think that I had any problems, of course. I don't remember what they taught me about controlling my temper. But it did help. I guess the biggest help was realizing how big of an issue that it was. In the end, it turned out good because I realized that I was getting so mad that I was scaring my mom to death. That is the last thing in the world that I wanted to do. So it helped me learn to deal with my temper."

Bobby also felt stress at school. "In elementary school, I was in the gifted classes. By middle school, I had slacked off and got by with a 'B' average. In high school, I did enough to get by, but I didn't care about getting 'As.' My stress was not around schoolwork—it was more peer interaction. A lot of my stress came from the change in people once we got to high school."

Bobby reached his peak stress point when he was in college. He had been dating a girl for over a year. During that time, "he remembered why he was in college" and his grades soared. She brought out the best in him and he was head over heels in love. And then . . . she dumped him.

"She broke up with me during semester break. The next semester, I had my lowest, worst GPA I had ever had. I had like a 1.8. I was depressed. It took me six months to recover. But I didn't take drugs."

Instead, Bobby went back to all the things that worked for him when he was feeling low. He made himself go to the gym every day. And he called on his friends for support.

"With some of my friends, we have the kind of friendship where we can just kind of spill our guts. And then with some of my friends, we always just goof off and have fun. Some of them were kids that I grew up with and some of them were new friends from college. My friends helped me a lot."

In the future, Bobby sees himself as a husband and father. As a man of 24, what are his views of marijuana now? Should drugs be legalized?

"Sometimes, I think that with the recreational drugs like marijuana, it wouldn't be a big deal if it was legalized. But you'd have the whole drinking-and-driving issue. You'd have to have some kind of control behind it. To me, that whole legalization thing would change some of the crime that goes along with it. Legalizing it would not be good for society, but because of the crime it might be better."

What will you tell your children about drugs?

"If they are 10 years old, I want to instill the fact that they don't need it. Drugs are not anything they need to be involved with. But I don't want to do it in such a way that they hear, 'Drugs are bad, drugs are bad, drugs are bad.'"

What will you tell your kids when they are 18 years old?

"I think at age 18 they are still too young to have a complete world view about it."

In your experience, what is the deciding factor on whether a young person decides to take drugs or not to take drugs?

"If I were placed in a different situation, I could have done it, if my family or my friends had been different. I don't think it was the basketball. I would have found something else. I think another thing that played into this is that I didn't want to let my parents down. That was definitely there. They may not believe it, but I have a lot of respect for my parents. Also, my mom was home after school. I had a lot of friends that were latchkey and both parents worked. The fact of knowing that she was there was a plus."

What message would you like to give today about drugs?

"I don't know. I would hate to say that it won't ruin your life because it really has ruined some lives. Not just Eddie. I could name at least 10 people from high school who had potential—big time—and who ruined their lives with drugs. These people were extremely bright and came from good families. One guy just got married, works for a restaurant, has been arrested several times, and he's still using drugs. It seems to me that those kids were more interested in doing it to be cool. That is how they got into drugs and they never got out."

CASE STUDY TWO

Ryan is 23 years old, has never tried drugs, and intends to stay drug-free for life. He is the younger of two children in a middle-class, African-American family. His father is an upper-level executive in an international firm. His mother is a full-time homemaker, a devout Christian, and volunteers in the community regularly.

The closest Ryan ever came to taking drugs happened when he was in elementary school. He was playing in the field with a neighbor. The other child decided to pull up some dead grass by the roots and try to smoke it. He lit it and took a few puffs. He kept urging Ryan to give it a try. Finally, Ryan gave in. But when he put it to his mouth, he burned his lip.

"It wasn't drugs. It was just grass in the field. But I gave in to peer pressure. As soon as I burned my lip, I thought, 'Man, this is stupid.' I decided that I would never give in to peer pressure like that again."

Ryan then laughed and said, "I didn't inhale."

Ryan said that it was his Bible beliefs that enabled him to keep his commitment to himself to stay free of drugs. At his church, drugs, sex, and alcohol were regularly addressed. Ryan knew what the Bible said about these matters and given a few moments, he could find the scriptures to back him up.

He believes that use of recreational drugs interferes with a person's ability to love God with his whole mind (Luke 10:25-27). He said that drugs make the mind and body unclean for worshiping God (Romans 12:1). He believes that drug use adversely affects a person's soundness of mind and the ability to exercise self-restraint (Titus 2:11, 12).

This final point was a big issue for Ryan. He liked to feel in control and conversely did not like feeling out of control. That is what he envisioned that drugs would do.

> *"Basically, I view drugs as something that cause you to lose control over your body. I didn't want to do that. It is hard enough to control myself anyway. I don't need something else to hinder my bodily functions."* —Ryan never experimented with drugs

But Ryan's brother was raised with these same admonitions, and yet he chose the other path. What were some other things that aided Ryan in staying drug-free?

For one thing, Ryan was used to adversity. He was a very small, shy, light-skinned black child in a predominately white school. Because of this, he didn't fit in with the white kids and he didn't fit in with the few black kids.

"School caused me the most anxiety. I didn't fit in with the kids at school. Because of my fair skin, I was always questioned about my race. They would say, 'Are you mixed? What race are you?'"

To add to the confusion, Ryan didn't sag his pants, use black slang, use black mannerisms in his walk or gestures, or give a lot of credence to "black power." He was well-mannered, soft-spoken, and could easily have gone unnoticed. But, he was one of the few black kids in a white school and at times the only black kid on his bus.

"Everyone wants to classify you. Everyone wants to put you in a group. Even at college, kids wanted to know, 'What are you?' I'm a person. Just a person. When I was young, I thought, 'Maybe if I was white, I would fit in better.'"

Ryan remembered one particularly painful childhood experience:

"Extra kids were on the bus so we had to be squeezed three people to a seat. A white boy got on and the bus driver told him to sit next to me. The boy said, 'I can't ride with a nigger.' The whole bus got quiet as the bus driver asked the boy, 'What did you say?' And he said it again. I told my mom what happened. I don't remember exactly what she said to me, but she helped me to realize that it wasn't my problem."

In reality, Ryan is a pretty good mix of everything. Yes, he is predominately black. But he is also white, Hispanic, Indian, and even Asian. He started realizing at an early age that there was more to him than either blacks or whites could see. Eventually, through the struggle at a young age, Ryan realized that he didn't need to fit in. He just needed to be himself.

By his early teen years, Ryan felt quite alone and unhappy. It was then that he decided to stop using his shyness and his color as an excuse for his isolation.

> *"I decided that I have to accept myself for who I am. I am still discovering things about myself, but I like myself. Also, I decided to be more friendly. I decided that I could not be shy and friendly at the same time. So I opened up and made myself talk to more people. The more I did it, the easier it got. I made friends with people of all ages."*—Ryan

Ryan had another obstacle at school. He was labeled LD (learning disabled) at the start and it took him years to break free of the classification and the implied limitations.

"I wasn't very good at school. It was hard to keep up with the other kids. I had a speech impediment, I was diagnosed as dyslexic, and I was a very poor reader."

Ryan spent five years in LD classes and slowly worked through his various challenges. But then he moved to a new school and resented the LD classes.

"The new school didn't have as much funding. LD classes were boring. It wasn't fun anymore and I wanted out. So I took it upon myself to get out. I was always in high math, but low English. So I started really paying attention to English and doing all my homework. By the end of middle school, I was in Honors English."

Breaking out of LD was a big boost for Ryan's self-confidence. In hindsight, he believes that he really did have mild dyslexia and he did need some help with his speech. But it was his decision to do whatever it took to escape from LD that would move him ahead in his educational achievement. Later, he chose to attend a predominately black high school. He figured that he could get the help he needed, and he did. At graduation, he walked down the aisle with a scholarship to North Carolina A & T University—a predominately black college. And, at his college graduation, he walked with honors.

Aside from racial and academic stress, Ryan also felt pressure from within his family. Whereas his mother and he were close, his relationship with his father was strained. "I don't know my dad. He is not a communicator. Our normal communication is that I'll try to say something. Then he will take it the wrong way. Then I'll try to explain it. Then he doesn't understand me. And then we stop."

Interestingly, Ryan learned the most about his dad from doing school assignments. "One time, I had to interview my dad for school. I found out he went to a predominately white college. I learned he went to college because my grandfather went to almost enough college to get a master's degree by working hard to pay for his own education. My grandfather told my dad how important it was to go to college and how much his education helped him. That was the first time I ever heard about that."

Did that conversation then lay the groundwork for future conversations?

"No. He was never there. He worked out of town three to four days a week. And when he was home he was always busy. Basically, he was a workaholic. He was always in his office working on his computer or he was working outside on the yard. That is one thing we did together. We worked on the yard. It wasn't really bonding, because we weren't talking, but it is a fond memory."

This lack of communication caused uncertainty for Ryan. On the one hand, his parents gave him a lot of freedom to make his own choices. But, on the other hand, they didn't always offer a lot of guidance, or even the courtesy of telling him what was going on in the family. He resented that.

"One time, we had a trip scheduled. Well, my parents had a trip scheduled. I didn't even know I was supposed to go along. Another time, I found out my car was for sale. I didn't even know. A friend of my mom's came up and said she was looking for a car and she knew that mine was for sale. I said, 'What are you talking about?' Later, I asked my mom and it was true. We were getting a new car and I was going to be given a different car to drive. But how did someone outside my family know about this before I did? That happened a lot in my family."

Ryan also noticed how much more involved other fathers were with their children.

"A lot of times I would see other young people doing things with their dads. One time, my dad and I played volleyball together and he was really good. I found out that he was good at basketball and other sports. And he did teach me a few things.

We did play catch. But I thought, 'He can do all these neat things, but he doesn't take time to teach them to me. What is the deal?' So I was resentful, especially when I saw the other kids and all the things their dads taught them."

Instead of letting resentment poison his spirit, Ryan tried to put his problems with his father into perspective.

"Seeing other kids in worse situations, I would say to myself, 'Ok, I don't have it that bad. My life could be 200 times worse.'"

And then there was his big brother, Fred. While they were young, Ryan looked up to his brother in awe. Fred was handsome, strong, smart, and talented.

"I wanted to be like him. I used to really look up to him. Especially, he played the drums really well. I thought, 'Wow! He's got a talent he can really use.' I even tried to play the drums to be like him. But once he started becoming a jerk . . . I remember one time I said to him, 'What's wrong with you? What are you doing?' And he said, 'I don't know'. The way he started acting when he started rebelling and using drugs, I started to think, 'You are an idiot.' This one thing, his drugs, cost him my respect. With his drugs, he worked his way downhill."

Ryan withdrew from his brother. He struggled with the loss of trust and respect that they once shared. He resented the emotional trauma that Fred was causing the family. So it was not an easy and carefree life that made it possible for Ryan to stay drug-free. He had plenty of reasons to be angry, to be mired down in self-pity, and to give up. And yet he didn't.

His faith was one of his main sources of strength from an early age. He felt that God was a real person, a Father of all, and one who could be counted on at all times. Ryan protected that relationship jealously by trying to do things that are pleasing to God—irrespective of what people would think.

"Prayer helped me a lot. You know the scripture, 'Throw all your burdens on the LORD' (Psalms 55:22). It really works. When I didn't do that—use prayer—my life got worse. I found that when I relied on myself, things took longer to get done and I was more stressed out. And I had good friends to associate with. I would do volunteer work with them every Tuesday night. It calmed me down and helped me keep things in perspective. I found that doing things for other people helped me to feel better."

Ryan also had some other coping techniques. Whereas some people use intense physical activity to reduce stress, Ryan used sleep. "When I was in high school and under a lot of stress, I used to take a nap after school. It was a good nap, about 45 minutes to an hour-and-a-half."

Another stress-relieving habit was picked up from his dad. For years, Ryan found this activity—or lack of activity—irritating. And yet, as Ryan got older, he adopted it. "This is a bad habit that I picked up from him. After a long day at work, he would plop down in front of the television. Generally, it was after dinner. And you really don't communicate when you are watching TV. We didn't communicate as a family much at my house. Even though we ate dinner together, we started watching TV while we were eating dinner."

Ryan found himself watching more and more TV as a way to zone out. To a lesser degree, Ryan used weight-lifting, biking, and running as a means to cope with stress. And he is always on the look out for new ways to manage stress.

"One thing that really helped was my mom. If I ever got into trouble, I always felt that I could go to my mom. We had a mutual respect for each other. She also knows my limitations and can tell when I'm doing too much. I would clench my fist a lot when I was stressed out and she would bring it to my attention. Just knowing that I was feeling a lot of stress would help me to focus on calming down."

One time a minister asked Ryan what was the biggest thing that helped him to avoid the pitfalls of youth and to maintain his Christian purity.

"I said, 'Seeing my brother's example and how badly things worked out for him. He left God and his life didn't work out. He didn't obey God's rules and he didn't obey my parents' rules. It really opened my eyes. And it really turned me more to God.'"

What will Ryan tell his children about drugs?

"I will be a little more concerned about drugs than my parents were. Basically, their message was that 'you don't need them.' But, I only remember one big talk on it and just a couple of other times. I think I was around 13 or 14 and I had already made up my own mind about it by then. So, I would reinforce it earlier and more often. Before I talked to them, I would build up their self-esteem and let them know who they are as individuals and that they don't have to fit in. I would also give them my viewpoint and the Bible's viewpoint. Drugs are not acceptable to me or to God."

*   *   *

Fred is five years older than his brother, Ryan. Nearly opposite in personality, Fred is confident, charming, strong-willed, and steeped in black culture. When he walks into a room, you notice. You notice, perhaps, because he is so calm and comfortable with himself. He wears dreadlocks, clothing that borders on being artistic, and a warm genuine smile. The fact that all of these look so natural makes Fred distinguished.

Fred graduated from a high school in Kernersville in the early 1990s and attended college for two years before dropping out. He classifies himself as a self-taught person.

"I know that I caused my parents a lot of stress when I was growing up. I know that now. I was very difficult."

Fred had his own ideas about things. He was determined to live life his way, even at a young age. One example of this was the way he approached school.

"All through school—elementary through high school—my parents would attend parent/teacher conferences. And the teachers would always say the same thing. Fred doesn't do his homework. I did not feel the need to do homework. Homework is to reinforce what you learn in class. I didn't need reinforcement. I could pick it all up in class. When it came test time to prove that I knew it, I could do it. But it was an ongoing issue at home."

Even in high school, when Fred admitted that it became "harder to pick up everything in class," he persisted in refusing to do homework. He was satisfied with his B-average at graduation because he did it his way.

Fred found communication at home difficult. His mom was home all the time, but he preferred to communicate with his father. And yet, communication with his dad was a challenge. Fred felt that his dad didn't understand him. His dad would try to be helpful, but Fred found his father's comments discouraging and negative.

"I remember being about seven years old. I wanted to make a birdhouse. I got a board and measured it, got a marker and drew out what I wanted it to look like. Then I wanted my dad to cut it out because he could use the power tools and I couldn't. But he asked, 'How is the bottom going to fit? Which side of the line do you want me to cut on? I was like, 'I just want you to cut it out.' He made it too difficult. Finally, I got tired of working with him. I said, 'Screw it. It's not worth it.' I threw it out."

Communication gradually deteriorated from there. By the time Fred was in high school, their relationship was tense and angry. It's not the way Fred wanted it to be. He wanted to be able to talk to his dad outside the context of father/son, or authority figure/subject. He wanted to be friends.

"I think in elementary and middle school you need to be parent/child, but also to be friends. That way, by the time you get to high school, when things really start to get difficult for the child, it will be easier to approach the parent as a friend. Then the child can say, 'This is what is going on,' 'I don't understand this,' or 'Why is this happening this way?' I wanted to be able to talk to my dad like that, but I didn't want to get into trouble for it."

So, Fred did the same thing that he did as a seven-year-old. He stopped asking his dad for help. He also moved away from the Bible values that he learned as a child.

> He set up his own value system and followed his own rules. He had his own rules about curfews, sex, alcohol, and drugs. He did what he wanted and bore the consequences.   —Fred, a teenage drug user

"One time, I crept out of the house, stole my dad's car, and got in a small accident. It could have been worse, but no one was hurt. Instead of telling my parents, I waited for them to find out for themselves the next morning. They were pretty angry. I was angry. I can't say what I was angry at. But I always felt that they were restricting me and saying 'no' for no good reason."

At one point, Fred's angry rebellion at home was so intense that his parents sought professional counseling. Both parents and both boys participated. But, after a period of time, it was discontinued because Fred refused to cooperate.

Though he was angry at home, Fred was happy with his friends at school. He and two buddies did not feel the need to join the redneck, prep, or drama groupies. They hung out together and that was enough. None of his friends used drugs and Fred doesn't even remember being asked to use drugs until his senior year.

"We had a good time at school. I would break out into song or do stupid stuff in the halls, and I think most of the kids thought I was on something, they just didn't know what. I was real eccentric and had a lot of fun."

To deal with the stress, instead of turning to drugs or drinking, Fred found solace in his friends, his music, and in the woods that surrounded his house. At that time, he felt drugs were a bad choice for him. He believed what he heard at middle school, that drugs will destroy your goals. And he believed what he heard at high school, that drugs affect your motor skills and your ability to make logical decisions.

But, in his junior year, Fred started hanging around the theater people. He described the group as "a dysfunctional family support group kind of thing." It was at this time that he started noticing more drugs at school and he started tuning in to the pro-drug conversations. In his senior year, he experimented.

"It was my second semester as a senior. So I knew that I was going to graduate. Right before school, a guy we'll call 'Bob' said, 'Do you have a car?' I said, 'Yeah.' He said, 'Let's go up there. I've got something.' I said, 'Ok.' We had two parking lots. One is on top of a hill. He rolled a joint and we smoked it. It was an impulse. Carefree. It was probably a Friday and I thought 'Why not?' I never thought, 'Oh, this is going to change my life.'"

Fred felt that he accepted Bob's offer because he could relate to Bob.

"He was a year younger than I was and I shared a class with him. I knew he was smart, and, like me, he wasn't doing any homework, but he would take a test and get a good grade on it. That is probably one of the reasons that I related to him. To a certain degree—I trusted him."

Fred's first experience with marijuana was less than euphoric. "It was an uncomfortable feeling. It was something that I wasn't used to. I felt edgy and uneasy. I was probably high but didn't recognize it. It took me longer to recognize sounds. As long as I was around Bob, I was fine. But when we went our separate ways to class, I started to get nervous and paranoid."

Fred's first class was an honor's level course. He was assigned to sit in the front row. He was worried that people knew, or the teachers would find out, that he had smoked pot. During the three hours that he felt the effects of marijuana, he worried that he would do something stupid, or that he would be called on for an answer. The experience was unsettling and he did not smoke pot again until he started college that fall.

"When I went away to college, I was distancing myself from my parents. My thinking was to get up there and to prove that I can work hard and get things done."

Finally, away at college, Fred had freedom he'd always wanted. No parental restrictions. He was in full control. But things did not go as planned.

"I got up there and I started partying. My classes weren't going well and I hated my roommate. He was smart and talented—but one of the most intense personalities I have ever met. He was angry and he would break things and play loud music like Metallica and throw stuff around the room. I got to the point where I would come to my room, drop off my books, and go across the hall to a friend's room. He always had pot. It was a way to relax."

When he left for college, he told his parents not to call. They took it literally. He missed them. He wondered if they cared.

Fred has mixed feelings on whether or not using pot affected his college performance and resulted in his ultimate decision to quit school. "I really partied too much. I made some mistakes. It affected my ability to focus."

On the other hand, Fred does not believe that it affected his motivation.

"I would slack off in my other classes, but I got all As and Bs in the classes that I really cared about. I got hired as an assistant to my professor and I worked hard even when it wasn't during my paid time. So I was able to work hard at the things I chose to work at."

He also met plenty of students who could keep their marijuana use under control.

"I hung out with a fair number of people on weekends who would smoke pot and drink. But, during the week, they could do their work. They were motivated to do what they had to do. I mean I know a lot of people who could have gotten As and high Bs and who instead got Bs and high Cs and they were fine with that. That was their compromise and they were secure with that. But me, on the other hand, I had had all my restrictions released when I moved to campus and I partied too much."

Like Jill in the other family, marijuana proved to be a gateway drug for Fred. He'd made a promise to himself not to take any hard drugs. "Anything you have to put in your nose or shoot in your vein is a hard drug."

He tried cocaine once. It was after he left college. He was with some out-of-state friends; they were using cocaine but weren't addicted.

"They weren't pressuring me and that is probably why I tried it. They said, 'Here it is, if you want to try it. But if not, we will understand because we're not going to push you into doing something you don't want to do.' "

Fred put a small amount of cocaine powder on the end of a key and snorted it. "For me, it woke me up and got me motivated. It was like drinking a pot of coffee. It was like taking No Doze—but without that weird shaky feeling. But coke cost $80 a gram. It's not worth it."

Fred also tried acid and that was more to his liking.

"I enjoy acid. It is like when you were a kid and your imagination was running wild. You could sit there and imagine really vibrant things. Acid does that. You can see different colors and you can laugh for hours on end about the silliest things. You can also have a bad trip. I've never had a bad trip, but I did have an emotional one. One time, I was on acid and my mom called. She was feeling depressed. Things had not gone as planned for her and my dad was out of town. I kept my composure while I was on the phone with her, but after she hung up I cried for a while. This was the first time she reached out to me and because of that it made the trip much more intense."

Fred said that most people should not try acid—ever.

"After you try acid, you are a different person. You will never be the same. You have seen things in a completely different way. The average person should not do acid. I would have no problem if everyone tried pot one time. But with acid, it is too easy to have a bad trip. Someone explained it to me like this. 'If you smoke a lot of pot and are just stoned out of your gourd, in two hours you'll be fine. But, after an hour into your acid trip, you start to have a bad time, you have six hours to go. There is nothing anyone can do. The only thing you can do is go to the hospital and get a shot to make you go to sleep.'"

Fred feels that there is a place in his life for drugs, as long as they are not an obsession.

> *"Pot was an obsession for a while . . . I would literally stay awake in my bed thinking about it. And I thought, 'Man, this is kind of ridiculous.' And I realized that I don't ever want to be addicted to any kind of drug or anything to where I have to sit there and think that I need that thing."*
> — Fred

Fred has never completed college. He believes that he can learn whatever he needs to learn while he is on the job.

"If I need to learn something, I know where the library is. I have had a bunch of different jobs. I feel that I can walk into a situation and if I don't know what is going on, I can get a book and learn it before you know that I don't know it. Many of my jobs I go into not knowing anything, but I learn it really fast. I am a self-learner."

Fred one day hopes to have a wife and children. What does Fred plan to tell his children about drugs?

"First of all, I've already decided to tell them that I've used marijuana. In school, they lump marijuana in with all the other drugs like heroin and LSD. And, I think, as far as illegal drugs, it is one of the most mild ones. I think I would say that I would prefer them not to do drugs, even marijuana. But I would want them to wait until they are out of high school if they did choose to use drugs. When you are in high school you are too easily influenced. You are trying to figure out so much stuff. Drugs would throw too much on to your perceptions and it will just make it that much more confusing."

Should marijuana be legalized?

"I think drug use is definitely becoming more prevalent. I am not opposed to people smoking pot. But I don't think it is right for it to be legalized."

At age 24, drugs were still a part of Fred's life, though not daily or even weekly.

"This is the path I have chosen to walk. Drugs give me a fair amount of perspective. I don't buy pot anymore. But if I am with my friends and someone has some, I'll smoke it. Just like someone else might have a beer or a glass of wine."

*   *   *

When the stories were all told, I searched for common factors that affected the teens' choices about drug use. Key factors seemed to center on control, connectedness, and coping skills. These three Cs became my yardstick for measuring the similarities and differences of the teens.

CONTROL

How the teens related to the concept of control seemed to be a major factor in how they responded to the temptation to use drugs. Fred, a drug user, wanted total control. He viewed control from his parents, teachers, or the law as a negative—something that restricted or interfered with what he wanted. From an early age, he decided for himself that homework was a waste of his time; his parent's rules, Bible's principles, and the law were too restrictive; and it was okay to work hard at the things he enjoyed, while ignoring assignments he did not value.

It seemed that he spent so much of his youth fighting for control, that once he finally aged out and got it—he didn't have the discipline to use it well. Without the discipline and the strong work ethic that homework is designed to produce, he didn't stand a chance at succeeding at college. This is when escaping with drugs became a regular habit.

This issue of control also affected his decision to use harder drugs. His friends set the example, by using cocaine in front of him, and then left him in control. Fred admitted it was the perfect pitch for him when he said, "They weren't pressuring me and that is probably why I tried it."

This strong desire for control worked to Fred's advantage when he was home from college and realized he was dependent on marijuana. Not liking outside control, he determined that he would never let anything—drugs or otherwise—control him to the point to where he *needed* it.

Jill, a drug user, also resisted control by authority figures, and instead, submitted to the control of her friends. She adopted their clothing, music, interests, and yes, even their choice to use drugs. As she explained, "I started smoking pot so that I could fit in and go with the crowd."

And go with the crowd she did. She went sneaking out, hanging out, cruising, and schmoosing.

It appears as though she also used drugs as a way to *defy* authority. When Jill was under the influence of drugs, she mocked her mother and reveled in the notion that her mother was clueless. She believed her teachers knew she was high but found satisfaction in the fact that 'they could not prove it.' She scored another point when a fellow student reported to her manager his suspicion that Jill used drugs and the manager said 'she didn't care.' And finally, Jill found a way to defy the law. She and thousands of others submitted to the eye-winking search at the Tom Petty concerts and then openly smoked marijuana on public property right in front of police.

Bobby and Ryan, both drug free, viewed control by authority figures as a protection. Bobby believed the "Just Say No" warnings that marijuana is a gateway drug and that using drugs can lead to bad consequences. Ryan respected his family's rules and allowed Bible principles to govern his decisions. Both these teens also had a high regard for the law of the land.

COPING SKILLS

It is not how many problems teens have—but how many *unresolved problems*—that increase their risk for drug abuse. By far, Ryan had the most problems, but he solved them by accepting help and employing positive coping techniques.

Ryan developed an arsenal early, as he faced so many problems at a young age. Sometimes it was as simple as adjusting his attitude. Regarding discrimination, his mom helped him to realize *who* owned the problem—it was the *disrespectful* person. When it came to peer pressure, again, he coped by realizing that he didn't *need* to fit in, he *needed* to be himself. He dealt with the pain of his father's low-involvement by saying, 'My life could have been 200 times worse.'

Other times, he had to work through his problems. Like so many teens, he felt alone, unhappy, and isolated. To cope, he decided to solve the problem. He made a conscious decision to accept himself, be more friendly, and talk to more people. It worked! And when he got tired of LD (Learning Disabled) classes, he worked his way out of them.

Finally, to deal with generalized stress, Ryan used the power of prayer, spent time with friends, did volunteer work, slept, watched television, ran, biked, and lifted weights.

Bobby, too, excelled at employing positive coping techniques. First, he *questioned* peer pressure and its validity. He realized that he did not need drugs to fit in, to have fun, or to cope with problems. When this decision cost him some of his older friends, he coped by looking at what he did have. He realized, "I still had plenty of friends and I didn't need that (drugs). I liked my life."

When it came to generalized stress, Bobby found a way to metabolize it. By playing a hard game of basketball, he converted emotional pain into physical pain. The physical pain eked out one drop at a time as he worked up a sweat. The sweat either evaporated into thin air or was washed away in the shower. Competitive sports didn't make his problems go away—but after sweating it out on the basketball court, the stress was manageable. He felt empowered to work on his problems with clearer eyes and increased energy.

Fred used a variety of coping skills, both positive and negative. One skill he learned early is summed up in his seven-year-old words, 'Screw it. It's not worth it.' Quitting is sometimes a positive choice, but not when it was something he really wanted—be it a birdhouse, a healthy relationship with his father, or a college education.

By high school, Fred had developed a positive method of dealing with peer pressure. He decided that he didn't *need* to join a peer group. He and two buddies created their own group and mystified the other students by breaking out into song, pulling silly antics, and indulging their free-spirited imaginations. This, along with music and spending time in the woods around his house, were enough to mitigate his daily stress until he reached the eleventh grade. Then, he changed his friends—to friends who used drugs—and, eventually, he experimented with marijuana.

In college—without his friends and the woods—marijuana became his coping method of choice.

Jill seemed to be the least prepared to cope with the problems common to youth. When she was bored and her friends suggested smoking marijuana, she went along with the group. When the high school culture overwhelmed her, instead of keeping her goal to join extracurricular activities, she withdrew and shrank back.

Like the others, she highly valued her friends, but she chose friends who were not solving their own problems, let alone helping Jill to solve hers. Jill chose friends who were sad and depressed, raising the possibility that she suffered from undetected childhood depression. Left untreated, this would place Jill at increased risk of drug abuse.

Jill also had a tendency to *avoid* facing her problems—choosing to act 'crazy' or do 'stupid' stuff—rather than *work* on a solution. But, by far, Jill's favorite method of coping with problems was to *escape* by smoking marijuana. She discovered that in a drug-induced state—even though for just a few hours—she could magically change her whole world. It was as easy as breathing, breathing in the intoxicating smoke of a marijuana cigarette. Unfortunately, it seemed like the more time Jill spent in her alternate world, the less motivated and the less capable she was to succeed in the real world.

CONNECTEDNESS

Research shows that the most important connection for teens is their relationship with their parents.

> The number one reason teens give for *not* using drugs is that they don't want to *"harm the relationship* between themselves and the caring adults in their lives."

Turning this around, teens can sometimes use drugs to punish their parents. Jill admitted, "Probably part of the reason I was smoking pot was out of rebellion because she (my mom) couldn't talk to me and I was mad at her."

Instead of feeling loved, understood, accepted, and cared for—the definition of connectedness—Jill sensed that her mother thought: "Jill is the bad child and she just wants to get attention. We can't trust her." Whether her mother felt that way or not, Jill was operating under this perception. The fact that she felt loved and accepted by her father was not enough to mitigate the pain caused by the perceived rejection by her mother.

Research also indicates that the second most powerful connection for school-aged children is their schools. Again, Jill did not feel as though she was an important part of the school, that she belonged, or that she had established any special connections with teachers or adults at school.

Add to this the fact that she was well-connected to drug-using teenagers and to teenagers older than herself—and she now becomes a student at increased risk for drug abuse.

Her brother, Bobby, claimed he wasn't well-connected to either parent, and said, "Our family life still drives me crazy to this day. My parents would not take any of my advice. They didn't really listen to me." And yet, he also said that one reason he did not use drugs was because: "I didn't want to let my parents down. That was definitely there. They may not believe it, but I have a lot of respect for my parents."

Bobby felt a sense of connection with his school too, stating, "I love(d) high school."

He also had powerful connections with his peers, but unlike his sister, he chose friends that helped him deal with stress in a positive way by engaging in sports and by talking things out.

Fred, the oldest in the other family, apparently had a very accepting, loving, and understanding mother—but he yearned for a strong relationship with his father. However, by the time he was in high school, their father/son relationship was strangled by tension and anger. Fred decided to disconnect. Later, his parents disconnected by taking literally his instructions not to call him while he was at college. It was then that his life began to spin out of control and he chose to disconnect from college stress by using marijuana regularly.

Fred didn't mention that he felt particularly attached to his high school or that he bonded with any adults—which was likely impeded by his stand on homework. He did connect well with his friends and when his friends were drug-free, so was he. When his new friends used drugs, he gradually relaxed his attitude about drugs and eventually used them too.

Fred's little brother, Ryan, was extremely well-connected to their mother. Ryan even credits her with much of his success in mastering positive coping skills. While his poor connection with his father was disappointing, he resolved this by learning to be content with what he had.

Ryan developed a strong connection at school, attending the high school of his choice, asking for help, and happily receiving the assistance he needed. He also took the initiative to seek out and maintain friendships of his choice. And finally, he was well-connected to God. He felt that God was a real person, a Father of all, and one who could be counted on at all times.

* * *

After analyzing the four stories, it was clear that parents of drug-free children cannot take all the credit any more than parents of drug-using children must shoulder all the blame.

Two children can be born to the same parents, but that does not mean that each child will relate equally well with each parent. Also, there is no guarantee that each child will relate to themselves or to the challenges of life identically.

These stories made it clear to me that raising children is a *partnership* between the child and the parents. Sometimes the parents put one brick up and the child does the same. Sometimes the parents put one brick up and the child takes down two. In the end, each one is accountable for how he or she contributes to the partnership. And though the primary craftsmen in the partnership are the child and his parents, other significant influences include adult role models in the child's life, school culture, friends, the laws of the land, and, yes, even God.

Best of all, this inquiry helped me to understand my role and responsibility as a mother in my own family. I could now differentiate the roles and responsibilities of my husband, my children, and myself. The better each of us did our parts, the healthier we would become as a family and as individuals.

And finally, these four teens helped me understand why four of the nine children in our family turned to drug abuse. Our family was a step-family in which each child had lost a parent in a car accident. My mom was killed by a drunk driver when I was two-and-a-half years old. My three step-brothers lost their father to a reckless driver.

The trauma from these losses manifested itself differently in each child. Because we were not helped to put our loss or our pain into words—it became a significant *unresolved* problem. For me, it broke my trust and I believed that people, especially women, could leave me at any moment. Because of this, I strongly resisted bonding with my new mother. The actual pain from my loss remained buried until I became a mother. Only then—as I gazed into the eyes of my children—did I realize all that I'd lost.

But, on the positive side, I had a wonderful relationship with my father. We were soul mates. Like Ryan's mom, my dad was able to help me solve my problems. For instance, I didn't like his new wife. Bear in mind that I was only eight years old and I didn't ask for another mother. So I complained that she treated me unfairly, and I didn't like her method of discipline which occasionally included a slap in the face. I had never been slapped in the face and I considered it a gross display of disrespect. I wanted him to control his wife or get rid of her.

My dad patiently listened and then explained that he could not allow me or any child to come between him and his wife. I would be grown and out of the house before I knew it, while they would live together as husband and wife for the rest of their lives. He did agree that the slapping would cease, but that was the only thing he would intervene on.

Then, he gave me this bit of advice, "Patty Jo, you can't change other people. So you better change yourself." At first, I thought that he didn't care. But then I thought about his words and realized that he was right. I couldn't change her. The only thing I could control was *my* behavior. As a result, I learned self-control. This was one of many times when my father had just the right words at the right time, and I still go to him for advice. In short, we were, and are, strongly connected. Because I had few unresolved problems and one strong connection to a parent—I was at low risk for drug use. Incidentally, my mom did a remarkable job rearing nine children in a stepfamily.

At the other extreme, was my sister Diane. She remembers the day our mother was killed. Diane was upset that her mom was going to the movies and leaving us with a babysitter. So Diane was angry with her mom the last time she saw her. Because our mom never returned, little Diane was not able to reconcile this.

Children often blame themselves for all kinds of problems, such as their parents' divorce, their fights, their sicknesses, and even their deaths. If these misconceptions are not resolved, a child can engage in self-destructive behavior, which includes drug abuse.

Diane was perhaps the least connected of all the children and it seemed that the children in our family who had the most unresolved problems and the poorest parental connections were indeed at greatest risk for drug abuse.

Three "Cs" for evaluating risk for drug or alcohol abuse

Control
Coping Skills
Connectedness

Photo left as seen in *Kernersville Magazine* inviting the public to a free seminar: *Understanding Today's Youth.*

The program highlights practical tips for parents and mentors, with an expanded focus on the Three Cs.

To date, this is the most requested seminar Sawvel presents around the country.

www.UnderTheInfluence.org

Clowns & Face Painting & Dancing in the Street

Jots & Sonshyne, Las Vegas clowns for 20 years, know how to captivate a crowd. They bring juggling, balloon art, pranks, and face painting to the many festivals and celebrations in town.

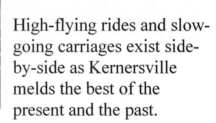

High-flying rides and slow-going carriages exist side-by-side as Kernersville melds the best of the present and the past.

www.KernersvilleNC.com

14

School Board Policy Change

Lesson 14: Look for a natural fit

Shortly after the 1998 school year began, Mr. Owensby casually asked me if I'd heard about the new drug-testing policy in the high schools. I hadn't. I was pleased and yet confused.

Drug testing was just what Glenn High School had asked for in 1996. Apparently, it was now available in all the high schools in the district. But it seemed odd that the newspaper and the people that worked so hard to make this happen were not informed first. Also, I wondered what was the new policy and how did it come into being.

I went to see Angela McReynolds. She explained the new two-pronged drug-testing policy. The *voluntary* leg is called "It's My Call." It was patterned after Carver's successful drug-testing program. *Students* make the call to remain drug and alcohol free. They sign a pledge and are randomly tested. It is a way for students to take a public stand against substance abuse.

The *mandatory* leg is called "It's Our Call." In this case, the *school* makes the call. All role-model students must join this program. A role-model student is one who participates in any extracurricular activity, including sports and civic clubs. If students want to be role-models, then they must sign a pledge and be randomly tested.

The program is not punitive. Drug-test results are confidential. If a student fails the urine test for drugs or alcohol, the student and parents are notified by the testing facility. If the family accepts free counseling, then the school is never notified and the student remains eligible to participate in extracurricular activities. If the family refuses, the principal is notified and the student is removed from the program.

Disqualified students cannot enroll in the program again until they complete the counseling or wait 365 days. For athletes, this means that they are off the team until they are back in the mandatory "It's Our Call" program.

Middle schools offered only the *voluntary* leg of the drug-testing program.

The results of my interview with McReynolds didn't appear as a story in the *Kernersville News* because a story had not been authorized. However, I kept this new information tucked away for future use.

Meantime, my writing career was stalling. My goal was to write for one new market per year. It was November and my goal was unmet. In desperation, I attended the North Carolina Writers Network 1998 Fall Conference in Winston-Salem.

I found out that the *Downtown Winston-Salem News* was looking for a lead writer. This small monthly specialty paper is published by Carter Publishing Co. Inc., which is owned by John Owensby.

Before going to Owensby, I went to John Staples. He thought this would be a good opportunity for me. He was unsure how Owensby would respond—but the periodical did need a writer.

It was at this subsequent meeting with Owensby that he and I resolved the rift that had persisted since the "Drugs in Schools" series.

He told me frankly, "I know that you can write this. I know that I can depend on you. But I don't want you taking over the *Downtown* newspaper. I don't want you running it."

"I can understand that. You just tell me whom to interview and what you want."

When the discussion was over, we agreed that I would write the cover story, an inside story, and a downtown "Vox Pop" for $100. As usual, I would supply all the photos except the cover shot.

As I rose to leave, Owensby smiled and said, "Patty, you're just like me. You see the hill and you take the hill."

A few days later, Owensby had me back in his office. It was the first week in December. The newspaper needed extra stories to balance the increased holiday ad copy. Owensby suggested that I write a four-part series on domestic violence. He also wanted me to write a few stories on animals.

Animal stories are popular with readers, but I wanted to get back into the schools. I wanted to see how the students responded to the new drug-testing policy. I wanted to see if it was making a difference. Did the students want it or were they merely tolerating it? What about the principals? And how did this whole policy come about in the first place?

"I'd really like to write about the schools," I said cautiously. "We haven't written anything about the new drug-testing policy. I'd like to see what the principals and the students think about it. The community probably wants to know more about it too."

Owensby thought about it for a moment.

"Ok. We'll do a series on the schools too. You can interview the superintendent, the two high school principals and the two middle school principals."

I had two and a half weeks to write two large series. Because of this, my interviews overlapped. I would go directly from a domestic violence interview to a school interview. This turned into an unexpected blessing.

My first interview was on December 7th with Kernersville Police Chief Neal Stockton. He told me that the department's theme for the year was "zero tolerance for domestic violence."

"You have themes at the police department?" I asked.

"Sure. Next year our theme is going to be 'zero tolerance for drugs.'"

"What do you mean 'zero tolerance for drugs' ?"

"In the past," said Chief Stockton, "if we saw kids smoking marijuana on a street corner, we might take away their drugs and give them a warning. We thought we were giving the kids a second chance. But we found out that the kids lost respect for the officers and the law. And a few years later, we were finding these same kids stealing cars and breaking into stores. So now, every person caught with drugs will pay a consequence—even if that means doing community service. We will have zero tolerance for drugs."

Three days later I interviewed Principal Coplin at Glenn High School. He welcomed me with a big smile and a handshake.

"Come on in," he said warmly and led me down the hall to his office.

He was extremely pleased with the new drug-testing policy. It was just what he had asked for in 1996. Coplin started the school year with an "It's My Call" kickoff assembly. Reverend Seth Lartey, a local motivational speaker, talked to the students about staying drug-free. It got them excited about the program. Coplin reported that parents were supportive too.

"I am not aware of any parents that did not encourage their kids to sign up," said Coplin. "We have gotten no negative calls. Zero. In just a few short months, it is already accepted as part of the system."

Coplin believed that the importance of partnership was the biggest lesson from the 1996 "Drugs in Schools" initiative. From the student voices, to the community meetings, to the solutions meetings at the schools, to the strong new policy passed by the board—it was all a remarkable example of partnership. This partnership told the young people in Kernersville that we—as a community—*care*.

He felt that it was important that the partnership continue. Drug testing was a tool, but it could not take the place of increased involvement by parents and the community.

Most of the students in the drug-testing program at Glenn High School were enrolled because they had to be. They wanted to play sports and be in clubs. The number of kids in the voluntary program was negligible. Coplin believed he knew why the voluntary sign up was so low.

"Part of the success of the Carver 'It's My Call' program," said Coplin, "was the use of incentives."

Carver gave stylish "It's My Call" T-shirts, pencils, pizza parties, and other incentives to students in the drug-testing program. Coplin wanted these incentives for his students. And he wanted the incentives to come from the community.

Eight hours later, I interviewed Superintendent Martin. He explained very eloquently what happened between August of 1996—when it appeared that the whole initiative had died—until August of 1998 when the drug-testing programs were rolled out in the schools.

It was a huge undertaking to be the first school district in North Carolina to institute a comprehensive alcohol and drug-testing program. This was quite a feat, especially considering that the school district ranked as the 110th largest in the United States. As with any large organization, it is difficult to make sweeping policy changes.

"Many players had to come together and step up to bat," said Martin, "for such an all-encompassing drug/alcohol urinalysis testing program to come into place. And Chuck Chambers, CEO with Sara Lee Direct, was probably the next one to come forward. Chuck was really hoping eight years ago that this voluntary drug testing would catch on with all the WS/FC high schools. When Kernersville was unable to find the money to fund the drug-testing program, Chuck decided that something must be done. And the school board knew if Kernersville needed stronger drug policy, so did the other WS/FC schools."

Chambers was on the board of the United Way of Forsyth County at the time. The local chapter of United Way was the highest per capita giving branch in the entire United States. Sara Lee Corporation, Chambers' employer, was the biggest contributor.

Martin credited Chambers with recommending that United Way help the students with drug prevention and testing in the schools. But United Way did not want to be associated with drug-testing. Instead, it earmarked $50,000 for drug prevention education and materials. Ultimately, this funded the Life Training Skills program now taught in all the middle schools. While Chambers did not solve the funding problem for drug-testing, he did get the ball rolling again.

"Another thing that helped to move us ahead," said Martin, "was a letter we got from a student expressing dismay about the use of drugs by high school students and athletes. School board member Donny Lambeth said, 'Let's find out more information on drug-testing.' So our attorney, Doug Punger, got to work. But we still needed to find the money to fund the program."

That was when Sheriff Ron Barker stepped up. He had a pool of money confiscated in drug-related cases. He suggested a grant of $50,000, Martin said, which the school board could utilize any way they wanted in the prevention of drugs or crime for students.

The money was offered to the schools in March of 1998, but first the school board had to confirm that it was okay to use the money for drug-testing. In August, the U.S. Attorney gave them the go-ahead.

Step One won the bid as the drug-testing agency. It does all the testing, handles the paperwork, and provides the counseling. Step One implemented its first round of student testing in November, 1998.

I asked Martin why the newspaper wasn't told months ago that the school board was considering such sweeping policy change. After all the work that we did, why had we been out of the loop?

Martin said, "Sometimes new ideas have to be nurtured behind closed doors until the ideas are strong enough to be shared with the public."

As we wrapped up the interview, Martin thanked "the community of Kernersville for the vigilance and interest that actually rippled all over Forsyth County."

He added, "And finally, I want to thank Carver High School for piloting this program successfully for so many (eight) years."

This led to a conversation about Carver. Carver's big advantage was its incentives. Over the years, up to 90 percent of the students volunteered to take a drug test. The other high schools now had the same "It's My Call" program, but very few kids *voluntarily* joined.

"So far," said Martin, "no one has filled this need. The school board specifically denied the use of any money for the purchase of T-shirts or other incentives for the students. This needs to come from the community."

I silently recalled that Chief Stockton was ready to roll out the new "Zero Tolerance for Drugs" theme. I also thought about Glenn's Principal Coplin and how he had asked for incentives.

I asked Martin if he would restate his last quote as more of a challenge and perhaps specifically target the Kernersville community.

He smiled and said, "Think of the message it would send to the kids if the community pulled together and got them 'It's My Call/It's Our Call' T-shirts. The T-shirts give the kids a tangible way to stand up against drugs. It will show that the community still cares and is going to stay actively involved. Absolutely, I hope the community will recognize our students and provide some incentives."

I decided to wait until Martin's story was printed and then personally deliver a copy to Chief Stockton.

My final interview for the series was at East Forsyth, with Principal Kurt Telford. He was beginning his first year as a high school principal, after replacing Judy Grissom.

He was initially concerned about the mandatory leg of the drug-testing program. He did not want students to shy away from sports or clubs just because they had to join the "It's Our Call" program. He believes that extracurricular activities are important because they teach skills that cannot be learned in a classroom.

Telford said that some parents called and asked questions about the new policy. Some raised questions about intrusion or invasion of privacy. But, in the end, it did not reduce student involvement. "In reality, this year our numbers have actually increased for students in extracurricular events," said Telford.

How did Telford promote the voluntary "It's My Call" program?

"I told the kids, 'If you feel like you might be tempted to use drugs or alcohol, it would be a great opportunity to sign up for 'It's My Call.' Or, if you want to prove that you don't use drugs or alcohol, or you want to stand up for being drug-free, 'It's My Call' is the right program.'"

It was clear how the school officials felt. I needed to talk with a few students.

Jeremy Reid, a senior at Glenn, said, "It shows that only a select few take drugs. It shows that it is not the whole school that does this. I did not feel embarrassed to sign up. Most of my friends are signed up. None of them had a complaint. All of us felt like we have nothing to hide. I think it is a great idea."

At East Forsyth, Alicia Ferrell, a senior, told the *News* what it was like to take the drug test. "An administrator came to my class and asked to speak to me for a moment. That is a pretty common thing. Then I went with her to the office where I filled out a form with my name on it. Basically it said that I agreed to take the test. Then they gave me a bottle of water to drink and told me to tell them when I was ready. Then I took a container (urine cup) into the restroom and when I brought it out I watched them seal it."

How did she feel about the test?

"I did not think it was difficult or embarrassing. No one followed me into the bathroom. I had complete privacy. Probably the worst thing about it was the inconvenience. But when you are in school, most kids don't mind getting out of class, even for a drug test."

How did Ferrell feel about the drug-testing program?

"This program shows that using drugs is wrong. And now, in everyday conversation, it lets people know that using drugs is not okay. Everybody makes mistakes. But it is your choice whether you want to let a mistake become a habit. With this new testing, if a student does make a mistake and then fails the drug test, her parents will get called. I think the student will learn sooner from her mistake in this case, than if there was no 'It's Our Call' program."

Did she feel that mandatory drug/alcohol testing is justified for students who want to be involved in extracurricular activities and sports?

"I feel that the reason a lot of kids do drugs in high school is because drugs are around and so it doesn't seem so bad. As a young child, I remember hearing about drugs and I thought drugs were a terrible thing. But in high school, drugs are talked about so much that it is almost normal. So you go from a child believing that drugs are the worst thing you can do, to when you grow up and you realize that drugs are really all around you. Casual drug talk is just common conversation at school, on television, in the neighborhood, and at work. So this program helps to change all that."

Where can it go from here?

"I think that other schools in other counties might realize that having a drug/alcohol testing program is not that difficult. I know that some people thought it might be discriminating or complicated. But it is really easy. The kids really don't mind it. None of my friends have a problem with it. So, maybe our program will help other schools to see that most students and most parents don't mind the program. And a lot of them even support it."

I was genuinely excited about drug testing in school. However, I found a flaw in the program. It came to my attention that student role-models were being asked to do something that adult role-models were not required to do.

When students fail this drug test:
- Students get free help
- Police are never called
- Nothing is recorded on their school record
- It's kept a secret—even from other classmates because students remain in sports and extras.

The role-model students had to be tested for drugs. This was based on the principle that they are leaders. But what about the adult leaders at school? Aren't teachers, counselors, principals, and superintendents leaders? Why aren't they subject

Who paid for drug testing?

Photo by Kay Disher, permission Kernersville News

Sheriff Ron Barker
Pinning a badge on Rus Smith, age 5.
(Sheriff Barker served from 1969-2002)

Photo by Michael Cottingham/ News

In 1998, Forsyth County Sheriff Ron Barker offered the Winston-Salem Forsyth County (WS/FC) Schools a grant of $50,000. The schools used this money to pay for student drug-testing. This allowed the WS/FC schools to be the first school district in North Carolina to institute a comprehensive alcohol and drug-testing program.

Where did the money come from?

Aptly, the funds came from a pool of money confiscated in drug- related cases!

http://www.forsyth.cc/sheriff/

to random drug tests? After all, many industries require random drug-testing. At Sara Lee, you are subject to random drug tests if you do something as simple as build a box. It should be much more necessary for those adults who shape the people of the future—our children! I wrote a column saying:

> The definition of "lead" does not allow for a public and a private set of values. The definition does not make room for a leader to tell others to take an action he is unwilling to perform himself.
>
> Regarding the schools, would not true leadership therefore involve random, mandatory testing of all the role-models?
>
> Think how much easier it would be for the student body to support this action if all the school board members, principals, teachers, and all other adults in the school system were bound by the same standard of mandatory drug-testing.
>
> That bold leadership could not help but earn the respect and admiration of the entire community, including the student body.
>
> This type of leadership is not new. It was introduced in the 1950s by Dr. W. Edwards Deming. At the time, America was not interested in this leadership method based on example, quality, and excellence. So Dr. Deming took his management system to Japan and in 30 short years helped them transform that country from a non-player to a tough world competitor.
>
> "True quality demanded a totality of commitment that began *at the very top*," according to the book, The Reckoning. Author David Halberstam convincingly demonstrated Deming's principles through the history of the automotive industry. He showed that real leaders lead by doing it first. For example, when Nissan's profits were down, the management always took pay cuts first, before asking the rank and file to make the sacrifice.
>
> Likewise, the school board and adults employed by the school district could be true leaders if they made the sacrifice of submitting to random, mandatory drug-testing, in addition to asking the student to submit.

I made it clear that I was not speaking against the "It's My/Our Call" program. I was asking for a *real* commitment from the top down. I was asking for a *'do as I do'* policy.

When the last of the series ran, I picked up extra copies and waited for my next opportunity to see the Police Chief.

15

Police Accept the Challenge

Lesson 15: Share your vision

In January, 1999, Owensby asked me to write a series on shoplifting. Ultimately, it won a prize in the North Carolina Press Association contest. More importantly, though, it gave me a reason to meet with the Chief.

At the end of our interview, I gave Chief Stockton several back issues of the *Kernersville News*. The papers highlighted pictures and quotes from the Kernersville Police Department (KPD). The last paper in the pile was dated December 22nd. It featured the superintendent's story. I pointed to Martin's challenge.

I suggested that as the police department was starting the year with "Zero Tolerance for Drugs,"—T-shirt incentives might be a good fit.

Without hesitating, the Chief said, "I think we can do that."

He asked me to come back the next morning.

When I arrived, the Chief had a team of officers assembled.

"Right now," I said, "less than half the students in Kernersville have joined the drug-testing program. Pretty much, the only kids in the program are the ones that *have* to join. But at Carver, 80 to 90 percent of the students sign up year after year. The difference is incentives. And the superintendent has challenged the community of Kernersville to provide incentives—like T-shirts—for its students."

I explained that incentives could help change the conversation at school from "most kids in my school use drugs"—to the truth. Most students *don't* use drugs. Two out of three teenagers don't use drugs, but they are not the ones doing all the talking. The T-shirts, along with newspaper stories, will give the students in the majority a voice—a way to be seen and heard. When the students know the truth—when the kids can feel the support of their fellow students and their community—it will be easier for them to choose a life free of drugs and alcohol.

When I was done, the Chief looked at his officers and said, "I brought you together to see if you thought we could do this thing. It goes along with our theme of Zero Tolerance for Drugs and it's an area where the police department could take the lead."

"I'm not sure," I said. "Glenn has about 1,000 students and East Forsyth has about 1,400. But I don't know how much it costs to buy and print a T-shirt."

"How much would it cost?" asked an officer.

Officer Mike Brim, who had T-shirts printed for his Police Day Camp, said that Sara Lee usually gave a discount to non-profits. As a rough estimate, he thought it might cost about $6,000 if about 80 percent of the students signed up.

Photo reprinted permission of *Kernersville News*

Chief Neal Stockton

In the 1998-99 school year, the Kernersville Police Department (KPD) adopted a new theme: Zero Tolerance for (illicit) Drugs. When the public school superintendent issued a challenge for someone in Kernersville to provide T-shirts as incentives for students to join *It's My Call* –a voluntary drug-testing program– the KPD took the challenge and piloted *Kernersville Cares for Kids (KCK)*.

"In the past, if we saw kids smoking marijuana on a street corner, we might take away their drugs and give them a warning. We thought we were giving the kids a second chance. But we found out the kids lost respect for the officers and the law. . . So now, every person caught with drugs will pay a consequence–even if that means doing community service." —Chief Neal Stockton (serving 1984-2009)

After a little more discussion, the Chief asked if the team wanted to tackle the project. He was confident that if the police department took the lead, the community would step up with the funds. The officers voted to go ahead with the project.

When I got back to the office, I told Owensby that the Chief accepted the superintendent's challenge. The Police Department would lead the way in providing T-shirts. Owensby was pleased but a little hesitant.

"We want to do this thing right," he said. "First, the Chief needs to make sure that Don Martin accepts his offer to provide T-shirts. And then, we'll do a story on this. We need a picture of them on the front page. Maybe we can get them shaking hands in front of the statue at the Police Department."

Owensby also suggested that the police come up with a slogan for the project. Brainstorming quickly, he and I came up with *T-shirts for Teens*. However, this slogan did not make ownership of the project clear.

On another occasion, the Kernersville Police Department had initiated a community project and the credit ended up going to the Forsyth County Sheriff's Department. The Chief wanted to make sure that the community of Kernersville and the police department got credit for their work.

So I asked myself, "What is this really all about?" It is about the community showing that it *cares*. It cares about its teens and their choices. That was it! *Kernersville Cares for Teens*.

Somehow, the new slogan, accompanied by the Chief's commitment, provided the necessary catalyst to send my mind whirling in a whole new direction. The Chief had made it clear that while the KPD had the manpower to *work* a project, they did not have the time to *create* it.

I began thinking. What would be the best way to market the idea to the students? Carver always had a highly energized kick-off assembly. Once, they even hosted Maya Angelou to inspire the students. Maybe, the Chief could get Governor Jim Hunt, who dubbed himself the "Education Governor," or a role-model like Michael Jordan, to talk to the students.

What about a fundraising committee? The officers needed help raising money. Why not have the schools notify the parents via the newsletters and the automated telephone messaging system? Maybe *parents* could help raise the money.

Other questions surfaced. Who would design the T-shirts? How would they be distributed? Should we offer any incentives to the middle schools? What kind of publicity would inspire the students and the adults?

A week later, on January 26, I drafted two letters to the Chief. The first closed by saying, "When we have the photo and the slogan we will alert the public as to the way they can support the project." The second letter contained a basic head-to-toe skeleton of the project, which the team could flesh out.

A few days later, the team of six officers was joined by three new people: Angela McReynolds, Carver's Ginger Amos, and a man from the local telephone company. Amos, who looks faded and fifty on the outside, has the heart and soul of an 18-year-old cheerleader. She heartily commended the police department for supporting the local students and assured them that they would make a difference.

She shared Carver's strategies of assemblies, daily announcements, pizza parties, and more.

McReynolds, who personifies the modern businesswoman, also commended the police. She suggested that the students be given control over the logo. Let them create it. Set out the rules and let them see what they can do. She also recommended that the school principals and the school resource officers be invited to the next meeting.

Near the end of the meeting, the employee from the telephone company spoke. He was certain that he could get a $5,000 grant from his company for the project. He convinced the team that money would not be a big obstacle, so we didn't waste a lot of time talking about fundraising.

One unsettling thing happened during the meeting. Momentum was running high as we fed on Amos' energy. She was talking about how the anti-drug message is all-pervasive at Carver. She said that the principal talks about it, the teachers talk about it, and the kids talk about it.

"Why, the teachers at Carver," said Amos, "even know which of their students are in the "It's My/Our Call" program and which few are not."

McReynolds interrupted, "The teachers can't promote this during class time. Class time is for teaching."

I glanced at Amos who obviously had teachers who were "breaking the rules." She just covered over it quickly by saying that there were lots of ways to help the kids to promote the project.

After the meeting, I asked Amos about the incident.

"Was it just me?" I asked. "Or did you get the feeling that Angela was slamming the brakes on the project?"

"Oh," said Amos, "that's just the way Angela is. She calls herself the devil's advocate. Don't worry about it. Teachers talk about lots of things in class that aren't in the textbook."

*   *   *

Kernersville Cares for Kids became the name of the project at the next meeting. Some people took offense at the word "kid," but the team didn't want to limit the project to teens. Besides, *Kernersville Cares for Kids* or *KCK* had a nice ring to it.

The police also came up with the idea of a victory party. The school with the most students in the "It's My/Our Call" programs—East Forsyth or Glenn—would get a party at school. The party would include music with a DJ, hot dogs, and soft drinks, all served by police officers. This proved to be one of the most powerful ideas in the whole project.

Officer Craig Brackens was appointed as the project coordinator. However, the Chief made it clear that he wanted me to stay involved.

Both principals responded to the good news with enthusiasm.

"I think it is super," said Glenn's Coplin, "that the Kernersville Police Department is going to take the lead in giving our students incentives. That is the missing element. The kids who did not have to sign up because they were not involved in extracurricular activities need an incentive to look at the positive side of joining the program. They need an incentive to be proactive and take a stand for a drug and alcohol-free life."

"I think it's great," said East's Telford. "For schools to be successful we have to have commitment from the teachers, the parents, and the community as a whole. I praise Chief Stockton."

The story with the photo was printed in the *Tuesday News just* as Mr. Owensby had envisioned it. It clearly stated that while the Kernersville Police Department was taking the lead, it needed the community's help. The police set a goal to raise $8,500 in three weeks. Readers were told how to address their checks and where to mail them.

Martin said, "I hope that other WS/FC Schools will follow. I hope their communities will get involved and show they care like Kernersville."

In the final paragraph, I did a little editorializing. "Community response will indicate the reality of the slogan *Kernersville Cares for Kids*."

Kernersville's Mayor Larry Brown evidently wrote the first check and I was sent to interview him. The Mayor challenged the community "to dig into their wallets and give a few dollars to *Kernersville Cares for Kids*." He further stated, "And I challenge the corporate community to recognize the value of the children in Kernersville and to help make *Kernersville Cares for Kids* (KCK) a success."

At that time, pledges totaled $2,000. One corporation had 500 employees that made a group contribution. So the story said that over 500 people had already supported the project. It seemed that as long as the telephone company grant was awarded, the money would take care of itself.

At the next police KCK team meeting two weeks later, each school had a representative. Vickie Lail, an assistant principal, represented East Forsyth, and Jane Dietrich, a teacher in charge of the school's S.A.V.E. (Students Against Violence Everywhere) club, represented Glenn. Three SROs from the sheriff's department and McReynolds were also there. The expanded team totaled 12, including me. Each person received a packet that I'd compiled from the previous meetings and discussions. It put everyone on the same page—literally.

<u>Define:</u> This is a leadership project by the Kernersville Police Dept.
<u>Purpose:</u> To demonstrate actively to the students of Kernersville that the community of Kernersville cares about them . . .
<u>Goals:</u> 1) Help kids help themselves. Give them the tools and leadership.
2) Clearly demonstrate Kernersville community support with real adult volunteers and real dollars
3) Keep it fun and simple.

Five chairman positions were listed, followed by a blank space. The goal was to fill each chairman's seat by the end of the meeting. Officer Dean Adams and Angela McReynolds volunteered for the School Assembly Team. McReynolds, a former art teacher, also agreed to help Officer Mike Brandon on the T-shirt Design Team. Ginger Amos took the lead on the Marketing

Team, Officer Dean Adams headed up the Distribution Team, and I agreed to be in charge of publicity.

One committee was not even discussed—the fundraising committee. This was not an oversight, because there was already $2,000 in pledges. And there was the solid promise of money by the telephone company employee.

Commitment is Key

Profound change often hangs by the thread of one committed person. Though different people fill that role as time marches on, that person is always someone who cares deeply, connects with others, and is convinced that change is imminent. Chief Neal Stockton personified commitment to Kernersville.
—Patty Jo Sawvel

www.UnderTheInfluence.org

16
Kicking Off the Project

Lesson 16: Leadership makes a difference

"Free food! Free food!" the young black man yelled.

About 1,000 of his peers shouted back, "Free food! Free food!"

When he and the crowd achieved a potent and predictable rhythm, he added a syllable and changed the chant to "All sign up! All sign up!" As enthusiasm swelled, he added another syllable and changed to "Take the challenge! Take the challenge!" The whole episode climaxed when he returned to two syllables and yelled, "Beat East! Beat East!"

It wasn't planned that way. But that is what can happen when students are given a chance to promote their ideas, their way. The chanter, Alan Brown, was one of three Students Against Violence Everywhere (S.A.V.E.) students introduced by Jane Dietrich at Glenn High School's kick-off assembly. He connected with the students in a way that no one else at the assembly did. And the kids loved it.

> *"In my entire teaching career, I would have to dig to recall an assembly where the kids got more excited."* —Jane Dietrich, GHS teacher commenting on a student-led drug-testing promotion

Before she and the S.A.V.E. students spoke, Officer Mike Brim had introduced *Kernersville Cares for Kids* and the incentive ideas. After the S.A.V.E. kids spoke, Principal Coplin capitalized on student enthusiasm and moved the student body to make a commitment. Then he introduced Tanya Crevier, a motivational speaker.

Crevier is less than 5'4" tall and she played *professional* basketball. So when she talked about "impossible" goals, the kids listened. She kept the drug-free theme going and specifically encouraged the kids to take the pledge.

This was probably one of the best-orchestrated and most powerful assemblies I've ever attended. I watched the audience file in as 1,000 separate individuals and I saw them leave as one solid team. Every student knew what he or she was being asked to do—sign the pledge and be willing to be tested.

At East Forsyth's kick off, the students were divided into four sections and four separate assemblies were held. Officer Mike Brim addressed each group. He told them about the T-shirts. He told them about the Victory Party. And, as he had at Glenn, Brim told the students about a free computer for the winning school.

At the time, East was in the lead with 51 percent of its students pledging, while Glenn lagged at 40 percent. The East kids got most excited about the free food and music at the Victory Party, but their enthusiasm paled when compared to Glenn's response. It just wasn't the same—to be told by an adult instead of being persuaded by your peers.

In addition to the lack of peer leadership, there was a lack of top leadership. Principal Telford delegated the kick-off talks to Assistant Principal Vickie Lail. Also, instead of dovetailing Brim's presentation with an entertaining motivational speaker, three adults got up and talked about college and career center opportunities.

I noticed an "are we done yet" look on the faces of many of the students. By the time the assembly concluded, student energy was low. I wondered if the students remembered or even cared about Brim's KCK announcement.

The kick-off assemblies proved to be reliable indicators of each school's success in promoting the pledging.

East, which had a rather lethargic assembly, never did pick up much speed, and only gained 43 signatures, or a mere three percent in the four weeks following their kick-off. Their strategy was passive and their principal was nearly invisible on this issue. Telford was aware of this and said he planned to change it after spring break.

"I plan to utilize that teachable moment just before class starts," said Telford, "by talking with different classes on the intercom. I will ask the students to help us. If they think about it, they will not only be helping East Forsyth, they will be helping themselves."

He also planned to talk to students as he passed them in the halls or on the sidewalks. He felt that students respond when their principal takes a personal interest in them.

Until then, the responsibility for the pledging rested mainly on Assistant Principal Vickie Lail. She and the adults at school became the "tellers" and the students became the "hearers." Finally, before spring break, the kids started promoting the program.

"Initially, we put information into the hands of all the teachers about our competition with Glenn. We asked first period teachers to hand out the brochures and to talk it up. This week (the *end* of March), S.A.V.E. kids put up posters and set up a sign-up table and are personally encouraging kids to sign up," said Lail.

I visited the S.A.V.E. sign-up table and when students signed the pledge I briefly interviewed them.

"I'm signing up," said Jessica Allen, "because I want to be a positive role model for younger kids. I read the pamphlet and I want my younger brothers and sisters to know that I stand for being drug-free. And the S.A.V.E. students talked to me too."

"Christine Eschleman (a student) came into my fifth period class," explained Dawn Carswell, "and I decided to sign up because I am going to be drug-free anyway. It is something positive."

E. J. Furchess signed up voluntarily before the incentives and East's promotion. Later he joined S.A.V.E. and began to promote the "It's My/Our Call" program. "I go up to kids," said Furchess, "and ask them if they are signed up. I explain the benefits."

Maria Antunez, who was also manning the S.A.V.E. sign up table, said, "This is a good program because it keeps kids off drugs. But also, the competition is good with Glenn. We love to compete with Glenn."

East was slow getting started, but S.A.V. E. coordinator and teacher Helen Prince was optimistic. She said, "I think the competition has made a difference. It has boosted awareness that it is important for students to be drug-free."

Meantime, since the kick-off assembly at Glenn, students and administrators alike had grabbed the ball and were running for a touchdown. Principal Coplin got on the intercom and encouraged his students daily. He gave them pledging updates and reminded them of their goal—to beat East. "The students love competition with East," Coplin told the readers of the *News*.

> Glenn High School Principal Adolphus Coplin talked to his teachers. He let them know that this was important to him.

He wanted them to talk with their students. As an incentive, if the Glenn Bobcats bested the East Eagles, Coplin would have a cookout for the first period teachers. Soon, classrooms were competing with classrooms and grade levels were competing with grade levels.

Teacher and S.A.V.E. Coordinator Jane Dietrich made it easy for the teachers to get involved. She gave them the tools and the topic. They received a pledge form for each member of their classes and were asked to talk about drugs and under-age drinking.

> On the student level, popular cheerleader Ashley Spaugh took over where Alan Brown left off. She started a dialogue with the students when she wrote an editorial in the school newspaper titled, "Do You Have the Courage?"—to sign up and take a stand.

Then, Spaugh and student athlete Beth Gray teamed up and started visiting the classes. As real role models, they gave five-minute spiels on why they pledged and why others should too. They made sure the students knew that the test was merely a urine test. They reminded the students that the party and the competition with East were dependent on *team* effort.

The S.A.V.E. students put up posters and manned sign-up tables before and after school, and during lunch.

A tremendous amount of energy was expended in Glenn's promotion, but signatures were slow to come in until someone read the fine print. On the back panel of the *It's My Call/It's Our Call* (IMC/IOC) pledge brochure was this question: *What happens if I sign the pledge card and my parent does not? Will I be included in the program?* The answer read: *Yes. By signing the pledge card, however, you agree that your parents can be notified of your test results.*

Though there was a line for parents to sign the testing consent form, only the students were *required* to sign. Evidently, students were losing or forgetting forms that went home. Once the kids realized they could sign for themselves, the process went faster. (Later this was amended to require both signatures.)

> It was apparent at Glenn that *some* of the students were genuinely interested in promoting a drug and alcohol free life. *Most* of them were interested in getting incentives and having fun. But whatever the case, *all* of them were hearing daily anti-drug/anti-alcohol messages.

By the end of March, the Glenn Bobcats closed the 10-point gap between them and the East Eagles. Spring break created a natural half time. The contest would resume when school started back on April 5. It would all be over on April 16.

Meantime, money to support KCK was trickling in slowly. The police department had set a goal of raising $8,500 by March 1. Ten days after the deadline passed, they had raised barely $2,000. I wrote a Vox Pop question to see if people *believed in* the incentive initiative.

Of the people randomly pictured and quoted, four out of five residents supported the KCK incentives. They said that it showed the kids that the town of Kernersville cares about them.

The youngest person interviewed, Brian Riding, "didn't think Kernersville should give the students that sign up anything." His viewpoint was that people don't need to get something as a reward when they do the right thing. If it is the right thing, you should do it for the sake of it being right. He did add, along with two other people, that he thought drug and alcohol testing was good.

Part of the Vox Pop question stated that donations for the KCK initiative were being collected by the police department. I hoped that the community—which said that it cared—would prove it by sending in money.

But, it didn't! In six weeks, only $166 had been added to the $2,000 already collected by the Kernersville Police Department. Even more telling was the origin of the contributions. In all, they came from the mayor, 10 local businesses, a KPD fundraiser, and me.

By this time, the man from the telephone company had been told that KCK would not get a $5,000 donation. Time was running out. On April 16, the contest between the schools would be over and the teens would expect their T-shirts.

The meetings at the police department became more intense. The Chief was very clear that the police department had accepted the challenge. The bottom line was that, regardless of what the community did, it was up to police to make sure the kids had T-shirts this year.

Ultimately, the duty of raising the money fell upon the Chief and his officers. Mike Brim later described the tremendous pressure this put on him and other officers. He had to do his usual job and then worry about raising thousands of dollars in just a few weeks. One thing that made this especially difficult for him was that he also raised money for his Police Day Camp (PDC) for children. He didn't want to strain his PDC relationships by asking for more money.

When the day came to pay for the T-shirts, the police had the money. They did not raise $8,500, as originally intended. This would have allowed KCK to share T-shirts with other schools who wanted to garner local community support. But they were able to raise $6,000 to purchase T-shirts for all the East and Glenn students in the program and to fund the Victory Party.

Betting On Kernersville

In 2013, when many newspapers across the country were downsizing, *Kernersville News* Publisher and Managing Editor John Owensby (right) invested in a new press which was custom built from the factory.

Owensby said, "With this new press, we are betting on the *Kernersville News'* future and the future of Kernersville." To his left is his daughter, Meredith Owensby Harrell, associate publisher and editor.

http://www.kernersvillenews.com/

144 UNDER THE INFLUENCE

Photo by Kay Disher, permission *Kernersville News*

Above: EFHS student Michael Babyak holds the East Eagles CD holder which he designed.

Above: T-shirts designed "by students for students" as *KCK* incentives for enrolling in the *It's My Call* voluntary drug-testing

"The pledge and the test (random urine drug-testing) make it easier to say no for students who find themselves in a bad situation. Basically, everyone I hang out with is in the program. All of us like the program. It helps keep drugs away from the school, the students, and out of athletics."

Michael Babyak, athlete

http://www.wsfcs.k12.nc.us/efhs
http://www.wsfcs.k12.nc.us/ghs

Above: Youth leaders helped create the message and the design for promotional items.

17

Victory

Lesson 17: Keep questioning

Glenn High School's spirit was at an all-time high. Hundreds of students rocked to the rhythm of *their* music being blasted across the athletic field by D.J. Todd Pegram.

Students excitedly talked with their friends as they freely roamed around the field. Others tossed a football or kicked a soccer ball. Many put on their new "It's My Call" T-shirts and signed them. Some teens sat on the bleachers and watched.

About a dozen policemen, including the Chief, served the students hot dogs, potato chips, and soft drinks. About a dozen volunteers from Kernersville Shepherd's Center joined the officers. Together they gave the students free food and free-flowing commendation.

Yes, the police had kept their word! They really knew how to throw a party and the students loved it. Virtually all the kids were there—honor roll and barely passing, popular and ignored, athletes and couch potatoes, musical and tone deaf—and everyone in between. This pledging drive pulled the school together because *everyone* could be a part of it. On this day, Thursday, May 13, 1999, everyone was a winner.

"When Mr. Coplin gets done talking trash to the other principal (Kurt Telford)," said one Junior Reserves Officer Training Corps (JROTC) student at Glenn, "and telling him what a good time we had, he will want this for his school. Next year, the biggest challenge will be from East Forsyth."

> Glenn students were pictured on the front of their hometown newspaper, as expected. But they were surprised and elated to see their party on the 6 o'clock news, on two local stations, both of which did live broadcasts from the stadium.

All of this positive attention occurred because 86 percent of Glenn students signed a pledge and about 10 percent of them were tested. This fact was pretty amazing because most of the students were in the program *voluntarily*.

Personally, I was happy that so many students at Glenn pledged and were having fun. But did it really make a difference? Did all this activity help the students to see the truth about drug use?

Had anything changed since the 1996 survey? Did over half the kids still believe that 70 percent of the students were using drugs monthly? Did 92 percent of the students still believe that "most students in my school use drugs"?

Randomly, I asked 31 students, "Eighty-six percent of the students signed the pledge, but what percentage of students do you feel are *really* drug-free?"

Answers ranged from a high of 90 percent to a low of 20 percent, but 60 percent was the average answer given. That meant that, on the average, they believed about 40 percent were using drugs. Wow!

In just one campaign, fueled by the community-supported T-shirts, the students at Glenn High School had their vision of drug use almost completely corrected. Scientific research had shown that Kernersville was following the national average of 36 percent of the students using drugs and now the kids were seeing the truth. Now students could see that "most students in my school do *not* use drugs."

This was victory! This was something to throw a party about. Excited, I went to Principal Coplin and told him about my findings.

> *"Changing student perspective about drug use is half the battle. Kids can encourage other kids not to be on drugs. When people say they are on drugs, that can't be the cool thing to do. If we can get the majority of kids to think of drugs and alcohol negatively, this new attitude will catch on."* —Principal Adolphus Coplin

The superintendent was also pleasantly surprised with Glenn's high pledging rate. When I told him about my informal survey and the positive shift in student opinion, he promised to do a bona fide study of the effects of the "It's My/Our Call" program and the use of community-based incentives.

Angela McReynolds presented the findings from this study at the WS/FC Board of Education meeting in June.

"Our numbers for drug violations have gone down this year. In the 1996-97 school year, 148 offenses occurred in the high schools. Typically, this figure will go up. They went up in 1997-98 to 167. This year, 1998-99, if you will note, we went down. Middle school stayed about the same (there is no drug testing in middle school). But in our high schools, where we have drug testing, we went down 22 offenses," said McReynolds.

"The month by month," interjected Superintendent Martin, "was of special interest because we did not start testing until November. If you look for the three years running, the months of August, September, October, the numbers (of violations) are almost exactly the same. If you really look at the numbers month by month, you will find more dramatic decreases in the third year once the drug testing got started in November."

From August through October, when students *pledged* to be drug and alcohol free—but no testing was being done—drug and alcohol violations remained about the same. But as soon as the testing began in November, violations began to decrease notably.

A chart showing how many students were enrolled in each high school, how many kids were in the drug testing pool, and what percentage of students that represented was shown to the board and printed in the *Kernersville News*.

High Schools' It's Our Call(IOC)/It's My Call(IMC)

School	Students in (IOC/IMC)	Students in school	Percentage Participating
Carver	707	837	84%
East Forsyth	922	1395	66%
Glenn	843	965	87%
Independence	0	249	0%
Mt. Tabor	631	1476	43%
North	642	1275	50%
Parkland	301	909	33%
Reynolds	733	1477	50%
South Park	59	131	45%
West Forsyth	874	1674	52%
Totals	**5712**	**10388**	**55%**

A board member asked why some schools had only 33-52% of their students participating in the drug testing and other schools had 66-87%. McReynolds explained that incentives made the difference. The top three schools—Glenn at 87%, Carver at 84%, and East at 66%—all had incentives.

"[W]e had an incentive program this year spurred on by the Kernersville Police Department. We did a kind of battle of the drug testing instead of the bands. We had a T-shirt designing contest and if you enrolled you got a free T-shirt. East and Glenn's memberships shot up dramatically," said McReynolds.

In fact, from August of 1998 until the end of February of 1999—when there were no incentives—Glenn remained near the bottom of the schools with about 40 percent, while East was a mediocre 50 percent. It was only in the last eight weeks—when incentives were promised—that Glenn more than doubled its pledging and East made a significant improvement.

> By all measures—increased student involvement, corrected student perception, and decreased drug violations—the drug-testing program and the T-shirt incentives were a success in Kernersville.

Finally, the community of adults and students was *moving*. Public opinion in Kernersville was very high in support of both drug testing and T-shirt incentives. For the first time, I really felt that the *Kernersville News* really deserved the NCPA Community Service Award. It looked like *Kernersville Cares for Kids* was going to be even bigger and better next year.

"Before KCK, a lot of kids would brag about using drugs or getting drunk. And the kids who weren't doing these things would keep silent. They didn't want to get teased."

Voice of an anonymous student

Principal Adolphus Coplin rallied his students at Glenn High School to enroll in the *It's My Call/It's Our Call* random drug-testing program. By all accounts, they set **a new national record for public high schools.** Coplin is pictured holding the KCK (*Kernersville Cares for Kids*) trophy for 2000-01. (Photo by Patty Jo Sawvel)

Percentage of GHS students in drug-testing program

1998-1999	87%
1999-2000	97%
2000-2001	98%

"KCK has transformed our school. The recognition and incentives from KCK has made being drug-free the cool thing to be."
Glenn H. S. Principal Adolphus Coplin

http://www.wsfcs.k12.nc.us/ghs

"We are pleased, very pleased with the responses from both high schools," the Chief told the readers of the *News*. "I think it really makes a difference when our community shows that it cares by supporting the good decisions our young people make. We are planning on providing these incentives every year with the possibility of expanding to the middle schools in Kernersville."

I never told the readers about the burden they put upon their police. The police agreed to take the lead, but not to do it all. Virtually no one sent in a check, even though nearly everyone supported the *Kernersville Cares for Kids* initiative. I suppose that everyone thought *someone* was sending in money. It didn't really matter why there was a problem raising the funds, but the fact that it got to be such a burden contributed to the unthinkable happening.

Pledging vs. Testing

From August through October, when students pledged to be drug and alcohol free—but no testing was being done, drug and alcohol violations remained about the same. But as soon as the testing began in November, violations began to decrease notably.

—Public WS/FC School Board Meeting Report

Framing History – Old & New

Artist and author Richard Hedgecock preserves the past in his downtown studio. Above, Körner's Folly is the town's largest tourist attraction with daily tours and tales. This 1880s seven-level home boasts 22 rooms with murals, carved woodwork, and 15 fireplaces.

Beneath the Oaks

Pick up a copy of *A Walking Tour of Historical Homes* at the Chamber of Commerce for a self-guided tour of downtown's incredible and authentic historic homes.

18

We Can't Do It

Lesson 18: Know your people

"Patty, I don't know how to tell you this," said Chief Stockton, "but we just can't do this again this year."

He was quiet and waited for a response. About 30 days earlier, in the April 27th edition of the *Kernersville News* he said the police department would provide incentives again. Now, he was saying that the department could not. Saying "we can't do it" went against the very root and fiber of the Chief.

The Chief was a man who kept his word at all cost. Since childhood, he was conditioned to push through pain, adversity, and seemingly unbeatable odds. He had experienced the power of putting his will—sheer determination—behind his word. But evidently, that wasn't enough.

Stepping back in time for a moment—if we look at the forces that turned boy Neal into Chief Stockton—we can get a historical glimpse of the community that shaped him.

A pivotal lesson in keeping his word occurred in 1964, when Neal was nine years old. He wanted a new bike, a $47 candy apple red bike with a white seat. His father, a policeman, couldn't afford to buy that bike any more than most of the other fathers in Kernersville. If Neal wanted the bike, he would have to buy it for himself. So he got a job working in the tobacco fields.

Getting a job in Kernersville at that age was pretty common, but what he did next was highly unusual. He went to W. J. Johnson's hardware store and applied for credit. Johnson gave his word that he would hold the bike for Neal. Neal promised to make weekly payments and have the bike paid for by the end of the summer.

Neal found that giving his word was much easier than keeping his word. Working tobacco is hard. Everything is done by hand. A boy can spend hours bent over in the summer heat of 90 degrees or hotter. To outsmart the sun, the workers often start at 6 o'clock in the morning. But that only trades one problem for another. Heavy dews drench their clothes so much that they have to wear raincoats into the fields.

The tobacco plant itself is hard to deal with. Tobacco is gooey. The plants ooze a tar that stains the hands. The residue was so sticky that Neal had to sand it off his hands with pumice soap. His clothes couldn't be washed. The tobacco wouldn't come out. So he wore the same clothes day after day to the fields until the clothes were thrown out. But Neal kept his promise. At the end of the summer, he'd earned a brand-new bike. He'd also earned self-respect and the respect of his parents, his peers, and W. J. Johnson.

The Chief was also accustomed to enduring personal discomfort for the benefit of the group. When he was 15 years old, he played centerfield for the All-star Senior League Baseball team. At the Southern U.S. Championship games, Neal was horsing around with some other boys. He hid behind a door, ready to spook a guy. The guy heard about Neal's plan and slammed the door against him. The bottom of the door caught Neal's big toe nail and stood it straight up.

Neal didn't tell his coach, Ronald Osborne. Neal thought he would bear the pain and play the game the next day. But in the middle of the night, his foot began to swell and throb. The pain of telling the coach paled in comparison to pain of his injury. In the wee hours of the morning, Osborne called in a surgeon. The nail was removed. Before the game, Neal's baseball shoe was opened up. A plastic cap was put on the end of his toe. And the whole mess was bound up with tape.

Neal played in the game. He played it with no sleep and with extreme pain. And the team won the 1971 Southern U S Championship game. This team was made up of farm boys pulled from a population of about 2,000 people. They beat out teams from Texas, Puerto Rico, and Florida who were pulling from a population of over 100,000. Neal knew his team depended on him and he came through for them.

Right now, Chief Stockton knew that he had made a homerun with the kids and the adult community with his *Kernersville Cares for Kids* program. He believed in the program and he knew the program needed to continue.

"We have to stay in front of kids," he said, "because they have so many opportunities to make a wrong choice. *Kernersville Cares for Kids* helps us to stay in front of kids and helps them to think about their choices. Today kids don't hear enough about choosing to be drug-free from TV, the churches, or their parents."

The Chief was especially sensitive to the powerful role parents play in a child's life. His father had successfully convinced him not to smoke, drink, or use drugs. The Chief's father, Grady Harden Stockton, was a policeman and ultimately the Chief of Police in Kernersville.

"He didn't lecture me," said Chief Neal Stockton. "From the time I was a little kid, he told me his 'war stories.' He showed me pictures of people who had hanged themselves or been shot or killed in a car wreck. He didn't say, 'Here's what happens.' He showed me a picture and said, 'Here's a guy who was drunk and hit a bridge.'"

> The method worked and it worked for two reasons. For one, young Neal loved his dad and wanted to grow up to be just like him. He had a deep respect for his father's work in the community. Also, his dad took the time to convince him of the effect of using mind-altering substances. His dad was so successful that Neal didn't have his first drink until he was 24 years old and he never used drugs.

"Kids today are so smart," said the Chief. "They *know* so much, but they don't *understand* the cause and effect of drug and alcohol use. *Kernersville Cares for Kids* shows them that the community *cares* and helps the kids to look at the total picture. It gives kids a chance to have a second thought about using drugs or drinking. So many times, it is the second thought that can change a life."

Obviously, the Chief believed in *Kernersville Cares for Kids* on both a personal and a professional level. So what had caused him to break his word? *Kernersville Cares for Kids* (KCK), which benefited over 2,000 local high school students, was just too much for the handful of police officers to bear. When the Chief made the promise, he was still hoping that the *News* readers would respond to the numerous calls for financial support. When he and his men had to carry the entire burden, it was too much.

"It just isn't fair to put all this on my officers," he said. "We just can't do it again."

Also, the Chief's personal life had been turned upside down in the 30-day interval between our "I will" and "I can't" conversation. Just four days before Glenn High School's Victory Party, his father died.

He attended Glenn's party because it was his duty and he wanted to be there. But his father's death was to take a greater toll than he expected.

For one thing, he would now carry the full responsibility of caring for his mother. But more importantly, when Grady Harden Stockton died, Neal Stockton lost more than a father. He lost his role model, his hero, and a large part of his daily life.

"From the time I was big enough to walk around," said Neal Stockton, "I wanted to be a police officer. I would put on my daddy's hat and grab his night stick and dress up in his clothes."

In 1968, he watched proudly as his father was appointed Police Chief of Kernersville. With his new schedule of nine-to-five replacing his old schedule of 5 o'clock in the evening until 1 o'clock in the morning, the two had more time for hunting, fishing, and being together.

When Neal graduated from high school, he quickly finished his Associate's Degree at Forsyth Technical Community College in Police Science. On August 28, 1975, just shy of his 20th birthday, Grady Cornelius "Neal" Stockton was hired by the Kernersville Police Department. He worked the same night shift his dad first worked. That is when he really got to know his dad.

> *"A man's role model is everything. My daddy, I knew him as a man after I was at the department. It means a lot to know a person as a man and not just as your dad. You need to see them both ways."*
> —Chief Neal Stockton

Less than a decade later, in 1984, Chief Grady Stockton had a heart attack and subsequent bypass surgery. This was a turning point in Officer Neal Stockton's life.

Mayor Roger Swisher and Town Manager Kelly Almond asked Officer Neal Stockton to be the new Chief. He had just completed his four-year degree at Gardner Webb College in Administration of Justice. Oddly, Officer Neal Stockton did not want the job.

> *"I really liked the streets. I liked the arrests. I liked the action. I had no ambition of being the Chief. The difference between being an officer and being the Chief is the difference of being a player and being a coach. I still wanted to play ball."* —Chief Stockton

Ultimately, after talking to his dad, his friends, his fellow officers, and his neighbors, he decided to accept the new responsibility.

At the same time, his dad asked more of him. Though Grady Stockton had two sons, the older son Billy had married at the young age of 16 and it was Neal that carried most of the family load. This was to intensify.

"Daddy depended on me to carry him through retirement. I gave a lot of myself to his care. My daddy trusted me and I did the man things. He trusted me to do that—to make decisions and to do repairs."

The new Chief also carried his father literally. "After his heart attack he was afraid that he would have another one and he didn't want to be alone. We went fishing a lot. After the surgery his legs didn't work right. I would help carry him in the boat and others would help too."

Just before his father's death, on May 9, 1999, Chief Neal Stockton was taking his dad to seven different doctors. At the first of April, the doctors gave Grady Stockton six weeks to live.

"He was 78 years old," said Chief Neal Stockton. "He was as hard as an oak table. He was a strong man. He had a strong mind and a strong body. *Everyone* knew he was strong. I wasn't prepared for his death because I knew that he had always done better than the doctors had predicted because he was strong. So I expected him to live another six months when they said six weeks."

Five days before he died, Grady Stockton gave his son Neal his favorite watch. It was a Christmas present from his officers back in 1981. He wore it every day. Chief Neal Stockton put it on and hasn't taken it off since.

The day he died, Chief Neal Stockton was at his father's bedside. The 78-year-old man had a smile on his face. He breathed out his last breath so heavy that the Chief said it was like someone punched the air out of him. And then the man, the father that was so central in the Chief's life, was gone.

"I was under a lot of pressure," said Chief Neal Stockton. "Things had changed. I was caring for my mom. *Kernersville Cares for Kids* was the biggest group effort the Kernersville Police Department ever did for the community. We were wearing so many hats and it just wasn't fair to my people to do KCK alone.

> *"Kernersville Cares for Kids shows them that the community cares and helps the kids to look at the total picture. It gives kids a chance to have a second thought about using drugs or drinking. **So many times, it is the second thought that can change a life.**"*
> —KPD Chief Neal Stockton

19

Finding a Better Way

Lesson 19: Find the real leaders

I'd been thinking all along that the police effort wasn't really a *community* effort. It wasn't really *"Kernersville" Cares for Kids* because hardly any of the residents were involved. As it stood, it could be more properly termed *Kernersville Police Department Cares for Kids.* So when the Chief said that the KPD could not sponsor KCK again, I wasn't surprised and I wasn't disappointed.

"That's great," I said. "Because you weren't supposed to do it all in the first place. This was supposed to be a *community* initiative. We'll take it back to the community."

The Chief assured me that the KPD would fully support the new leadership of KCK.

Immediately, I went to Owensby and told him the news. I asked if he would hold another community meeting like the one in 1996. After all, he had started this awareness, the police had successfully piloted KCK, and now he could keep it going.

Owensby agreed that it sounded like a good idea. He asked me to compile a guest list and get back with him after he completed the 100-mile run for which he was training. So at the end of June, when his race was done, we met. Enthusiastically, I explained that the superintendent, the police chief, and the two principals agreed to address the audience.

When I had finished speaking, there was a big pause. Owensby leaned back in his chair and said, "I've made some changes in the direction I'm headed. I don't think we are going to do that meeting."

I was shocked and confused. I thought we just needed to finalize a few details. I was not prepared for his decision, but I knew it would be useless to argue.

The meeting *had* to happen. The 1999-2000 school year was scheduled to begin on August 9th. The principals wanted to start the school year with the "It's My/Our Call" focus. They needed to know if they could tell the kids the community would provide incentives again.

I went to see John Staples. I explained that the community meeting was too important to cancel. We needed to find someone to help us.

"Whom could you recommend," I asked Staples, "that I could talk to? We need someone who can get the job done. We need someone who knows how to raise the money and get the community involved."

"Arnold King," said Staples.

King has a strong reputation in Kernersville. If he backs something, other people will back it. Also, if King is involved in a project, it usually succeeds. Interestingly, Staples said that King wasn't always that way. It was only after he made some serious money in real estate that he became so active in the community. It went along with a saying Staples used to quote to me, "You have to do well to do good."

Staples took me to the next Rotary Club meeting and introduced me to King.

King let me know right away that he was called upon to do many things for many people, so he was accustomed to saying no. He gave me 30 minutes to present my case. He asked very pointed questions.

Why was *I* doing this? Why didn't the *newspaper* call the meeting? Was Mr. Owensby going to give press coverage and acknowledgement to the supporters as he did for the "Christmas Stocking Fund"?

Who was going to get the credit for this? If Owensby got involved, would *he* take all the credit? King had a disagreement with Owensby. He wasn't interested in putting a feather in Owensby's cap, but he might be interested in helping the kids.

What did we *really* want? Money? Eight thousand dollars is not that hard to raise. Did the incentives really work? Was there any *proof* that drug use was down?

King grilled me for an hour—making us both late for our next appointments. But in the end, he gave his full support, permission to use his name, and a list of half-a-dozen people to add to my guest list. He also agreed to be chairman of the fundraising committee.

King was immeasurably helpful in sorting out the purpose of the meeting and asked, "Is this a meeting of movers and shakers, or is this a meeting of people who are in a position to write a check?"

We decided on the former. What we really needed was strong leadership on several committees. Once we had broad leadership and commitment, the money would follow.

> I made an appointment to see Owensby on July 6, at 3:30. Two hours prior to this, I had lunch with John Staples and asked him to critique my pitch. When I had finished, Staples asked, *"What if he says no?" "We're not asking his permission,"* I said impatiently. *"We are going to have this meeting with or without him. It would just be a whole lot easier if he were part of the team."*

Staples's question clarified my reason for meeting with Owensby. Out of respect for all that he had done for the students and KCK, we were giving him an opportunity to join the team before we moved ahead without him.

When I met with Owensby, I took a notepad and explained clearly that the meeting was set for July 15, at 8 o'clock in the morning at Town Hall. The speakers were going to be Chief Neal Stockton, Superintendent Martin, Principal Telford, and Principal Coplin.

"What about the money? You can't have a program if you don't have money. That was a big problem last year," said Owensby.

"A local businessman has come forward and offered to lead the fundraising," I said. "So the meeting is going to happen," I quickly added, "and KCK is going to

Finding a Better Way 157

continue. What I'm asking you is, do you want to be a part of this? Will you support this in the newspaper?"

Owensby leaned back in his chair and thought for a moment.

Finally, he said, "Since you work for the newspaper, the newspaper's reputation will be involved whether or not I choose to get directly involved. The newspaper has to be careful of what it gets involved in. Some things can come back and bite you. The funds for instance….. if they are mismanaged and the newspaper is at all involved, it could come back on us."

"The funds," I assured him, "are handled by the police department. They opened a special account so that all the money would be handled prudently."

He liked that. He decided to call Chief Neal Stockton on the spot. He asked the Chief about the upcoming meeting, the KPD's intentions of supporting KCK, and how the money was to be handled.

By the time he got off the telephone, his mind was made up. He was in.

> Owensby told me that KCK needed to be set up with three co-sponsors. He recommended that the Kernersville Police Department, the *Kernersville News*, and the WS/FC Schools fill those roles. He would represent the newspaper, the Chief would represent the police, and he wanted Superintendent Don Martin (and no substitute) to represent the schools.

The purpose of the co-sponsors, he said, was to provide assurance to all contributors that KCK was stable, safe, and supervised. It also would clearly establish who received credit for the success of the program. I agreed to make the telephone calls to put his ideas in place.

Next, Owensby suggested getting co-directing sponsors. As we had six committees that would be led by community leaders, we agreed that the committee chairpeople would be the co-directors.

Lastly, and probably most importantly for the moment, he asked if I wanted to send invitations to the meeting on *Kernersville News* letterhead. I declined, stating that I thought blank letterhead would be more neutral, but his offer showed me that he was 100 percent committed.

I wondered how he came up with all those ideas so fast. Perhaps Owensby's decision to cancel the meeting a few weeks ago had not been as arbitrary as it appeared. Maybe he had thought about it so much that he decided it would be too much work. After all, it had been too big a burden for the police department. But after today's meeting, and after his conversation with Chief Stockton, perhaps he could see that he could *help* without having to do it all.

The next day, I went to the Chamber of Commerce and got a list of all the civic clubs in Kernersville. As an afterthought, I asked the secretary, "If you were going to have a leadership meeting and you only wanted people there who are involved and who get things done, whom would you call?"

She quietly reached into a file folder and gave me the "Kernersville Chamber of Commerce 1999 Organizational Chart."

My goal was to get 30 people—the right people—to this meeting. This was my spiel:

"Hi, this is Patty. I'm calling to invite you to a Special Leadership Meeting at Town Hall next Thursday (July 15) at 8 o'clock in the morning. It is a youth-oriented initiative that has proved highly successful. It is invitation only. May I put your name down?"

Only a few people confirmed immediately. Most people asked, "How did you get my name?"

"Well," I replied every time, "evidently you are recognized as a leader in Kernersville because you are on my list. You must have gotten involved in the community in the past. Anyway, it is RSVP and we guarantee you will be out in one hour. May I put your name down?"

A few more people were satisfied with this, but most went on to ask, "What is this all about?"

To this I would say, "The speakers will be the police chief, the superintendent, and the two high school principals. It is about the incentives for kids who make drug-free and other good choices at school. Last year, eight out of ten high school students in Kernersville responded to the program. The kids want it back and the schools want it back. So we are going to meet to see if we can get it back. May I put your name down?"

By the end of the day, 25 local leaders had confirmed. By the end of the week, over 30 people were on the list.

On Tuesday, I wanted to call people to remind them of the meeting, but I didn't want to appear overbearing. I also had the challenge of providing coffee and refreshments with no budget. I happened to see Officer Mike Brim and he said the police department would make the coffee. He also suggested that Bojangles and other fast food places often donated food for community events. I made the calls and food was promised.

That set the groundwork for follow-up telephone calls on Tuesday.

"Hi, this is Patty. I'm calling to let you know that we will be serving coffee and refreshments at 7:30 at the Special Leadership Meeting at Town Hall. That way, people can have a chance to visit for a few minutes because we will be starting the meeting promptly at 8 o'clock. I'll see you Thursday."

Meantime, I made 35 packets to hand out at the meeting. The first page was a Vox Pop column. The question was: "Around the time of the Colorado and Georgia school shootings, Kernersville high school students were focusing on a drug-free initiative. An average of eight out of ten students responded to the community incentives and took a stand against drugs. Does this student response make you feel more comfortable with the safety of Kernersville schools? Do you think the community should provide incentives again for the new school year?"

All five people interviewed for the column wanted the kids to have incentives again. Next in the packet was a front-page story featuring five students from Glenn and East. The third sheet had two highlighted quotes. The first said, "The new 1998-99 drug-testing policy had a measurable positive effect." It was followed by a quote from the Chief explaining the value of community incentives.

A chart showed clearly that Glenn (#1) and East (#3) were leading the school district in participation. There was a picture of Superintendent Martin shaking hands with the Chief, and highlighted in yellow: "But while the Kernersville Police Department is taking the lead, they cannot do it alone." Also highlighted was Principal Coplin's quote, "The kids who did not have to sign up . . . need an incentive to look at the positive side of joining the program."

A fact sheet completed the package. It explained the difference between the mandatory "It's Our Call" and the voluntary "It's My Call." It gave a three-sentence history of KCK. The handout ended by answering three questions about incentives:
1) What was Glenn and East participation like prior to incentives?
2) What happened in eight short weeks after incentives were provided?
3) How did schools with incentives compare with other schools in the district that did not have incentives?

On the meeting day, I left the house at 6:30 and stopped at the Bagel Station, Dunkin Donuts, and Bojangles. At 7:20, I arrived at Town Hall. Harlam Beachem, the housekeeper, graciously helped me set up the room. At 7:35, guests started to trickle in. At 7:59 the meeting commenced.

Our speeches were brief and skillfully dovetailed, a skill I had learned from Glenda Keels, president of the Downtown Winston-Salem Association. One day, she had mentioned how busy she was. Among other things, she had to write a speech for the mayor, as he was going to speak at their annual awards ceremony.

"*You* write the speech for the Mayor?" I asked.

"Of course. How else could the mayor speak at all the clubs and occasions? How could he possibly keep up with everything? He *depends* on us to do this when we ask him to speak," she said matter-of-factly.

So when it came time for this meeting—I wrote *sample* speeches for the Chief and the superintendent. The Chief's presentation focused on community safety.

"Kids who feel well connected to their families and their communities," he said, "are less likely to have a problem with either drugs or violence." He then showed that KCK was a proven way for the community to make that connection.

When his five minutes were up, he introduced Superintendent Don Martin. Martin thanked the community of Kernersville for laying the foundation for drug policy change back in 1996. He provided evidence that drug violations decreased when drug testing was instituted. He also thanked the community for providing incentives through KCK during the 1998-99 school year.

Principal Telford developed the theme of school safety. "Especially, in light of the recent violence in Georgia and Colorado," said Telford, "this program helped kids to feel safer at school."

The school shooting in Georgia was of particular interest because the boy responsible for the gunfire was a former resident of Kernersville. When people across the nation asked the question: "Could that have happened at our schools?" the answer in Kernersville was "yes".

Principal Coplin spoke last. That was not an accident. He is a passionate man. He loves kids, loves the drug-testing policy, and loves KCK. His job was to take all the information that our previous speakers had used to fuel the minds—and to light a flame in their hearts.

Coplin told the audience that incentives were at the *heart* of the successful program at Glenn. KCK and the "It's My Call" program had *transformed* his school.

> *"I would like to come to you with a **plea**, a call for action. It's not just to raise money, but to give us true support and to come together. That's what we're here about—**transforming our entire community**."*
> —Principal Adolphus Coplin

I overheard someone say, "I was expecting someone to stand up and say 'Amen' after Mr. Coplin got done!"

Chief Stockton then introduced me and I led the group in a page-by-page review of the pictures and highlighted quotes that were in the packets. The goal was to give this group of decision-makers tangible proof that KCK was real, it was important, and it was credible.

Chief Stockton then proposed a motion to make KCK a permanent focus by the leaders of Kernersville. "If the motion passes," he said, "we will quickly organize into committees. Time has not allowed for a question-and-answer period, but we feel confident that you can make a decision based on three things:

1) this has been publicly reported on in dozens of stories in the *Kernersville News* for the last six months
2) all those who took the lead—the police department, the schools as represented by Dr. Martin, and Mr. Telford and Mr. Coplin—have spoken to you about the success of the first year of the program
3) the community—made up of the parents, teachers, residents and kids—has made it known that they want to have this successful program again."

The decision was unanimous. I passed out sheets that itemized each of the six KCK committees, one per page. Each sheet stated the name of the committee, the purpose, and the responsibilities. Below this was space for one committee chairperson and ten teammates.

"*This* (I held up the six committee sign-up sheets) is KCK. This is the kind of commitment that it is going to take to provide incentives for the kids. Now I assure you that you are not being asked to support a project on its dry run. This program is a proven success with the kids. And because it has already happened once, a certain amount of structure has been laid down that you can depend on."

I reviewed the goals and responsibilities of each committee: fundraising, T-shirts, publicity, trophy, victory party, and middle school involvement. Finally, I pointed to two officers on the perimeter of the room. Each officer was assigned to organize three of the committees. The audience was invited to sign up.

I expected the group to rush over to the officers and sign up for a committee. Instead, there was a moment of silence. . .then people began to talk. Bob Reed, city executive of BB&T, said that his bank would give a $1,000 savings bond to each high school. The principals could have a random drawing for all the kids in the drug-free program.

Owensby, who has a reputation for being prudent, if not tight-fisted, offered to donate all the printing for promoting KCK.

Rick Bagley, the school board member who in 1996 suggested legalizing drugs, wrote the first check and donated $100.

Ivey Redmon agreed not only to join the Trophy Committee, but to write a check for the full cost—$300.

I watched the consensus build to a climax and then gradually abate. The room grew quieter. People felt good. But I was concerned that no one was moving toward the officers. No one was signing up for the committees.

Suddenly, and dramatically, Arnold King stood up!

"*I'll chair the fundraising committee.* Which officer has that sheet?" he asked.

As he moved toward the officer, eight people followed him and joined his team. After that, others moved away from the table. By the time the meeting was over, each committee had at least one person on the team. Some teams were full.

At 8:44, less than an hour after commencing, the meeting was over. I counted it as a big success for five reasons. Firstly, everyone who said they would be there was there. Secondly, people left the room with more energy than they came in with. Thirdly, every committee had a start and 30 out of the 35 attendees joined a committee. Fourthly, the community support was broad and represented several facets of the population. Lastly, we accomplished what we set out to do. KCK was back.

"Why did you do it?" John Staples asked me. "Why did you arrange this meeting? What was your motive? Don't tell me now. Think about it. Write it down."

His question was both intriguing and unsettling. Did I have a selfish motive? Was I doing this to make myself a hero? Why did I do it? After giving it considerable thought, here is what I concluded:

Since becoming a reporter, I have been cautioned to remember that I am a *reporter* and not a *creator* of the news. My instructions were to let the community do as it would do. And yet, the more I became aware of the problems, the more I felt responsible to the community. So while I was cautious, this is why I took action.

> I viewed the community as my neighborhood. If someone posted a "lost puppy" sign at the end of my street and I canvassed door-to-door asking everyone if they had seen the puppy—that would be going beyond the call of duty. But if a puppy, fitting the posted description, came and sat on my porch—I would be irresponsible and lacking in honor if I did *not* take action.

Regarding *Kernersville Cares for Kids*, the "puppy" sat on my porch three times before I was able to return it to its rightful owner—the community. First, in 1996, the students made it clear that they needed more adult leadership, a community voice, and *tangible* support so that they could win the battle against illegal drug use and under-age drinking. In a very passive manner, I contacted a few companies who might be able to fund the drug-testing program that Glenn High School requested. Then I left it up to Principal Coplin and the companies to sort it out.

The "puppy" was back in the fall of 1998. By then, a new drug/alcohol testing policy had been instituted in the schools. During an interview, Principal Coplin told me that the kids *needed* community support—incentives. The community of Kernersville needed to adopt its students and take an active interest in their drug and alcohol choices.

He told me this as a reporter and as a member of the community. This time, due to my increased interaction with the public as a newspaper reporter, I was able to identify a *natural placement*. The police department wanted to focus on "zero tolerance for drugs" and was also looking for a better connection with the community. It was simply a matter of introducing the "lost puppy" to the person looking for a dog.

Unexpectedly, in June of 1999, the "puppy" was back on my porch. This time, however, I had a better understanding of *who owned the puppy*. It was the community of Kernersville—not just the police department. And eventually, I came to understand that extremely complex question: *Who* is the community?

Who is the community?

For me, the answer lies in a similar question asked of Jesus Christ. *Who* is my neighbor? The man asking the question in the story was really asking: Whom am I *obligated* to love as my neighbor?

The Great Teacher showed that *you make yourself a neighbor* when you help others in need. Being a neighbor and loving a neighbor involves knowledge, choice, and action.

So too with the question: *Who* is the community? The community is made up of people who through knowledge, choice, and action *make themselves part of the community*—by helping out when they see others in need.

So though I couldn't put this into words when I called the July 15 meeting, it did influence *whom* I invited. I invited people who had proven that they were the *community*. And now, though the puppy and I have remained close—it has been adopted by the real community.

20

A REAL Community Organization

Lesson 20: Give real leaders real authority and real recognition

I spent the weekend reviewing the sign-up sheets from the meeting. Two teams, fundraising and the victory party, had chairpersons and full teams. The middle school team had a chairperson but no teammates. The other three teams had teammates, but no chairpersons.

I called each attendee with this spiel:

"Thanks for being at the Special Leadership Meeting last Thursday. I was calling to get your fax number so I can send you updates on the program. Oh, and I wanted to congratulate you for putting yourself on a committee. Just a quick update—two of our committees are full, but we need some more leadership. Do you know someone who might want to chair a committee or volunteer with the program?"

Amazingly, this worked well. Victoria Cullingham agreed to leave Arnold King's team to chair the publicity committee. It proved to be a great match.

Before making the switch, I called King. As chairperson of fundraising, I did not want to take his teammate without his permission. He did not know Cullingham and was quick to acquiesce. Then he suggested that I call his good friend Kim Simser to see if she would like to chair a team. Simser decided to head up the T-shirt team, and again it was a perfect match.

Ivey Redmon was the only person on the Trophy committee and he signed as a teammate. When asked about whom he knew that could join his team, he was quick to think of his friend and neighbor, Pam Role. By the end of the conversation, Redmon agreed to chair his team. By the end of the day, two more teammates were added.

Officer Mike Brim chaired the victory party team. He had only two teammates, but said he would recruit volunteers from within the police department.

The last team to consider was the middle school committee. I had met Dana Caudill Jones at the Special Leadership Meeting. She wanted to sign up as a teammate for the middle school team, but after some persuasion, she agreed to take the chairperson's role. My arm-twisting proved to be a mistake.

The middle school committee was new and untried. Unlike the other committees, there was no script to follow. Also, it was later decided that just one person should meet with both schools. That negated the need to build a team, but it also meant that there would be no support for the leader. This job ended up being so different from its original expectations that Jones asked to be excused. At the first steering committee meeting, the superintendent recommended that Southeast Middle School Principal John Beaty take the role.

Exactly one week after the Special Leadership Meeting, all chairpersons received a fax that itemized their teammates, their committee's purpose, and their responsibilities. The first steering committee meeting was set for August 26th. Each team was to have a meeting prior to that date. To add incentive and accountability, each chairperson was promised a *Kernersville News* story on each team meeting.

It seemed to work. Every team had a meeting prior to our group meeting, except the middle school committee.

The trophy team was featured first in the *News*. The purpose of the trophy and the progress of the team formed the core of the story. The secondary theme honored the leaders, and put out a call for more leaders and more funds.

Redmon and Role were grandparents and heavily involved in the community. I asked, "Why did you choose to take on one more responsibility by joining yet another club, 'Kernersville Cares for Kids'?"

Redmon did it for his grandchildren.

Role said, "I find that the more I give to the community, the more I understand how the community works."

King and his fundraising team were featured next. Again I asked *why* they got involved.

"I took the chairman position for fundraiser …," said King, "because I believe in the program and it needed to be done."

> "This (KCK) is a good program. If you live in a community, you have to give back as much as you can."   —Bob Reed

"I would like to see," said Amy Macumber, mother of three, "every resident and every youth get involved in this program. Everyone could give at least a dollar to support this program."

There was a call for support at the end of all the committee stories. Readers were told how to contact KCK.

Before the August 26th meeting, a fax reminded the chairpersons that they would have five minutes on the program to update the group on their team's progress. Any questions would be brainstormed after all the presentations were made.

The meeting started promptly at 8 o'clock in the morning. I quickly laid out the purpose of the meeting. We were here to acknowledge the progress of the teams, offer support, and clarify the vision.

King gave the first report. I put him first out of respect for all he had done, and because I knew he would set the tone for this new group. He reported that his team had already raised $1,875. He planned to target the Chamber of Commerce members. He said there were 1,000 businesses in Kernersville and half of them were Chamber members. He was going to have a KCK flyer mailed out with the Chamber of Commerce's newsletter. His teammates would follow up with telephone calls.

King shared his telephone script with the group. It was a soft-sell that asked chamber members to review the insert and consider making a small donation to KCK.

The script let people know that the *Kernersville News* would publish the names of all contributors, both businesses and individuals.

Kim Simser, who was next, really did her homework. She came to the meeting with a handout that detailed the number of T-shirts, the cost, the delivery date, the student art contest deadlines, and more.

Victoria Cullingham was equally prepared and enthusiastic. In just a few short weeks, she and her team had come up with an entire publicity campaign. They were making bumper stickers, flyers, posters, and banners. To increase awareness, she was organizing fundraising events at the middle schools.

Ivey Redmon's team had studied hundreds of pictures before deciding on a torch for the top of the trophy. The torch reminded them of the excellence and commitment of the Olympics. It was formed out of beautiful heirloom quality crystal and one of the three flames was engraved with the words "Pass on the Excellence."

After Officer Mike Brim gave an update on the victory party team, we considered the questions. Everything was decided by consensus. In the final 30 minutes of our first meeting we made nine decisions.

1) The $10,000 fundraising drive would be completed by November 1.
2) The Glenn vs. East sign up competition would end May 1. The winner of the victory party would then be announced.
3) The trophy competition would be *district* wide and would end May 1.
4) The T-shirts would be ready for distribution to the students November 15.
5) The KCK logo for all publicity items would be a torch.
6) The official KCK colors would be gold and burgundy.
7) The trophy top would be a crystal torch. The base, yet to be purchased, would carry the history of the winners from year to year. (School name, year, percentage.)
8) Donations would be sent to a KCK post office box and the official telephone number for KCK would be the police department phone number.
9) The next steering committee meeting was set for September 24th.

When the room cleared, I felt exhausted but ecstatic. Eleven people, Owensby, Martin, one officer representing the chief of police, the two high school principals, the five committee chairs, and myself, all united in flawless harmony. We moved ahead at lightning speed. The meeting was everything a common unity could produce. It was my first experience with this phenomenon.

I called my brother, Roger Bailey. He is a year and a day older than I, and has always been my closest friend. Since early childhood, we have shared our hopes and fears, victories and defeats. When I called him, bursting with excitement about our first board meeting, he was sitting at his desk—the director's desk—for a large non-profit.

"It was great . . amazing!" I said.

I told him all about the meeting and how well everyone worked together. Then I said, "Now I know why you love your job so much."

There was a pause.

"I do like my job," he said, "but boards don't always work that well together. To make nine decisions in 30 minutes is not the norm."

"Why is that?" I asked.

"Sometimes you get people appointed to boards that really don't want to be there. Their appointments might be mandated. Sometimes people are defending their own interests instead of fighting for the cause. Sometimes there are personality conflicts. There are lots of reasons why boards don't work well, but I'm happy that yours does. Just realize conflicts might come up."

> "Sometimes you get people appointed to boards that really don't want to be there. Their appointments might be mandated. Sometimes people are defending their own interests instead of fighting for the cause. Sometimes there are personality conflicts. There are lots of reasons why boards don't work well, but I'm happy that yours does. Just realize conflicts might come up." —Roger M. Bailey, non-profit director

Thankfully, our meetings continued to maintain a high level of momentum and cohesiveness. We had occasional discord, but it was resolved in a matter of minutes.

*   *   *

In September, when Arnold King gave his report, he was clearly dissatisfied with his team. Evidently, many of his teammates did not personally know the chamber members they were soliciting. Because of this, their telephone calls were not bearing the anticipated fruits. King knew that it makes a difference *who* asks for the money. People tend to give more money and to give it more readily to people they know. But what was King really saying?

"Are you saying that you can't raise the money?" I asked.

"No," he said. "I'll raise the money." And he sat down.

Kim Simser said she had similar problems with her team members. They weren't doing their jobs.

I paused and looked around the room. Everyone was quietly looking at me, the facilitator, to see what I would do.

"Everyone in this room is a leader," I said. "You were given a team to help you get started. But you are in charge. If you don't like your team, build a new one. It is up to you how you manage your committee."

With that said, we moved ahead. Some people used the teams they were given, some people reorganized, and some people did most of the work themselves. All of them got the job done—which is the definition of leadership.

At our October meeting, King reported that his team had raised $6,310. His newspaper ad thanked 63 contributors. King announced that he was shifting his campaign focus from businesses to churches.

A REAL Community Organization   167
Key People & Presidents

While it is impossible to picture everyone who stimulated KCK's growth and development, below are some additional leaders that contributed greatly.

Arnold King

John G. Wolfe

This small editorial and writing staff keeps the *Kernersville News* printing papers three days a week. It keeps the paper going while "stringer" reporters tackle investigative or community service projects. (L-R) Jennifer Owensby, Duncan McInnes, Bob Kalbaugh, Wendy Freeman Davis, and Meredith Owensby-Harrell, associate publisher and editor.

Kim King

Capt. Mike Brim

Clarence Lambe

Howard Gaither Photo
Dr. Eunice M. Dudley

Jim Wilhelm

Buddy Collins

Duane Long

Presidents of *Kernersville Cares for Kids* 1998-2013

Photo Gil Goodrow
Patty Jo Sawvel
Founding-2001

Mike Willard
2001-2002

George Groce
2002-2005

Bob Prescott
2005-2009

Doug Kiger
2009-current

Simser had already ordered the T-shirts, Redmon found a craftsman for the trophy base, Beaty was coordinating the middle school contest, and Brim was on track for the Victory party.

Cullingham was doing a remarkable job with publicity. A giant score card, displaying East's and Glenn's percentages, was planted near the downtown library. Nineteen thousand KCK flyers were distributed in the *Tuesday News*. Five hundred yellow and red KCK posters were printed for the downtown Halloween event. Thousands of KCK bumper stickers were printed.

When the five-minute presentations were done, we focused the rest of the meeting on helping Cullingham. First, we asked, how we could encourage and empower the students.

Beaty said middle school students watch high school students. Maybe some role models from Glenn and East could visit the two middle schools. The principals agreed to work it out.

Owensby knew Dave Odom, the basketball coach at Wake Forest University. Perhaps he would endorse the drug-free students and KCK.

Martin suggested that this be televised. This would encourage the students *and* raise public awareness. He would contact Channel 12 to see if it would air this and some public service announcements (PSAs) that featured students. He said Lee White, who filmed for the school district at Cable 2, could produce the PSAs.

Beaty remembered that Alec Zumwalt, a graduate of East Forsyth, had signed with the Atlanta Braves. He promised to ask Zumwalt to do a PSA for television.

Someone noted that most of the television stations had early morning talk shows and one had a program "What's right with our schools." Cullingham said she would ask local stations to feature students promoting "It's My/Our Call" random drug testing and the KCK program.

Martin also suggested that when alcohol and drug awareness week arrived, Lee White could center his Assignment Schools program on the schools that were leading in the "It's My/Our Call" program.

Finally, King suggested that it would be easier to collect funds if KCK was a bonafide non-profit. I agreed to contact local attorney Joseph Anderson about acquiring non-profit status.

December's meeting was just as powerful.
- A date was set for filming 20 student PSAs.
- KCK bumper stickers would be handed out at the Downtown 2000 Celebration
- The *Kernersville News* would write a story when the T-shirts were distributed

Problems were resolved quickly. Redmon said the cabinetmaker was not keeping his promise—he had not even started to build the trophy base. However, King, a former trophy shop owner, gave Redmon the name of a dependable craftsman and when Simser realized she did not have a vehicle to pick up the 2,500 T-shirts, the police immediately came to the rescue.

The way we worked together reminded me of a symphony. Everyone *knew* his part and *played* his part. KCK wrote its own sonata, which was greater than the measure of any single individual. I, "e pluribus unum," felt it was a rare privilege to conduct it.

> The way we worked together reminded me of a symphony. Everyone *knew* his part and *played* his part. KCK wrote its own sonata, which was greater than the measure of any single individual. I, "e pluribus unum," felt it was a rare privilege to conduct it.
>
> This imagery came back to me so often that in late March, I wrote a column about the KCK symphony. I noted the *harmonious blending* of the WS/FC Schools, the Kernersville Police Department, and the *Kernersville News. In the first movement,* Dr. Martin *trumpeted* a challenge.
>
> The Kernersville police sounded a powerful *drum-like* response. In time, six community leaders took *first chair* positions and created their own *sections.* The kids heard the *music* and eight out of ten responded. Schools in neighboring counties were beginning to hear the *beat* and ask questions.
> All were invited to join the *movement.*

Preserving Legends

For years, photographer Gene Stafford (right) has captured the people and places that best reflect the spirit of Kernersville.

Above, the Gazebo at Harmon Park, donated by Margaret Burks in memory of her beloved husband, Leo. Top right, Brady Mullinax, the inspiration for the town's Honeybee Festival.

21

Kernersville Kids Lead the U.S.

Lesson 21: Good news is not always popular

On April 24, 2000, when the pledges were tallied, 1,027 of the 1,059 students at Glenn had entered the drug-testing lottery. That was 97 percent of the students. It was more support than anyone thought possible—*students* supporting drug testing.

> In 2000, record numbers of students enrolled in the drug-testing program: Glenn High School—97 percent
> North Forsyth High School—93 percent
> Carver High School—92 percent

Other high schools in the district had nearly as much participation. North Forsyth finished second at 93% and Carver placed third at 92 percent. In all, nearly 8,000 students in Forsyth County joined the "It's My/Our Call" program.

Glenn clearly led the district. Did it lead the nation? I called Rhonda Turner, coordinator of North Carolina Safe and Drug-Free Schools.

"Drug testing in the schools is so new," said Turner, "that no one is collecting this data yet. In North Carolina, we have 11 educational agencies doing drug testing, but most of them test only for sports or extracurricular. So 97% could be the highest in the nation."

Turner referred me to Gerald Kilbert, chairman of the *national* program. Introducing myself as a newspaper reporter, I asked Kilbert if Glenn led the nation.

"I feel 97 percent is probably the highest in the nation," said Kilbert. "But it is difficult to verify because there is no national database and so little money is behind the program. I will send a challenge to all the state consultants to see if any school is claiming to have more than 97 percent."

Kilbert kept his word and sent me a copy of the message he sent to over 50 state consultants. He listed my email address for responses. No one responded. So, May 2, 2000, Coplin and the crystal flamed trophy were pictured on the front of the *Kernersville News* with a story headlined, "Glenn High May Lead U.S. in Drug-Free Commitment."

Thinking that Kilbert, a *national leader* in the "War on Drugs," would be pleased, I emailed him a copy of the story. I invited him to come to the Victory Party on May 10th. He could meet the students, Principal Coplin, KCK members, and the community.

I even asked him, "Who else should know about the great things happening at Safe and Drug-Free Schools and Communities? Can you forward this story to all your other schools in California and to all your consultants like Rhonda Turner around the nation? How do we let President Bill Clinton know about this great accomplishment?"

"I'm not certain as to how you want to proceed," he replied coldly. "You will need to map out your own strategy."

Apparently, he did not see Glenn's successful program as something to put in the spotlight. He did *not* offer to take the story to the Commander-in-Chief, President Clinton, or to any other people fighting the "War on Drugs."

Instead, he cautioned me "that many districts do not see drug testing, even voluntary testing, as a quality response to the problem. There is no research base that I know of that says drug testing is the way to go. In addition, many communities do not want the legal challenges that go along with such a strategy."

What was he saying? Decision-makers at schools didn't have proof that drug testing is effective. Why? Because even though drug testing had been going on in schools across America for nearly 10 years, the commanders and leaders in the "War on Drugs" never bothered to study it? And even now, with 97 percent of the kids at Glenn backing this strategy, the chairman of the national program gave no indication that a database *would be established.*

Imagine! In a literal long-term war, soldiers are attacking by land, air, and sea. When it comes time to make the report, the commander in chief asks the officer in charge, "How is the parachuting operation fairing?"

"I don't know, sir," he replies.

"Haven't you been dropping young soldiers into enemy territory for about 10 years now?"

"Yes, sir. We keep dropping them but we have no idea how effective it is. We never set up a database."

"Well," asks the Chief, "what about the ground troops?"

"I don't know. We've kind of lost touch with them. But they are out there somewhere making a difference."

"What about the marines?"

> How can you have a "War on Drugs" when you don't know what your troops are doing and you don't look to see what is working? And if you have a big success and you don't study it—how can you hope to repeat it? Finally, what kind of leadership are the students of America getting when it comes to fighting drugs and underage drinking?

In reality, Kilbert was *shocked* that I quoted him in a newspaper story about drug testing. He reprimanded me by email and wrote, "Also, I must say, that I do not appreciate being quoted in any article without having been told that I was going to be quoted. I think your quote is close to what I said, but it is strictly an opinion, which you couched as 'feel.' It is my suggestion that you inform people that you intend to quote what they say before doing so without their permission."

So KCK took Kilbert's advice and mapped out its own strategy. It looked for ways to get the kids the recognition they deserved as role models of the nation. First, all the national television stations were sent a letter signed by the superintendent, police chief, and publisher. An East Forsyth Eagles T-shirt was also placed in the package.

In the letter to Nancy Tellem, the listed contact for CBS, I wrote: "<u>At Glenn High School, 97 percent of the students signed a pledge to be drug-free and backed it up by agreeing to a random drug test.</u> **All sources indicate that this is a national record.**

The topic of drug testing teens and the *War on Drugs* is of primary interest to the public, according to national polls. **We invite CBS to visit our school and to see how these students feel about drug testing.**"

No national stations responded. I even made some long-distance telephone calls and still had no response

> "Does there have to be something terrible—like a shooting—to grab the media's attention? If Glenn was the national champion in basketball, it would have been on national television. Why is being the national leader in student drug testing any less important?"

On the bright side, President Bill Clinton, N.C. Governor James Hunt, N.C. Senator John Edwards, N.C. State Board of Education Chairman Phillip Kirk, and N.C. State Superintendent Michael Ward, all responded with thank-you letters.

Letters and T-shirts were sent to the other nine high schools in the district and to numerous drug and alcohol related agencies across the country. In all, over 50 letters were sent. Everyone was invited to attend the Glenn Victory Party to meet the students.

Four local television stations came to the Victory Party. The students loved the attention and eagerly responded to the reporters' questions. Two questions dominated the interviews: Why did 97 percent of the kids agree to take a drug test? And, why did three percent decline to sign up?

> **Jeff Hagerty of Fox 8 asked a GHS student *why* he was one of the 97% who enrolled in the drug-testing program.** *"People don't look down on you anymore if you don't take drugs. I signed up because I am proud to be drug-free."* —Televised Unnamed Student

As Hagerty completed his interviews, it was refreshing to hear him say, "I'd much rather report on something like this than a car crash, a fire, or kids getting into trouble with drugs."

Angela Starke of Channel 45 got to the root of why three percent didn't sign up.

"They either got too involved," said senior David Coplin, "felt like they were being forced to do something they did not want to do, or some of them felt like it was their right (to refuse to sign) and that was fine."

Principal Coplin was pleased with the positive news coverage of his students. He told the *News,* "The students are looking for support. They are looking for our community to support them with efforts like this."

KCK captured clips of the television reports and passed them on to the students at Glenn. The students added these to their PSA television ads they had produced a few months earlier. Four students from Glenn and 15 students from the district's other nine high schools were filmed and aired on Cable 2.

Lee White, who worked for the school system, filmed the PSAs. He turned these sometimes-shy voices into dynamic student messages by adding music, graphics, and live sports clips.

KCK made sure every school had a copy of its students' video. Many schools aired these videos in-house so that everyone could see the sports stars, student government leaders, and other role models telling why *they* chose to live without drugs and alcohol.

The *Kernersville News* ran photos of the PSA students, along with their quotes and a summary of their achievements.

One of my favorite quotes was by E. J. Furchess III, vice-president of the S.A.V.E. club at East Forsyth. He was pictured in his "Real Eagles Don't Do Drugs" T-shirt and said, "Doing drugs is like putting holes in your parachute. You feel free until reality hits you. So in other words, don't mess up your life."

"One of the biggest steps in growing up," said Brook Evans, in her Carver varsity cheerleader outfit, "is making your own decisions. . . Make an example of yourself and others will follow you."

Brandon Isaiah, a senior at Parkland school who was selected for the USA Today All-State football team, and All-Conference in football and basketball, was decked out in his team jacket and jersey. His hat was from the University of Virginia where he had already signed on.

Isaiah said, "Athletics is a skill. Education is a gift and a great opportunity. Getting involved in drugs may lead to your missing out. Sense is common. You should use it to see that you don't miss out on these great opportunities . . ."

Glenn's Senior Class President, Russell Lauten, was wearing a necktie and a team jacket. He said, "On the road to success, it is important to understand the consequences of one's actions. . . One of the most important decisions you will make in life is to keep yourself drug-free. In doing so, you have made one right step on your road to success."

The county school board honored the students at a board meeting earlier in March and an unusual thing happened. After I showed the members the KCK donation jugs being used in the community, school board member, Jeanie Metcalf, asked me to pass a jug. In a matter of minutes, school board members put in over $100. Dr. Martin later told me that he had never seen this happen at a school board meeting.

At the May school board meeting, Coplin proudly accepted the KCK "It's My Call" trophy. We called it the "Oscar" of recognition. He gave the credit to his students, but everyone knew that the kids thrived under his leadership.

People who understood Coplin knew that this trophy represented much more than a district-wide win; it was the apex of three of his highest endeavors—serving God, promoting education, and directing young people. Coplin had become serious about these goals as a junior in college. Prior to this, his life centered on making music and having fun. He was a sax player in "The Love Street Gang" at Winston-Salem State University. The reggae band was pretty good and the 1970s group is pictured in the book *African Americans in Winston-Salem Forsyth County*.

In his junior year, Coplin married and changed his goals from making music to teaching music. Then he tweaked his goals again and decided he could have more impact on children's lives as a principal. Much of this was due to the mentoring and friendship of Preacher Nathaniel Miller.

"He picked me up as a son," said Coplin. "He had a love for music himself and he was also an assistant principal. He told me, 'What you need to do is go on to grad school and get a master's degree in administration.' So I quit my entertaining and concentrated on school."

Coplin had been without a father in the home since he was about six years old. His mother, a high school drop out, had married in the 11th grade, had three children, and then became a single parent. His mother's response to these events laid the foundation for Coplin's love of education.

Coplin's mother, Frances Crosby, worked by day as a housekeeper in a hospital and attended school in the evenings. After completing her high school education, she went on to Winston-Salem State University to earn her nursing degree. Eventually, she became a teacher in the nursing program at the university.

Coplin saw his mother's life transformed by the power of education. He saw her advance from cleaning up after others to teaching people to save lives. Her students bettered their lives and benefited others—all due to some well-placed education.

She showed her children determination and persistence.

"I remember the time she had shingles when she was working on her master's degree," said Coplin. "She was sick and itching all over the place—but it didn't stop her from working on her degree. It didn't stop her from completing it. So when I'd come to an obstacle, I'd think, 'Mom didn't give up so I'm not going to give up either.'"

Both his grandmothers, Flossie Curley and Laura Robinson, instilled in Coplin a passion for helping children.

Robinson felt like she helped raise thousands of kids. Coplin remembered what his grandmother always told him, "The teachers used to come and ask me to do things to help the students like I was the principal. I was a friend to the students. I would sit down and talk to them about school or their troubles."

Robinson wasn't a teacher or a principal. She was a custodian at Bolton Elementary School in Winston-Salem. To her, her students, and her administrators, it was a very important job.

"Her work brought her pleasure," said Coplin. "She was content. She was appreciated. Still today, she is nearly 90 years old and has been retired over 20 years.

Her principals and teachers still come by to see her. She understood that it takes everyone in a school, even the custodian, to care for the kids."

This strong backbone of education shaped his life. Being principal wasn't a career choice, it was his "destiny".

"I saw being a principal," said Coplin, "as a way to fulfill my mission as a Christian on earth. Help kids. Educate kids. Seek and save the lost."

"God led me right here," he added. "I knew I had this job several years before I got here. Not in a haughty sort of way. But I knew it was God's will. I wanted Glenn High School. I knew several people here. Circumstances and God made it possible."

Saving kids from drugs was right in line with Coplin's mission to "seek and save the lost." He told his students real-life stories—like the one about the boy at his high school who was so smart that after he did his own homework, he wrote papers for some friends of Coplin.

"He was sharp," said Coplin, "but he got involved in drugs and marijuana. Now he is a vagabond. He can't think straight. He can't even think for himself. He didn't have to end up like that. Maybe his story is part of why I am so passionate about this."

"Without being drug-free," said Coplin, "the academics are irrelevant. If students are going to waste their lives using drugs, there is no sense in even graduating. Students who use drugs are like the walking dead."

Coplin held parents accountable and gave them no-nonsense advice. "Don't be scared of your children. Sometimes we can be afraid to say what is on our mind. It hurts to tell our children that what they have been doing is wrong and it won't be tolerated. But we have to have the courage to tell our children the truth."

Coplin, a husband and father, also admonished parents to bring up the topic of under-age drinking and drugs often.

"If we are watching television," said Coplin, "or reading the newspaper about someone who has been busted for using drugs, I ask my children, 'What do you think about that?' I also remind them that I never want to get a call from the police telling me to come pick up my child because he had been drinking or using drugs."

All this history had reached a climax at the May school board meeting. Coplin's life was crystallized in the flame of that trophy. He had "sought and saved" 97 percent of his students. It was a remarkable and memorable testimony of the power of leaders who really care.

Coplin said, "When I leave this school one day, I would like to say that . . .I had the challenge of changing the student drug-usage perception . . . and I would like to know that I had an *impact* on the school in that particular area. It is important and I am proud of meeting the challenge."

22

Middle Schools Come Aboard

Lesson 22: Applaud others

When the 2000-01 school year began, Superintendent Don Martin asked for increased participation by the middle schools in the *It's My Call* Program. Specifically, Martin wanted *Kernersville Cares for Kids* to spearhead the campaign.

Oddly, the two middle schools in Kernersville lagged the county average of 14% enrollment, with Kernersville Middle School coming in at 8% and Southeast Middle School at 10%.

This was not due to neglect on the part of KCK. On the contrary, KCK sponsored cash prize "Drug-free Essay" contests in each of the schools. The winning essays were printed in the local newspaper along with a photo of the student. Also, the middle schools held fundraisers for KCK and contributed over 10% of the annual KCK budget.

Apparently, even though voluntary drug testing was available in all the middle schools since the 1998-99 school year, few middle schools were promoting it. Instead, the local middle schools saw themselves as cheerleaders for the high school students.

To turn this around, Martin suggested that Nancy Dixon, the WS/FC Schools Program Specialist for the Safe and Drug-free Schools, Principal Coplin, and I talk to the middle school principals in Kernersville. Then, he invited us to talk with all 16 middle school principals at a principals' meeting.

> From the beginning of the meeting, it became obvious that the middle school principals believed that drug testing—even if it was 100% voluntary—was inappropriate for middle school children. After all, children in middle school generally are only 10-13 years old.

Nancy Dixon shed some light on reality. "The average age of first use of inhalants is 11," said Dixon, "and for alcohol it is 12, and for marijuana it is 13."

She went on to add, "Our average drug violation in the WS/FC Schools is a student, age 15, who has been using drugs for two to three years. That means the student got started when he was 12 or 13."

It was clear that drug problems often begin in middle school, so middle school would be the appropriate place to begin a pledging and testing program. But the principals were hesitant to sign up a large percentage of their students at the risk of having their school look bad if, in fact, several students tested positive.

Here, Principal Coplin saved the day. Speaking from experience he told the principals that drug testing was not about catching bad kids. It was about changing student perception of drug use.

> "Students tend to believe what they see. If students see that most kids in their school are in the It's My Call program and that most kids don't use drugs, then they will be less likely to use drugs. In my school, drug violations are down since the students started pledging in the It's My Call program." —Principal Coplin

Lastly, I spoke on behalf of *Kernersville Cares for Kids*. While 14 of the 16 middle schools were outside of Kernersville, KCK still wanted to give all the schools an incentive to promote the *It's My Call* program. I suggested individual plaques, a trophy similar to the high school trophy, or perhaps flags. It was their choice.

As the discussion ensued, one thing became clear. The middle school principals did not want recognition to go to the top school. They wanted recognition for *every* school that met a certain expectation. In the end, it was decided that every middle school that achieved 50% enrollment in the voluntary drug-testing program would receive an "It's My Call/Drug-Free" flag.

Four months later, Kernersville Middle School Principal Debbie Brooks announced that she wanted her school to be the first to qualify for a flag. She turned the project over to Catherine Rusch, the faculty advisor of the Hawk Leaders. Hawk Leaders, then in its third year of operation, is a group of 32 eighth graders with excellent character and academic achievement. They receive special leadership training, at the YMCA Camp Hanes, about one hour northwest of Kernersville, where they are challenged to walk on ropes, climb flagpoles, and top walls—all as a way to learn teamwork and leadership.

On January 11, 2001, Rusch set the possibility before the Hawk Leaders. She explained that the testing and pledging was all voluntary and that drug use usually begins in middle school.

> "I asked the Hawk Leaders if they were willing to promote the program in the school." —Hawk Leader Coach Catherine Rusch gave her youth leaders a CHOICE. They CHOSE to own the program.

After some discussion, they decided to accept the challenge. Each Hawk Leader signed a pledge and then the group divided into three teams and formed a plan. Each team drew a giant thermometer, and as they collected student pledges, they colored in the red mercury. This way, the whole school could readily see the rise in student support of voluntary drug testing.

Beginning with the eighth grade, a newsletter was sent to all the parents. Then, on January 16th, every eighth grade student received a copy of the *It's My Call* brochure and pledge form.

Amazingly, just three days later, 81 students returned the forms signed by themselves and their parents. Once the eighth graders were on board, they went to the seventh graders and asked them to follow their lead. Lastly, they went to the sixth graders.

In the next 60 days, Kernersville Middle School soared from 20% to 66%. In fact, it finished the year as number one in the district for middle schools. Southeast did not fare so well—probably because it had an interim principal who took over in January. It only managed to advance from 10% to 16%.

However, Hill Middle School in Winston-Salem qualified for a flag at 50%. At this school, the SRO, Deputy Dobson, made this her personal project. She was well-liked by the students.

> *"Every time I see students, I ask them if they have taken the pledge to be drug-free. I feel that it is so important for kids to make a decision early to stay drug-free. And I encourage students to encourage their friends to join the program."* —SRO Deputy Dobson

The high schools did well too. Unbelievably, Glenn High School topped its old record by one percentage point, finishing out the year at 98%. North Forsyth came in for a strong second place at 96 % under the leadership of Principal Ron Jessup and his assistant principal Sandra Hunter. Carver came in third at 81% under the leadership of Principal Dan Piggott and Ginger Amos, and Principal Kurt Telford led Kernersville's East Forsyth High School to a fourth place at 78%.

We had fun that year with the recognitions. We created a "Club 90" award for schools that achieved 90% or more. And, we had a "Triple L" award for **L**eaders **L**eading **L**eaders. This award went to Catherine Rusch and the Hawk Leaders, Deputy Dobson, and Ginger Amos.

The top schools were recognized by Mayor's Proclamations, recognition ceremonies at the Town Alderman meetings in Kernersville and Winston-Salem, and at a televised school board meeting. Angela Starke, TV 45, went to the Glenn High School Victory Party and newspaper stories on all the achieving schools were sent to the remaining schools to "share the secrets of their success."

However, from an organizational standpoint, it was a hard year for *Kernersville Cares for Kids.* Several board members left at the end of the prior year due to sickness, relocation, or other commitments.

One key person who left was Arnold King, the fundraising chairman. Right up front he promised he would stay only one year and he was true to his word. However, before he left, he advised the board to become incorporated as a bona-fide non-profit.

To attract more members for the 2000-01 school year, we had a community meeting at the YMCA shortly after the school year began. Fifty people attended and five joined the board, but none wanted to spearhead the fundraising.

Several board members pitched in and the middle schools once again held fundraising events. KCK was still short of the needed funds, so I got permission from Owensby to write a "free newspaper story" on any company that would contribute $200 or more. Several companies responded and the budget was met.

By all accounts, it was a great year for KCK and for the schools. But I was getting exhausted. So, at our final board meeting for the school year, on May 31, 2001, I made an announcement. After giving a seven sentence history of KCK I said:

> In 2000, KCK became incorporated. On April 10, 2001, KCK became an official 501(c)(3) non-profit. Now, we are at a crossroads.

My life too has changed. I've been with KCK since the beginning. It started out being a 5-hour-a-week commitment, then a 10-12-hour-a-week effort. Now it is taking 20 hours a week and sometimes 40.

My responsibilities are changing. Since 1996, my children have grown up. My baby turns 17 next month. My grandbaby just turned three and another is on the way in July. I promised my husband that when my children were grown, I would get a real job and contribute toward our retirement savings.

Also, in 1999, I signed a contract to write two books. One was just published last month. The other—I have yet to keep my word to complete.

Finally, most of you know that I am one of Jehovah's Witnesses and like many others, we take our religious commitments *very* seriously. I have made some promises concerning my faith that I need to fulfill in the next two years.

So, I plan on staying involved in KCK as a board member, but I cannot continue to give 20 hours a week. So, what can we do? What do we need to do to keep KCK going and growing?

Nancy Dixon and I talked and we feel that we are ready for a part-time Program Manager. We met with the Winston-Salem Foundation to look at the feasibility of getting a grant to help us through this transition, if that is what the board wants. It looks very promising.

So now, it is up to the board to decide: Do we want to pursue getting a part-time program manager? Do we want to build our capacity so that KCK is a permanent entity in Kernersville?

The board voted unanimously to pursue the grant.

www.UnderTheInfluence.org

Middle Schools come aboard 2001

Kernersville Middle School (KMS) Principal Debbie Brooks broke through the myth that "middle school is too young for drug tests (a discreet urine sample required) and was awarded an "IMC Drug Free" flag from KCK. KMS had 66% voluntary enrollment and Hill Middle school squeaked in at exactly 50% student sign up. After that, 90% voluntary enrollment became the norm at the local middle schools.

"It's become "cool" for students to sign up for "It's My Call" at our school." Principal Brooks

Principal Debbie Brooks

Photos by Patty Jo Sawvel, *Kernersville News*

2002 KMS Hawk Leaders inspired 91% of their classmates to join IMC voluntary drug-testing. Above (L-R): Sandra Fruchtenicht, Bryson Childress, Keelie Murdock.

Fast Fact

"The average age of first use of inhalants is 11 and for alcohol it is 12 and for marijuana it is 13. Our average drug violation in the WS/FC Schools is a student, age 15, who has been using drugs for two to three years. That means they got started when they were 12 or 13." –Nancy Dixon, WS/FC Schools Program Specialist for Safe and Drug-Free Schools.

http://wsfcs.k12.nc.us

"I had the most fun making videos (five minute "join IMC" videos created by the students and aired in school) because we got to put in the bloopers. We wanted the videos to be fun to watch and to challenge the students to do better than last year. The videos made a big difference." –Bryson Childress

Keeping the Spirit Alive

Charlie Snow opened *Snow's Ice Cream & Sandwich Shop* in 1947 and fed the mind and body of "neighbors" in town for 39 years. Charlie built his restaurant in an alley that was only 11 feet wide, but deep enough to seat 45 people.

Charlie Snow and his bride-to-be Virginia Warren in 1948 at the 4th of July Horse Show.

In 2009, retired Principal David Fitzpatrick decided to honor his delicious boyhood memories of time spent at *Snow's* by opening *Fitz on Main* in the very location and with the same spirit of Charlie Snow's restaurant.

23

Thirty Days of Madness

Lesson 23: Ask for help

When Nancy Dixon and I looked at the facts, we realized that we had placed ourselves in a nearly impossible situation. Though we both had some grant writing experience, this grant application was due in less than 30 days.

It dawned on me that, in my singular grant writing episode two years prior, there were four months to perfect my application. Additionally, Jeffrey Swaim, the grant director of The Arts Council of Winston-Salem and Forsyth County, genuinely supported my goal to receive a $2,000 Regional Artists Project Grant.

That grant writing experience served as my tutor for my current commitment to KCK. In my first grant, I had asked for an Arts Grant to pay for an editor to coach me through the process of converting the "Drugs in School" series into a book. It would entail more than merely pasting together a bunch of old newspaper stories. I wanted to weave the student voices with the community response in such a compelling way that it would rock the nation.

When I took drafts of my first grant application to Swaim, I could tell that he wanted my application to have its greatest chance of success before the judging panel. He didn't just give me cursory approval—'yes, I had met the requirement.' He worked hard to help me see the vast difference between getting a bank loan and an Arts grant.

> *"I know you are passionate about this, but it's not coming through in your application. You are appealing to artists. Go home and watch Anne of Green Gables."* —Jeffrey Swaim, Grant Director, The Arts Council of Winston-Salem and Forsyth County

It just so happened that I loved Anne of Green Gables and had a copy of the series, so I sat down and watched it! I think it helped. I went back in and edited that first grant application. I wrote:

> I've always been consumed by people's life stories. But, I have never been content just to hear them. Stories speak to me. I not only collect them, I sort them, frame them, and share them. Like the *Chicken Soup* books, I have collected strands of vivid stories. But I am no longer content with a nice collection of threads. I yearn to become adept at weaving an entire tapestry around a dynamic centerpiece that speaks to me. The desire to accomplish this will not let me rest. Daily I add bits and pieces to my collection of materials

for this project. It is extremely important that this literary work materializes the way that I envision it. And, for that to happen, I need some one-on-one assistance in the form of an editor. Because, like even the best artists or athletes, I can not see myself. I need someone that can let me go as I am internally called, answer any questions as they arise, point out my choices and crossroads, and speak up when I get out of focus. After interviewing several prospects for this position, I found an editor who has the ability and the commitment to be my personal mirror.

In the end, I did receive the grant. Equally important, I found that the grant writing process enabled me to distill, crystallize, and clarify my goals. It helped me discern the difference between *who I am and what I do*, and, *who I want to be and what I want to do*.

So, when the KCK grant writing opportunity presented itself, it was with this sense of nostalgia that I accepted. I imagined that the process would be clarifying and useful beyond its monetary value.

However, this time there was no Swaim to encourage me. In fact, at our first meeting with James Gore at The Winston-Salem Foundation, it became apparent that we would be swimming upstream.

"Why should the Foundation fund this? This program is for Kernersville," Gore asked.

"Well, Kernersville is in Forsyth County," I replied.

"I know," he continued, "but we try to fund programs that are going to help *all* the kids in the county, not just the ones in Kernersville. Besides, Kernersville is a very supportive community. Why don't you go to them for funding?"

I knew what he was thinking. It was the same perception problem I had with the people who lived in Kernersville. Kernersville teens might have a drug problem, but the problem is worse for kids who live in the inner city of Winston-Salem.

And, to a degree, this is true. Sad as it seems, students living as short as 15 or 20 miles apart have totally different childhoods. Some inner city kids in Winston-Salem hear gun shots and see drug deals go down on a regular basis in their neighborhoods. In contrast, the vast majority of Kernersville's youth escapes that fate for their entire childhood.

However, drug use in Kernersville did mirror the national average and KCK was addressing it. Best of all, KCK was having a positive impact and its success could be scientifically measured.

In fact, Nancy Dixon sent me an email on August 31, 2000, about the annual safety surveys conducted at each school. Students were asked: Have you ever seen someone under the influence of alcohol or other drugs at school?

> Dixon's email stated: "In the 1997-98 survey (the year prior to drug testing), 70% of students at **Glenn** reported "yes" to the above question. In the 1999-00 survey, (only) 37% of **Glenn** students reported "yes" to the above question. Now, unfortunately, neither **North** (Forsyth High School) nor **Carver** (High School) enjoyed such a decline. North declined 4% between 1997-98 until 1999-00 and **Carver** increased about 4%." —Nancy Dixon, Safe & Drug Free Schools Specialist
>
> **Dixon drew the conclusion that while all three schools had high enrollments in the drug-testing program and all three had incentives—only Kernersville had *the community connection* that KCK created. In her opinion, it was the connection with the community that was causing this phenomenal positive change on the high school campus, not drug testing alone.**

In the grant, we were seeking to build "social capital" or "the power of human interaction." I felt that this and other positive proofs made KCK a prime candidate for grant funding. Gore seemed less concerned with the question of whether it worked, and more concerned with whether or not it would work for *all* the county kids.

He asked, "How is this different from Crosby Scholars? They do drug testing and they are set up in *all* the schools."

Thankfully, I was familiar with Crosby Scholars. It helps students find money for college. As a homeschool mom, I needed to know how to find scholarships for my children, so I had volunteered as a Crosby Scholars advisor for the 2000-01 school year.

As an advisor, I went to Glenn High School and met with 31 tenth graders on four occasions to help them with their college planning. Also, I joined them at their Saturday seminars, where they learned to improve their study habits and excel on the SAT. By the end of the year, I'd helped them move one step closer to their goal and I obtained the tools necessary to help my own children obtain scholarships for their education.

"Crosby Scholars' *main purpose*," I explained to Gore, "is to help students get a college education. It appeals specifically to college-bound students."

> *"Drug testing is one **small** component of the program. KCK's **main purpose** is to help students stay drug-free. It is open to all students in Kernersville and it gives students **a voice in the community**, it gives them incentives, and it creates a positive peer group that **changes their perception of drug use at their school**."*
> —Patty Jo Sawvel, explaining the true nature of KCK

Even as I said this, I made a note to get a letter of support from Mona Lovett, the executive director of Crosby Scholars, whom I knew personally.

By the end of our initial interview, Gore had raised some good questions: Why did we need a part-time program manager? How were we going to support this staff person after the first year? What was the town doing to show its support?

However, Gore, unlike Swaim, did not seem to be committed to helping us write our best possible application. I left the meeting feeling that he would have a hard time justifying grant money for students who lived in "Pleasantville" when there were thousands of students in the county in dire straits.

This, of course, did not deter us. After all, the application would be judged by a panel, but it did mean that we were on our own.

The next hurdle came in finding time to write the grant with all the attention that it deserved. As it turned out, prior to accepting the grant writing privilege, I'd accepted a scholarship to attend the Wake Forest University Addiction Studies Program for Journalists, in Scottsdale, Arizona. This program coincided with the 63rd Annual Scientific Meeting of the College on Problems of Drug Dependence (CPDD) and I was invited to attend both programs from June 15-19, 2001.

This fell right in the middle of my grant writing month. So, I packed up all the grant writing material and took it on the plane with me to the beautiful Fairmont Scottsdale Princess in Arizona.

Thankfully, one of my fellow journalists who was also a professional grant writer understood my dilemma, and agreed to help me write the grant during our "off duty" time.

Her insights were priceless as she outlined the need for an "outcome" based approach. With her help, we refined and revised the rough draft that Dixon and I wrote before I left Kernersville. She also gave me tips on letters of support to add credibility to our request.

Because of her kind assistance, I was able to give 100% effort to each of my endeavors on this trip. I started my day at 4:00 a.m. and worked for two or three hours on the grant. Then I took a daily swim, enjoyed a nice walk, and finally made my way to enjoy a long day of classes from 8:30-5:00. At some point in the day, my fellow journalist reviewed my work and made suggestions, thereby setting things up for my next day's work.

The Addiction Studies classes were phenomenal. We were listening to real scientists—the ones who actually do the studies—present their findings. For instance, we learned that when a random group of monkeys has unlimited access to alcohol, some will become alcoholics and some will not. By means of testing, scientists can actually identify monkeys that are genetically predisposed to becoming alcoholics. But, if a random group of monkeys has unlimited access to cocaine, *all of them* will become addicted. Cocaine is one of the most addictive substances known to man and to monkeys.

Our instructors used slide shows, handouts, books, and plenty of question and answer sessions to educate us about addiction. To be perfectly honest—though it was a red carpet affair—we were expected to work.

For those of us who came looking for answers, that's exactly what we did; we worked! And yet, I wasn't sure what I was going to do with my newly found knowledge.

More perplexing than the new answers I'd found were the new questions that they raised.

> How do *I* view addiction? Is it a moral problem, a medical problem, a behavioral problem, or a social problem? The point of the Wake Forest University Addiction Studies Program for Journalists program was to convince journalists—by means of science—that addiction is a disease. A health problem.

An illustration was given of a man who is genetically predisposed to diabetes. He may choose to eat lots of sugar and carbohydrates, drink beer, refuse to exercise, and he may remain healthy for a long time. But, perhaps, when he turns 40, something changes. He begins to feel light-headed and very thirsty. He goes to the doctors and is told that he has Type II diabetes. His body has undergone physical changes and while treatment may help the disease, it will not cure the disease.

It is the same with the disease of addiction. Some people can use drugs or alcohol for years and then one day physical changes occur in the brain. They now have the disease of addiction, which causes them to seek drugs compulsively—beyond their control. Like diabetes, addiction is never cured, it is controlled.

Another example used in the program to help us understand addiction was that of Hollywood actor, Robert Downey, Jr. Downey claimed to be addicted to drugs since the age of eight and could not seem to find a drug treatment program that worked for him.

In 1999, Downey explained to a judge how he experienced addiction when he said, "It's like I have a loaded gun in my mouth and my finger's on the trigger, and I like the taste of gunmetal."

His addiction was so uncontrollable that neither of his loves—for Hollywood acting and for his son—nor fear of returning to jail or prison—was enough to prevent him from compulsively using drugs. Downey had the disease of addiction and he needed help, not more jail time.

I weighed all this evidence very carefully, because, frankly, I always thought that drug or alcohol addicts were "bad" people. I thought they made bad choices by breaking the rules (using illegal drugs or drinking to the point of drunkenness) and then they reaped the ensuing bad consequences. I never thought that perhaps they were people who made choices similar to other people, but because of their genetic makeup they were prone to develop the disease of addiction. Then, once they had the disease, it was incurable and difficult to control. This possibility is something I would ponder for years to come.

Meantime, when the two-day Addiction Studies program was over, I attended the CPDD conference. It was there that I heard the most shocking and unexpected announcement about drugs: Alan Leshner, the director and spokesman for the

National Institute on Drug Abuse (NIDA), began his speech by addressing the prohibition campaign which was coined as the "War on Drugs."

> *"As a metaphor for drug abuse or drug addiction, the "War on Drugs" is a good metaphor. But, you don't wage war on an object such as drugs. This ("War on Drugs") has become a symbol of national failure. It is a pointless metaphor."*
>
> —Alan Leshner, director of the National Institute on Drug Abuse (NIDA), stated at the 63rd Annual Scientific Meeting of the College on Problems of Drug Dependence (CPDD) June, 2001.

Later, I had a chance to confirm this statement with Leshner. He told me that I heard him correctly. Officially, it was no longer correct to say that America is involved in a "War on Drugs." Oddly, Leshner's announcement was made on the 30th anniversary of the "War on Drugs" prohibition campaign. In this campaign, the United States government, aided by other countries, intended to reduce the *supply* of illegal drugs.

Another speaker at the CPDD conference said, "President Bush, when introducing the Drug Czar said, '*Demand* is where we have to deal with this (problem), not *supply*.'"

I thought about that. What kind of a "war" is fought so poorly that virtually every teenager in America can come in contact with the enemy—drugs—on a daily basis? Leshner was right, it was a national failure.

On the other hand, if the river of supply flows so abundantly that virtually any citizen could begin an uninterrupted daily habit of marijuana use, then how could someone conclude that targeting supply is *not paramount*?

But then, another piece was added to the puzzle.

Leshner continued, "President Bush put in for funding for NIDA and it will be the largest funding increase in NIDA's history. NIDA's funding will increase over its 2001 funding by 16%." He later added, "We need to use science as the vehicle to improve the quality of drug treatment available."

It appeared to me that this was a shift in policy. America was no longer trying to reduce supply. Instead, additional funding would be steered toward finding a cure for addiction. Once addiction was no longer an issue, it might be one short step to legalizing recreational drugs.

Obviously, all of these new ideas—garnered right from the source—would take a while to sort out. But I believe I witnessed a landmark change in United States' policy on illegal drugs.

While I came to the convention to get educated, I came to share the success story of Kernersville. This town had its own "War on Drugs" and it was winning.

I showed dozens of scientists and attendees newspaper stories about Glenn High School's 98% enrollment in the drug-testing program. And, I passed around pictures and quotes from student leaders in all 10 high schools in Forsyth County that were proud to tell the world that they didn't want or need to take drugs.

While telling my story, I stumbled upon one of the most dynamic ways to convince students that underage drinking and illegal drug use are harmful.

> As I was wandering around the NIDA exhibits, I saw a woman wearing a large button that read: I Dissected a Rat's Brain. The pin did exactly what it was supposed to do. It made me ask questions.

It turned out that, in an unforgettable learning encounter, this woman was invited to dissect the brain of a drug-addicted rat.

The idea fascinated me. That would be a lesson that no one—no teen—would ever forget. I immediately asked Wake Forest University (WFU) professors David Friedman and Kent Vrana if we could arrange for students from Kernersville to dissect a rat's brain. I thought the request was reasonable because WFU ran two of the largest addiction studies in the country, funded by the National Institute of Health (NIH), and it used rats for its experiments.

While this was not feasible, the professors arranged to have other lessons that would have a similar learning impact. For instance, while the students could not dissect brains, the scientists would let them hold and examine real brains—even a human brain. Also, graduate students would help the teens observe live rats—some sober and some under the influence of drugs, and Professor Vrana would show the students the same slide show he showed the journalists at the Addiction Studies Program.

It was this new idea that excited me more than anything else and it gave me the impetus to give the grant all the attention that it deserved. All in all, I spent over 40 hours writing and revising the grant and that is in addition to the countless hours that Dixon dedicated to the project.

Just to be sure that our application was perfect, I asked my brother Roger, the director of Smart Start in Davidson County, and Bert Wood, president of Step One, to compare the guidelines with our finished product to make sure that we addressed all of James Gore's concerns. As successful grant writers, they knew what to look for and made some additional suggestions.

We made the final adjustments, and with the help of volunteers from the Kernersville Police Department, we hand-collected 25 letters from students, public officials, and members of the community. Finally, on July 2, 2001, I hand-delivered the grant application to the Winston-Salem Foundation.

Signs of Significance

Fourth of July Park is no ordinary city park. While it sports the typical picnic shelters, playgrounds, tennis and basketball courts, and walking trails, it is also home to a ramped up skate park created in collaboration with the town's avid skateboarders. Additionally, dogs have their own fenced in Doggy Park. This too was created with the help of pet loving people. Separate areas are provided for large and small dogs.

One of the many historical markers is located just a mile from the 4th of July Park at the crossroads of Main Street & Mountain Street.

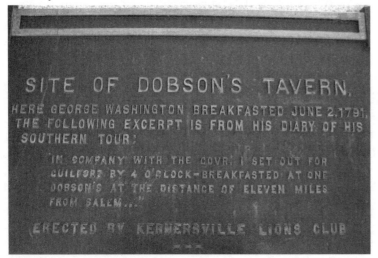

Presidents
Visit
Kernersville

George Washington

George W. Bush

Bill Clinton

24

KCK Gets a New President

Lesson 24: Focus on the positive

Our first board meeting for the new school year was held on September 13, 2001, just two days after the bombing of the World Trade Center. While there was a general feeling of uneasiness, the board was hopeful that this was going to be a good year. Dr. Martin even commented that he'd gotten a call from the Winston-Salem Foundation and he was very confident that KCK would get the grant.

One week later, we received our "I regret to inform you" letter. The letter advised me to contact the Foundation to find out why we were rejected, so I did. I was told that a vacancy on KCK's board and a lack of clear vision were contributing factors.

But in the application process, I'd explained to James Gore that as a young non-profit, which follows the school year, these items were historically resolved each September at our Leadership Meeting. I really believe that the overriding factor was that the Winston-Salem Foundation was already funding Crosby Scholars and felt the two programs were too similar.

The rejection by the Foundation was quite a blow to KCK: People were getting tired; it was difficult for a handful of volunteers to support 5,300 students every year; and, KCK *really needed* a part-time program coordinator. Now it was clear it was not getting one.

However, even as this opportunity faded a new one arose. On September 25 and 26, Glenn High School Principal Coplin, Tammy Thompson, a KCK board member who was also the Teen Director for the YMCA, and I went to Charlotte, North Carolina, to attend the *Healthy Community Institute for Non-Profit Excellence*. This free two-day intensive seminar was sponsored by the BlueCross/BlueShield of North Carolina Foundation.

The invitation for this was originally sent to my brother, Roger, as he is the director of a non-profit. He'd already attended this program, highly recommended it, and passed the invitation along to me. Much to my surprise, the *Institute* allowed KCK to attend.

The program was just what we needed. It was dynamic, well-presented, and completely user-friendly. It did not give us any manpower, but it gave us much better tools.

The program also gave KCK a reality check.

> The BlueCross BlueShield Healthy *Community Institute for Non-Profit Excellence recommended* that, in a healthy non-profit organization, *each* board member should: serve or chair a major committee, make a generous personal donation, be directly involved in fundraising, and bring in new money. When I suggested this, the board members—mostly overcommitted school principals—didn't receive it well.

It came back to the age-old question that continuously haunted KCK. Does Kernersville really care about its kids and its drug problem? Or, do they just want the schools to solve the problem?

In the mind of the five principals sitting on the board, it wasn't their job to raise the money and the manpower for *Kernersville Cares for Kids*. That was the community's job. It was the principals' job to take the money and manpower into their schools and to spearhead student-led anti-drug campaigns. I had to agree.

On September 27, the day following our return from Charlotte, KCK had a Special Leadership Meeting at Town Hall to garner new volunteers to carry the load for the 2001-02 school year.

Our meeting had an unusual theme—*Why are we here?* Briefly, I explained that KCK is here to set the record straight. Most kids don't use drugs and, yet, without adult leadership they are afraid to speak up in front of their peers.

'*Why am I here?*' I thought. After I wrote the "Drugs in School" series, I saw a need for the healthy kids to have a voice and a need for all the kids to see that the town was paying attention to them.

I told the group, "One teen recently told me, 'Before KCK, a lot of kids would brag about using drugs or getting drunk. And the kids who weren't doing these things would keep silent. They didn't want to get teased. But with KCK, now we can speak up—because the whole school is talking about how it is better to be drug-free and how we don't *need* drugs.'"

I then let the group know that after four years of volunteering, I was taking this to a new level. A grant from the Arts Council was giving me an opportunity to write a book about Kernersville and the way it is empowering its youth to stay drug and alcohol free. "So that opens the way for a new president and new leadership," I said. "We have six board positions open for people willing to work hard for the kids."

I then addressed—*Why are you here?*

"Only you can answer that," I said. "But I can tell you why you were invited. Some of you are members of the Kernersville Alumni Association and you have expressed an interest in reaching out to the students of today. You want to preserve the history of what it means to be a student in Kernersville and to keep the future history positive and powerful.

"Mayor Brown is here because he has supported KCK financially and otherwise, and is looking for a small office space for KCK. The rest of you were recommended by someone in the community as leaders who have been known to make a difference. So that is why you were invited."

Next, Chief Neal Stockton told why he is so committed to KCK. Then Principal Coplin and Glenn senior John Kivett gave a first-hand account of how KCK makes a difference in the schools.

Kivett said, "Some students who use drugs join the *It's My Call* program knowing they can be tested, because they *want* to get caught. They don't have anyone to turn to for help. Their parents are not there for them and they don't know what to do."

Of course, if they test positive for substance abuse, they get free help and if they accept it, they get immunity from disciplinary action at school or with the law.

Finally, I wrapped it up by asking, "Now is the time to answer that question— *Why am I here?* For some of you, you will see that you have a place on our board. You want to help shape the future of KCK and the students in the greatest way possible. It is a big commitment. Every board member must serve on a committee. We are having a six-hour board retreat on Friday, October 26. We have monthly board meetings and everyone brings something to the table.

"For some of you, you may see yourself as a volunteer on a committee. And, for some of you, you may wish to support the program by contributing financially. Now is the time to answer the question—*Why am I here?*"

At that point, everyone was asked to look at the committee sheets and to fill in the positions they were interested in. Once again, much to my amazement—and yet I fully hoped for and expected this—all six board positions were filled!

> Best of all, after this meeting Mayor Brown approached me and asked, *"Why don't you ask the Town of Kernersville for money?"*

"Can we do that?" I asked. The Mayor assured me that we could. First though, he suggested that prior to making a formal request, we give each alderman a letter of request and an information packet that included news clippings and a list of contributors.

At the October 2 Town Hall meeting, we made a formal request to the Board of Aldermen for $10,000. The Town's attorney John G. Wolfe, III, suggested that the Board of Aldermen review KCK's records and intents before deciding whether or not to support KCK.

The next day I hand-delivered all the requested materials to Wolfe. Meantime, Mayor Larry Brown gave me a lesson in how "the real world" works. He suggested that each KCK board member and all the KCK student leaders write a letter of request to the aldermen. Perhaps, most importantly, the Mayor suggested that Police Chief Stockton talk to each alderman personally, prior to the next meeting. Finally, he advised that KCK have its "big guns"—the superintendent, the Police Chief, and the newspaper publisher—at the upcoming meeting.

Each alderman also received a copy of a story on KCK that appeared in *The Next Step Newsletter*. This substance abuse prevention magazine told the KCK story to a statewide and national readership. Interestingly, I was invited to write the story by Susan Rook, whom I met at the Addiction Studies for Journalists program in Scottsdale, Arizona.

After following the Mayor's suggestions religiously, we again made our request on November 8. The board asked a few questions. Mainly they wanted to know if 100% of their grant would benefit Kernersville's students. I explained that the Kernersville schools include students who lived in Winston-Salem, but the Town's funds would only be used for the schools in Kernersville.

The board voted unanimously to grant KCK $4,000 annually, with the stipulation that the money be used for incentives for the students and not to pay for staff salary. The board also promised an additional $2,000 if the County Commissioners would donate $6,000.

However, the County Commissioners—like the Winston-Salem Foundation—could not seem to justify giving KCK a donation when Kernersville is not an underprivileged or special needs area.

Regardless, the Town's grant of $4,000 was a big boon for KCK. It lightened the load of annual fundraising, but more importantly, it sent the message loudly and clearly that Kernersville really does care for its kids.

The KCK Board Retreat, held October 26th, was equally successful. Local business consultant Bob Camp led the 16 board members—100% attendance—through a leadership activity and then asked members to identify the strengths and weaknesses of KCK.

The weaknesses were the same unresolved issues that surfaced year after year, but now the board was facing them. Roger Stockton, a newly-retired resident, volunteered to chair the fundraising and was soon thereafter elected to be KCK's vice-president. Mike Willard, a minister at Main Street Baptist Church, volunteered to find four KCK liaisons to work directly with the student leadership teams in the schools. This was the latest attempt by the board to increase its connection with students, as KCK had yet to find a way to bring the students to our daytime board meetings. Willard was later voted KCK's new president.

Carol Bennett, a retired teacher from East Forsyth High School and voted Wal-Mart's Teacher of the Year, organized a new program for KCK called "Win Some Wheels." This took place on Halloween night when 3,000 people came downtown for a celebration. "We Support Our Students" posters—printed for free by the *Kernersville News*—were displayed in virtually all the downtown storefronts. On the night of the event, Carol and a team of students signed up over 1,000 children for a free bike and skateboard give-away that took place at the end of the evening. Bennett was later elected as KCK's new treasurer. And Fermin Bocanegra, a pastor at Iglesia Cristiana Wesleyana Church, offered to spearhead a campaign to reach the growing Hispanic population in the schools more effectively.

These four new board members came directly from the Special Leadership Meeting just a month earlier, and all of them proved that they came on board to work! Willard, the new KCK president, kept his word and found four liaisons—Bill Wyramon, Kim King, Carol Bennett, and Tom Hancock. They went to the four

Town Government Supports KCK With Funding

In 2001, **Mayor Larry Brown** (left) suggested that KCK ask the Town for money. That year, the Board of Aldermen approved $4,000 to help fund KCK. This added a new level of stability and recognition to the value of KCK to the Town of Kernersville. Pictured next, Principal Debbie Brooks (KMS) rallied her students to a new middle school record of 91%, Principal Jim Wilhelm (EFHS), Principal Debbie Blanton Warren (SEMS), and Principal Adolphus Coplin (GHS).

"I was in the audience the day Kernersville Cares for Kids *first presented its request for funding at the Board of Aldermen meeting and I've always supported KCK. I believe it is a great program that we can be all be proud of. When our new middle school was added (East Forsyth Middle School), I suggested that we raise the contribution to $6000 and the board approved."*

–Mayor Dawn Morgan, 2011

http://toknc.com

Mayor Dawn Morgan

schools to support the student leaders in their drug-free campaign. Willard also enacted an Executive Committee to handle day-to-day matters and reduce the amount of KCK board meetings.

However, as can happen with any new idea, it is sometimes taken too far. By significantly reducing the frequency of the full board meeting, KCK actually began to lose its connectedness. Some KCK board members, who at one time complained that monthly meetings were too much, now began to ask if KCK was still alive. Obviously, plenty of work was still being done, but, because the full board was not sharing in the process, they were not gaining momentum from the success.

One of the best successes of the year happened on May 30, 2002. Forty middle and high school students attended the first "*I Saw a Rat's Brain*" field trip at Wake Forest University. It was fascinating to watch the students as Dr. Kent Vrana presented the same slide show that he used at the Addiction Studies Program.

One student asked, "Is it wrong to use drugs?"

Dr. Vrana explained, "Scientists don't get involved in the moral issue of drug use. They look at the science. Science tells us that using drugs causes changes in the brain."

Then, one-third of the teens were escorted to the Human Performance Lab. Wake Forest University graduate students introduced the teens to a simulator car. Students sit in the driver's seat, take hold of the steering wheel, and then "drive" down a road that is projected on the screen in front of them. At first, the video is set to project a path as it would be observed by a typical sober driver. Then, the video is changed to simulate how the very same path would appear to a driver who is drunk or under the influence of marijuana. Due to slowed mental perceptions and slowed reflexes, the obstacles appeared to jump out at the driver with very little warning. The student drivers, of course, crashed, and they learned first-hand that it is dangerous to drive while impaired.

While some students drove the car, Dr. Anthony Liguori, an associate professor at WFU, invited others to step into a balance box that was specifically designed to deceive their eyes and their feet about their true position in the box. It gave the students a means to feel how the world might appear if they were under the influence of drugs or alcohol.

At the same time, another third of students, under the leadership of Sara Ward, a WFU graduate student, were led to a lab to observe white rats. Ward asked for volunteers and then used the following exercise to demonstrate *why* rats seek drugs: Ward instructed Kernersville Middle School student, Peter Coutuse to push a lever. Each time he did, he received a Cheetos as a reward. As it was just before lunch, Coutuse was willing to push the lever countless times to get his reward.

Then another student was selected to push the lever to receive a reward. This student pushed the lever and was rewarded with cat food. She declined her reward. Thus, Ward effectively demonstrated that part of the process of addiction is based on how a reward makes the research animal feel.

KCK Board 2001-02

Upon the advice of business leader Arnold King *Kernersville Cares for Kids* applied for non-profit status. On April 10, 2001, the IRS recognized KCK as a 501 (c) (3). Pictured above is the first "official" board at its first planning retreat held on October 26, 2001. Bob Camp facilitated the retreat – leading the group to discern KCK's strengths, weaknesses, and goals for the year.

Row 1: Tammy Thompson (Sec), Patty Jo Sawvel, Debbie Brooks (Principal KMS), Carol Bennett (Treas), Nancy Dixon (WS/FCS), Debbie Blanton-Warren (Principal SEMS). Row 2: Fermin Bocanegra, John Owensby (Co-sponsor), Roger Stockton, Adolphus Coplin (Principal GHS), Mike Willard (President). Row 3: James East, Dan Adams, Dr. Don Martin (Co-sponsor), KPD Chief Neal Stockton (Co-sponsor). Not pictured: James Wilhelm (Principal EFHS), George Groce (VP)

"Some students who use drugs join the It's My Call (voluntary drug-testing program) KNOWING they can be tested because they WANT to get caught. They don't have anyone to turn to for help. Their parents are not there for them and they don't know what to do."
—Glenn High School Senior John Kivett spoke to the above group at the September 27, 2001 KCK Leadership Meeting.

Kim King, a KCK liaison who attended the program, said, "This showed kids how addiction works in rats and how people can act like rats. In this type of learning, it is one thing for kids to hear words; it is another thing for them to learn by hands-on experience. This really makes kids think."

The final third of the students followed WFU graduate students into a lab where they saw real rat, monkey, and human brains. After a brief explanation of *how* the brain functions and *how* drugs and alcohol affect the brain, students were invited to put on a pair of surgical gloves and actually hold the brains.

As stated so well by middle school student Kishara Ashley Warren, "My favorite part of the whole field trip was picking up the brains."

The overwhelming majority of students agreed with her and I did too. There was something almost sacred about holding a human brain. It was dead. It was preserved. But it was real and it almost gave off an energy. I can't explain it, but each year that I accompanied the students on this field trip, holding a human brain had the same affect on me. It made me realize that brains are fragile and we need to be careful with them.

At the end of the session, all the groups of teens had a chance to visit each of the three labs. Oddly, none of this seemed to affect their appetite. When the lab work was done, we immediately went to an on-campus pizza party sponsored by KCK. The students were joined by WFU graduate students—who love pizza—and they told the teens why they chose addiction studies for their graduate work.

After lunch, there was a pinning ceremony so that each participant sported a silver dollar sized pin with a pink cartoon mouse that said, *"I Saw a Rat's Brain."* The surprised little mouse was standing on the names of the sponsors, Kernersville Cares for Kids and Wake Forest University. When the kids wore their pins to school, they did what they were supposed to do; they started conversations about the field trip.

Principal Coplin told me that when his group returned to school, one of his students came rushing into his office.

"This student explained what addiction is. He was amazed at how out of control someone using drugs could be. This was not a kid whom I would have expected this type of reaction from. He is popular and likes to have fun. So, while I was not there at the field trip, I could see by my students' reactions that it was powerful. I want to know how I can get more of my students to participate in that program."
—Principal Coplin, sharing a student's response to the Rat's Brain Trip

As the school year ended, I thought about everything that happened over the past nine months. Then it dawned on me, that even though KCK did not get the Winston-Salem Foundation Grant, KCK had accomplished nearly every goal it outlined in the grant application.

KCK developed student-based teams by assigning each school a KCK liaison and sent over 100 students to Camp Hanes for the same leadership training that worked so well for the Hawk Leaders. Thankfully, most students could pay the $20 fee, so only a few scholarships were needed.

To reach the Hispanic population, Southeast Middle School SRO Frank Martinez teamed up with the school system's graphic designer, Timothy Porter, to create a brochure in Spanish featuring Hispanic students telling why they chose to be drug and alcohol-free. The school system printed the brochure and made it available to all the schools.

The town of Kernersville gave KCK a small office at Town Hall. It wasn't very big, but it was big enough to store KCK records and create a presence in the community. Later, it was returned to the Town, as KCK found that it really didn't need a storefront. It just needed funds and manpower.

The Special Leadership Meeting and the board retreat, both promised in the grant application, went on as planned and were very successful. And the increased media coverage became a reality as over 30 KCK stories and photos were published in the *Kernersville News* over the course of the year.

KCK even reached out personally to 25 schools in Forsyth County, the bulk of which had students in Winston-Salem. This outreach occurred on January 8, 2002, when Superintendent Don Martin asked me to share the secrets of KCK's success at a joint principals' meeting.

I held up a photograph for the 60 middle and high school principals to see.

> *"This woman is 86 years old and in her bathrobe. She has her favorite dog on her lap and a big smile on her face. Do you know who she is? She's my high school principal. I just saw her in Michigan a couple of weeks ago. Do you know **why** I went to see her 25 years after graduation? Because she cared. She made a difference in **my** life."*—**Patty Jo Sawvel at a principals' meeting.** {See a photo of Principal Baker on the About the Author page}

"I have a lot of respect for you and the difference you make with your students," I continued, "and I want to share some success stories that are happening right here in this school district."

Each principal was given a packet of newspaper stories that featured the winning strategies of their fellow principals who'd led their schools to 90 percent or greater participation in the county's *It's My Call* drug-testing program.

After briefly reviewing some highlights, I concluded by saying, "This packet is yours to keep. And whatever you do, watch out! Twenty-five years from now, when you're still in your pajamas at noontime, one of your former students will probably sneak up on your doorstep and thank you for taking the time to care and for pointing him in the right direction."

The meeting was fun and, more importantly, it inspired positive leadership throughout the county. The greatest results were seen in the middle schools.

WFU Annual Rat's Brain Field Trip

Wake Forest University gives youth leaders REAL answers from REAL scientists. Young people, ages 10-18, visit the college campus and receive hands-on training

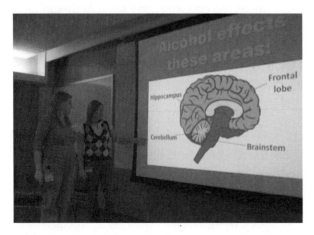

Brittani Canals holds a real human brain with classmates.

When students gently cradle a human brain in their own hands, they realize just how fragile and wonderful our brains are. *"My favorite part of the whole field trip was picking up the brains."*
–Kishara Warren

Reprinted with permission of *Kernersville News*

Wake Forest University professors and graduate students volunteer their time every year to host a field trip for 60 students from Kernersville's schools. Youth then become advocates for choosing "no drugs/no underage drinking."

http://www.wfu.edu/

By year end, 'Leap at Kennedy Middle School,' which allows failing students to complete two years of course work in one year so they can get back to their correct grade, went from last place in the county at 7% voluntary drug testing, to 59%. This won 'Leap' a KCK flag.

Mineral Springs Middle School went from 33% to 69% and Hill Middle School went from 50% to 82%. These three schools are all in Winston-Salem and they all sought and won the KCK flags.

Of course, the Kernersville schools did well too. Under the new leadership of Principal Debbie Blanton Warren, Southeast Middle School jumped from 16% to 81%. Then, Principal Debbie Brooks and her Hawk Leaders broke the barrier by beating every middle school and every high school in the nation, except Glenn, when they had 91% of the students signed up for voluntary drug testing. Principal Coplin and two Glenn seniors, Marquitas Broadway and Tim Murphy, once again led their school to the number one spot with 93% participation.

Middle Schools Set New Records
(students in voluntary drug testing)

LEAP sprang from 7 percent to 59 percent
Mineral Springs jumped from 33 percent to 69 percent
Hill climbed from 50 percent to 82 percent
Southeast zoomed from 16 percent to 81 percent
Kernersville soared to 91 percent

This told me that KCK was not just helping Kernersville; it was having a significant impact on the students in inner-city Winston-Salem too.

And, looking at the Winston-Salem Foundation grant application, there were only two things that KCK did not accomplish. It did not implement a fundraising strategy, and it did not hire a part-time program coordinator.

So, once again, I found that the grant writing activity had its own rewards, independent of the decision to fund, or not to fund, the proposal.

One final observation was surprising. Though I'd resigned as the president of KCK, this did not really save me much time to write my book. I ended up being involved in nearly every project that KCK initiated. Apparently, after many years of volunteering, I'd become addicted!

Treasure Hunting in Kernersville

Over 50 artists and craftsmen offer their goods at **Country Cupboard** on Highway 421 near Triad Park.

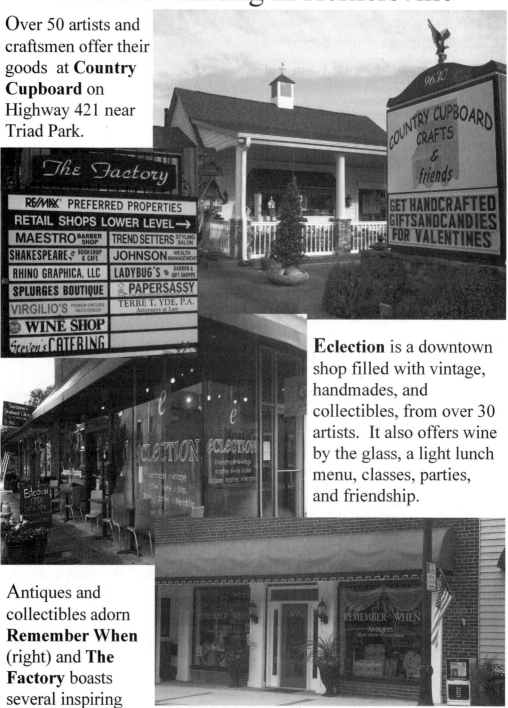

Eclection is a downtown shop filled with vintage, handmades, and collectibles, from over 30 artists. It also offers wine by the glass, a light lunch menu, classes, parties, and friendship.

Antiques and collectibles adorn **Remember When** (right) and **The Factory** boasts several inspiring boutiques to explore.

http://discoverkernersville.com/

25

Letting Go

Lesson 25: Be open to new ideas

"Sometimes you just have to let go."

These words kept surfacing in my mind as I felt myself being pulled in two different directions as the 2002-03 school year began. On the one hand, I felt deeply obligated to write the book I'd promised to the Arts Council in 1999. On the other hand, I felt deeply committed to keep KCK going and growing for the students of Kernersville.

"The problem," I had told fellow board member Nancy Dixon, "is that I can't drive the train and write a book about it at the same time."

That is when she uttered these sagacious words, "Sometimes you just have to let go." At the time, I wasn't easily convinced.

"What do you mean let go?" I asked.

"You know," she explained, "like a mother has to let go of her child. At some point, the child has to walk on its own. If the mother is always there to hold the child's hand, then how will the child learn to walk on its own?"

"Well," I countered, "what if it doesn't? What if it doesn't survive on its own?"

"That's the real world, Patty Jo," Dixon said. "We all want the best for our children, but they don't all survive. That's life. But, if people really want KCK, then they will figure out a way to keep it going."

I thought about what she said for a long time. It was the Fall of 2002, and KCK was beginning its fifth year. Maybe it really was time to let go. Maybe it was time to test if Kernersville really wanted KCK. Consequently, I let go. I still attended some board meetings, but I didn't volunteer for any projects.

*   *   *

George Groce, a former alderman in Kernersville, became the new president when serious family health issues made it impossible for Willard to continue. At a board meeting under Groce's leadership, the challenge of getting students on the KCK board was finally resolved.

In reporting on the past year's activities, I noted to the board that while the liaison strategy seemed promising at the onset, it hadn't worked. The KCK liaisons told me that though they went to the schools with ideas and free literature, the student leaders didn't seek any active assistance from the adults.

At the same time, the students said that they really didn't understand *why* the adults were there. So, most of the adults ended up spending a lot of time standing around feeling rather useless.

Oddly, the liaison project was an important lesson on how *not* to help kids. In a partnership, it doesn't work for adults to figure out arbitrarily what the kids want or need. The only way to know is to ask them. Strangely, in this attempt to increase KCK's connection with the students, the students actually disconnected because they were not part of the decision-making process.

So, the unresolved question surfaced again. How can we get students on the board? The obvious obstacle was that KCK held its board meetings on school days at the very time that students were in classes. KCK was unwilling to have evening meetings to resolve this conflict.

> In the 2002-03 school year, the question of how to get students to daytime board meetings—held while school was in session— was resolved by the newest principal on the KCK board, Principal Debbie Blanton-Warren.
>
> She told the board, *"We can just bring the students with us to the board meetings. Students leave school all the time during class hours for sports or other activities. This wouldn't be any different."*
>
> From that point forward, students attended board meetings.

The other principals and the superintendent nodded in agreement and in short order it was decided the principals would select one or two students from each school and provide transportation to the board meetings.

Once there, students reported to the board about their schools' promotion campaign of the It's *My Call* pledging and testing program. Though it would be a few years before the students initiated a KCK project of their own accord, the mere presence of students at the board meeting reminded all the adults why KCK was here—it was here for the kids.

The following school year, 2003-04, the KCK student leaders opted to design one poster from each school for the downtown storefronts. But, here again, while the idea looked good on paper, it simply did not work well in reality. The students were unclear about what needed to be on the posters, so the *Kernersville News* ended up contributing four times the work to print four different posters.

Additionally, there was the problem of which poster to hang in which storefront, as most store owners were not willing to hang four posters in their windows. Finally, it was decided that, at least for the time being, KCK would produce one annual poster that would follow the old format.

That same year, the community reached out to KCK in a new way. Bruce Boyer, the president of the Kernersville Chamber of Commerce, told Groce that KCK had been named the recipient of a fundraising partnership with the Winston-Salem Warthogs. In 2004, KCK received a $1,400 check from the Chamber.

The following year, 2004-05, KCK board member and former principal in Maryland, Carey Reece, suggested that KCK promote the Safe Homes program at East Forsyth and Glenn high schools. In this program, parents sign a written statement pledging the following:

- I will actively supervise all the gatherings of youth in our home or on our property, or ask another responsible adult for help to do so.
- I will not allow the possession or use of alcohol, tobacco, or other drugs by youth in our home or on our property.
- I will set expectations for my children by knowing where they are, whom they are with, what they are doing, and when they are to return home.

Once the pledge is signed, parents' names and telephone numbers are kept in a database at each school. So, when students ask to attend a party, parents can check the database to see if the host family has pledged. They can also telephone the family directly.

As Reece explained, "This has many benefits. First, parents are making a statement. Second, this pledge list becomes a networking tool for parents who are looking for other families who share their values. Third, the list can be used for support groups. Parents can compare parenting techniques and get ideas for solving problems. Fourth, if kids are saying 'everyone is doing it,' parents can show them that other families are taking a stand too."

Initially, I was against the promotion of this, not because I disagreed with the concept, but because KCK would be taking on another responsibility, when it was barely carrying its existing load.

Benefits of the Safe Homes Program
(as shared by KCK board member Carey Reece)

1) Parents make a statement or pledge.
2) Each pledge becomes a networking tool.
3) The list of pledging parents can be used as a support group
4) If kids say "everyone is doing it," the parents can show them that other families share their rules and values.

But after giving it more consideration, I realized that this—empowering the parents—would actually complete the circle of commitment. This was the missing link!

The community proved its commitment by funding KCK, and the students proved their commitment by enrolling in the pledging and testing program. Safe Homes provided a tangible way for parents to prove their commitment by signing a pledge to provide safe homes and supervision for student gatherings.

I wanted to know what the teens thought about this idea and I wanted to know what high school weekend parties were like in Kernersville. So, Principal Trish Gainey arranged for me to interview five students from East Forsyth High School for a newspaper story.

Kyle Phelps, a senior, started off the story saying, "I was afraid to go to parties for a while because of the movie image. I thought kids would be bouncing off the walls, breaking things, and breaking the rules. That's what I thought parties were like in high school."

Because of this, Kyle opted to decline party invitations until he was in 11th grade. When he did attend his first party, he found out that local parties are not like the Hollywood hype. "Parties here are different in that they are not as crazy. People are not running around in their underwear. But parties are the same in that there is drinking and some drugs and a lot of times no adults are there," said Phelps.

The other East Forsyth role model students who were interviewed all said they had been to parties where drugs and alcohol were present and adult supervision was missing.

But how did the students feel about the Safe Homes program?

"I think it is a good idea," said Kyle Phelps. "But what are the consequences for the parents? Are parents really going to be willing to stick by their pledge or are they going to turn their heads the other way?"

"There are parents," said Brandon Mills, 12th grader, "who don't care enough to say something or they have already given up on their children. How are you going to reach those parents?"

In contrast to their concerns about the Safe Homes program, the students really did see the benefit of the *It's My Call* pledge.

"If students sign the pledge," said Sarah Edwards, 11th grader, "and they are tempted—they can say 'I shouldn't do this. I could be tested.' They remember that. But how will you know if parents who pledge are keeping their word?"

Oddly, the students were *not opposed* to supervised and drug/alcohol-free parties. To them, the presence of an adult is *not* the deciding factor on whether they choose to attend a party.

Will Teens Attend Parties Supervised by Adults?

"If my friends invite me to go to a party, then I want to go. I want to be with my friends and it doesn't matter if there are adults there.
—Katie Lewis, EFHS Senior

However, there is something that will cause these students to leave a party.

"I will leave a party, if very few of my friends are there or if the main focus of the party is drugs or alcohol." —Brandon Mills, EFHS Senior

To find out more about the national Safe Homes initiative visit www.pride.org.

---

*   *   *

Groce's term expired at the end of the school year. Bob Prescott, also a former alderman, was elected president for the 2005-06 school year. KCK momentum was ebbing, as the organization struggled to stand on its own, but it held to its course. Money was collected from the Town, a few businesses, and the Bucket Brigade led by the Kernersville Police Department. The programs, the *I Saw a Rat's Brain* field trip and the victory parties all happened without a hitch.

East Forsyth High School won the Victory Party sponsored by the local police with 74 % of the students enrolled in the drug-testing program, while Glenn High School hit rock bottom with only 50% of its students enrolled.

Many of the middle schools were now outperforming the high schools and Southeast Middle School in Kernersville won the Victory Party sponsored by Kernersville Parks and Recreation, and led the entire county with 88% enrollment. That year six middle schools qualified for a KCK flag.

Glenn High School Grad Promotes KCK

Michael Church, GHS class of 2003 earned his business and marketing degree at University of NC in Greensboro in 2007 and immediately created the Town's most successful glossy magazine with a readership of 25,000 in 2013. Since its inception, Church has promoted Kernersville Cares for Kids programs and events.

Church joined the IMC *voluntary* drug testing program at Glenn. He noted, "The accountability and knowing that the teachers and parents cared enough to have a program that would steer us in the right direction and keep us from making critical mistakes meant a lot to me."

Home Drug Testing Kit

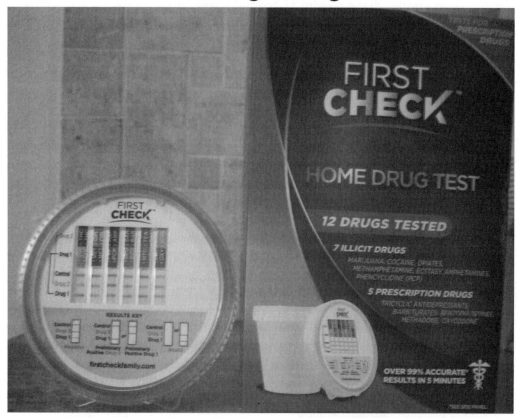

Why Would I Want to Give My Teen a Home Drug Test?

† Home Drug Testing gives your teen an easy way to say "no" to drugs. He can honestly say, **"I can't. I don't want to fail my *parents*' drug test."**

† Home Drug Testing **allows parents to hold their teens accountable** for the choices they make.

† Home Drug Testing **allows parents to get help for their teens sooner.** In WS/FC Schools, the average person who fails the drug test is 15 years old and has been using drugs for two years. Early intervention is key.

† Home Drug Test Kits are **affordable at $12-40 and easily available** at WalMart and most drug stores. Cost includes a professional lab confirmation of any positive test results.

http://www.drugtestyourteen.com

26

Getting a Better Grip

Lesson 26: Positive actions plant seeds for future opportunities

During my "letting go" years from 2002-2006, an opportunity arrived that allowed me to get a better grip on the bigger issues of drugs and student drug testing.

This opportunity directly resulted from my attendance at the Wake Forest University Addiction Studies for Journalists Program in the summer of 2001. As it turned out, Sue Rusche, who was co-director of the Addiction Studies Program, was also on book publisher Thomson Gale's advisory board for their upcoming publication: *Drugs and Controlled Substances: Information for Students.*

When editor Stacey Blachford needed writers for the upcoming book, Rusche recommended her recent *Addiction Studies* graduates. Because I was on the list, Blachford called me. I was elated because Thomson Gale is a world leader in educational and library reference publishing.

Blachford explained that this 500-page reference book was designed to help high school and college students research the scientific, social, legal, and historical issues of 50 commonly abused drugs.

In exchange for a 6,000 word entry, I would receive $1,100 and a spot on the "Contributors" page listing my name and professional affiliation.

As much as I wanted to accept this offer, I told Blachford that I would have to think about it and call her back. It wasn't a matter of value. With teenage children, I always needed more money and a byline with Thomson-Gale would be a valuable asset. But this offer presented a matter of honor. I had to do some soul-searching to decide if this would help or hinder my progress on the Arts Council book.

On the one hand, this project would force me to take a good look at the legal and historical aspects of drugs and substance abuse. This was something I'd never done before. So I could view this offer as an opportunity to receive a small financial incentive for doing something that I probably needed to do anyway.

On the other hand, I had to ask myself, "Am I using this as an excuse to procrastinate? Is my interest in this project really a symptom of avoidance behavior? Am I quick to accept this so that I don't have to face the fear of proceeding with my own book?"

Ultimately, I decided to accept the offer. Blachford gave me a choice of 20 different drugs. I chose cocaine because it's a very well-documented drug and its highly addictive nature intrigued me.

The most interesting thing I learned from the project is *why* drug laws became necessary. By tracing its history, I found that when cocaine was separated from the coca leaf by a German chemist in 1860, the drug was *presumed innocent* of any addictive or toxic effects. Within three years, cocaine was added to a wine, Vin

Mariani, which was endorsed as a health and energy aid by Pope Leo XIII, Thomas Edison, and over 7,000 physicians worldwide.

About that time, cocaine powder, up to 99.9% pure, became available in the United States at local grocery stores or by mail order. Soon, cocaine was commonly found in America's medicine cabinets and it was used to treat children's toothaches, morning sickness of pregnant women, allergies, fatigue, flu, and countless other ills.

The accepted and widespread use of cocaine, amidst the general population, allowed for one of the largest, long-term case studies ever done on cocaine. By the 1890s, cocaine's toxic, addictive, and sometimes sudden-death effect on America's families was undeniable. Public opinion began to shift and, in 1910, President William Howard Taft named cocaine as Public Enemy No. One.

In 1914, cocaine was one of the first drugs to be banned when Congress passed the Harrison Narcotics Act. Other laws were passed in the decades that followed. Nearly 100 years later, in the 1980s, when an epidemic of cocaine use was fueled by the advent of *crack* cocaine, tougher drug laws, like the Anti-Drug Abuse Act of 1986 and 1988, were passed.

These laws were determined to keep drug dealers from exploiting the young and the poor with a cheap, but dangerous, "fix" for their problems. The new laws demanded harsh penalties for first-time offenders. In fact, the Federal Trafficking Penalty for a first-time offender convicted of possessing five grams of crack (one tablespoon) is a mandatory minimum sentence of five years in prison without parole.

> Cocaine is still believed to be the most addictive substance known to man and it is still illegal in the United States, except as a local anesthetic.

This research told me that drug laws arose out of the need to protect people. Once a government knows the facts—that something is dangerous and threatening public health and safety—it has an obligation to protect its citizens. Government protection is important because misinformation spreads faster than the truth. Also, erroneous information appears to mutate like a virus, making it difficult to anticipate the current pro-drug propaganda. But, if the federal government bans a drug, then while potential users may not discern the truth about the drug, they do know that they are breaking the law if they choose to use it.

> Even as late as the 1980s, the myth that cocaine is not addictive was very pervasive. **Len Bias and Don Rogers**—two promising young athletes who died from cocaine in 1986—might have believed this myth.
>
> Or, maybe they believed the myth that recreational drugs can make you better than you are.
>
> Or, maybe it was some other misinformation that induced them to experiment. Whatever the case, a law was in place to protect them and tougher laws followed their deaths.

When the research was done and I submitted the manuscript to Stacey Blachford, she asked me to write another entry. I declined, explaining that I could not justify this because I was committed to writing my own book. Instead, I referred her to Brian Sine, a recent graduate and aspiring writer from the University of North Carolina, Greensboro.

However, Blachford called again, a few weeks later. She explained that she was in a pinch and really needed one more writer. Reluctantly, I accepted and wrote an entry on psilocybin—hallucinogen-producing mushrooms. This was one of the final entries for the book and it had a short deadline. I was able to complete this second entry in about one month, as compared to three months that it took to complete the first entry.

Three years later, in September of 2005, I received an email from Chandra Howard at Greenhaven Press, an imprint of Thomson Gale. Apparently, my name was still in the company directory, and she asked if I would like to accept an assignment for their "At Issues" book series for students.

My book was progressing well, so I told her that if they had a title on *Teen Drug Abuse*, I would take it; otherwise, I wasn't interested. I reasoned that a *Teen Drug Abuse* title would help me move 10 years of past research into the present.

As it turned out, she asked me to create a book on Student Drug Testing. Instead of writing the book, my job was to research articles, books, government reports, and other information published within the last two years and to pair opposing viewpoints into head-to-head/pro-con debates.

Once the articles were chosen, my job was to write a 150-word introduction and to edit each selection for word length. In this way, high school students could easily access public media about debatable current topics such as gang violence, Social Security, Satanism, and my assignment—Student Drug Testing.

> I believed I knew a lot about drug testing, but quickly found out that I was wrong. First and foremost, not all student drug-testing programs are created equal. Some are punishing and seem to be designed to "catch bad kids," while others are non-punitive and designed to help students get back on track without public embarrassment.

In punitive or punishing programs, students who fail the drug test are temporarily suspended from their sport or extracurricular activity. They are generally reinstated when they meet certain guidelines or attend required intervention. The problem with intervening suspension is that the whole school is given visual notice that a student has a drug or alcohol problem. This public shaming can undermine mutual respect and call into question the intention to *help* the student. Instead, the humiliation may actually harden the offender in his course of action.

On the other hand, non-punitive testing programs, like the one found in the WS/FC Schools, treat students with respect.

> Non-punitive testing programs allow students to keep their *privacy and their dignity* if they fail the drug test. As long as students *accept free help*, they remain on the team or in the club and no one knows except their parents and the principal. The idea here is to *"help good kids who made a bad choice."*

Doing the research for this book showed me how important it is for communities to clarify their *intentions* for creating a drug-testing program. Did they really want to help children and create a safe way for students to get help with a drug problem? Or, did they want to hurt, embarrass, or punish students who developed drug problems? Oddly, regardless of what the words in the drug policy state, the students quickly uncover the real intention and that affects their level of support for the program, which ultimately decides its success.

It was also surprising to discover how differently schools can administer the actual drug test. Some schools test 100% of the students involved in sports and extracurricular and they test them on a pre-announced date. This greatly increases the chances of cheating, because students only have to take evasive action for one day.

According to experts, a student can cheat by taping a balloon filled with a buddy's clean urine to his leg and then transferring the urine into a collection cup in the privacy of the bathroom. By taping the balloon to his leg, the urine maintains body temperature which is the first test the sample has to pass. Using a buddy's clean urine insures it will pass the laboratory test.

Students also use herbal drinks or diuretics to mask and dilute their samples. These are readily available at vitamin stores or on the Internet and they really work. Other students add adulterants to their urine sample *after* it's in the collection cup. Labs are getting better at detecting these additives, but new additives are constantly being manufactured.

More worrisome than cheating is the fact that cheating techniques can be dangerous. As with any information, sometimes cheating techniques are misunderstood. There have been reports of students *drinking* bleach instead of adding it to the urine collection cup to cheat the test. Though drinking bleach is rarely fatal, it burns the esophagus and causes nausea and vomiting. Worst of all, it simply doesn't work!

In contrast, at the WS/FC Schools, students are randomly selected on a monthly basis throughout the school year. They do not know they will be tested until they are already at school and sitting in class. So there is little possibility of the balloon trick, since few students want to carry around a bag of urine for the entire school year. Also, there is no time to do the multi-hour herbal flush. And students proceed directly to the designated testing center on campus so there is virtually no opportunity to retrieve an adulterant from their lockers.

One of the most amazing discoveries to come from this project was the realization that the adult community mirrors the student community when it comes to being a silent majority. Just as drug-free students let drug users dominate conversations in school about drugs, so, too, the majority of adults who support non-punitive student drug testing keep silent, while a tiny group of anti-testing adults are responsible for virtually all the anti-drug-testing propaganda.

In the course of my research, it shocked me to see just how small the minority is, and yet what a powerful voice this group has developed. In checking the background of each author of the included selections, I found that in nearly every case the authors of the anti-drug-testing articles were directly linked to the American Civil Liberties Union (ACLU). This organization is taking the lead in opposing student drug testing.

I also came across one of the most insightful research reports to date: *School Connectedness: Improving Students' Lives* by Robert Blum at Johns Hopkins Bloomberg School of Public Health. In this research report, Blum effectively demonstrates that a strong sense of bonding, belonging, and ownership—between a student and his or her school—measurably lowers the risk of illegal drug use. Surprisingly, it is not the students' bond with their peers that makes the most significant impact.

> According to *School Connectedness: Improving Students' Lives* by Robert Blum at John Hopkins Bloomberg School of Public Health: It is the students' healthy bond with the adults—teachers, staff, janitors—that makes a positive difference.

This made me realize *why* KCK makes the drug-testing program at the schools in Kernersville so much more effective than the same identical program in its sister schools throughout the county.

KCK bonds the students with their adult community. By means of KCK, teachers personally take an interest in each student, trying to encourage 100% participation. Principals and School Resource Officers (SROs) notice *all* the students and try to get them *all* in the voluntary drug-testing program. It becomes the one thing that every student can support and belong to. And even outside of school, community leaders and the local newspaper pay attention to the students, display their posters, and give money to the program.

This was highlighted in the final chapter of the *Student Drug Testing* book. Ashley Coffman, a reporter for the *Kernersville News,* wrote a newspaper story heavily peppered with quotes from students, school administrators, and Police Chief Neal Stockton, to demonstrate that random student drug testing, coupled with KCK, promoted a sense of belonging in the schools.

She also reported that on October 19, 2005, the nation's Drug Czar, John Walters, and the Deputy Secretary of the US Department of Education, Ray Simon, honored the WS/FC Schools' successful drug-testing program by holding a national press conference for the Office of National Drug Control Policy at Carver High School. At this conference, the school system was presented with an $800,000 grant for drug testing.

When the book was nearly done, I received an exciting telephone call. Thomson Gale wanted to upgrade the book to a hardcover with full-color illustrations. The company was going to use it as the forerunner for a new series titled: *Issues that Concern You.* I was told that I would receive an additional $500 for writing an introduction and two appendix sections.

The first appendix was titled: "What You Should Know About Student Drug Testing." The second was titled: "What You Should Do About Student Drug Testing." My goal was still the same. I had to write all of these sections in an unbiased manner so students could debate and sort things out for themselves.

When I received my five free copies, they were beautiful and, best of all, this project forced me to look at the other side of the issue. *That*—the ability to see both sides of the issue—was worth more than money can buy.

During these "letting go" years, I also worked on my book with editor, Ed Friedenberg. Friedenberg made it easy for me to write because he was a good listener, a gentle teacher, and genuinely interested in my story and in my success.

He took long pauses—sometimes for days—before responding to one of my questions. And, he was careful to select precisely the right words for his response. Friedenberg was careful not to color my story with his perceptions, but instead he tried to be the truest mirror possible—helping me to see for myself what was there and what was not.

In fact, Friedenberg rarely answered my questions. Instead, for every one question I asked him, he asked me two or three additional questions to nudge me into searching within myself for the answers.

Early in our partnership, Friedenberg met me at various restaurants when he came down from his mountain home in Floyd County, Virginia, to see his doctors in Winston-Salem, North Carolina. Later, as his health declined, I took lunch and a chapter to his farm in the mountains.

By July 14, 2003, I'd completed 12 chapters. And by the day of his death, on July 14, 2006, my 79-year-old friend had helped me to complete 22 chapters. I thought my book was done and in the final paragraph of my memorial column I wrote:

> Now that Ed is gone and the manuscript is done, I have the daunting privilege of finding an agent and a publisher for my book. But I'm not alone. Ed left me a helper. He left his gentle whisper. As with his children and his grandchildren, Ed's whisper will always be there to guide me.

However, when I sent the manuscript off to readers, they all had the same response. Where is the rest of the story? What ever happened to *KCK?*

Oddly, I couldn't see it. I didn't realize that the story wasn't done yet and after receiving about 30 rejection letters from prospective publishing agents, I put the book away and again turned my attention to KCK. The following year, 2006-07 would prove to be a turning point for *Kernersville Cares for Kids.*

27

New Voices

Lesson 27: Truth is powerful

During the 2006-07 school year, principals lamented the low enrollment of sixth grade students in the voluntary drug-testing program. It wasn't a problem with the kids. They wanted to join *It's My Call*. The problem was with their parents. Many parents felt that testing a 10 or 11-year-old child for drugs was not only unnecessary, but it was inappropriate. Consequently, parents refused to co-sign the drug-testing form.

Their refusal presented a question: How can we best educate the parents? I asked Principal Debbie Blanton-Warren if it might be helpful to write a feature story in the newspaper highlighting parents who had been pleased to enroll their 6th grade children. This would let parents learn from other parents who faced the same decision. She liked the idea and quickly gave me the names of two families to contact.

What happened next was totally unexpected, but exactly what the community needed. One of the parents told the truth. She shared her own childhood experience of middle school. And this wasn't just any parent. This parent, Tammy LaRue, was the president of the Parent Teacher Student Association at Principal Warren's school.

Because LaRue was so frank, I asked her to sign a permission slip authorizing the use of her story. It's not that her account was particularly graphic, but permission was needed, because in a small town, *truth can be a two-edged sword*. It can cut to the heart of a matter and resolve a problem quickly, for which the public is grateful. However, it can also hurt the truth-teller, when "respectable people" feign shock and disbelief that a role-model adult admitted to poor choices as a child.

Publisher Owensby ran the story on the front page of the free paper—the *Tuesday News* dated February 13, 2007—and changed my title from the question: *Is 6th Grade too Young for Drug Testing?* to the statement, *Not too Young for Drug Testing*.

In the opening words, LaRue courageously stated, "When I was in the sixth grade, my mother didn't have any idea that in a few years I would be using drugs. I was a straight A student and in the gifted program."

LaRue went on to explain that she started using drugs in the 9th grade and immediately her grades began to fall. In fact, she failed the second semester of freshman English and several classes thereafter.

"I tell my daughter, Britni, that drug and alcohol use leads to ditching school; ditching school leads to bad grades; and bad grades affect every other aspect of your life including your opportunity for college, your self-esteem, and your social circles," LaRue continued.

Because of LaRue's experience, when Britni started the 6th grade and brought home the *It's My Call* permission form, both mother and daughter signed it. Britni pledged to stay drug-free and to take random tests, and her mother gave permission for her daughter to be in the program.

"That's why I feel so strongly about this program," LaRue concluded. "If we had drug testing and drug education like this when I was in middle school, I might not have made the choice to use drugs."

Principal Warren agreed that middle school is the right time to make a commitment to stay drug-free.

> *"Middle school is the time when students begin making life-long choices. The earlier they get on the right path, the easier it is to stay on that path when peer pressure increases."*
> — Principal Debbie Blanton Warren

Britni LaRue supplied the student's perspective when she said, "I think this program is really important because it shows kids that you don't have to do drugs to be popular."

> *"I think this program is really important because it shows kids that you don't have to do drugs to be popular. At our school, over 80 percent of the kids are in the program and the test is not a big deal."*
> —Britni LaRue, middle school student

Connor Hinds, who also joined *It's My Call* in the 6th grade said, "I don't think 6th grade is too young. When I was in 5th grade, I had a friend who told me about his older brother who took drugs. His brother died in a car crash."

Connor's mother, Debbie Hinds, told why she co-signed her son's permission slip even though he was so young. "Statistics show that children are using drugs and alcohol earlier," Hinds said.

> *"I would rather know if my child is using drugs and be able to do something early, than not to know. I am very supportive of drug testing."*
> —Connor's mom, Debbie Hinds

Three days following LaRue's public confession, Bruce Boyer contacted me. As president of the Kernersville Chamber of Commerce, Boyer wanted to know if KCK wanted to be the recipient of the fundraiser, *Kernersville Day at the Warthogs* baseball game. He explained that this program generated $1,200-1,400 dollars.

After consulting with KCK President Bob Prescott, I met with Boyer and asked him, "Does KCK have to sell tickets to the baseball game?"

"No," he said. "The civic clubs sell the tickets. They find sponsors to buy blocks of 50 tickets. KCK receives two dollars for every ticket sold and an additional dollar if people actually use the ticket to attend the game." Boyer explained that the

Chamber and the civic clubs pocket zero dollars from this project. All the funds go to the designated non-profit organization.

This sounded too good to be true. "*Why*," I asked, "would the civic clubs do this for *KCK*? I mean, I know they have their own projects. So why would they do this?"

"The civic clubs," Boyer explained, "are members of the Chamber of Commerce. And one of the purposes of the Chamber is to make Kernersville a better place to live. We all know the problems that come with drugs: vandalism, theft, and ruined lives, and so this is a way for the community to do what is right and help prevent this problem."

His explanation made sense. It also made me realize that Kernersville as represented by the Chamber was proving that it cared for the town's children. The civic clubs were stepping back from their own agenda and stepping up to the plate to help KCK.

"What is KCK's role in this?" I asked.

"The Civic Council would like KCK to be active in planning on-field activities before the game. This is *Kernersville* Day at the Warthogs—so we want the community to come and spend the day at the ballpark."

Boyer explained that this was the second time the Chamber had reached out to KCK. The first time, three years previously, the Chamber reached out, but KCK did not reach back. KCK simply accepted the check without contributing to the success of the community-building project. So KCK was passed over for the next two years, with the money going to the Kernersville Police Camp for children, and then to the local YMCA.

If KCK wanted to be named the recipient again, KCK would need to accept responsibility for planning and organizing pre-game on-field activities to draw Kernersville residents to the game.

Boyer asked me to bring several board members and students to meet with the Civic Council at the Chamber. We scheduled the meeting for the same day as a KCK board meeting. Here too, an exciting change was about to happen.

Prior to this particular board meeting, KCK students saw themselves as reporters to the board. They literally read from hand-written sheets and informed the board about how they were spending their KCK allocation and how the student body was responding.

Sometimes the reports were quite interesting. Some students or their SROs used movie cameras and filmed humorous or informative "commercials" about drug testing. These two or three minute clips were played on classroom televisions during morning announcements and were well-received by the students.

Other students reported on pizza parties or ice-cream socials for classrooms with 100 % participation. Some schools rewarded teachers, because they had been very instrumental in motivating their students.

Though the student board members would respond to questions or to the adult board's generous praise, for years the students' communications were reactive rather than proactive. That changed on April 12, 2007, at approximately 10:30 a.m.

At that time, the students' routine reports had long passed and the board was in the middle of scheduling the *I Saw a Rat's Brain* field trip, when Glenn freshman Annie Orchard suddenly blurted out, "Why can't we have a booth at Spring Folly?"

Instantly, the group froze. It was *not* because this 15-year-old had interrupted the adults, who included the Superintendent, the Police Chief, the newspaper Publisher, and a dozen other adults. It was because this was the *first time* that a student ever initiated a project for KCK. For a long moment, no one spoke. We all looked at Annie.

I'm not sure what everyone else was thinking, but one question came to my mind: How would this organization—whose sole purpose was to support the students—respond?

Dr. Martin leaned back in his chair and all eyes moved to him. It was obvious that he was silently contemplating this new possibility. Then he slowly asked the board, "Could we have a booth at Spring Folly?"

Before anyone could answer, Annie stole the floor again and defended her idea. She said, "My dad and I had a booth there and we sold some things we made. It was fun and a lot of people go to Spring Folly."

Jim Pryor, director of Kernersville Parks and Recreation, supported Annie's analysis saying, "About 20,000 people come to Spring Folly."

With that, the board voted unanimously to support Annie's idea, even though the festival was a mere three weeks away. Mina Cook, of Unlimited Success, and I agreed to co-chair the event.

Cook is a joy to work with because she has superb organizational skills, fresh ideas, and she makes sure everything gets done, even if she has to do it herself. Therefore, when she agreed to set up and tear down the booth, schedule the student volunteers, provide all the games and prizes, and create a *Look What Happens When a Community Backs Its Students* poster—I knew that it was safe to erase all these responsibilities from my to-do list.

That left me with the tasks of scheduling adult volunteers for the booth, creating a new tri-fold KCK brochure, working with Melissa Marvin at the *Kernersville News* to create a publicity campaign, and acquiring a free space for KCK at Spring Folly.

This last task was accomplished when we met with Boyer later that day about *Kernersville Day at the Warthogs,* since he was also a coordinator for Spring Folly.

Annie and several other students and adults from KCK met at the Chamber that afternoon. Once again, she spoke up. "Why don't you let high school students, like cheerleaders and soccer players, do demonstrations on the field?" Annie asked.

The group liked that idea. Then I asked, "Why don't we take it one step further? Why don't we offer free sports clinics and have high school students work with younger students?"

Brad Phillips, assistant principal at Annie's school, said, "We are already set up to do that because we offer clinics during the summer—but students have to pay for it."

The group continued to brainstorm and ultimately decided to offer clinics in cheerleading, soccer, softball, and tee-ball.

Noting how excited the students were getting, I wondered how we could ensure that plenty of children attended the clinics. "Why don't we sell tickets through the schools? That way, we can be sure that plenty of children attend. And we can give the schools an incentive, by letting them keep the two-dollar profit from each ticket for their own drug-free campaigns," I suggested.

This fit nicely with the Civic Counsel's goals. They would sell tickets to raise money while the schools sold tickets to raise student participation.

All agreed with the new ideas and we divided the responsibilities. Brad Phillips took the lead in coordinating the clinics with both high schools, and Mina Cook organized family-fun activities that included a game table, face painting, and bubble making. As the KCK event chair, my job was to coordinate the schools and the Chamber, create flyers, write newspaper stories, and complete a new KCK tri-fold brochure to be used at Spring Folly and Kernersville Day at the Warthogs.

Once again, I found myself up to my armpits in volunteer work. The first event to arrive on the calendar was Spring Folly. This downtown festival was scheduled to begin Friday, May 4, at 6 o'clock in the evening. At about 5:30, a light drizzle clouded my windshield as I waited in the drive-thru lane of my bank.

Immediately, I began to worry and wondered if the Chamber would cancel the Folly. Everyone at KCK—students and adults alike—had worked so hard to make this a memorable debut. Would this rain drown that little flame—that tiny student voice—that had started this whirlwind of activity?

Moments ticked by as I contemplated this unpleasant possibility. Then, almost like someone sounded a signal, business owners shielded by umbrellas, began streaming out of downtown storefronts carrying tents, chairs, and plastic tubs. Quickly, they set up their booths in the streets.

A warm feeling of relief swept over me as I realized that these people were not going to let a little rain keep them from enjoying one of the happiest homegrown festivals in the community. The show was going to go on.

By 8:30, on opening night, a large crowd gathered in front of the main stage. Some staked out their places with lawn chairs, others stood around the perimeter. Still others prepared to dance. All of them were anticipating an evening of Motown music with *The Crystals,* who recorded Top Ten hits in the 1960s.

The next day, Guy Lombardo's Royal Canadians took the stage at 3 o'clock in the afternoon. Exile—a versatile band that plays rock, pop and country—wrapped it up on Saturday night.

Though the music was fun, the bedrock of Spring Folly consists of dozens of civic clubs, businesses, crafters, and ordinary people like Annie and her dad, who had set up tables to sell carnival food, crafts, or ideas. These tables lined the two main streets that intersect in the dead center of downtown.

Most of the vendors had goods for sale along with a hardy stock of free items. It was the freebies that motivated adults and children to go from booth to booth collecting key chains, pencils, magnets, candy, and other goodies.

When guests arrived at the KCK booth, we invited them to play a game. We asked them a question and when they answered correctly, they won a prize. For older kids or adults we might ask: What are the names of three drugs that are commonly abused? Or, why is it a bad idea to drink and drive?

We kept offering questions until each guest qualified for a prize. In this way, everyone was a winner with KCK. For very small children, we often asked: "What should you always do before you take medicine?" We gave them hints until they drew the correct conclusion: Ask your parents to help you.

For the duration of the Folly, the KCK booth was staffed with at least one adult board member and one student. My student volunteer, Brandon Hall, was also featured on the front of the new KCK brochure and as we handed it out, several visitors recognized him.

Brandon, an accomplished athlete who genuinely enjoys reaching out to others, took charge of the question and answer game. I kept the prizes stocked and handed out KCK brochures and bumper stickers. Before long, I wondered just how many visitors would stop at our booth during our watch from 2 to 4 o'clock on Saturday afternoon. So, we started counting.

Much to our amazement, even though it rained intermittently, over 100 people visited the KCK booth. A few engaged us in lengthy conversations, but most guests passed through quickly, and nearly all commended Brandon for his work.

The next day I polled three principals, three Unlimited Success representatives, and KCK board member, Carey Reece, who also staffed the booth. They all reported that the event was a very positive experience.

Mina Cook probably summed it up best when she said, "It was great to have a presence there to tell parents and kids from the elementary schools what they have to look forward to in middle school—especially as peer pressure increases—and it was great for the current middle school and high school students to see us out there."

Everyone agreed that KCK should make this an annual event.

Spring Folly invigorated KCK with new energy and it proved to be a wonderful dress rehearsal for *Kernersville Day at the Warthogs* one month later. Even though the baseball event lasted only five hours, it required much more planning and manpower than the multi-day Folly.

We had to bring together dozens of high school students and coaches to work the clinics, arrange the clinics side-by-side to run simultaneously and in a safe manner, and direct children to the various clinics. Stadium officials gave us only one hour to set up the clinics and the clinics were only opened for only one hour prior to the game. After that, everything had to be removed from the field so it could be prepped for the game.

At the same time, we had to set up our KCK booth in the stands, which included game tables, face painting, bubble blowing and an information table—all of which would be available before, during, and after the ballgame.

In addition to this, we had a welcome table on the outside of the stadium and numerous activities inside the stadium *during* the game. These included honorary first pitches by Glenn and East Forsyth baseball pitchers, photos with the mascot, and KCK certificates presented to the event sponsors on the baseball field.

Obviously, this event required an unbelievable amount of cooperation among the Chamber, the Civic Council, the students, the schools, the newspaper, the stadium, and KCK. By game day, we had all proved to ourselves that this community cared for its children and the students cared for their community.

Vans were packed with supplies the night before and we were ready for the day's events, when a predicted thunderstorm decided to pick June 3 as the day to let the weathermen be right.

The storm, bearing heavy rains, started in the morning and refused to leave. To add to our disappointment, the officials declined to cancel the game until 2:00 p.m. So, instead of being able to salvage the day early, with another activity, students and adults were required to "stand ready," until the official announcement was made.

Even though *Kernersville Day at the Warthogs* was rescheduled, school was out and the high school baseball players had already departed for summer leagues. We had similar issues with the other clinics. Nearly all the former volunteers were either already committed or they were going to be out-of-town on our rain date, July 1. This left us less than 30 days to totally reconstruct the clinics and, frankly, we were tired.

Then I remembered Peggy Essex Smith. I'd interviewed her for the *Life After Retirement* section of the Chamber's Town Brochure earlier in the year. Smith, age 76, played professional ball for the Chicago Colleens in her younger years, and was still playing softball and winning in the Senior Olympics. Her son, Stan Smith, a local banker, played for the Red Sox in 1979, the year they won the pennant. Together, this mother-son duo hosted the baseball clinic.

Annie and her dad joined Coach Carl Albert and his daughter, Kayla, to host the soccer clinic. And, before we knew it, the program was back on track. That year the Chamber presented Bob Prescott, president of KCK, with a check for $1,457. Best of all, even though we had to construct this event twice, there was a true and measurable connection between the students and their community.

The students also made a strong connection with the school's drug-free program. At Southeast Middle School 88 % of the students participated in the *It's My Call* program. Principal Warren's school also received the *Standard and Poors Research Award* from New York for narrowing the achievement gap and Southeast was one of 100 schools in the United States to receive the *School to Watch* designation for having a stellar middle school.

Dossie Poteat, principal of East Forsyth Middle School, built two years earlier, rallied his students to 91% participation in the voluntary drug-testing program.

However, it was Principal Debbie Brooks of Kernersville Middle School who claimed the top prize for the school district and likely the entire nation with 93% participation.

One key to Principal Brooks' success was a letter written by the mother of 6th grade student, Brandon Winbush. I met Brandon while searching for role model students to feature in the new KCK brochure. Principal Brooks recommended him, and then, as she checked her records, she discovered that he was *not* enrolled in the *It's My Call* program. Thinking this was a simple oversight, she called Brandon's mom.

It turned out that Brandon's absence from the program was not an oversight. His mother was actually resistant to the idea of having her young son tested for drugs. However, once Principal Brooks fully explained the program, Brandon's mother co-signed his permission form. Principal Brooks asked this mother to write a letter, sharing her feelings in a letter so that it could be shared with other reluctant parents of 6th graders.

Tavonda Winbush wrote:

> As a concerned parent, I was not warm to the idea of *It's My Call*. I thought the program was a way of indirectly giving the school permission to single out my child. But after doing some research and talking with other parents, I realized that a program such as *It's My Call* was created to protect our children from the influences of drugs and alcohol, and to give them a head start on a brighter future. This program has been a great tool for my husband and me to talk with our son about the dangers of substance abuse. *It's My Call* is a great asset to our community, and I would highly recommend that all parents sign up for this program.

In addition to this, Principal Brooks also adopted one of her 6th grade teacher's strategies. Mrs. Amy Simmons, who achieved 100% participation in the *It's My Call* program in her classroom, personally placed telephone calls to parents who refused to co-sign the permission form.

She explained to parents that signing the form enabled their child to participate in the *It's My Call* program—which over 80 percent of Kernersville's middle schoolers supported. Co-signing allowed their child be a part of something that is really big and really important to their child's peers.

> Signing the form does *not* mean their child will be tested. It means that their child *may* be chosen for testing. However, the parent is called prior to the test and, at that time, the parent can decide whether or not to allow the testing.

By separating *It's My Call* into two separate decisions, this teacher made it easier for parents. This approach allowed parents to support their child's wish to pledge immediately, while deferring the decision on the testing until the issue actually arose.

Simmons went a step further by reassuring parents that if middle school students fail the drug test, it's a secret from all people, except the principal, the student, and the parent. Additionally, middle school students retain all their sports and extracurricular privileges, even if they do not accept intervention, because the program at this level is completely voluntary.

Principal Brooks found that the mother's letter, combined with personal telephone calls, solved the 6th grade problem.

> By the spring of 2007, Kernersville Middle School enrollment in the *It's My Call* voluntary program soared from 68% to 93%.

At the high schools, while Carver came in first with 89%, both high schools in Kernersville took the next two places. East Forsyth claimed second place by maintaining its average of 74% and Glenn finally broke free of 50% and zipped up to 71%.

It was clear to me that strong leadership by school principals and increased community involvement—which was becoming stronger each year—were keys to Kernersville's leading the district, the state, and the nation.

However, one question lingered: Was there any evidence that all this testing and pledging reduced drug use and underage drinking by the students?

> A leader is best
>
> when people barely know he exists,
>
> when his work is done,
>
> his aim fulfilled,
>
> they will say:
>
> we did it ourselves. —Lao Tzu

> # We Respect Our Students
>
> **8 out of 10 students signed a pledge to stay drug/alcohol free and to take a random drug test.**
>
> ### Kernersville students Lead By Example.
>
>
>
> - East Forsyth High School
> - Glenn High School
> - East Forsyth Middle School
> - Kernersville Middle School
> - Southeast Middle School
>
>
>
> For donations or other information:
> Kernersville Cares for Kids
> P.O. Box 553
> Kernersville, NC 27285
> or call 345-7754
>
> ## Kernersville Cares for Kids
> www.KernersvilleCaresForKids.org
> This is a non-paid community service printing courtesy of *Kernersville News*

Every May – right before the Town's largest downtown community festival – about 500 of the above posters are displayed in business windows. As 20,000 visitors and local residents celebrate Spring Folly, they see for themselves that in Kernersville, ***Kernersville Cares for Kids*** **is more than a name, it is a way of life.**

Kernersville has learned to give its youth what they want. It begins by LISTENING. In Kernersville, kids want:

- **Respect**
- A public voice
- **Training in leadership and public speaking**
- Meaningful connections with caring adults
- **Opportunities to do REAL things in their REAL community**
- Genuine help given in a respectful manner when needed
- **Recognition for their support of community values**
- To be partners in decisions that affect them

http://www.kernersvillecaresforkids.org/

28

A Study of the Test

Lesson 28: Test the test

According to the findings of a 2006 study done in the WS/FC Schools, drug and alcohol use among students has not been eliminated, but it has been measurably reduced. Students participating in the voluntary (It's My Call) or mandatory (It's Our Call) random student drug-testing (RSDT) program were LESS LIKELY to have used:
- marijuana (30 day, 12 month, and lifetime use)
- inhalants
- prescription drugs
- hallucinogens
- cocaine
- alcohol (either heavily or frequently)

When compared with the students NOT ENROLLED in the RSTD program, these students reported FEWER:
- "troubles" at school (i.e. behavior problems, skipping, suspension)
- academic issues
- legal problems
- fights with other students
- arguments with parents

This is a significant bounty because the WS/FC schools are not just interested in having drug-free schools. School officials are interested in creating successful schools.

A successful school by their definition is not just a school that academically educates its students. A successful school enables its students and their families to be successful too. It accepts its role as part of the village and seeks free-flowing interchanges in all directions.

By definition then, a successful school is well-connected to the families it serves, the local community to which it belongs, and the greater community. In this way, it creates a sense of belonging for the future community—the students. This is, after all, the real goal of education: To create healthy, responsible citizens who can carry their load and have something extra to share.

It was this sense of connectedness—this belief in belonging—that helped the WS/FC schools to grant permission to *Kernersville News* to survey the students in 1996. The newspaper became the artery—the lifeline of accurate information—between the schools, the families, and the greater community. Once the whole village knew the shocking reality of the situation—that drug and alcohol use in this model community were identical to national averages—the village united and created its own solution to its problem. Hence, a comprehensive random student drug-testing program—with a voluntary and a mandatory component—was instituted.

However, community involvement and ownership of the program did not stop there. Instead, in two different communities, the local village stayed involved and has reaped outstanding rewards.

First, is the Carver Nation. This school served as the prototype for the RSDT (Random Student Drug Testing) program. This predominantly black high school finds itself in a large city, with a large daily newspaper (The *Winston-Salem Journal*), and 10 high schools. It doesn't get any special attention from town when it comes to drug testing or community recognition.

So, Carver reversed the flow and started actively reaching out to its community. It has built its own support system and has literally become a village within the village—hence, Carver Nation.

Carver Nation generates community involvement, incentives, and recognition for its students and the teenagers can feel the support. In response, Carver leads the district in high school student participation in the RSDT program.

In the second case, the Kernersville community created KCK. This non-profit—which was set up specifically to raise money and awareness to empower the students to live substance-free lives—celebrated its 10th anniversary in 2008.

Evidence is clear this community organization makes a difference. The middle and high schools in Kernersville consistently lead the district in participation in the RSTD program and hence reap the rewards.

In Kernersville, the greater village—town government—endorses and allocates funds to support *KCK*. The mayor, the police chief, the newspaper publisher, the superintendent, and the five school principals are all part of the KCK board.

It's real here. In Kernersville, the schools belong to the community and the community belongs to the schools. After all, the future community is filling the desks of the schools. So, this model of mutual ownership creates free-flowing interchange. This interchange and sense of belonging results in more successful students and families. And, whereas families are the foundation of the community, it ultimately results in a healthier and more successful village.

Returning to the micro-level, random student drug testing increases students' sense of belonging to each other, their school, and their community. This is for several reasons.

> Students view this drug-testing program as fair, helpful, and caring. If a student fails the random student drug test in *this* school district—there is no punishment.
>
> - Police are never called.
> - Nothing is recorded on the permanent school record.
> - The student body doesn't have a clue because the student continues in all his or her academics, sports, clubs, and other activities *as long as* the student accepts free help.

When students refuse help, they are required to drop all extracurricular activities *until* they accept help or until 365 days have passed. Currently, 76 percent of the students accept free help.

> "Help" doesn't just mean help to quit using drugs or alcohol. Help means getting to the root of the problem, which could be anything from undetected learning disabilities, to loneliness, to sexual abuse. Once the student learns to resolve or cope with the painful problem, the "need" for substance abuse diminishes.

Because of the helpful nature of the program, students actively promote it to each other. And this is one program that all students can belong to, whether or not the pupils are academically inclined, athletic, club-oriented, or otherwise connected.

Aside from connecting students—as they promote this out of sincere conviction or even just to win the district trophy—it connects students to their school. In Kernersville especially, principals, teachers, and even the janitors talk about the need to stay free of drugs and alcohol. So when the students join the RSDT program, they know that they are meeting the expectations of the adults in their school. And, as expected, they get visible recognition and acceptance from their leaders.

On top of this, the students of Kernersville receive the visible support of their greater community. Posters—which the students create—are commercially reproduced and adorn the storefronts of local businesses. Money is transferred from the community coffers to fund the students' initiatives for incentives to promote the RSDT. The students see their faces, their schools, and hear their voices in their local newspaper—the *Kernersville News*. These students *know* that they are important to their community and that they belong to the village.

This sense of belonging is critical to the success of the student, according to a 2005 study published by Johns Hopkins University. The report, "School Connectedness: Improving Students' Lives," noted:

These seven qualities seem to influence students' positive attachment to school:

- Having a sense of belonging and being a part of a school
- Liking school
- Perceiving that teachers are supportive and caring
- Having good friends within school
- Being engaged in their own current and future academic progress
- Believing that discipline is fair and effective
- Participating in extracurricular activities

These factors, measured in different ways, are highly predictive of success in school. Because each of these seven factors brings with it a sense of connection—to oneself, one's community or one's friends—it is clear that school connectedness makes a difference in the lives of American youth.

Clearly, *Kernersville Cares for Kids* and random student drug testing make a real and measurable impact on the students' choices in Kernersville. This was something to celebrate!

www.UnderTheInfluence.org

29

Retreat

Lesson 29: Brainstorming builds momentum

At the conclusion of our final board meeting for the school year, we suddenly realized that nine years had passed. Quickly, board members scrambled to arrive at a date to plan KCK's 10th Anniversary. June 22, 2007 was chosen and Principal Trish Gainey offered to host the retreat in the new administrative wing at East Forsyth High School. Superintendent Don Martin said he would buy breakfast for everyone and facilitate the meeting.

At eight o'clock on the designated morning we enjoyed a healthy, yet elegant array of breakfast foods that included eggs, fresh fruit, warm breads, and cold juices. The meeting commenced quickly because three of us, Annie Orchard, Chief Stockton, and I, could only stay for one-half of the two-hour retreat.

After Annie received a special award for outstanding student leadership, Martin asked us to consider the KCK vision. He did this partly to indulge me, as I'd recently discovered that KCK board members varied widely in their perception of KCK. Probably most opposite in viewpoints were Bob Prescott—current president— and I, founding president.

Prescott told me that to him, KCK is like a giant snowball. You just let it go and it keeps getting bigger. However, to me KCK is like a child. You hold on to it. You feed it, you nurture it, you protect it. And most of all, when it finds its voice, you listen to it. It is not that either vision is right or wrong, but it seemed to me that the board could increase its unity by adopting a common vision.

Without too much ado, the group opted simply to reaffirm the mission statement on the front of the new KCK brochure:

> *Kernersville Cares for Kids (KCK) was created by the people of Kernersville for the students of Kernersville to lead by example. Primarily, KCK raises money, awareness, and community-connectedness to strengthen our students to do their part to keep themselves, their schools, and their community drug-free.*

Then the fun began. Martin asked, "How can we celebrate the 10th Anniversary of KCK?"

Unfortunately, I didn't take careful notes, as I was caught up in the moment. But someone suggested that we do a special event at Spring Folly next year. Another suggested we do a fundraising event for the endowment. Still another board member, probably a principal, wanted former students to return to their alma mater to speak at a PTSA meeting and testify how KCK helped them personally.

Then, Martin said, "Maybe we could invite people to some kind of a KCK activity and have Cable 2 film the event."

Bruce Boyer, a guest at the retreat, suggested, "The film could feature student role models, maybe the students who ran the sports clinics at the baseball game."

"Maybe," Chief Stockton added, "we could get students from 10 years ago—some of the first students to join *It's My Call*—and show them as adults."

"That's a great idea," I added. "As a matter of fact, I just read in the newspaper about Jeremy Reid who is now a Highway Patrolman. He was in the newspaper 10 years ago, when he was at Glenn High School. He promoted drug testing at his school."

"I agree that using role model students for a 10th Anniversary video is a really good idea," said Kathy Jordan, director of the county's Safe and Drug-free Schools program, "because students don't respond to 'Do this. Don't do that.' That doesn't work with kids today."

Later, Jordan said, "What about putting some of the students on National Public Radio. They have a segment called *This I Believe*. Students could tell their story."

Annie Orchard brought the discussion back to the local level. She asked, "Why don't the high school students go to the middle schools and elementary schools and talk to the younger students?"

"Maybe we could have a field day," Brandon Hall, an East Forsyth High School student suggested.

"I'd like something like that at my school," Principal Debbie Brooks said. "We really need to target the transition grades, like the fifth graders who are transitioning to middle school and eight graders who will be next year's high school students."

"Maybe," said Mina Cook, "we could do this during Red Ribbon week. (Red Ribbon week is celebrated annually in October. Millions of children and adults wear red ribbons to unite nationally in a stand against drug abuse.) At the end of the program the high school students could give the children stickers that remind students to *Lead by Example*."

"I'd like to see the high school students speak to the students in the D.A.R.E. (Drug Abuse Resistance Education) classes in the elementary schools. I think it would be good for the older kids and good for the younger children," Brad Phillips said.

"Maybe the middle school students could speak to the elementary school children," offered Principal Dossie Poteat, "while the high school students speak to the middle school students."

Ideas were still being generated when Annie, and the Chief, and I slipped away to our appointments. I was happy to leave early. By necessity the meeting would continue without me proving to the board—and probably more importantly to myself—that Patty Jo Sawvel was dispensable.

According to a report at the November KCK board meeting, the remaining 13 attendees addressed the current KCK projects and decided to keep them all, while adding more student leadership opportunities.

Fundraising was also discussed and it was suggested that adult and student board members participate in fundraising. Also, a KCK Fun Run in partnership with Kernersville's Parks and Recreation department was brainstormed in quite a lot of detail. However, once again, none of the fundraising initiatives actually materialized within the following 12 months.

Four weeks after the retreat, *Kernersville News* reporter Jennifer Schneider asked the *Vox Populi* question: How do you feel about drug testing in the school?

All five randomly chosen respondents agreed that drug testing has a place in the schools. Three qualified their comment. One said it should be random. Another said testing should occur if there is probable cause. The third said the random testing should only be for students in extracurricular activities rather than random testing of all students.

To the left of the *Vox Populi*, publisher John Owensby printed a lengthy editorial titled, *Stifling Drug Use*. The column cited the 2006-07 drug testing results for the WS/FC Schools. It reported that of the 2,047 students tested for eight different drugs, including alcohol, marijuana, cocaine, amphetamines, opiates, barbituates, creatinine, and benzodiazepines, 97.7% of the students passed the drug test. An additional 250 students were tested for anabolic steroid use and 100% of them passed the test.

Mina Cook was quoted in the editorial and attributed the town of Kernersville's outstanding success in the drug-testing program to three key factors.

> Mina Cook stated:
> 1) Drug testing is promoted as helpful and not as a tool to shame or embarrass.
> 2) Students are extremely active in promoting the program to their peers.
> 3) KCK keeps "drug use in the forefront of public dialogue."

Cook ended her quote by saying, "Thanks to KCK, drug use isn't going to end up on the back burner either in our schools or our community."

Summer passed quickly and before the 2007-08 school year began, Bob Prescott announced that he was running for political office as town alderman. If he won on November 6, he might step down as president of KCK.

In the past, I'd been asked to step up, at least temporarily, when others stepped down, so I decided to clarify my role early. A few days prior to the first annual board meeting in September, I wrote a letter to Superintendent Don Martin. In part it read:

> *I will be unable to accept any leadership positions or be part of any events planning committees, except for the 10th Anniversary video, if the board decides to move ahead with this . . . I feel that after our*

> *recent summer retreat, KCK, as an organization, now has the history, unity, clarity, and vision to make this year the best year ever. I will continue to fulfill my responsibilities as a Board member, which includes volunteering for a pre-assigned shift at special events.*

He probably chuckled when he received the letter, because at this point I'd pretty well established myself as one who begins the year with determination to let go and ends the year fully engaged and nearly overwhelmed. This year would be no different.

In September, the meeting maintained its positive momentum, yet, despite that, I came away with no new commitments on my plate.

At the end of the month, Mina Cook, began a series of Healthy Student Carnivals at four middle schools. Kernersville's East Forsyth Middle School hosted her first carnival and Cook used games and prizes to teach students how to make healthy choices about stress reduction, diet, cleanliness, and substance abuse.

The carnival kicked-off the school's annual voluntary drug-testing drive, and according to Principal Dossie Poteat, this coupled with the video antics of his SRO Officer Derrick Crews, helped the school claim No. 1 in the district with 95.1% enrollment by the end of the school year.

Then, as suggested at the KCK summer retreat, Cook provided student leadership training. She chose Monday, November 12, because school was closed for Veteran's Day and it was one day prior to KCK's next board meeting.

Nine KCK students met with Cook, representing all 5 middle and high schools in Kernersville. According to Cook, though she'd done many leadership camps for students over the years, this was the first one for students directly involved in a community coalition.

By the end of the four-hour session, the students had a clear vision of their roles in KCK, a plan, and a united voice. At the next day's board meeting, it was obvious that they were now operating as a team.

> At 10 a. m., the students went to the front of the room and held up large, handwritten poster boards. The students explained to the adults what *they* wanted to do this year for KCK. The students were clearly leading!

They wanted to double the size of the KCK booth at Spring Folly and at the Warthogs game so that they could have more of a presence in the community. They wanted to go to the elementary and middle schools to talk with younger children about making healthy choices and staying drug free. They wanted to do a skit and have a raffle and they wanted to have special T-shirts to wear during their volunteer activities.

In about ten short minutes, the students lit a fire of enthusiasm that propelled KCK to a new level of commitment and cooperation. When Kathy Jordan next presented the findings from the summer retreat, it was clear that the students' vision and the KCK vision were an exact match.

Before concluding, Jordan again raised the question: How can we best let the community of Kernersville know that we have been supporting the students for 10 years? The question of how to celebrate KCK's 10th Anniversary was presented, but there was no deliberate effort to answer it.

Instead, Bob Prescott gave a quick accounts report, noting that the Town gave KCK $6,000, the bucket brigade raised about $800, and Kernersville Day at the Warthogs generally raised about $1,300. Prescott suggested that each school be given an additional $300 as each had already spent its annual allocation by November 13.

Principal Gainey recommended that the schools defer accepting the $300 and instead give the money to student leadership teams for their T-shirts, stickers, and other items they requested.

After that, Superintendent Martin suggested that the assignments be parceled out before the meeting ended. In that way, everyone would know who was taking the lead on each project.

Annie Orchard suggested that Glenn and East adopt Kernersville Day at the Warthogs because the high school students do most of the volunteering at the sports clinics. Her assistant principal, Brad Phillips, quickly offered to chair the event because he could easily use last year's game plan.

To simplify the project, I suggested that KCK cancel the rain date option, because it is too difficult to reinvent the clinics once school is out. The board agreed.

Prescott then asked, "Do we have a volunteer for Spring Folly?"

Principal Debbie Brooks immediately said, "I'll do it." Mina Cook offered to work with her. Then George Groce brought back to the fore the students' request for T-shirts. Groce knew a company that could print the shirts.

Prescott asked if the T-shirts could bear the new logo that is featured on KCK's bumper stickers. However, Annie Orchard said, "If the students are the ones that will be wearing the T-shirts, then it would be best for them to design them. They know what they want to wear."

> "We as adults can get in the way of the kids. So we have to be careful that we don't take over or kill the ideas of the kids. It is our job to make their ideas happen."
> —Jim Pryor, director of Kernersville Parks and Recreation

All agreed that KCK had to be careful to nurture this new relationship with the student leaders.

Next, Chief Stockton set the date for the annual Bucket Brigade on May 16, 2008, and Prescott promised to organize the *I Saw a Rat's Brain* field trip at Wake Forest University.

Groce noticed that every KCK event—the baseball game, the Bucket Brigade, and Spring Folly—were all slated for the month of May.

"Why don't we make May KCK month?" Groce asked. "I'll talk to Mayor Curtis Swisher about this. Curtis will do this for us."

The hour was passing quickly and nearly every major initiative was nailed down. Prescott asked John Owensby, "Can we push KCK in May in the newspaper?"

Owensby agreed and then asked the principals, "What are you hearing from parents?"

"Resistance is getting less," said East Forsyth Middle School Assistant Principal Deborah Smith. "I can count the refusals on two hands!"

Prescott, who skillfully facilitated the meeting so that all in attendance had a voice, closed the meeting by acknowledging, "The enthusiasm today was GREAT."

Usually the room clears fairly quickly, but on this day people stayed and talked. Everyone could feel the positive momentum in the room and it was so refreshing no one wanted to leave.

Best of all, I left the meeting with nothing on my plate. All the assignments were quickly and willingly snatched up by other board members. It was enough to convince me that KCK was not only standing, it was walking on its own.

To confirm that this was a landmark meeting, I emailed the board and asked them: What went right today?

Generally, an email of this nature results in spotty replies. But in this instance, nearly 100% of the board took the time to reply to this inquiry. In a nutshell, the adult board members credited the success to the enthusiastic and united leadership by the students. In turn, the students credited Mina Cook's leadership training.

Two students, Jalen Hatton and Brandon Hall, noted that the "students-only" meeting was more "relaxed" and "less intimidating" than the KCK board meetings. It was a safe place for them to share their ideas and develop a team plan, before addressing the adults.

Amber Murdaugh, a seventh grade student said, "It changed the way I presented by giving me more ideas to share with everyone."

Caitlin Amos, an eighth grade student, probably stated it most literally. "I feel the last KCK meeting was more powerful because we put the ideas on posters and this let the board members *see* our thoughts better."

The next KCK board meeting was set for Tuesday, February 12, 2008. That was three months away and I wondered: Who will come up with a 10th Anniversary idea? If something isn't put on the calendar soon, the school year will end without a celebration. I decided to wait and see.

Saturday "Students Only" Meetings

"I feel the last KCK meeting was more powerful because we put the ideas on posters and this let the board members see our thoughts better."

–Caitlin Amos, 8th grade, commenting on the value of Mina Cook's student meeting prior to board meetings.

Mina Cook and Kathy Jordan from the Safe and Drug Free School Program were each instrumental in helping the students with leadership meetings and planning community events that included games, educational materials and prizes.

Kelly Hall

Wendy Ward

In 2009, Friends of KCK were very involved in the KCK student leadership development. Pictured above, Heather Camp and Henrietta Barrett during a "students only" meeting. From 2010-12, Kelly Hall and Wendy Ward led the kids.

http://www.kernersvillecaresforkids.org

The Spirit and the 2020 Vision

Mayor Roger P. Swisher
1964-1985 and 1987-1991

"Roger Swisher was complaining one day about the way things were done in Kernersville," John Staples recalled, "and someone asked him, 'If you don't like it, why don't you do something about it? Why don't YOU run for Mayor?' So he did and he was a very good Mayor."

THAT is the spirit of Kernersville: *Don't complain about a problem, do something to fix it.*

Mayor Roger Swisher was fond of quoting Winston Churchill: *"He who fails to plan is planning to fail."*

Kernersville's 2020 Plan

Kernersville has a "perfect" vision of its future and it's right on target to make it a reality. In 1996, individuals and elected officials collaborated on the future of Kernersville – resulting in the 2020 Plan. **"Every family, every business, and every community needs a plan,"** said Arnold King, chairman of the 2020 Strategic Planning Committee, **"and this is our tool for measuring incoming opportunities to see if they are helping us to meet our goals as a community."**

http://www.kernersvillenc.com/docs/2020-update.pdf

In 2008, after serving as mayor, Curtis Swisher was appointed as the town manager. Curtis is the nephew of Roger.

Arnold King
2020 Strategic Planning

30

10th Anniversary

Lesson 30: Ask someone who knows

I waited until the day before the scheduled board meeting and then went to see Bruce Boyer at the Chamber of Commerce. He's a busy man, but he once told me that he would talk to anyone about anything if the person would buy him lunch. So, I did.

I told Boyer that I was not acting in an official capacity. My visit was merely to collect some 10th anniversary ideas to present to the board at the next KCK meeting. Our goal was to raise community awareness, increase student involvement, and raise money for the KCK endowment fund.

Boyer suggested a faculty basketball game. It was a natural fit for a school-based program and these had been successful in the past.

"That's one possibility. What's another option?" I asked Boyer.

> *"You could have a major luncheon and invite corporate sponsors to buy tables for $400 each. Food is only $10 a plate which allows businesses to write off everything but the cost of the meal."*
> — Bruce Boyer, Chamber of Commerce

Boyer then went on to sketch out the entire idea, complete with possible locations, menu suggestions, and even some options for the guest speaker. Not surprisingly, his favorite speakers were all sports giants and, of those, I liked Wake Forest University Football Coach Jim Grobe the best.

"Wake Forest," Boyer explained, "the smallest school in the ACC attaining champion status can help the small town of Kernersville keep its kids drug-free," Boyer said.

"Actually," I added, "Wake Forest already partners with KCK in the *I Saw a Rat's Brain* field trip and they are home to the largest alcohol and research center in America, so it's a perfect match."

"And," Boyer said as he smiled, "people will pay to see and hear Jim Grobe."

Before lunch was over, Bruce suggested that KCK join the Chamber. The cost was nominal at $100, but, if we were members, he could use the Chamber website and newsletter to promote KCK. I promised to mention this to Prescott.

Immediately upon leaving the Chamber, I emailed the KCK's three co-sponsors and the president.

Amazingly, we were all able to meet at the Superintendent's office two days later by tying in Prescott by telephone. I gave everyone a typed copy of Boyer's plan and demonstrated how this idea would meet all of KCK's objectives.

If we could sell 400 seats for $40 each, we would raise $16,000. Subtracting fees for the speaker, food, and other event expenses, we could hope to net $10,000 for the endowment. Best of all, this idea was modeled after the Kernersville Foundation's successful fundraising event. And the Rotary Club was able to sell all the tickets for the Foundation's event in just seven days!

All in attendance agreed that the idea was worthy of board consideration. We mapped out a game plan and then presented it at the next board meeting, which had been delayed until February 19.

Prior to the meeting, Mina Cook once again hosted a KCK Student Leadership Retreat to enable the teens to plan the Spring Folly event. Once again, the students arrived well-prepared and ready to lead the way. They stood in front of the adult board and opened the meeting by explaining that they wanted more space, more activities, more adult and student involvement, and a new location at the festival. All their wishes were granted.

Then Mina Cook was unanimously elected to the KCK board. Later that morning, when we needed a volunteer to build a KCK website, Cook and two students—Zach Gignac and Annie Orchard—offered to take charge of the project.

The sixth item on the agenda was the KCK 10th Anniversary idea. Superintendent Martin explained the idea and offered to acquire the speaker. I offered to sell all the tickets—believing at the time that I had about 60 days to do so. I also volunteered to work with the students to create a 10th Anniversary Video. Owensby offered to print all the posters, tickets, flyers, and newspaper announcements. The board voted unanimously to proceed with the project and to join the Chamber of Commerce.

Once again, the students and adults left the meeting with a keen sense of new possibilities. The next meeting was set for March 25th.

As there was not yet a speaker or a date for the 10th Anniversary Luncheon, I turned my attention to the KCK video. First, I met with Chris Runge, station manager for Cable 2, as he, TJ James and Doug McBride would be producing the video. Runge suggested Kernersville's downtown Fourth of July Park for the filming location and he advised us to keep it simple. Then, the student leaders and I met three times before the actual filming.

The students had some great ideas. A couple of the girls wanted to script some conversations and role-play scenes that showed why they joined the drug-testing program. Two of the boys wanted to bring in former students who joined the drug-testing program in high school and who were now playing college or professional sports. These local athletes included Josh Howard, then playing for the Dallas Mavericks, and two athletes playing for Wake Forest University, Chris Paul (basketball) and Chris Degeu (football).

Someone else wanted to film Wally, the mascot of the Warthogs. And I thought it would be cool to have students randomly sneak up on downtown business owners and thank them for displaying the *We Respect Our Students* Posters in their storefront windows.

Prior to the filming, Runge nixed the idea of student acting, as he could virtually guarantee that the students would be disappointed with the results. Also, there was not enough time to coordinate filming with the schedules of the former student athletes. And, though Wally was filmed, the Warthogs were later replaced by the Winston-Salem Dash team, and so the footage was cut.

Instead, Runge recommended that the students come to the filming with ideas in mind but no scripting.

> ## Chris Runge's Advice for filming a Cable 2 KCK Video
> *"The main thing to remember is NOT to prep them too much. We want this to be as natural and as believable as possible . . . . We want the beauty and the pureness of the kids to shine through."*

So on the morning of the filming, April 14, 2008, as the students and I ate breakfast at the picnic tables in the park, I didn't put up too much of a fuss when the students wanted to visit and have fun, instead of glancing over their notes on the history of KCK and *It's My Call*. Like most of us, they were pretty confident about what they knew and how they would express themselves. . . until they actually looked into the single-eye of the camera. Suddenly, their minds went blank and these formerly fluent students began to stammer.

The most common remark I heard them say to me was: Don't let them print that! I don't think any of them were happy with their solo debut.

However, we were working with professionals, and our day of filming only got better as time went on. Next, the Cable 2 crew recommended that the students divide into two groups. One went to the swings and the other to some short steps. Each group was encouraged to talk about KCK and *It's My Call*.

This time, the film crew stayed at the fringes of the group and zoomed in from a distance. When the group not-on-camera became engrossed in the moment and forgot about the filming, the crew sneaked up and captured some authentic enthusiasm.

Next, the students walked downtown and randomly chose businesses that were showcasing their *We Respect Our Students* posters. That is when the magic began.

When the students walked into Richard Hedgecock's art studio, he greeted them warmly, thanked them for their gratitude, and engaged them in a heartfelt conversation.

> *"Richard Hedgecock was so kind and so supportive of us. And, he was so knowledgeable about KCK. He posed good questions to us about our neighborhoods and how we were spreading the message to stay drug free."* —Zach Gignac, KCK youth leader

When the students went into the deli, Bob's NY Italian Subs, they had similar results. Bob Bender and his wife, Dawn, warmly welcomed the students and commended them for staying away from smoking, drugs, and alcohol. Bender spontaneously presented some "learn from me" lessons, which proved to be so colorful, that the students were transfixed. I came back later to hear "the rest of the story" and featured him in a column.

Next, the students made three prearranged visits to see the Chief of Police, the president of the Chamber, and the publisher of the *Kernersville News*. Spontaneous visits were not possible as the three men in charge were all on-call. However, this didn't seem to alter the authenticity of the experience for the students or for the adults.

What made this an indelible memory is the fact that the students had seen these three businessmen often at the KCK board meetings. But, they never had a one-on-one encounter where they could see them as individuals.

> After meeting Chief Neal Stockton, Chamber President Bruce Boyer, and Publisher John Owensby at their places of work—the students gained a new perspective.
> *"They really do support us and they really do respect us."*
> —Caitlin Amos, KCK youth leader

By the end of the day, the student leaders felt a real connection to their community. They felt cared for.

Brandon Winbush summed it nicely.

> *"Without the community, I really and truly don't think the program would be as successful as it is today."*
> —Brandon Winbush, KCK youth leader

After the filming, we all went back to the park for lunch. Originally, I was going to order pizza for all the kids. But then, I decided to ask what *they* wanted for lunch. Someone suggested *Subway's* five dollar foot-long sandwiches.

Annie Orchard took the orders and I was amazed to hear the students rattle off their favorite subs, complete with toppings, condiments, and cheeses, with no two subs being the same. Then, KPD Officer James Osborne, who was our personal attendant for the day, went to pick up the order.

I suggested to the students that as KCK was also building a website, perhaps I could shoot some snapshots as the students played in the park. They immediately came up with various poses on the slides, the monkey bars, the swings, and the stairs. Then, I saw a long fallen log and suggested the students all balance on it and face the camera. One of the students suggested that they join hands and another took it to the next level and suggested they all raise their hands up in a victory shot. That feeling was captured on film and pictured on the bottom of the 10th Anniversary Endowment Luncheon program.

However, at this late date, April 14, KCK still did not have a speaker or a confirmed date for the luncheon. It was not that the Superintendent was not trying. At the end, he was making daily telephone calls, but Coach Jim Grobe was not able to commit to a speaking engagement. Finally, Martin decided to ask Wake Forest University's head basketball coach, Dino Gaudio.

Finally, on Thursday, April 17th, when I came home from work, the following email was waiting for me: "WE HAVE A SPEAKER!! Coach Gaudio can speak on May 15th - I told him his time commitment would be from noon until 1:15 pm."

This was great, but I had to work the next day, and we did not have a confirmed location or any publicity for the event. At Martin's suggestion, Principal Debbie Brooks stepped up and took over the event set-up and menu responsibilities. Then, on Saturday, I called Owensby at his home.

"Dr. Martin was able to get Coach Dino Gaudio for KCK's 10th," I told him, "but that gives us less than 30 days to sell the tickets. Can we put a story in the *Tuesday News?*"

"Sure. Why don't you go ahead and write it and send it in," Owensby said. Then he authorized me to work with Chris Manuel who would design an ad, a flyer, and luncheon tickets on Monday.

> The beauty of working on such short notice is that you realize just how much you can do with limited resources.

For instance, with the story on Gaudio, normally I would have conducted a telephone or in-person interview. As it was, I had to settle for Internet information from newspapers and the Wake Forest website. But, that was really all I needed.

After introducing the event in the first paragraph of the front page story, the next two paragraphs stated:

> Gaudio brings with him 25 years of coaching experience and the endorsement of his belated best friend and mentor, Skip Prosser, who said, "Dino has got to be considered one of the best teachers, coaches, and recruiters in the country."
>
> As a father who values young people and a coach who has led teams to championships, Gaudio was invited by Dr. Don Martin, superintendent of the Winston-Salem/Forsyth County Schools (WS/FCS) to recognize and inspire the town of Kernersville for taking its "team of young people" to the top spot in the nation with its commitment to staying drug-free.

This was followed by a challenge from Martin and a small introductory paragraph to let the community know just how well their students were doing in supporting the drug-testing program.

> According to Mina Cook, director of Unlimited Success and Partnership for a Drug-Free NC in the WS/FC Schools, "The middle schools in Kernersville have a 200% higher enrollment and the high schools have a 150% higher enrollment in the *Its My Call* drug-free program than the district average for middle and high schools. So,

community support groups like KCK really do make a significant difference in the schools."

Currently, over 90% of the middle school students and over 75% of the high school students are in the drug-free program. Why are students flocking to the *It's My Call* pledging and random testing program?

One reason, according to Connor Hinds, an 8th grade student at Southeast Middle School: "We want our schools and our community to be drug-free."

The story concluded by inviting businesses to purchase luncheon tables seating eight for $280 or individuals to buy tickets for $35. The *Lifestyles* section of the *Tuesday News* had an ad, which doubled as a flyer, announcing the *Lunch & Listen with WFU Coach Gaudio* slated for an 11:30 a.m. buffet with the program to commence at noon.

The location—First Christian Church—was the only facility large enough in Kernersville to house the event, and it was commonly used for community gatherings. Additionally, the rental was waived if KCK used the in-house catering service which, in fact, has an excellent reputation.

Prior to writing the story, two things happened. Several weeks earlier Bob Prescott alerted me that for the first time since its inception, the *I Saw a Rat's Brain* field trip had to be cancelled due to grant restrictions at Wake Forest University. I felt bad because I knew just how much the 30 high school and 30 middle school students looked forward to the whole trip. It was a genuine VIP experience to be guests on a college campus, connect with the scientific community, and share a pizza lunch with student leaders from neighboring schools.

Then, just days prior to writing the story, I went to see Bruce Boyer.

Immediately, Boyer asked me, "Why did you pick May 15 to do your KCK fundraiser luncheon? You know that it is so close to Spring Folly that it will be hard to sell tickets. People make a huge commitment to Spring Folly and this has been a tough year for a lot of businesses."

"This was the only day," I explained, "that Dr. Martin could get the speaker for the event. He's been trying since February, and we just got a speaker yesterday."

"Well, I'm really involved in Spring Folly," he said, "and so I won't be of much help until after it's over. But if you get me a flyer and a photo of Coach Gaudio, I'll send a notice to all the Chamber members."

I knew that Boyer was doing all that he could do and once he realized that I had not utterly disregarded his earlier suggestions, he did all that he could to support the project. In fact, he helped me quickly sketch out a marketing plan.

Boyer suggested that tickets be available at several locations in town. I had no idea where the best locations would be, so he suggested the Chamber, the YMCA, the bank BB&T, and the *Kernersville News*. He also suggested that I post flyers at the library and other public buildings, approach the Town about buying a table, and get a letter of support from the Mayor.

He then suggested that County Commissioner Dave Plyler emcee the event and outlined a quick program that included Principal Coplin, Principal Poteat, Bob Prescott, Annie Orchard, Mayor Pro Tem Kevin Bugg, Superintendent Martin, and, of course, the keynote speaker, Coach Gaudio.

Before I left, Boyer asked me who was going to be selling the tickets for the event. I told him that I was. He looked shocked.

I said, "You told me the Rotary Club sold 400 tickets for the Kernersville Foundation in just one week. So it can be done."

He looked at me and said, "That was a whole group of people and they *know* people in town. They have connections."

He didn't say anymore, but for the first time, I was starting to question whether I *could* sell the tickets. And as I pondered that, somehow the two thoughts—first, that the kids' field trip had been cancelled, and second, that it was going to be difficult to sell the tickets—intertwined and a new idea came to mind.

> What if we invite those 60 students to the 10th Anniversary Luncheon? What if the corporate tables are packaged to include seven adult tickets with one student ticket? In this way, companies can eat lunch with a student and show him that the community really does care.

Quickly, I emailed Martin with the idea, as he'd left the marketing up to me, but I wanted to be sure this was a good idea from the school's perspective. He loved the idea and that became a key factor in selling the tickets.

www.UnderTheInfluence.org

Changing with Time

John G. Wolfe, a descendent of the town's namesake Joseph Kerner, serves as Town Attorney. His office is located in the historic Pinnix Drug Store.

The 1870s Norfolk-Southern Train Depot has been restored in the center of town, preserving another important part of local history. Freight trains still operate in Kernersville.

Police Chief Neal Stockton retired in 2009. In 2012 he was elected to the Board of Aldermen.

31

Selling the Tickets

Lesson 31: Keep it fun

At first glance, it appeared that I had 30 days to sell tickets. But I marked off three days to develop marketing materials, and six days that fell on weekends, and an additional three days for the caterer's final count deadline.

> I was left with a mere 14 days to sell 400 tickets.

Nonetheless, I took heart in the fact that if the Rotary Club could sell 400 tickets in a week, perhaps I could do the same with twice the time. In reality, I was too embarrassed to ask people in the community to help me on such short notice.

Monday at 3:00, once the newspaper story and flyer were proofed for print, I met with Dave Plyler, a nominee for County Commissioner. He agreed to emcee KCK's celebration and then asked how I was planning to sell 400 tickets in so few days. I'd been so focused on the newspaper publicity that I hadn't had time to think about a sales strategy.

"I think first I'll mail letters to businesses," I said.

"How much will that cost?" he immediately asked.

"Humm. I don't know. I don't really have a marketing budget," I replied.

"How long would it take?" he fired back.

I thought about that. I only had 14 days to introduce, revisit, and close the sales. "That would take too long," I conceded.

Plyler looked at me for a long moment. I think he was wondering what he'd just gotten himself into. He'd already committed to emcee the event, and now he was probably wondering how successful the luncheon would be. I just waited and let him wrestle with his doubts.

Then he surprised me. He said, "I've been in radio advertising most of my life. In the media business, 24 hours is referred to as the universe. Within that universe are hours, minutes, and seconds. My point is: You can do a lot in 10 seconds."

His perspective on time was encouraging and downright inspiring. I dropped the idea of snail mail and decided to go right for primetime, face-to-face interviews.

> Plyler told me that in his business it usually takes eight contacts to make a sale, so I'd better get started.

Before he left, I asked Plyler to give me the names of businesses that might be interested in supporting KCK. He gave me 10 names on the condition that I refrain from using his name. I agreed. Of the 10, four of these businesses eventually bought tables with an additional two buying at least two tickets.

While Plyler aimed to encourage me, he also wanted me to be realistic. In his final parting, Plyler said gravely, "It is going to be *difficult* to sell 400 tickets so quickly."

For the first time, I felt scared! I wasn't afraid of personal failure. That has never bothered me as long as I can look myself in the mirror and know that I did everything within my power to accomplish my goal. It was more a fear of disappointing the kids.

> We'd told them (the KCK youth leaders) that we were having a 10th Anniversary Luncheon where they could meet their community and show their video. What if no one came? What if the kids walked into an empty arena? That could not happen.

To alleviate my fear, I knew that I needed some quick successes. Who would absolutely buy a table? Superintendent Martin led the way by recommending that each school in Kernersville buy a table, with the high schools buying two. After all, if the community was coming to meet its students, the schools needed to step up and have a presence.

This made ticket sales easier because I could guarantee the business community that each of the five schools and half-a-dozen people from central office would be there to honor Kernersville and its students. All-in-all, 8 tables were purchased by the schools.

Next, I went to BB&T, the bank that manages KCK's money. I met with Jeff Jordan, the city manager. I tried to be calm, but by now it was Tuesday, April 22, and I felt panicky. I gave him a copy of the newspaper story, told him how important this was to the kids, and then asked if BB&T would sponsor a table. Jordan put his hands in his pockets and explained that these things take some time. "We support KCK," Jordan explained, "but big corporations don't turn on a dime."

He wasn't saying "yes" and I needed his name on the list, so I pressed, "But you *have* to, you're our bank."

"We *have* to?" he repeated with practiced pleasantness.

"Yes. You're our bank. If our own bank won't support us, who will?" I pleaded.

Jordan studied me for a moment. His face was calm and he was wearing a pleasant smile. It's the kind of smile that says one thing on the outside when people are thinking something different on the inside. Nonetheless, he acquiesced, "We'll sponsor a table."

Immediately, I said, "Great! When can you send a check?"

"In December," he said dryly.

"The reason I'm asking is because KCK has no operating capital. We have to give the catering company a check three days before the event and that is just two weeks away. So we need people to pay as soon as possible," I said.

He breathed a heavy sigh and then said, "We've already cut our checks for April. We'll send a check the first of May."

Before I left, he added, "Oh, why don't you go to the YMCA? I'm on the board there. Tell them that Jeff Jordan said they *have* to buy a table."

"Can I do that?" I asked Jordan.

"Sure," he assured me. "I'm on the board and they *have* to do what the board members say."

"Great. Thanks," I said.

Before stopping at the YMCA, I went to see Bruce Boyer. I showed him the list which included 8 tables for the schools, one table for Unlimited Success, and now, a table for BB&T. Boyer said KCK was off to good start and had me mark 2 tickets for the Chamber. Additionally, he said the Town would no doubt buy a table, which they did.

On my way out the door, I mentioned Jordan's suggestion that I tell the YMCA that they *had* to buy a table. Boyer, not privy to the entire interaction, smiled and said, "Tell them that I said they *should* buy a table."

Little did I know, but I was in for a big lesson. John Coulter, executive director, was not in, but had agreed that the YMCA could distribute the tickets. When I arrived, the staff recommended that I talk with Chris Brady. Since Brady was unavailable, they suggested I return at 5:00.

When I met her at 5:00, it was clear that she was very busy. She wanted to know why I had tried to contact her twice in the last 24 hours.

She asked me, "What's the rush? Why all the aggression?"

It stopped me for a moment. I wondered silently: Was I being too aggressive?

"The newspaper," I explained, "said that the YMCA would have KCK Luncheon tickets available, and I wanted to be sure to deliver your tickets as soon as possible."

She told me that Coulter had not mentioned this to her, but she would take the tickets and the flyer. Then I asked if the YMCA would like to sponsor a table. She said that John Coulter would have to decide that. She would call him and ask.

I said, "Tell him that I talked to Jeff Jordan and Bruce Boyer, and they said the YMCA *has* to buy a table. And we only have two weeks, so can you let me know as soon as you know?"

She was clearly agitated at this point and said a bit acidly, "You want me to let you know as soon as we know."

"Yes."

The very next day, Brady called.

She said, "We are not able to commit to a table at this time. That's what you want, right? You wanted me to call as soon as possible, right?"

I thought long and hard about my first two sales attempts. In my fear, I panicked. I was actually doing more harm than good. I apologized to Brady and the YMCA did buy two tickets.

The next day, I didn't have to go to work, so I spent all Wednesday selling tables. I woke up early and decided that instead of randomly calling on businesses, I would contact KCK's original sponsors. And to save time, instead of making face-to-face appointments, I would do everything over the telephone, fax, and email.

> Hi. This is Patty Jo Sawvel from *Kernersville Cares for Kids*. Did you know that 10 years have gone by since KCK first began? (wait for response) I know, it's unbelievable! And you were one of KCK's founding sponsors. We could not have done it without you. So, I'm calling to invite you to KCK's 10th Anniversary Endowment Luncheon. You probably read about it on the front page of the Tuesday paper. It's a lunch and listen with Coach Dino Gaudio. The reason we are having it is so the students can meet their community and see for themselves that Kernersville *does* care for its kids.

I then explained the details and asked them to sponsor a table. Most people wanted to have some information faxed or emailed, so I prepared five pages to send: a copy of the newspaper story, a copy of the flyer, a list of the businesses already onboard, a quick fact sheet on KCK, and a "Benefits to Buying a Table of Eight."

The "Benefits to Buying a Table of Eight" stated:
- The table will be named for your company
- You will be in good company
- You will be recognized at the event
- You will be recognized in the program
- You will be recognized in the *Kernersville News*
- *TAX DEDUCTIBLE*
- *Supporting one of the most successful drug prevention plans in the US (KCK went to Washington, D.C. as a model program.)*

With this new approach, I relaxed and had fun. Tony Alford, a property developer, bought the next table and then Bob Prescott sold two tables, one to Fidelity Bank and one to the law firm of Thomas & Bennett. After that, Hillary Clinton came to town and Prescott let me know that he couldn't sell any more tickets, as he wanted to focus on politics. I appreciated his honesty.

Next, I talked with Ivey Redmon, the first KCK trophy team leader. He bought a table and named it, "In memory of Doris Redmon" his beloved and belated wife.

It was Redmon's sponsorship that sparked an idea for the most fun sale of the entire event. I called Margaret Burks because she had money and a beloved and belated spouse, Leo F. Burks.

After saying my spiel, Burks said, "Let someone else do that for a change. I donated $61,000 to the gazebo and do you think anyone knows that?"

"I know," I confided. "A picture of your gazebo is on the cover of the Chamber brochure and you donated it in memory of your husband."

"Well," she said grudgingly, "you're one of the few. Do you know that the day the gazebo was dedicated, John O. put a picture of two men eating in the newspaper, rather than the gazebo?"

She went on to tell me how she had worked at Modern Cleaners until she was 79 years old.

"Mrs. Burks," I said playfully, "you're making it hard on people like me, because the President would like to see all of us working that long!"

She countered, "You should!"

"That's what my dad says," I responded. "He says find a job you can do for the rest of your life and do it!"

That was the turning point. Burks laughed.

"Call Modern Machine. I bet you don't even know where that's at," she challenged.

"I do. Doesn't Mr. Bennett own that?"

"No!" she said adamantly. "He likes people to think that! Someone wrote a newspaper story and you would have thought that he owned it."

I did not think it wise to confess to this sin at the moment, so I let her remark slide by.

She continued, "Mr. Avalon Potts owns that, the same man that owned Modern Cleaners and the same man that I worked for.

Margaret Burks was the toughest, but most entertaining customer. *"I need to sic you on Avalon (Potts). See if he will buy a table."* Burks and Potts each sponsored tables!

I picked up on this new idea and added, "Actually, he is one of our founding sponsors. If he buys a table, will you?"

There was no response, so I added, "I really need to sell these tables for the kids. It would mean a lot to me."

She agreed, gave me Potts' telephone number, and instructed me to call him at 7:00 o'clock the next morning. So, on Tuesday, April 29, I placed the call and followed my notes carefully.

"Mr. Potts," I began enthusiastically, "Margaret Burks asked me to call. She said she worked for you. I'm trying to get 50 kids to hear Coach Gaudio at the 10th Anniversary KCK Luncheon—the program that keeps kids off drugs. Our program is well-supported by an average of 8 out of 10 students in town. If you sponsor a table, Margaret Burks will too. For $280 you can make a lot of kids happy!"

I don't know if Burks called him ahead of time or not. I think not, but without hesitation he said, "I believe we'll try to do that."

I didn't know at the time, but this phrase, "I think we'll try to do that," is Southern or at least Kernersvillian for "yes."

Just to clarify I asked, "Does that mean you *will* sponsor a table?"

He confirmed and I immediately called Burks to set up a time to pick up her check. When I arrived, she was wearing an apron and invited me to sit in her kitchen. She was making fried apple pies.

She explained to me that fried apple pies are her trademark secret. She gives these tasty treats to people who help her with community projects. When she lifted the last pie out of the electric skillet, she gave it to me. Of course, it was delicious.

She then took me on a tour of her home, shared some political views, and finally introduced me to her family via photographs. I genuinely enjoyed our visit.

Another fun sale came when I had coffee with 70-year-old Henrietta Barrett. I'd met her about six months earlier when someone recommended her as the subject for my column. She had a fascinating story and we immediately felt as though we'd known each other for years.

At coffee, I explained my dilemma—the need to sell so many tickets in such a short period of time and so close to the expenditures from Spring Folly and in such a sluggish economy. I asked for her advice.

First, she told me that her husband, James Barrett, would buy a table for Edward Jones Investments. I asked if she was sure and she called him on the spot and arranged for me to pick up a check.

Next she listed off several businesses to call. Barrett told me exactly whom to contact and to mention her name. As the fundraiser for Kernersville's Shepherd's Center, she had an excellent reputation in town and was highly respected.

One of the names she listed was Parks Chevrolet. I mentioned that I'd already called them and I'd already faxed information. She told me to go see Mr. Hubert Parks in person and to use her name to open the door.

I did as she said and met with Parks. After a pleasant interchange, Parks said, "I think we'll try to do that." By now I knew to translate this as "yes" and simply asked if he wanted to be invoiced.

In time, I had to reconcile myself to the idea that I was not going to sell 400 tickets. There just was not enough time, as I was working 20 hours a week for a paycheck and my son, Clif, was graduating from college during these same two weeks.

However, tables were selling at a steady rate and sponsors were quick to give me referrals. In looking for ways to maximize sales, I asked myself: "Who has money?" I concluded that businesses who were currently advertising probably had money. So I scanned the *Kernersville News* to see who was advertising there. And I scanned the Chamber of Commerce town brochure to see who bought ads.

In the Chamber's brochure, I noticed that Bishop McGuinness Catholic High School bought a full-page ad. I contacted the school, and much to my amazement, I was informed that Gaudio's daughter attended there. The school sponsored a table.

Finally, I scanned the advertising in Kernersville's only glossy magazine *Kernersville Living*. There was a full-page ad featuring Dr. Amy Harper and I remembered from my cover story interview with her six months earlier that she is a genuinely generous businesswoman. When I asked her to sponsor a table, she and her husband, Overton, were elated. They were looking for meaningful ways to support the community and this was exactly what they had in mind.

On Monday, May 12th, when the final ticket count was due, I was pleased to report that 256 tickets had been sold. That represented 29 tables sponsored by the business community with an additional two dozen tickets sold as singles. Happily, all 50 students were sponsored by their community.

Honoring the People

In 1856, the town of Kernersville honored its young people by opening its first school in the old "Plunket Place." This school — which benefited people at the beginning of their lives — stayed opened during the Civil War. In 1930, Mr. Ad Linville used this building to honor citizens at the end of their lives, as they made their way to their final resting place. In 1965, Jack Pierce organized Pierce Funeral Service. Today, this historic building is home to Pierce-Jefferson Funeral Services. (see below)

How do you sell 400 tickets in 14 days?

"I've been in radio advertising most of my life. In the media business, 24 hours is referred to as the universe. Within that universe are hours, minutes, and seconds. My point is: **You can do a lot in 10 seconds.***"*

–Dave Plyler

http://triadtoday.com/TTabout/TTaboutDP.shtml

Dave Plyler, emcee for the first annual KCK Lunch & Listen '08.

A group of retired adults – who later became known as **Friends of KCK** – were instrumental in helping with ticket sales and with creating public speaking and training for the KCK youth leaders.

The *Kernersville News* featured KCK leader Brandon Hall in a story about the upcoming Lunch & Listen. Hall personally sold tickets for every luncheon event and was eventually joined by his fellow KCK student leaders. These youth genuinely enjoyed taking ownership of ticket sales and visiting their adult community.

KCK Youth Leader Brandon Hall

32

Community Hug

Lesson 32: Recognize success

Two days before the 10th Anniversary luncheon, KCK had its final board meeting for the year. I was given just five minutes on the agenda because the luncheon—though KCK's largest commitment—was nonetheless one of several events scheduled over the next 15 days.

I pondered: What could I say, in five brief minutes, to convey the dynamic possibilities of this celebration? I knew that without a common vision, we risked having a flat event where principals and students simply "showed up" to eat lunch. However, if we galvanized around a singular intention, we could create a three-dimensional expression—a virtual personification—of *caring*.

When it came my turn to speak, I gave everyone a copy of my speech, and then presented it.

> The purpose of this event is *more* than just to celebrate 10 years of success of helping students Lead by Example. It is *more* than a fundraising event for the KCK Endowment. The purpose of this event is to create a real *bonding* . . . an *embracing* of our students with their community and of our community with their students.
>
> We want to create a *flow*, a *movement*, a *connection* . . . and I saw this happen on April 14, when 10 of our KCK student leaders made the KCK community video.
>
> This video will be shown at the 10th Anniversary Luncheon. And here is what happened. First, we tried filming the students solo. Then, we tried filming the students in groups. And the magic just wasn't happening.
>
> Lastly, we went downtown and the students randomly walked into businesses and said, "Thank you for displaying our poster . . . We Respect Our Students."
>
> The store owners were visibly *moved* and *delighted* and they really welcomed the students and *bonded* with them.
>
> The students in turn opened up and asked questions. The students' most common reflection on the whole event was: "Wow. I never knew *how much* our community *really* cares about us."
>
> I could physically feel the energy shift in both the students and the adults. *This* is what we want to repeat at the 10th Anniversary Luncheon.

It is a simple recipe. We simply need to think . . . *thankfulness.*

In the brief two minutes that it took to say those words, the entire board clearly understood the expectation. More importantly, they emphatically embraced it.

Next, I called all the table sponsors. I wanted to refine their expectation of the luncheon and I wanted to avert the traditional 10% no-show rate that Boyer had warned me about. To accomplish this, I gave them an abbreviated version of my speech. Commendably, the few businesses that had an unassigned seat at their table used that ticket to sponsor an additional student.

On the day of the big event, I arrived at First Christian Church at 10 o'clock in the morning. Principal Debbie Brooks was already decorating the 35 white-linen table tops with multi-colored *It's My Call* centerpieces crafted by the art students at Kernersville Middle School.

I added a large two-sided card to each table to identify the sponsors and then placed a stand-up program in front of each place setting. The program, featuring a bold KCK torch in three shades of blue, perfectly complemented the centerpieces. Lastly, at Boyer's suggestion, I discreetly placed a few small donation invitations on each table.

Mina Cook completed the table dressing by giving each guest a complementary pencil, a KCK sticker, and a "Lead by Example" metal carabiner (snap hook).

Just moments after we were done, our guests began to arrive. Using a map of the tables, KCK student leaders showed the business leaders to their tables and then everyone stood in line waiting for Jennifer Hipply, the caterer, to begin serving.

Right on cue, the lines opened, Principal Coplin gave the invocation, and people began to eat a hearty meal of chicken, salad, green beans, rolls, and cheesecake. I glanced around the room and breathed in the excitement.

> My eyes stopped on Avalon Potts. He had two middle school students dressed in white shirts and ties at his table and he was visibly pleased to be treating these young men to lunch. The young men seemed to be enjoying their conversation with the half-dozen machinists at the table.

From my seat, which I chose in the very back of the room, I planned to witness the entire event, and remain invisible.

Just after 12 o'clock, when most people had finished their meals, Dave Plyler began the program. He introduced Bob Prescott, who thanked the business community for supporting the students and recognizing KCK's 10th Anniversary.

Prescott concluded by saying, "The town of Kernersville is proud of its students. Kernersville is the only town in the state that funds such a program as KCK."

His two-minute part was followed by Glenn sophomore, Annie Orchard. She told the audience that she'd been part of *It's My Call* since 6th grade, when she was invited to join the program by her health teacher. "Now," Annie clarified, "I'm in *It's My Call* because I like to be a role model for all kids. I like to be respected. And I have goals."

Annie then introduced the student video, but there was a problem with the equipment and it would not play.

Plyler gently minimized the problem and kept the program on track. As Mayor Pro Tem Kevin Bugg invited all the principals and KCK student leaders to the stage to read a Mayor's Proclamation, Chris Runge and his Cable 2 team slipped back to the audio center at the back of the room.

Part way through Dr. Martin's speech, Runge let me know that the problem had been solved. Discreetly, I walked to the edge of the stage and caught Plyler's eye. He came over and I explained that the problem had been resolved. He told me that it was probably best just to delete the video, but I insisted that it was very important to the students and was key to the success of the luncheon. He looked at me, as if to say,

Who's the professional here? . . . I've been doing these things for years," but ultimately decided to indulge my wish.

Before Coach Dino Gaudio spoke, Plyler once again introduced the video. Unbelievably, the video again failed to play.

Plyler gave them about one minute to resolve the problem and then said, "Apparently, it's just not meant to be." He then quickly introduced Gaudio.

Gaudio then gave an unexpectedly strong and compelling speech. We'd originally thought he would cite a few statistics, pat the town and the students on the back, and then talk about Wake Forest basketball.

But unbeknownst to us, he'd had a very personal experience with teens and drugs and he had come here to tell his story.
Below is a paraphrased version of his story:

> *A sixth grader came home from school one day and found his mom, his older brother, 22, and his older sister 19, who were normally at college, all in the kitchen crying.*
>
> *He asked, "What's the matter?"*
>
> *They said, "Dad has a terrible disease and he only has one year to live."*
>
> *The young man denied it and said, "My dad's fine. We just played ball together last week."*
>
> *They said, "No. He has cancer and only one year to live."*
>
> *Thirteen or 14 months later, his father passed away. Now he was in 7th grade. Every day he came home to a mom that was incredibly depressed.*

Every day when he came home, he'd say, "Hey mom, I'm home."

Then he would sit down and do his homework. He'd look out at the basketball court and he wanted to play ball, but first he would do his homework.

One day, he came in the house and said, "Hey mom, I'm home."

No answer.

He changed his clothes and said it again, "Hey mom, I'm home."

No answer.

He pushed open the door. His mom had taken her own life. He had a decision to make. Choice one: He could stay on the path his parents had led him on, the path of homework and school. Choice two: He could run with the wrong crowd.

He had these choices because at 5:00 no one was calling him in to dinner. And at 9:00 there was no one telling him to go to bed.

This kid chose to stay on the right path. He graduated high school in the top 10 of his class. He was part of the school team that won All-State in basketball and he won a basketball scholarship to the University of Tampa and played ball and earned his degree. Then he moved back to his hometown and he became a role model there.

I know because that kid played basketball for me in high school. No matter what your life is like, you don't have to go down the path of drugs. You can take the other path.

When you are faced with the choice personally, you have a decision to make: Am I going to keep doing what's right or am I going to give up?

When adversity rears its head, can YOU deal with it? The answer to that question will determine your goals, your decisions, and your success.

The crowd exploded in applause and it seemed that nothing could make the day any more memorable . . . except the video. Plyler hadn't seen the video, he didn't understand it's magic. It shined the light on the best of the community and the best of the kids. But it was the students' warm smiles, heartfelt enthusiasm, and genuine joy that made it the best thank you present the community could ask for.

At the end of Gaudio's speech, Runge approached me and said that this time the problem was really fixed. Apparently the CD player at this facility has a permanent pause so that if the video is not started with a few minutes of loading, it locks. The key was to load the CD immediately prior to the showing.

Quickly, I went back to the front of the room. However, I did not approach Plyler. I knew that he'd given me my last chance. Instead, I approached Dr. Martin. I explained the problem and the solution. I also told him why *he* was the only one in the room who could convince Plyler to give the video another chance.

Martin talked to Plyler and Plyler, with a smile, introduced the video for a third time. Thankfully, it played. It was indeed the perfect conclusion to the community's celebration of its homegrown KCK program.

When it was all over, the room was aglow with excitement. The people knew—in their own hearts—that this community had done something to really be proud of.

> *History is the witness of the times,*
>
> *the torch of truth*
>
> *the life of memory*
>
> *the teacher of life,*
>
> *the messenger of antiquity.*
>
> *Cicero*

A Voice Beyond Newspaper

In 2008, Chris Runge from Cable 2 filmed KCK Youth Leaders as they spoke with Downtown business leaders that were displaying *"We Respect Our Students"* posters in their front windows. The resulting video was aired at the 10th Anniversary First Annual Lunch & Listen and then broadcast on television. After that, Runge filmed annual videos of KCK which were aired on Cable 2.

http://www.wsfcs.k12.nc.us/Page/565

"It is a lot easier to follow the crowd and do bad things than it is to LEAD the crowd and do good things... The smarter person will remain drug free."
    –Rishawna Woods, senior at EFHS

In 2001, Lee White from Cable 2 filmed "stay drug-free" Public Service Announcements by youth leaders and aired them on television and in the local schools.

Richard Hedgecock, local artist, captured the printed words of youth leaders – such as "Lead by Example" or "Teens Go Green –Don't Pollute Your Body" or "Be Free of Drugs and Underage Drinking"– and literally framed their newspaper stories in picture frames to be displayed in the halls of the local schools.

KCK 10th Anniversary Lunch & Listen

On May 15, 2008 Kernersville experienced its first KCK "community hug". Businesses sponsored tables and ate lunch with students while listening to a powerful leadership presentation. About 250 attendees celebrated students who stay free of drugs and underage drinking.

"When the community showed up, it showed us that our work really meant something to them. It showed us that the adults really care."
Brandon Winbush, 14

Annie Orchard, 15, spoke at the Lunch & Listen
" I don't use drugs or alcohol because I have goals and want to achieve them in my life."

Britni LaRue and her mother, Tammy celebrated with KCK. In 2007, they'd spoken out in a newspaper story about middle schools.

WS/FC Schools Superintendent Don Martin (left) had lunch with keynote speaker Dino Gaudio, Men's Basketball Coach at Wake Forest University. He told a moving story at the L & L.

"When adversity rears its head, can YOU deal with it? The answer to that question will determine your goals, your decisions, and your success."   *– Coach Dino Gaudio*

Friends of KCK

Friends of KCK was organized in the 2009-10 school year to help youth leaders do REAL things in their REAL community. Benefiting from the expertise of caring adults, many of whom were retired, students learned the skill of public speaking, the art of meeting and greeting adults with a dynamic handshake, and the courage to personally present business people with the opportunity to sponsor tables or tickets to the *KCK Annual Lunch and Listen.*

Photo Wendy Freeman Davis

FOUNDING MEMBERS OF *FRIENDS OF KCK*
Left, Irvin Grigg, Carl "Ace" Clarke, Henrietta Barrett, Ivey Redmon, Heather Camp.

33

The Final Lesson

Lesson 33: There is no final lesson

At first glance it might seem that now was the perfect time to make my exit from KCK. After all, *Kernersville Cares for Kids* had achieved its goals and the connections between the students, the community, and the KCK board were sound.

However, there remained one unresolved problem. As a proverbial thorn-in-the-side, this problem would get all the attention a neglected 10-year-old problem can demand. It happened almost a year to the day. KCK once again found itself with a last-minute Lunch & Listen speaker, Super Bowl Pro David Rowe, and a date, April 21, 2009.

When the details were announced at the March 17th board meeting, KCK did not have a sales plan, ample time, or board commitment to sell the tickets. This occurred despite the fact that the board had determined, six months earlier, that it was going to repeat this successful event.

To compound matters, in the 344 days that passed between the two Lunch & Listens, the economy took a big hit. Major banks were failing, auto manufacturers were on the brink of bankruptcy, and unemployment was nearing 10%.

Lastly, for some reason unbeknownst to me, the Lunch & Listen planning committee, of which I was not a part, decided to *raise* the ticket price from $35 to $40. This was after the board was advised that other non-profits such as Kernersville Foundation had lowered their ticket prices, due to the current economy.

With all of this on the table at the board meeting, I raised my hand and volunteered to sell 10 tables. I was hoping my action would precipitate similar commitments by the rest of the board members, but it didn't.

To make it easy for them, I offered to give each school principal the names and telephone numbers of two previous table sponsors, if they would make the calls. They agreed but it was obvious that they were not very enthusiastic.

Immediately following the meeting, Principal Gainey, who chaired the Lunch & Listen, approached me.

> *"I don't think the principals should have to sell tickets."*
> —KCK Board Member Principal Trish Gainey

She was right and I told her so. The principals, who often work 60-plus hours a week, were already actively promoting anti-drug campaigns in their schools. And now, they were spearheading all the KCK projects, even this labor-intensive Lunch & Listen. If principals sold the tickets, then how could the community claim ownership in the organization? On the other hand, how did the planning committee expect that the tickets would be sold?

Oddly, 10 years into KCK's history, we were faced with Principal Coplin's original assertion, "I can tell you right now what the community wants to do about the drug problem. They want the schools to solve the problem."

I went ahead and emailed each principal the names and numbers as promised and then I set out to sell my 10 tables. In very short order, I found it to be much more difficult than completing the same task one year earlier. Immediately, I began to visualize how the 50 students would feel if they walked into an empty auditorium?

Of course, there would be 96 people there, because the five schools and school related organizations bought a total of 16 tables that seat six people each. But some of those tables included the students. From that vision arose a question.

> What would it mean if the tickets weren't sold? Would it prove that the community didn't care? Or, would it prove that the KCK board did not care enough to solve its problem of finding a fundraiser?

I knew that the real answer was found in the last question. But oddly, the teens would probably attribute the empty seats to a lack of community support.

Deciding that disappointed students were not an option and realizing that I was powerless to accomplish this on my own, I called for help. First I called Bob Prescott, KCK's president. Almost immediately Prescott said, "The front-page story in the *Kernersville News* was great. People are already calling me about the tickets. I don't think we'll have anything to worry about."

I was pleased with the story too, but I knew from last year that even the best of stories does not sell tickets. It only adds credibility to the sales call. Then I asked Prescott if he would sell tickets to the same two businesses that he approached last year. He quickly agreed and said he would call me with the results.

When he called back, Prescott said that the bank, which sponsored a whole table last year, could only buy one ticket this year. However, his contact filled the table with five other single tickets. Unfortunately, these ticket holders were high profile community and corporate leaders, who might have sponsored entire tables.

Prescott's report was the final reality check. Whereas it is one thing to sell 10 tables, it is quite another to sell 60 separate tickets.

Immediately I made more calls for help. Irvin Grigg, a retired businessman, and former board member with the Shepherd's Center, agreed to ask each current board member to fill one place at a table.

> As we talked, I explained to Grigg, *"It's hard enough to be a teenager in the best of times. But these are not the best of times. Some of our kids are coming home to stressed-out parents. And if the statistics are right, maybe one-out-of-ten of these kids is coming home to parents without jobs. So the kids are trying to believe that their education and their good choices are going to make a difference, but that's not the reality that they are seeing. Now, more than ever, the community needs to be there for the students."*

Without revealing his game plan, Grigg attended the next Shepherd's Center board meeting, and gave a speech so moving that Wayne Mabe from Bank of North Carolina called me to sponsor a table. When I asked him why he made the decision, he directly credited Grigg's speech. Grigg, incidentally, sold two tables to members of the Shepherd's board.

Next, I called John Staples, my mentor. Staples loves the community but doesn't like sales. However, he agreed to fill his table with lunch buddies and so we named a table for Kernersville High School's Class of 1954.

Nancy Bourn, whom I'd met a month earlier when writing her cover story for *Kernersville Living* magazine, agreed to sell six tickets and KCK named a table for Trend Setters Styling Salon.

Then I called and emailed the 14 KCK student leaders. Three of them responded and asked for more information. One personally accepted the challenge. East Forsyth High School sophomore Brandon Hall, who plans to go to college and then open his own business, saw this as an opportunity to get to know his business community. So, I wrote a story about him and put his picture in the newspaper. Hall sold 17 tickets.

However, the real breakthrough came when I met Henrietta Barrett and Heather Camp for coffee. These retired business women spent years working with the elderly at the Shepherd's Center. In fact, as its first executive director, Camp nurtured it from a seedling start-up to one of the healthiest and fruitful non-profits in Kernersville. And Barrett, whom Camp hand-picked, became one of the most effective and dependable fundraisers for the organization.

After briefly explaining KCK and the Lunch & Listen, I asked these ladies, "How would you like to spend some time helping the young people? These are people at the beginning of their lives, people who have their whole future ahead of them. They are full of new ideas, energy, and do you know what they want? They want someone to listen to them and to show them how to meet their goals."

Camp immediately said, "I'd love to mentor the students and work with them, but I don't do fundraising. I told the Shepherd's Center Board when they hired me 21 years ago that fundraising is the one thing I won't do and I haven't."

Her response was not what I'd hoped for. I paused for a moment. I knew in my heart that Camp, one of the most gracious people I've ever met, had a place in this. Perhaps we just saw her place differently. I thought about all the people she'd mentored and all the people that blossomed under her care. Then it became clear.

"Actually," I explained, "the KCK student leaders need leadership training. Last year, Mina Cook had "students only" retreats just before our board meetings and it made a world of difference in the way the students related to the board. Mina's meetings raised their confidence, forged kids from five schools into one solid team and helped them speak with one voice."

"They told the adults exactly what they wanted and the adults helped make it happen. It set the whole group on fire! But this year, the students didn't receive any leadership training, because Mina's grant expired and she is no longer on the board.

So now the students have reverted to being observers rather than leaders at the meetings."

As we talked about this, Camp could see herself doing this and enjoying it.

I turned to Henrietta Barrett, who helped me last year. Barrett said that she would help sell tickets, but she would not do it alone.

As we tossed around the possibilities, we realized that KCK really needs a permanent support organization, just like the symphony needs a symphony guild or the school's athletic departments need booster clubs. These support organizations don't dictate policy or programming, they simply become dependable supply lines of cash and community support.

In the end, we came up with the idea of *"Friends of KCK."* Camp and Barrett—who know the people and personalities in Kernersville—agreed to build a team of community volunteers if the KCK board wanted this resource.

This team could then lift the burden of ticket sales, publicity, marketing, student mentoring, and even the labor of set-up and tear-down of events—so that the principals are free to focus on the jobs that they do so well. Best of all, the increased broad-based community support would be an undeniable evidence of the name **Kernersville** *Cares for Kids.* And lastly, the funds from the Lunch and Listen could help build KCK's future by funding the endowment.

Though they were excited, Camp and Barrett let me know that they would not sign a lifelong contract. Instead, they would build a self-sustaining volunteer base, where seasoned volunteers recruit and train new volunteers so that the support system would continue even when they moved on. I, in turn, promised to help them in any way that I could, short of joining their team.

The possibility of *Friends of KCK* was extremely refreshing. I explained to the new founders that because *Friends of KCK* would be taking responsibility for many of the loose ends that I'd been managing, I could now take a very necessary and important step.

I told Camp and Barrett, "I think my presence on the board is now doing more harm than good. My coming off the board is similar to a parent's withdrawal when a child gets married. If the parent keeps showing up at the kitchen table every time the newlyweds have a problem, the couple will never learn to manage their own lives. So the issue at stake is *not* finding the best answer to life's challenges, but allowing the couple or the non-profit to find their *own* answers. In that way, they accept full responsibility for their choices."

Camp and Barrett both understood and agreed. We resolved to present the *Friends of KCK* idea to KCK's executive committee *after* the tickets were sold. Though Camp did not sell a single ticket, she did give Barrett and me a list of promising prospects. Barrett, of course, had a list of her own. And with that, we were off and running. In the end, we had 100 more people at KCK's second Lunch & Listen than at the first.

Though the event was an unquestioned success, there was some talk that perhaps KCK should limit its luncheon to every other year, as it was so labor intensive. However, I explained to Superintendent Martin why it is important to keep the Lunch & Listen an annual event, when I joined Camp and Barrett in his office on May 26.

> It is important to hold the Lunch & Listen annually because **this is the most meaningful proof of support from the *students' viewpoint.*** They love the incentives and the money the community gives them, but what they crave most is a powerful connection with the adults in their town.

> As Zach Gignac, a senior at EFHS, told me:
> *"We're always told that the adults in the community care, but when you actually see them there for you, then you believe it."*

It's the positive connection that inspires them and makes them believe that the town is watching, listening, and caring.

So while *It's My Call* is important, because it sets an expectation before the students, and whereas incentives are great because they reward the good choices that the students make, it is the physical embrace of the Lunch & Listen that touches the hearts of these students.

In essence, the effect of the Lunch & Listen is the very ideal that every community is looking for—a positive connection between the youth and the adults. Instead of canceling the very best program—the one that raises the most awareness, the most community-connectedness, and the most money—why not, instead, ask for more help?

In fact, that is the Kernersville way of doing things. When Spring Folly, one of Kernersville's most successful annual events, kept getting bigger and more labor intensive, it wasn't canceled. Instead, a call went out for more help.

Martin, of course, was in full accord. He agreed with Camp when she advised that annual events, historically, gain more momentum than non-annual events. Additionally, they are easier to support because people keep them on their calendars.

When we met with Martin, a full executive committee meeting was not possible, but Martin assured the women that the board would be delighted to welcome *Friends of KCK* as a support group. Finally, the 10-year-old problem of fundraising and friend-raising was solved.

However, that wasn't the only payoff. *Friends of KCK* laid the groundwork for the most profound demonstration of student leadership to date.

From Editor to Author

www.KernersvilleNews.com

John Staples, age 76, averages a book a year since retiring as editor of the *Kernersville News* in 2002. John still helps new writers and always has a story to share about his hometown.

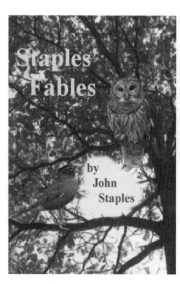

Staples' Fables is reminiscent of Aeosop's Fables. John is completing his 10th book in the series. *White Lies* is a thinly-veiled tale of Kernersville.

34

A Mountain Top Experience

Lesson 34: Keep Chasing the Question

How did she do it? How did Mina Cook transform 20 KCK students on the board into genuine leaders? What did she do in her "students only" Saturday meetings?

I asked myself those questions every time I attended a board meeting in 2008-2009. Since her departure the previous year and subsequent absence of any Saturday student meetings, the student "leaders" had reverted to voiceless observers.

As Jamaal Doran, a rising 12th grader from Glenn High School told me, "When I went to the KCK board meetings, I asked myself, 'Why am I here?"

> *"The board isn't requesting our ideas. They aren't hearing us. Why are we here?"* —Jamaal Doran, GHS rising senior

I didn't want that to happen again in the upcoming 2009-2010 school year. So, while I didn't know Cook's secret, I was determined to do what I could to give the students the leadership they deserved. And frankly, I was hoping to witness for myself that moment of transformation when the kids found their voice.

At the same time, Heather Camp and Henrietta Barrett had a few expectations of their own. In a late summer meeting they gave me the following ultimatum: KCK had to have all its board seats filled and have a speaker signed on *before* they would invest any of their time working as *Friends of KCK*.

I objected, stating that KCK needed both a president and a vice-president this year and it often went without a vice-president.

> *"If KCK can't get its own house in order, why should anyone else help?"* —Heather Camp, Friend of KCK

Barrett, in charge of fundraising and also a Friend of KCK, added:

> *"It's inexcusable to wait to the last minute to get a speaker and then expect the community to support you.* —Henrietta Barrett

KCK Youth Leadership Team
2008-2009

Jamaal Doran Annie Orchard Andrew Krivsky Tecora Logan

Haley Fulp Brandon Winbush Harrison Hollis Brandon Hall

Caitlin Amos Amber Murdaugh Yvette Parham Jena Reisenauer

Connor Hinds Zach Gignac

"When I attend get-togethers with my friends, I have a legitimate excuse to stay drug-free because we have random drug tests at school." —Zach Gignac

2009 2nd Annual KCK Lunch & Listen

FIVE YOUTH LEADERS spoke at the 2nd luncheon. (L-R) Andrew Krivsky (SEMS), Brandon Winbush (KMS), Jamaal Doran (GHS), Harrison Hollis (EFMS), and Zach Gignac (EFHS).

"We're always told that the adults in the community care, but when you actually see them there for you, then you believe it."
—Zach Gignac

KCK President Bob Prescott with keynote speaker David Rowe, NFL SUPERBOWL XI Pro. Rowe assured the audience of 350 adults and youth that if he could play sports in high school and then play for the "party team"– Oakland Raiders– without ever touching a drop of alcohol, they could resist peer pressure and stay free of drugs and underage drinking too!

EFHS Principal Trish Gainey hosted the L&L and played a major role in organizing future KCK events.

"We had adults and students all being reminded to keep our priorities straight and to care for each other. It showed everyone what Kernersville can be like when adults and students work together." —John Staples

http://www.kernersvillecaresforkids.org/

Additionally, they wanted help marketing KCK. Specifically, they wanted KCK students to speak at virtually every club, church, and civic organization in town.

I said, "Is that possible? Will the clubs let them speak?"

Barrett said, "Let them? The clubs are always looking for speakers and they love to listen to young people." Barrett then offered to call and organize speaking engagements . . . as soon as we had a Lunch & Listen speaker confirmed.

Thankfully, Captain Doug Kiger, a soft-spoken police officer with a strong propensity to follow rules, guidelines, and protocol, accepted the invitation to be KCK's incoming president. And newly retired Kernersville Elementary School Principal David Fitzpatrick agreed to support him as the new vice-president.

To acquire a speaker, I asked literally everyone. We wanted a speaker who lived a dynamic life and who cared about helping kids to stay free of drugs and underage drinking.

One of my housecleaning clients, Joe Gangloff, a former Marine and retired CFO from R. J. Reynolds Tobacco Company, referred me to Porter Halyburton.

Halyburton survived seven-and-a-half years as a prisoner of war after his Navy plane was shot down over North Vietnam. Now a nationally acclaimed speaker and university professor, Halyburton was just what we were looking for.

And he had a profound message.

> Prisoner of War survivor Porter Halyburton had learned the power of choice and the power of forgiveness. And having learned these under the extremest of tests, he'd retained the purest of lessons.

Now that would give the kids something to talk about when they went to the civic clubs!

Thankfully, after hearing the KCK story, Halyburton was happy to help.

After reporting the "met conditions" to Camp and Barrett, I emailed KCK President Kiger. He directly contacted the principals and asked them to invite their students to the September 19, 2009, KCK Saturday Leadership Meeting.

Amazingly, 17 of the 20 students showed up at the police station training room. And thus began our shared journey to explore the power of student leadership.

To begin, I followed the one tip that Mina Cook had given me:

> "The students may have been nominated by their schools, but make sure that it is their *personal choice* to be a KCK leader."
> —Advice from Mina Cook

So I asked the kids: Who owns KCK? They didn't really know. So I read the front of the KCK brochure: "Kernersville Cares for Kids was created by the people of Kernersville *for the students* of Kernersville to lead by example."

Then I asked them again: So who owns KCK? They said excitedly, "We do!"

Then I told them, "*You* create KCK every year with its projects and activities. Do you want to create it again this year?"

Again they answered in the affirmative.

Then Henrietta Barrett came forward and wrote notes on a poster-sized notebook while the kids called out ideas for KCK's three main projects: the Wake Forest University Rat's Brain Field Trip; Spring Folly; and the 3rd Annual Lunch & Listen.

As the kids warmed up and melded into one solid team, they suddenly commenced asking for more and more ownership.

They wanted to create a new brochure as the current brochure had many of the high school leaders frozen in time as middle schoolers. The students also wanted a new KCK dvd/video, brain fairs at their school so that *all* the students could understand the harmful effects of drugs on the human brain, and they wanted to buy a tent and T-shirts for their KCK work at community festivals.

Our four hour meeting was quickly speeding by when Jena Reisenauer, a sophomore at Glenn High School asked:

> *"Why can't we sell tickets to the Lunch & Listen?"*
> —Jena Reisenauer, GHS 10th grade KCK youth leader

This was quickly followed by, "Why can't *we* speak in the community?"

And just that fast, the kids became so energized and spontaneous that they crossed the line separating adult and student leadership.

Later, I realized that this miraculous phenomenon was not dependent on Mina Cook and it wasn't dependent on me. The fact became clear: Students discover their own power when they are under the influence of positive leadership.

Quickly, the kids sketched out how they would like to present their ideas to the adults at the next board meeting on September 29th. They concluded by asking for another Saturday meeting in October.

Ten days later, at the September board meeting, President Kiger invited the students to the front of the room—making it clear to all that KCK was indeed student led. As expected, the kids' energy invigorated the whole group, which further inspired the teens.

By the time the second leadership meeting came around, it dawned on me that I was teaching something called *leadership* but I really had no idea of how to put that concept into words. So, for the October meeting, I printed a Google search of the words leader and leadership. As we read through the 20-plus excerpts, the students clearly resented the "classroom" approach to this topic.

But it was a necessary task because it enabled us to wrestle out a concrete definition that made sense to us. We concluded: Leaders breathe life into ideas and move people to action.

> ### **WHAT IS A LEADER?**
>
> Leaders breathe life into ideas
> and
> move people to action.

So now, we had a good question to ask ourselves before we started any project or campaign: How can I breathe life into this so it comes alive and how can I move people to support it?

The leadership excerpts also noted that real leaders stand up and speak up for what they believe in. This provided a good segue to public speaking.

While the kids were willing to speak, I felt that it would be cruel and unusual punishment to give them the opportunity without also giving them the tools to do it well.

So for the second part of the meeting, Carl Clarke joined our team. Clarke was actually serving as editor of this book and was so moved by the KCK story that he agreed to conduct a one-hour public speaking workshop, followed by private speaking lessons for each young person over the coming weeks.

As the class found out, Clarke had quite a resume' as a retired teacher, coach, and principal. Additionally, he was a paid actor and even had a street named after him in Kernersville.

Clarke brought to bear all the confidence, authority, and conviction that he'd earned in the last eight decades and stole the show as he contrasted poor versus powerful speaking ability.

Then, he took his lesson a step further. Clarke sought out the shyest and smallest student of them all—little red-haired Drew Craven—and asked him to come to the front of the class.

Carl Clarke then walked to the back of the class. He asked Drew to introduce himself.

Drew looked down and managed to get out a barely audible whisper, "Hello. I'm Drew Craven."

Clarke said bluntly, "I can't hear you. Speak up! Talk to the wall."

Drew tried again and he did speak louder. However, it was not loud enough.

> *"Speak like you are somebody. Speak like you have something important to say. Don't say it to me. Say it to the back wall."*
> —Carl Clarke, Friend of KCK taught the youth public speaking.

Drew tried again and this time he did it! He felt the difference as did everyone else in the room.

The following month, students scheduled to speak in November participated in mandatory private speaking lessons with Carl Clarke.

First, students each wrote their own speeches based on their personal experiences in KCK and then they presented their 10-minute messages to Clarke one at time.

Several months later, wanting to witness the transformation for myself, I accompanied one student, Dusty Nguyen, for his lesson at Clarke's home.

Dusty had a halting speaking style and moved about nervously. I watched over the next hour as Clarke increased Dusty's awareness of his "stage presence" and helped him focus on his pace, pitch and power.

Later, Dusty's father called me and said, "I am so proud of my son. I heard his speech before he went to his class. Then I heard it when he came home. He is so motivated!"

By the time Dusty actually gave his speech at Caleb's Creek Elementary School, he had practiced it 30 times. He was so smooth that Kelly Hall said she couldn't believe it was his first speech. Kelly Hall was by now my official partner at the Saturday meetings and she witnessed Dusty's speech because her son, Brandon, was also giving a speech.

Interestingly, before Brandon gave his public speech, Kelly called to ask if Brandon could be excused from taking a lesson from Clarke. Brandon was loaded with classes and had a job and he didn't have much time. In addition to this, he was very happy with his speech and was accustomed to speaking up.

However, I knew that no matter how proficient a 16-year old-speaker is, he has plenty of room for improvement. Additionally, Clarke was a rare one-of-a-kind, no-nonsense speaking coach. So I insisted that Brandon comply.

Amazingly, when Brandon called to tell me how much he learned from Clarke, I didn't recognize his voice! In just one session, Clarke had shown this rather quiet young man how to project strength and conviction in his tone.

From that day forward, Brandon's "new and improved voice" became his daily voice. A few months later, Brandon Hall would be unanimously elected by his peers to be the first KCK president of the student leaders. And while his "new voice" cannot claim all the credit, it was a definite and measurable turning point for Brandon.

In November, our family went home to Michigan, but the Saturday Leadership meeting went on. Kelly Hall volunteered to lead the meeting. Hall loves kids and was finally living her passion as a first year teacher at Cash Elementary. In fact, her principal, Judy Jones, nominated Hall as "First Year Teacher of the Year." So the KCK team was in good hands.

Hall passed out some copies the book, *Two Souls Indivisible,* so the students could read the captivating account of Porter Halyburton's life before they spoke to the community.

Carl Clarke once again attended the November meeting to coach students one-on-one. And lastly, Kelly Hall and Camp and Barrett helped the kids memorize KCK facts and history in a friendly game rewarded by free gifts from local businesses.

In December, the kids were dismissed from the monthly Saturday meeting and I went to school instead. At a free One Day Training for Adult Leaders class, which was sponsored by Unlimited Success, Aidil Collins showed us how a group of high school students changed public policy. They were instrumental in influencing legislature to ban smoking in public places in North Carolina.

This was all accomplished under the direction of *Youth Empowered Solutions*, better known as YES. As the local director, Collins was here to show us how to be effective adult leaders for students who wanted to promote the *It's My Call (IMC)* drug-free program at their schools.

Collins admonished, "Adult leaders are there to influence, not to dictate."

She also defined prevention. "Prevention happens when kids discover the truth about a substance and they figure out who is telling them the truth and then they choose to become a light for the truth. That is prevention."

She then drew a triangle titled Youth Empowerment. The base was labeled *opportunity*—actually getting the IMC pledges or selling Lunch & Listen Tickets. But opportunity was maximized by *skill development* on one side—which included learning the truth and developing public speaking skills, and by *critical awareness* on the other side. Critical awareness was the constant asking of the question: Why?

She made the interesting observation: "Sometimes it is not solving the question, but sifting through the ideas that benefit kids most. And, if you, as an adult, answer the question, you keep the power. So hold them responsible for their own learning."

Over the next six hours, she provided the groundwork for KCK's remaining Saturday Leadership meetings. Needless to say, this adult skill development class skyrocketed our already successful Saturday meetings to a whole new level.

So at our next scheduled Saturday "students only" meeting on January 9, 2010, I invited two national reps from SADD (Students Against Destructive Decisions) to join us. Just a few years older than our Saturday class, these two college students were perfect role models.

> *"Leadership is not about other people opening doors for you.*
> *Leadership is about you opening doors for yourself."*
>   —Darian LeNeave, age 19, National SADD Rep, Guest Speaker

He then added, "By my leadership and caring I have changed lives. One of my friends needed someone to talk to so that he could stop doing the things he was doing to himself and I was there."

Laura Grubbs, age 22, told the students, "Our goal (at Carver High School) was to keep *It's My Call* on the front burner. We had daily morning announcements, a message board, posters, incentives, paid speakers, candy, and cookouts. Our school partner—Hanesbrands—paid for a lot of our incentives."

Then, their mentor, Ginger Amos, told the team, "*It's My Call* is a success at Carver because it is student driven. I'm the sponsor and I meet with the kids and we plan out our monthly programs, but it is the *students* that do the work."

The teens were visibly inspired and once our guests departed they got to work. Our mission was to leave this meeting with the plan and tools to raise each school's IMC enrollment and to beat Carver and take back the trophy.

To do this, we worked on our critical awareness by asking some tough questions. Why do we care if kids use illicit drugs? What problems are caused by illegal drug use?

After mulling this over I asked the kids, "Did you know that all drugs used to be legal? And, did you know that drugs that people think are brand new—like Ecstasy, Oxycotin, Adderall, and marijuana—have actually been around since your grandparents were kids? So why are they illegal as recreational drugs today?

> Did you know that all drugs used to be legal? You need to find out *why* the law changed.

We talked about *why* kids take drugs. Again, this was straight from the YES workshop. Teen drug use is primarily due to peer pressure; mental health issues such as depression and anxiety; and trauma, such as loss of a loved one, sexual abuse, or violence.

As we talked, I could almost see the wheels start to turn. The student leaders began to grapple with the truth and develop some compassion for their fellow classmates. Their role as leaders was taking on more meaning and by the time we broke into groups, they all decided that they wanted at least 90% of their classmates to be enrolled in the IMC random and voluntary drug-testing program.

Their motive stemmed from their desire to help their classmates to get free and private assistance to get back on the drug-free path if they needed it.

And they came up with creative and fun ways to promote the enrollment. They wanted to have candy giveaways, cash drawings, dog tag incentives, pep rallies, T-shirts, and room-to-room personal testimonials.

The following month, Heather Camp and Henrietta Barrett let me know that it was time to host a *Friends of KCK* Volunteer Meeting. So I took their list and added some current names from Leadership Kernersville and set the date for February 15.

Amazingly, even though we experienced so much rain, hail, and snow that we almost canceled the event, we had a record turn out. Though 25 were invited, 30 actually attended because some people brought a friend.

We let the kids do most of the talking. In five short minutes, I let the group know that these kids wanted to do *real* things in their *real* community and they needed adults with driver's licenses to take them to local businesses.

Kernersville's new Police Chief Ken Gamble spoke on the "Power of One" and Principal Dossie Poteat, who achieved a 90.9% student enrollment in the IMC at East Forsyth Middle School, spoke about the value of the Kernersville Village that is raising the children.

Heather Camp and Henrietta Barrett also spoke briefly about the *Friends of KCK*.

Then we had four student speakers, including Drew Craven who publicly praised Carl Clarke for "teaching him how to speak."

At the end of the meeting, 23 new volunteers signed up to help the kids. KCK now had some wheels and it was about ready to take flight.

Know Your Drug (& Alcohol) Definitions

Experimentation: Drug EXPERIMENTATION is using an illicit drug or using a legal drug in a way that it was not intended to be used or that was not prescribed to you by a doctor. Experimentation can happen once or many times.

Use: Drug USE progresses beyond experimentation and becomes regular. A person may develop a pattern of monthly, weekly, or daily use.

Abuse: Drug ABUSE progresses beyond use and is characterized by a craving for the substances. The drugs interfere with or cause problems in the person's life. It is also common for the person to lie to himself or others about his abuse. (also known as Substance Use Disorder SUD)

Tolerance/Dependency: Drug TOLERANCE happens when the person needs *larger doses* of the drug to experience the same effect. The DEPENDENT person ignores clear negative consequences, will often choose drugs over friends, family, or former personal interests, and will make excuses for his behavior

Addiction: Drug ADDICTION is a preventable disease that a person unintentionally gives to himself by using drugs or alcohol. For one person, one or two experiments result in "a switch being flipped" in the brain which causes addiction. Another person may abuse drugs for months or years without experiencing addiction. People with physical addiction to alcohol or drugs will experience withdrawal symptoms (tremors, anxiety, etc.) when they stop using the substance. Addiction is non-curable, but it is successfully treatable.

Recovery: A person with substance addiction can be helped to a state of RECOVERY. Recovery requires abstinence. He is never considered "cured" or "recovered" because a single indulgence of drugs (or alcohol if alcohol was his addictive substance) can trigger addiction behavior.
(http://en.wikipedia.org/wiki/Substance_use_disorder)

35

Grand Central Station

Lesson 35: The joy is in the journey

Five days following the *Friends of KCK* adult volunteers meeting, we had a "students only" Saturday Leadership Meeting. And once again, each student was given the personal choice: Do I want to sell tickets to the 3rd Annual Lunch and Listen?

Fifteen of the 20 students chose to do this and each was immediately paired with an adult. Four of the girls Haley Fulp, Jena Reisenauer, Mariah Scott, and Nicole Ward, chose to work with their mothers, who were also businesswomen. Drew Craven partnered with his grandfather and expert salesman, Bob Wilkinson.

The remaining 10 students were paired with community leaders who also made the specific choice: I want to provide transportation for students making sales calls.

Two days later, on Monday, February 22, each of the 15 student/adult teams was assigned a sales lead—a company which had sponsored a table at the last Lunch and Listen.

But prior to this, we had some work to do at our Saturday meeting. Again, believing that it is wrong to give students a job without giving them the tools to do it successfully, we learned *how* to give a Lunch and Listen sales presentation.

Each student leader—including those who chose not to sell—was given a professional 10-page sales kit. By using a clear plastic presentation folder with sheet cover protectors, it was sophisticated enough for an adult and simple enough for a student. And in fact, adults and students used the same sales kit. Best of all, the kits only cost $2.50 each to produce.

To design the kits, I tried to keep in mind my own door-to-door sales as a child, when I sold seeds, greeting cards, and other items to earn spending money. For me, the key to my confidence lay in knowing my product well and then knowing *where* to find the answers if anyone asked me questions.

With that in mind, the cover announced the name, date, and location of our event under a huge KCK logo. The second page had the basic KCK facts, followed by a flyer for the current event, last year's program which named all of last year's sponsors, a copy of the newspaper story featuring our speaker, and finally, a sales script.

> The script could be recited in two minutes and it was designed to breathe life into the Lunch and Listen and move people to sponsor a table.

To get the students familiar with the sales kit, Heather Camp and Henrietta Barrett played a game. They tossed a ball, another idea from the YES meeting, and whoever caught the ball was asked a question from the sales kit. When the student gave the right answer, he or she was tossed a piece of candy.

To keep the pressure off, all participants were free to ask for help when they were holding the ball. So everyone learned to use the sales kit at the same time.

There was an immediate incentive for students to learn to use their sales kits well. At the end of the meeting, we staged a competition. Camp and Barrett called out review questions and who ever raised his hand first and called out the correct answer received a point. The top four students received prizes from the community that included a set of diamond earrings, two free lunches, and a box of handmade chocolate truffles.

In addition to this, each of the students gave practice presentations to the other youths.

Then, Brandon Hall told his classmates how he'd sold 37 tickets the prior year using email and the telephone.

We had one final secret weapon to use against any residual fear or reluctance that might be lurking in our courageous student sales team. We called in a professional—Duane Long—and he gave the team a chance to address a real businessman.

Long, a serious but caring man and former director of the Kernersville Chamber of Commerce, was quick to school the students on the best way to approach businesses and on the power of a proper handshake.

> A firm handshake accompanied by a warm smile and direct eye contact *is* the key to connecting properly with adults in Kernersville.

So, if the students were serious about selling Lunch and Listen tickets, then mastering the art of a genuine handshake was critical for their success.

So, we practiced our confident and friendly handshake at every meeting and it became our standard mode of operation when we entered board meetings or approached adults.

This powerful meeting was led by Kelly Hall and *Friends of KCK*. They reported that because the students now had a full set of tools, they left the meeting prepared and excited to begin selling on Monday.

At that point, my role shifted. Now that we'd built an engine, my job was to shovel coal into the boiler and keep all these little trains on schedule.

To make sure that the student leaders remained in the driver's seat, I asked them to take the initiative to contact their assigned adult mentors. It was also the student's job to telephone the business prospect and schedule a sales appointment.

As for the adults, I recommended that they see themselves as the students' cheerleaders and wheels. Hopefully, they could listen to their students' practice presentation before going to the actual appointment. And I asked the adults to refrain from purchasing personal tickets until the students "earned it" by first giving a presentation.

And then, the fun began. By February 25, just four days into our sales kick-off 176 tickets were sold. Now 84 of these were purchased by the schools, but Brandon Hall sold an additional 37, followed by Drew Craven and Mariah Scott who each sold 12.

Interestingly, Mariah had given her first public speech just a month earlier at the Lions Club. Her former elementary school principal, David Fitzpatrick, was in the audience and he told me, "I couldn't believe it when I heard Mariah give her speech. I know her and when she was at my school she wouldn't speak in public if we offered her a million dollars. That proved to me what KCK can do for the kids."

When I told this to Mariah, she laughed and confirmed his observation. Then she showed me her speech. In the conclusion she'd written:

> *"KCK has helped me overcome my quiet and shy personality. Usually, I don't speak publicly, but that is also another wall that I have broken down since joining KCK."* —Mariah Scott

She ended up taking credit for six of the 12 tickets purchased by the Lion's Club, while her speaking partner, took credit for the other six.

Mariah also gave her presentation to Duane Long—her assigned lead. Mariah emailed to say that Mr. Long gave her an A+ on her presentation.

But most amazingly of all, Kelly Hall told me that she saw Mariah going store-to-store selling tickets downtown!

All of this good news went out in team emails and telephone calls to feed the kids each other's success stories so they could build enthusiasm and share sales ideas during the long 30 days between our Saturday Leadership Meetings.

By March 1, Brandon Hall sent me an email. "Hi. Sold a table to Carolina Physical Therapy, contacted Countryside Bowling—will let me know by end of week, Love That Music will let me know, going to Truliant, Juicy Java . . .Will be talking with Kernersville Police Department on March 9 and Mitchell and Bartlett this Wednesday. This is just an update: as of today 43 tickets sold, will be 49 if I get the KPD."

I forwarded his email to his teammates along with an email script that they could try.

At the same time, Dusty Nguyen was driven by his "wheels" Bobbie Wolfe to make a presentation at Körner's Folly—Kernersville's namesake historic site. Of course, the non-profit board could not use its funds to sponsor a table, but instead, individual board members bought six tickets and then named the table for the Folly.

Additionally, Bobbie Wolfe took Dusty to give his presentation to her husband, John Wolfe, the Town attorney, and Wolfe sponsored a table.

Then, as I was reading the *Kernersville News,* I noticed that Judge Ron Spivey was running for reelection. Knowing that he was part of the very first community meeting—before KCK was even conceived—I called to see if he wanted to sponsor a table. He did.

Drew Craven picked up on this idea and sold a table to Dave Griffith who was running for Sheriff. Drew also sold a table to Chick-fil-A, which was exciting to the whole team because Chick-fil-A bought breakfast for our 20 leaders at all of our Saturday meetings.

By March 3, 40 tables were sold. I emailed the team: "Hey team—we have half the tables sold now!!! This is FANTASTIC. We have never had so many tables sold before at this early date. Remember, our goal is to have all 80 tables sold by March 30 so that we can focus on our other activities . . . Keep up the EXCELLENT leadership."

In reality, at our two prior luncheons, we'd never sold a single ticket before March 3rd.

As the momentum picked up, it became a bit crazy. For a case in point, on March 10, six student speeches were given in the community. Calling and confirming with both the civic clubs and the students kept me busy, but it avoided any misunderstandings.

When I talked to the students, I reminded them to double check the directions, arrive 15 minutes early, and walk in with a smile and, of course, a KCK handshake. But really, what I was letting them know was that I cared about them personally and that I wanted them to call me when they were done and tell me all about it!

One of the speeches was actually a radio spot. WSJS emcee JR Snider interviewed Nicole Ward over the telephone and broadcast it live on radio while she was at school.

Nicole, an 8th grader at Southeast Middle School, was quickly distinguishing herself as a KCK leader by selling 12 tickets to businesses that had never before attended the luncheon, by completing the reading of Porter Halyburton's book, and by taking charge of the T-shirt selection for the student leaders.

On this same day, Nicole was scheduled to give a second speech to the Kernersville Chamber of Commerce with Michael Davis, a dynamic seventh grade student from Kernersville Middle School.

Michael and Nicole were at the Chamber by personal invitation. Bruce Boyer, the president, had heard them speak at the Kiwanis Club and they had left a lasting impression. In fact, Boyer told me, "These kids were the best speakers that we had all year. And what made it particularly impressive is that they came without any adults."

I explained to Boyer that we wanted the students to be real leaders in their real community. So once we gave them the tools, the adults stepped back and let the students make it happen.

That evening, Nicole emailed me. In an excerpt she wrote, ". . . I had an amazing time. The radio interview was kind of nerve racking at first, but I really liked it . . . it was like talking to you on the phone, very relaxed."

That warmed my heart and I wrote back, "I listened to your live broadcast and it was awesome! You really did a great job. I'm so glad that it was fun for you—

because your happiness in living by your good choices came through in your voice. Great job! Keep up the good work."

It was the constant student-adult exchanges like these that kept the steam in KCK and the drive of the kids at an all-time high. What is perhaps most astounding about this is that these 11-17 year old students were going to school full-time and most were very busy with sports. And yet, they *wanted* to get out in their community to speak and sell.

By the time the March 20 Saturday Leadership Meeting arrived, 50 tables were sold. At this meeting we had Ruth Fair, the aunt of KCK student leader Michael Davis, give a presentation on *compassionate* leadership. Earlier, we'd talked about *servant* leadership—where the leader makes other people feel special. Now, we were going to talk about compassion—awareness and empathy for those we are trying to lead.

Fair was a natural choice for this. As a *Friend of KCK*, she told me her story. It was so compelling, I wrote it and it was published in the *Kernersville News*. And now, here she was, telling it personally to the 20 student leaders. Below is an excerpt from her message.

"From my earliest memories, I felt that life was not fair. Growing up in a home where each girl had a different father, it was easy to compare the time and attention each dad gave his daughter. The fact was, my dad rarely came to see me.

I started to lie, because I did not like the truth. The truth was, my dad was an alcoholic and he didn't keep his promises and I was jealous of my sisters.

I got my attention by acting out. To compound my pain and frustration, when I was nine years old, a friend of my grandmother's began routinely molesting me.

I couldn't tell anyone because I knew that no one would believe me because I lied so much. By middle school I had earned the reputation of being a bully.

By age 14, I began smoking marijuana to calm the rage. By the age of 16, I was an emancipated teen.

From there I got an apartment and acquired a 19-year-old boyfriend who drank heavily. He moved me to Atlanta, Georgia. I had my first experience with crack cocaine. Mostly to afford this expensive habit I prostituted myself. Eventually, I landed in jail."

Thankfully, Ruth Fair reestablished contact with her mother—whom she had not talked to in 16 years—and the healing began. "At that point, I put my life in God's hands. I chose to help people instead of hurting others," Fair explained.

KCK Youth Leadership Team
2009-2010

Photo by Bob Kalbaugh, Features and News Editor, *Kernersville News,* reprinted with permission.

(L-R) Front: Juli Pascual, Dusty Nguyen, Mariah Scott, Nicole Ward (Secretary), Michael Davis, Alex Zilakakis, Dawn Jensen, Patty Jo Sawvel, Haley Fulp, Jamaal Doran, Monica Shi, Caitlin Amos, Dalinzae Hodge, Jazzmin Gentry, Drew Craven, (L-R) Top: Brandon Winbush(Vice-Pres.), Jena Reisenauer, Tecora Logan, Brandon Hall (President), Connor Hinds, Carter Maffett.

Members of this youth leadership team gave 33 presentations to civic clubs and groups in their Town during the 2009-10 school year. Students also created a positive peer influence at their schools by promoting life free of illicit drugs and underage drinking.

Additionally, they personally contacted business owners and sold 180 of the 450 tickets to their 3rd Annual KCK Lunch & Listen. Much credit for their success goes to the training and support supplied by the newly founded Friends of KCK.

Photo by Julie Knight

Police Chief Ken Gamble

Police Chief Ken Gamble (September 1, 2009) continued the strong leadership of the Kernerville Police Department in *Kernersville Cares for Kids*. Chief Gamble would like to see the *Cares for Kids* programs in other towns to help the youth.

"Kernersville Cares for Kids (KCK) is about developing student leadership. Youth become ambassadors. They become role models. They prove 'you can have fun without using drugs.' KCK supports youth leadership development." –Chief Ken Gamble

http://toknc.com

Fair pointed out to the class clearly *why* she started using drugs. It was not to have fun or to be a rebel.

> *"By using drugs, I didn't have to feel the pain or deal with any of the problems that I had."*
> —Ruth Fair, guest speaker at a KCK "students only" meeting

Then, she told the students how they could be compassionate leaders at their schools. "Approach the person who always eats lunch alone and ask if you can join her. If someone comes up to you who generally doesn't talk to anyone, don't blow that person off. Listen to what he has to say and respond back to him. It could be that he just got up enough nerve to approach you."

Fair then added, "Another thing you can do is to stand up against the ill treatment of others. For instance, if someone is bullying someone else, don't stand and watch it. Go report that person to a higher authority because the next time it could be you."

She concluded by encouraging the students to use compassion to break down the barriers with their peers and to become part of the solution.

Fair's speech really gave the kids something to think about.

> Instead of judging drug using or drinking students as "bad" or "selfish"—Fair helped them to see these classmates as people who were in pain and in need of help.

Incidentally, Fair was now living a role model life. She had accepted all the help she needed, had a wonderful job at a college and was working on her Bachelor's degree in Sociology.

It was while in this sober frame of mind that the students held an election. Again, this was the brainstorm of Heather Camp and Henrietta Barrett.

> Camp and Barrett suggested that the students elect a president, vice-president, and secretary so that they could learn organizational leadership.

Brandon Hall, who was by far the most proactive leader, easily and unanimously won the role of president after giving his speech.

Nicole Ward also won unopposed as secretary. Brandon Winbush edged out Jena Reisenauer by three votes for vice president, but Jena would come back the following year to win the seat of president when Brandon Hall went off to college.

In fact, when Jena became president, Nicole Ward would take the seat of vice-president, Tecora Logan would take her spot as secretary, and Vivian Le would fill the newly created position as KCK student historian.

Then, the students made a huge decision that reshaped their view of leadership. In past *Lunch and Listens*, the students were "Celebrity Leaders"—where the spotlight was on them.

However, this year, the KCK students voted to be "Servant Leaders" which shined the spotlight on their guests.

> **What would the youth leaders choose to be?**
> **"Celebrity Leaders"**—where the spotlight was on them.
> **"Servant Leaders"**— putting the spotlight on their guests.

Lastly, each student decided to create a personal leadership board. On the tri-fold board students put facts and photos that became their personal message to their community.

Incidentally, Brandon Hall took another opportunity to show leadership by initiating a "board party" at his house. Ten of the leaders came and worked together to complete the tri-fold boards.

These leadership boards lined the perimeter of the *Lunch and Listen* room, allowing guests to "see" the leadership of their students. Later, the boards were placed in public buildings around town so that everyone could enjoy them.

The next 30 days sped by. To add to the excitement, The *Kernersville News* ran ads to promote the luncheon. Also, *Kernersville Magazine* printed a full-page story on the KCK student leaders and a second story on Porter Halyburton in the Town's only glossy magazine. Both the newspaper and the magazine featured quotes and photos of the kids.

On April 19, we declared our Lunch and Listen a sell out! Friends of KCK and the student leaders had sold 450 tickets, up from 350 the previous year.

On April 24, four days before the Lunch and Listen, we had our final KCK Saturday Leadership Meeting. As one might imagine, we had 100% attendance and 100% attention. We did a dress rehearsal of the upcoming event and eagerly awaited Tuesday, April 27.

On the day of the event, all 20 KCK student leaders arrived at East Forsyth High School in Servant Leader mode. They helped set up the event, practiced their speeches in front of their peers, ate a "students only" lunch, studied the seating maps, and then went out to breathe life into the event and embrace their community.

As guests began to arrive, they were each greeted and seated—with a proper handshake of course, by a red-shirted KCK student leader.

Incidentally, having matching red T-shirts was Kelly Hall's idea. I voted against it, feeling that the students should be dressed up for this important event.

But Kelly thought it was more important that the students look like a team and the students agreed with her. As it worked out, this was a perfect way for guests to easily identify the 20 students who were serving them.

From 11 o'clock until noon, the red-shirts refilled drinks, visited with newcomers, and made sure all in attendance felt like celebrities.

Then, at 12 sharp, the 20 student leaders took their places behind the podium and faced the audience. Once again, the students completely owned their leadership and no adults sat with them.

When Porter Halyburton finished his dynamic speech, the students presented him with a red leader's T-shirt.

Then, KCK President Doug Kiger presented the annual KCK awards. Glenn High School came in first place in the high school competition with 82.9% of the students enrolled in the *It's My Call* drug-free pledging and random testing program. East Forsyth High School had 76% of its student body enrolled.

As Kiger noted, the Kernersville high schools had about 150% more students in the *It's My Call* program than the district average. Additionally, both high schools did better than they had in years. Principal Brad Craddock claimed Glenn's trophy.

Then Kiger announced that East Forsyth Middle School had an unbelievable 99.1% of its students enrolled in the *voluntary* drug-testing program. Principal Dossie Poteat was able to lead his school to a level never before achieved in Kernersville or anywhere else known in the nation.

Southeast Middle came in at 90.2% and Kernersville Middle finished at 87.2%. Again, this was all very significant as the middle schools in Kernersville have 200% more students enrolled in this voluntary plan than the average middle school enrollment in the district.

On that high note, President Kiger then announced the KCK student leaders special program—*We Need You*.

This was a new idea and it came from a question that Kelly Hall asked, "Why can't all the student leaders speak at the *Lunch and Listen*?" In looking for a way to make that happen, we came up with the brainstorm of having each student give a 15-second message. The goal was to use this time as a "teaching moment."

Once Kiger announced them, the students lined up and one-by-one approached the microphone. To help the speakers relax, we encouraged the students to take the focus off themselves and to speak up for students who didn't have a voice.

Some of the messages were very serious.

"**Parents**: We need you. We need you to know the truth about underage drinking. If you allow us to break the drinking law, we are six times more likely to abuse marijuana than teens who obey the law. Please don't allow us to drink alcohol."

"**Students**: We need you. We need you to stand up and speak up when you see anyone being mistreated. The best way to stop bullying is for *everyone* to come to the aid of the victim *every time* it happens."

"**Parents**: We need you. We need you to know the truth about teen smoking. The truth is, young people who smoke before the age of 18 are 10 times more likely to use drugs than their non-smoking peers. Please, don't allow us to smoke."

"**Students**: We need you. We need you to know that it is okay if you don't like yourselves. One study showed that 90% of graduating seniors did not like themselves. The good news is, you are the only person you can change. So make a choice to make one small change every day."

"**Parents**: We need you. We need you to know that sexually abused children are 26 times more likely to use drugs. If your child has ever been molested, know that your child may need professional help."

The students also had a little humor, such as when tall Brandon Hall towered over the microphone and said, "Mom and Dad: We need you. We need you both—that's right dad—to give us a hug every day—even if we are six feet tall."

And, there was plenty of thanks, as when our smallest and newest leader, sixth grader, Alex Zilakakis, said, "Mayor Morgan and Aldermen: We need you. We need you to keep creating a role model government by directly supporting *Kernersville Cares for Kids* even when the budget is tight."

Then, Michael Davis, Nicole Ward, and Brandon Hall each gave a three-minute speech. This was followed by a short final conclusion by Principal Dossie Poteat.

That was supposed to be the end of the program, but instead, KCK had a surprise planned. They knew that this was my last year with KCK and they wanted to tell me thank you.

So Dr. Martin, Mr. Owensby, and Captain Kiger—representing KCK's founding co-sponsors—presented me with a Service Award and kind words of thanks.

Then, the 20 student leaders gave me flowers and much more credit than I deserved. And I, of course, told the truth. This record-breaking year—in IMC drug testing enrollments and in Lunch and Listen attendance—would not have been possible without these 20 kids. They made it happen.

And with that, KCK came full circle. To the highest degree, the students—in word and deed—really were driving the KCK train.

However, a few misunderstandings needed to be addressed before I completely retired from the KCK board.

www.UnderTheInfluence.org

2010 3rd Annual KCK Lunch & Listen

All photos on this page were taken by East Forsyth H.S. Student Stephanie Smith

ALL 20 KCK YOUTH LEADERS SPOKE to a sell-out crowd of 450 people at this event. They had a powerful message: WE NEED YOU. The 20 leaders wore red-shirts and practiced "servant leadership" shining the spotlight on their guests and assuring that everyone felt cared for by the youth. (L-R) Michael Davis, Brandon Hall (Pres.), Nicole Ward (Sec.). Right photo: KCK Pres. Doug Kiger.

Keynote speaker Porter Halyburton (left) told the crowd that when he stepped through the gates, ending his torture and confinement as a POW in Vietnam the following happened: *"I looked back and I said, 'I forgive you' and all that hatred fell away. And that day, I left two prisons, the Hoalo and the prison of hatred. Forgiveness is the final lesson, a choice you make."*

Patty Jo Sawvel gets a surprise farewell hug from Brandon Hall and the youth team. Sawvel handed the baton to the next generation of leaders.

Principal Dossie Poteat sets all-time record for voluntary student drug-testing – 99.1% signed up at East Forsyth Middle School.

Compassionate Leadership

"Stand up against the ill treatment of others. For instance, if someone is bullying someone else, don't stand and watch it. Go report that person to a higher authority because the next time it could be you."
–Ruth Fair

Fair's nephew, (left) Michael Davis was a KCK student leader who invited his Aunt Ruth to speak at a KCK "Students Only" meeting.

Ruth Fair

"Plenty of kids have natural leadership abilities. Our job is to teach them to use their leadership to help others and to lead others in a good way."

–Kelly Hall, 4th grade teacher Cash Elementary KCK Volunteer & Board Member

Kelly Hall leads the monthly "Students only Saturday Leadership Meetings at the Kernersville Police Station.

http://www.kernersvillecaresforkids.org

Leadership From the Top

Even though *Kernersville Cares for Kids* is student-driven, it is leadership from the principals and staff– their listening and responding in a positive manner– that builds momentum within the student body.

"How do you get 99% of your students to sign up for voluntary random drug-testing? You make it important and you keep it fun."

–*Principal Dossie Poteat*
East Foryth Middle School

Principal Dossie Poteat, who repeatedly enrolls over 99% of his students in the IMC voluntary drug-testing program.

Principal Trish Gainey
East Forsyth High

"You can't teach them until you can reach them. In other words, our first job is to build a trusting relationship with each student and then the students will respond."– **Principal Trish Gainey**

Principal Brad Craddock of Glenn High School said, "My goal is to get to know every student by name. Having a positive influence begins by building relationships with my students."

36

Passing the Baton

Lesson 36: Transitions take time

"I want you to really hear me," Principal Trish Gainey said to me privately.

> *"It's great that the students are coming up with ideas, but sometimes we feel like they push us into a corner. We are made to look like the 'bad guys' if we can't let them do everything they think of. Maybe the adults can come up with the ideas and present them to the kids."*
> —Principal Trish Gainey

She then specifically referenced the Christmas Parade incident. I was glad that she brought this up, because though this happened six months earlier and I addressed it at the time, clearly it was not resolved.

And I was happy that Principal Gainey brought it to my attention, because she traditionally is courageous enough to say what everyone else is thinking.

Additionally, I sensed that some of the adult board members thought that since I'd turned my attention to student leadership, maybe this was a case of the tail wagging the dog. Maybe these weren't student ideas at all. Maybe I was just using the students as a mouthpiece for my own ideas.

At the next board meeting, President Kiger gave me some time to address this. I restated Principal Gainey's concerns and then reminded the board that I was just as shocked as they were at the November board meeting when the students announced that they wanted to have a float in the Town's Christmas Parade.

Kelly Hall had led that Saturday "students only" meeting, because I was with my family in Michigan. Furthermore, I would never suggest participation in a Christmas event because I don't even celebrate Christmas. I'm one of Jehovah's Witnesses and I honor Jesus in a completely different way.

But the real issue for the board was not the actual event. Some of the board members were upset because the kids had only given them a couple weeks' notice. In that short time, liability and insurance had to be addressed, permissions obtained, and a float had to be constructed.

As it worked out, Kelly Hall and the student leaders and *Friends of KCK* did all the planning, building, and acquiring of materials. And Assistant Principal Scott Muncie from East Forsyth High School drove the float to satisfy the liability requirements.

This issue came up again when the students wanted to have an "after party" at a restaurant immediately following the Lunch and Listen. It sounded easy. Penny Goodloe, owner of BOOMR'Z Restaurant, offered to host the party and to pick up the tab, but it would take tremendous planning to coordinate permissions, transportation, and supervision of 20 students off campus.

In the end, both events happened. And I conceded that when you are working with kids, they are bound to come up with plenty of ideas—some feasible and some not. So I suggested that the board expect this and set up a protocol.

In short, I recommended that they treat these children the same way that they treated their own.

"When my children were younger," I explained, "they might come to me all excited and ask, 'Mom, can we go to the movies with Mary tonight?' Then I would ask: 1) What is the name of the movie? 2) What is the rating? 3) What time is it playing? 4) What about transportation and who will be with you? 5) What night of the week is it?"

"If my children said it was Wednesday," I continued, "I'd say, 'You know that we don't go to the movies or do other social activities on school nights. But, what about Saturday?'"

So I was not framed as a "mean mom" because I tried to support their good ideas and say yes as much as possible. But, they knew our rules and their ideas had to work for everyone.

In a similar way, the adult KCK board could come up with some parameters regarding lead time, cost, and other factors that could be used as a measuring stick for all future ideas.

Whatever means the board chose to solve this problem, one thing was for sure:

> It would be a mistake for the adults to come up with the ideas and dictate them to the students. That would not be leadership, that would be school.

Another visceral feeling on the board was that the students should not *have* to sell tickets to the Lunch and Listen.

But here again, it was just a matter of getting the adults and the students on the same page. The students were not "pushed" or "browbeaten" into selling tickets.

This was *their* idea! It gave them an opportunity to do something real and something measurable in the *adult* community. This was a thrilling adventure for them, especially once they were assigned their own personal set of "wheels."

I was getting emails from the kids, like the one that Dusty Nguyen sent on March 11. He wrote, "Do I need your permission to go to a store to see if they would buy a table? And what other places could I go to sell a table, because I still want to help out."

Dusty ended up selling 19 tickets. Nicole Ward sold 21, and Drew Craven sold a whopping 36. However, it was Brandon Hall who raised the bar when he personally sold 69 tickets.

In all, the 20 KCK student leaders sold 180 tickets. The schools bought 90. And the *Friends of KCK*—primarily led by Henrietta Barrett and Irvin Grigg—sold the remaining 180 tickets.

Could the adults have sold all the tickets without the kids? Sure. But that would have robbed the students of the personal opportunity to breathe life into their idea—the definition of being a real leader.

And they would have missed every word of encouragement, every smile of approval, every ounce of community solidarity that happened each time an adult drove them to an appointment, or an adult bought a ticket, or an adult commended them for a job well done.

On the flip side, could the students have sold all the tickets without the adult leadership? Not likely. After all, these 11-17 year olds have limited life experience. They needed and craved constant adult feedback and direction. And this brought up another issue that was bothering some adult board members. Some principals felt that I was calling the students too much, perhaps bothering them.

But from the parents' and the *students' point of view*, it was an honor for the students to receive a telephone call from a caring adult. In fact, at the celebration at BOOMR'Z, most of the "roast" was spent with students giggling and impersonating me calling them on the telephone.

> From the parents' and the *students' point of view*, it was an honor for the students to receive a telephone call from a caring adult.

Jamaal Doran, the group's only senior and the leader that gave the invocation at the *Lunch and Listen*, probably said it best, "Hello Jamaal," he said mimicking my voice into hand, "How are you?" Then, in his own voice, "Great, Miss Patty Jo." "Good. Good," he replied in my habitual double affirmation. "Did you meet with John Staples today? How did it go?"

Each time he nailed my conversation style, his peers laughed and then someone else would pick up one of my weird mannerisms.

But one thing was clear, these students knew me and they knew that I knew them. They thrived on having an adult that cared enough to call.

That brought up the third and final point that I discussed with the board. I really felt that the KCK youth deserved a paid director. I wasn't interested in the job. I really wanted to take Kernersville's success story and give the kids a national voice.

But I asked the board:

> "What was it that made this year so dynamic? It is that we *invested* in the kids and gave them more time, more tools and more adult leadership to do REAL things in their REAL community."

To me, a paid director is like the glue that holds all the pieces together. Or, maybe a director is like the eye of a needle. All events and ideas thread through this one eye and then that thread can be used to stitch together the students, the schools, the adult community, and the board—uniting the fabric of the Town into the strongest and healthiest community possible.

As my final pitch, I asked, "Why does a police force of 50 capable officers need a chief? Why does a school system with 50 competent principals need a superintendent? So why does KCK—which serves 5,000 local students—need a director?"

The board did see a need to reassign some of the leadership responsibilities when I left, as Kelly Hall was a full-time teacher and a full-time mother of two. She made it clear that whereas she could coach the 20 student leaders at monthly Saturday meetings, she would not be able to man Grand Central Station.

Ultimately, the board decided to give modest stipends to teachers at each of the five schools to help the 20 leaders and train even more student leaders on-site at each school. And this was definitely a move in the right direction.

Of course, the real litmus test for any board action is to ask, *"From the students' viewpoint,* how effective is this strategy?"

With all of that said, I closed my presentation by highly commending the KCK board for a job well done. Then I shared with them two brief stories.

Drew Craven recently told me that he was at a party with his friends. "We saw a couple kids to go into the woods to use marijuana. We had to decide what we were going to do. I told my friends that I didn't want to do that. They said that they didn't want to do that either. They listened to me," Drew said proudly.

> The ability to stand up and speak up to peers—at the very point of decision—that makes our student leadership powerful.

And I believe that when we train our students to speak up in front of 10 or 100 or 450 adults, it makes speaking up in front of their peers so much easier.

But it doesn't always happen that way.

> One of our student leaders told me that he or she experimented with drugs. When I asked the student *why*, the student said, *"Drugs are so glorified in popular music and in the movies that it makes it seem like they really can't be that bad."* The peer pressure brought to bear by the entertainment community in the U.S. is real. It is extreme and it is intense. KCK's work is highly relevant.

Thankfully, this student immediately recognized drug use as a mistake. The student told his or her parents and received the needed help. And this was limited to a one-time regret.

So make no mistake. What KCK does for its students is relevant. It is necessary. And it keeps kids from being fooled twice.

Noting the facial expressions around the table, I think that this story had more of an impact on the KCK board than probably anything else that I'd shared with them. They were determined to keep KCK going and growing. And I now felt free to retire from the board.

KCK Youth Leadership Team
2010-2011

Photo by News Reporter Wendy Freeman Davis, reprinted with permission of *Kernersville News*.

Youth from the local high schools and middle schools spearhead the promotion of *"It's My Call"*—a program designed to give students the tools to make the choice to remain free of illicit drugs and underage drinking. Pictured back to front,(L-R): Jena Reisenaur, Brandon Hall, Nicole Ward, Carter Maffett, Brandon Winbush, Conner Hinds, Drew McIntosh, Christopher Hinton, Kendal Dodd, Mariah Scott, Jazzmin Gentry, Dawn Jensen, Drew Craven, Alex Zilakakis, Silvia Ruiz, Brooke Ramsey, Tecora Logan.

"If students fail the random drug-test, they are not punished. No one at school finds out. They are given FREE HELP to get back on the drug-free path."

–Nicole Ward, KCK Youth Leaders Vice-President 2011-12

2011 4th Annual KCK Lunch & Listen

It's all about the kids! Kernersville youth embrace their adult community while sharing a meal and a motivating speech that raises new possibilities.

(Right) Kelly Hall, leader of the youth team's Saturday Leadership Meetings, reviews the final details before each of the 20 youth meets and greets the guests. Each youth leader spoke at the event with a WE THANK YOU message.

Keynote speaker Captain Ivan Castro (left), the only blind officer serving in US Army Special Forces
(pictured with Korben Hiatt)

"One of my greatest challenges in being blind is being in need of asking for help. A lesson for you for life experience is to ask for help. That is an integral part of life. We are not on this earth alone." –Captain Ivan Castro

37

The Handoff is Complete

Lesson 37: It is okay to let go

On Tuesday, April 26, 2011, *Kernersville Cares for Kids* celebrated its 4th *Annual Lunch and Listen.* I sat among the 250 attendees and heard guest speaker Captain Ivan Castro tell the audience that if a blind U.S. Army Special Forces officer could run marathons and rebuild his life, then surely students could overcome any obstacle.

> Captain Ivan Castro—the only blind officer serving in the US Army Special Forces—encouraged the students to always take the hard right instead of the easy wrong.

I watched proudly as the 20 student leaders did a variation on the 15-second *We Need You* messages by changing it to a gracious *We Thank You.* Yes, KCK had survived without me and I couldn't be more proud.

However, some of the teens told me that KCK had lost some momentum. There were fewer public speaking opportunities and less involvement in ticket sales for the student leaders this year. But I told them that this was to be expected.

If I were literally to hand a baton to another runner, I would slow down and make absolutely certain that the new runner had the baton firmly in hand before I let go. So, KCK slowed down out of necessity.

I encouraged the student leaders to be patient, to communicate their needs, and to keep up the good work.

And in taking a closer look, while the format of leadership training was different than the previous year, there was new growth in other areas.

> Kelly Hall, who took charge of the Saturday "students only" meetings asked the youth some important questions early in the year.
> *"What is another way that we can connect with the community? What festivals does our Town have that we can get involved in?"*

That led to the students' first involvement in the Annual Honeybee Festival—held every third Saturday in September, drawing a crowd of 10,000 people.

When the Kernersville Police Department suggested that KCK design a mural for the police department's Clean Slate program, Kelly Hall initiated a friendly competition. Ultimately, the mural created by Carter Maffett, an 8th grade student at

Community Festivals and Events

Youth Leaders love being active in their adult community festivals.

KCK student leaders set up their tent and activities for children of all ages. Everyone wins a prize! Additionally, KCK distributes information on how to help children grow up drug-free.

KCK Three Co-sponsors 2011-12

Photo Wendy Freeman Davis
Winston-Salem Forsyth County Schools
Superintendent Don Martin

Photo Julie Knight
Kernersville Police
Chief Ken Gamble

Photo Wendy Freeman Davis
Kernersville News
Publisher John Owensby

Kernersville Cares for Kids

President
Captain Doug Kiger

Vice-President
David Fitzpatrick

Treasurer
Curtis Swisher

Secretary
Dana Caudill Jones

East Forsyth High School
Principal Trish Gainey

Glenn High School
Principal Brad Craddock

East Forsyth Middle School
Principal Dossie Poteat

Kernersville Middle School
Principal Sharon Porter

Southeast Middle School
Principal Stephanie Gentry

Board Members 2011-12

First Christian Academy
Principal Bonnie McDaniel

Bishop McGuinness H.S.
Bob Koepf, teacher

Safe & Drug-free Schools Program
Kathy Jordan

Community Rep
Kelly Hall
Saturday Leader Coach

Community Rep
Bob Prescott

Community Rep
Wendy Ward
Saturday Leader Coach

Kernersville Cares for Kids (KCK) was created by the people of Kernersville for the students of Kernersville to *lead by example*. Primarily, KCK raises money, awareness, and community-connectedness *to strengthen our students* to do their part to keep themselves, their schools, and their community drug free.

KCK board photographs by Wendy Freeman Davis, Governmental Affairs Reporter for the *Kernersville News*

KCK Youth Board Members

Jena Reisenauer
KCK President
GHS

Nicole Ward
KCK Vice-Pres.
GHS

Tecora Logan
KCK Secretary
GHS

Vivian Le
KCK Historian
SEMS

Connor Hinds
GHS

Ariel Thomas
FCA

Jacob Hauk
FCA

Sierra Clontz
FCA

Matthew Hecht
FCA

Jonah Compton
FCA

Carly Toccoa Keenan
EFHS

Mariah Scott
EFHS

Taylor Marsh
EFHS

Brandon Winbush
EFHS

Caitlin Amos
EFHS

Carter Maffett
EFHS

2011-2012 School Year

Drew Cone
EFHS

Caroline Caporossi
BMHS

Emily Corsig
BMHS

Caitlin Ferguson
BMHS

Tory Bowers
BMHS

Kayla Hatton
EFMS

Chris Hinton
EFMS

Meagan Piatt
EFMS

Kyndal Dodd
EFMS

Sabrina Martin
KMS

Drew McIntosh
KMS

Madison Cone
KMS

Silvia Ruiz
KMS

Alex Zilakakis
KMS

Zane Willard
SEMS

Michaela Smith
SEMS

East Forsyth Middle School, was selected, and then painted on a 4x8 sheet of plywood by the students to become a mobile mural for use around town.

Carter's mural, *Many Hands, One Voice*, features five hands with wristband logos from the five public middle and high schools in Kernersville depicting support for KCK and the *It's My Call* program. This was later updated to seven hands as two private schools, Bishop McGuinness Catholic H.S. and First Christian Academy, joined *Kernersville Cares for Kids.*

The goal of the project is to place a mural over graffiti because taggers generally respect art and will take their spray paints elsewhere.

It was clear that the teens really thrived under Kelly Hall's stellar leadership and she was assisted by Nicole Ward's mom, Wendy. As Caitlin Amos, a sophomore at East Forsyth High School said, "Mrs. Hall is a very hands-on leader and we really liked working with her."

In inquiring about the adult KCK board, President Kiger told me that all the previously elected board members held their positions, and Kelly Hall, Wendy Ward, and Dana Caudill Jones were elected to serve on the board. Hall and Ward each have a child that serves as a KCK student leader, but Jones was interested in the KCK board because she was inspired by one of the student leaders.

Jones, a Town alderman for many years, knew of KCK from its onset. As a matter of fact, she was at the initial Leadership Meeting and planned to serve on the Middle School Committee, but then declined when I changed the expectations.

But in 2010, her family's company, Caudill Electric, hired KCK student leader Brandon Hall. One day, she sat down with Brandon to get to know him better as a person. She asked him how school was going.

"He shared a few things and then he told me about KCK and Carl Clarke," Jones said. "He told me that he was apprehensive about speaking in front of adults but that he worked with Mr. Clarke. I could really see that he was excited. KCK was doing more than helping him make good choices. It was giving him resources. I could see the light bulbs turning on in his eyes. I could see his growing confidence."

> *"I like to see us bring resources to young people to build strength of character and to help them be a leader to their peers and show them how to give back to their community. I wanted to make sure that this continued and that KCK lived up to its name, so I got involved."*
> —Dana Caudill Jones

According to KCK President Doug Kiger, Dana Caudill Jones was one of two people that really stepped forward in the 2010-11 school year. "When we needed someone to help with the ticket sales," Captain Kiger said, "Dana said she would make the calls and she did it."

In preparation for the 2011-12 school year, Jones is currently scheduling public speaking opportunities for the student leaders, bringing in adult community leaders to present leadership ideas at Hall's Saturday meetings, and arranging for more public speaking training for the team.

Kernersville Magazine, by publisher Michael Church, recently featured Mariah Scott (left) and Nicole Ward in a story about KCK. Mariah told the readers that she was tempted by friends to sneak alcohol. *"I was able to be strong. I was able to say, 'No thanks, I'm good.' Instead of me being embarrassed, I think they were embarrassed that they asked . . . Kernersville Cares for Kids has made a difference in my life. I used to be very shy and now I speak up. Helping other kids is my favorite part of being a KCK student leader."*

http://www.kernersvillemagazine.com

The other person to step up was East Forsyth High School Principal Trish Gainey. She helped with most of the KCK projects and especially focused on the *Lunch and Listen*.

In a newspaper interview, I learned from Principal Gainey that she was an unlikely candidate for a public school principal, because she was actually a very mediocre and sometimes struggling student in high school.

Like many students, she did not let herself be defined by her grades or test scores. Instead, she excelled in and built self-esteem by her participation in Girl Scouts and sports.

Early in life she learned to stand up for the underdog and overcome any obstacles in her path.

In her own words, "I am always out to prove myself."

So I asked her, "Why are you so committed to KCK and determined to see it succeed?"

Principal Gainey responded, "I think the reason that I have stepped up is that we have principals that do not know the history of KCK and I'm not willing to let it falter. They do not understand what it took to get us here. When Dr. Martin and I retire, we need to be sure that we have led our newer board members so that they can step up when we are not here."

KCK has one other asset that will likely insure its success. As Mayor Morgan told me at the last luncheon:

> *"I believe that it's the students' enthusiasm that makes KCK such a success. Students leading students really does change attitudes about drug and alcohol use."* —Mayor Dawn Morgan

She added, "Patty Jo, I believe that this *high level of student commitment* insures that Kernersville Cares for Kids will continue to be an important part of our community for years to come."

Though she could not have predicted this, it looks like the students will soon bolster KCK in a way that's never been done to date.

As Brandon Hall attended his final KCK board meeting before heading off to North Carolina State University, he promised the board:

> *"When I come back in four years, I plan to join the KCK board."* —KCK Student Board President Brandon Hall

This will make him the first person to experience KCK as a student leader and then return to serve the community as an adult KCK board member. And if I know Brandon Hall, he will recruit his peers to step up and follow suit.

One Year Later—Remarkable Growth in 2012

Support for Kernersville Cares for Kids and the random drug testing program was at an all-time high in the year following the original publication of this book. Remarkably, 84 percent of all the middle and high schools students in Kernersville joined the "It's My Call" drug testing program.

As 9th grader, Sierra Clontz said, "This program is not just a meeting or a pep rally once in a while. *It's a way of life.* It's me saying, 'I am pledging to steer clear from things I know will have a negative outcome in my life.'"

Genuine community care is at the very heart of this successful program. Care can be measured in many ways. For youth, they believe it when they see it. Zane Willard, also a 9th grader noted, "I see Kernersville caring for kids right before my eyes. I see caring adults who want to fix this problem. This really leaves an impression on me."

For adults, *care* is often measured by how much financial support that it attracts. Here again, support for KCK has exceeded previous years. KCK board member, Bob Prescott organized a golf tournament and raised over $5,000 this year, twice as much as last year. And when Kernersville Foundation handed KCK President Doug Kiger a check for $2,800, he was told that more people earmarked their donation to be directed to KCK than to any other program. Additionally, the Town of Kernersville once again awarded a $6,500 grant to KCK.

The community heartily embraced the students at another successful Lunch and Listen. Former convict and recovering addict Fred Moore keynoted the event and enthusiastically engaged the question of the day, "How do you make a good decision?"

The KCK board also made some landmark changes that continue to keep the program viable. One of the biggest adjustments entailed replacing the monthly Saturday student leadership meetings with "in school" meetings. Each month, all the student leaders and the six KCK school coaches meet for one hour in the morning at a host school. This allows more students to attend and it's had some beneficial results.

"The new format of the KCK meetings gives *the coaches* a better understanding of how to *work together* to guide and support the KCK student leaders so they can feel comfortable being role models for their peers," observed KCK Coach Ginnie Tate.

It also empowers the students. According to KCK Coach Alicia Cone, "I have seen a transformation in our student leaders. The students have taken ownership and are *applying positive peer pressure to persuade their classmates* to stay drug, alcohol and tobacco free."

The student meeting that I observed in November 2012 was powerful. Guest speaker General James R. Gorham (retired National Guard 2012) told the youth that he was willing to die for what he believed in. Then he challenged the students, "Will you sacrifice your reputation, your popularity, or your coolness in order to defend what you know to be right and to help others to stay free of drugs and alcohol?"

All of this—the increased student engagement, the community's unprecedented backing, and the board's strong leadership—give me the answer to the number one question I am asked when I speak to other communities about this program: How is KCK doing now that you have stepped aside? Irrefutably, *Kernersville Cares for Kids* is alive and doing well!

Additionally, Dr. Don Martin, who will retire in June 2013, approved for this book, *Under the Influence: The Town That Listened to Its Kids* to be used in all 32 middle and high schools in the district as a resource for health and Physical Education classes. In support of this, special training was offered to 110 teachers in December 2012, with online instruction available for those who could not attend. And while Dr. Martin authorized a grant for $7,510 to spark funding for the project, it was the community—individual businesses—that actually sponsored the classroom sets of books and proved to kids throughout the district that Forsyth County cares about its kids.

It's refreshing to know that as KCK enters its 15th year of operation in 2013—it is solidly embraced by a community committed to its success. Knowing this gives me freeness of speech to recommend to communities across the nation a program that genuinely empowers youth to work together to steer clear of drugs and underage drinking.

As Kernersville's Mayor Dawn Morgan said so aptly, "Helping students actively promote a drug-free and alcohol-free lifestyle to their peers really works. It's a good model and other communities should consider using it."

> *"I believe KCK encourages students to Lead by Example and leaders make a difference within the community."*
> —Captain Doug Kiger, KCK president

> **Leaders breathe life into ideas &**
> **move people to action.**
> —*Inspired by Kernersville Cares for Kids*
>
> http://www.kernersvillecaresforkids.org/

Three Youth Who Lit A Fire

Annie Orchard, age 15, interrupted an adult KCK board meeting on April 12, 2007, to ask, *"Why can't we have a booth at Spring Folly?"*

This was the first time a student ever initiated a KCK project and the board fully supported her. It marked the beginning of students having a genuine voice on the KCK board and primed an artesian well of ideas that is still flowing.

Jena Reisenauer, age 15, on September 19, 2009, asked, *"Why can't we sell the(Lunch and Listen) tickets?* This moved 14 of her peers at the Saturday "Students Only" leadership meeting to join her and resulted in a brand new adventure and community connection for everyone. Jena was voted 2011 KCK student president.

Brandon Hall is a quiet leader. He is a doer. Brandon was the only student to sell tickets in 2008, and sold 17 for $35 each. In 2009, he sold 39 and in 2010, he sold 69. His motivation? *"I plan to open a business here after I return from college. So this is a way for me to get to know my community."* At the age of 15, Brandon Hall already saw himself as a useful part of the adult community. In 2010 , he was unanimously voted the first KCK student president and in 2011, he was awarded KCK's Kiger College Scholarship. He'll be back and plans to serve on the KCK adult board.

KCK Youth Board Members

Carter Maffett
KCK President
EFHS

Taylor Marsh
KCK Vice-Pres.
EFHS

Zane Willard
KCK Secretary
GHS

Vivian Le
KCK Historian
SEMS

Brandon Winbush
EFHS

Drew Cone
EFHS

Jacob Hauk
FCA

Sierra Clontz
FCA

Nick D'Andrea
FCA

Jonah Compton
FCA

Garrett Grounds
FCA

Ariel Thomas
FCA

Karina Johnson
FCA

Michaela Smith
GHS

Tecora Logan
GHS

Kyndal Dodd
GHS

2012-2013 School Year

Anayanci Calvo
EFMS

Frank Vereen
EFMS

Alexa Langley
EFMS

Addison Watson
EFMS

Matthew Brown
EFMS

Sabrina Martin
KMS

Felicia Elliott
KMS

Madison Cone
KMS

Brett Surmons
SEMS

Jazmine Calvin
SEMS

Coach Tate
EFHS

Coach Curry
GHS

Coach Smith
EFMS

Coach Cone
FCA

Coach Lineberry
KMS

Coach Derrah
SEMS

Students Enrolled in Random Drug-testing
WS/FC Schools HIGH School Enrollment

High School	2010-2011 % enrolled	2011-2012 % enrolled
Atkins	12.4	46.7
Carver	**94.9**	**94.9**
East	**77.2**	**84.4**
Carter Voc	14.8	30.5
Glenn	**78.8**	**82.7**
Middle College	35.0	47.8
Mt. Tabor	51.2	49.7
North	54.8	45.6
Paisley IB	60.3	62.9
Parkland	49.4	48.3
Reynolds	45.3	44.6
Reagan	64.3	68.9
Walkertown	(new school)	32.8
West	64.6	64.0
WS Prep Acad.	53.9	71.2
Early College of Forsyth	100.0	100.0

Students Enrolled in Random Drug-testing
WS/FC Schools MIDDLE School Enrollment

Middle School	2010-2011 % enrolled	2011-2012 % enrolled
Clemmons	**85.0**	**86.9**
East Forsyth	**99.4**	**92.6**
Flat Rock	43.6	26.0
Hanes	2.8	8.9
Hill	44.2	43.5
Kennedy	61.3	6.2
Kernersville	**83.3**	**84.9**
Meadowlark	19.0	5.0
Mineral Springs	39.3	24.0
Northwest	67.3	44.0
Paisley	56.9	47.3
Philo	4.3	1.6
Southeast	**75.2**	**74.3**
Jefferson	6.6	20.2
Walkertown	52.0	27.9
Wiley	42.0	24.5
WSPA	44.5	48.0

Giving Kids a National Voice

Fox 8 with anchor Bob Buckley and cameraman Eric Sander were the first **TV team** to move *Under the Influence* beyond Forsyth County. Deb Mitchell (far right) spotlighted KCK in the 2011 Philanthropic Awards.

Reporter Anna Johnson (left) wrote a front page story in the **Sanford Herald** about KCK kids.

Sanford, NC Radio hosts Margaret Murchison of WFJA (left) and Lil Barrett of WDSG spread the research on how to drug proof young people and take positive action.

Jim Longworth, **TV host of abc45,** interviewed students about why they choose to stay drug free.

Austin, Texas anchor for KXAN Sally Hernandez (left) and **Cable 8** Greensboro Glimpses anchor Jay Lambeth (right).

For over 10 years, Cable 2 of Forsyth County, managed by Chris Runge and TJ James, have given teens a voice on television.

TJ James

Chris Runge

A Brief Look at the National Picture

So where does the country go from here? On a national level, the government—which apparently no longer has a war on drugs—has some tough choices to make.

Legalization?

There is going to be increasing pressure to legalize recreational drugs. In large measure, the pressure will be money-driven because the illegal drug trade is one of the most profitable businesses in the world. Some would argue that if Americans regularly consume huge amounts of drugs, why not legalize the drug trade?

It might seem that in this way the government could control the safety and quality of drugs and the country could benefit from increased tax revenues. This line of reasoning will likely become almost impossible to resist if addiction become *curable*.

However, this logic reminds me of the faulty thinking that led to the sexual revolution in the 1960s after the advent of the birth control pill. Apparently believing that unwanted pregnancy was the primary negative consequence from engaging in sex outside of marriage, people failed to predict that multiple sexual partners would lead to other problems, such as skyrocketing diseases, emotional turmoil, and the breakdown of family stability. This last item, the eroding of the family unit—the cornerstone of society—has cost the country dearly.

In like manner, the real risk of legalized recreational drugs is *not* addiction. The real risk lies in tipping the balance for millions of people in favor of impaired judgment versus sound-in-mind thinking; self-indulgence versus self-control; disconnection with reality versus courageously facing the facts; and no doubt countless other risks people are not aware of yet.

A Health Problem?

In 2011, President Obama stated that drug abuse is a public health problem. And, according to a survey released August 15, 2011, adults across the nation agree with him, at least when it involves children.

The press release about the survey stated: "**Adults rate drug abuse** and childhood obesity as the **top health concerns for kids** in their communities, according to the fifth annual survey of the top 10 health concerns for kids conducted by the University of Michigan C.S. Mott Children's Hospital National Poll on Children's Health." {For the complete report visit www.uofmhealth.org/news/top-ten-national-poll-0815}

In view of this, and taking into account the current escalation in youth drug abuse, why not treat this like any other pervasive childhood disease? For instance, tuberculosis TB testing is still done in many schools because if it remains undetected, it can have dire consequences for the carrier and for those around him.

Looking at a TB model, why not *randomly* test (so there is no chance to cheat) all students from age 11 through graduation? And then, if students fail the drug test, give them the help that they need. As with any other health issue, there would be no need to punish, criminalize, or make public the child's health issue. The goal would be to genuinely respect the child and help him resolve the underlying issues that are causing the symptom of drug abuse.

But how much would that cost? To put that into perspective, it might be helpful to find out how much it costs to ignore the problem.

According to the U.S. Department of Justice dated February 2010, "The trafficking and abuse of drugs in the United States affects nearly all aspects of our lives. **The economic cost alone is immense, estimated at nearly $215 billion.** The damage caused by drug abuse and addiction is reflected in an overburdened justice system, a strained healthcare system, lost productivity, and environmental destruction."

{For the complete report Google "what is the cost of drug abuse to society" or visit www.justice.gov/ndic/pubs38/38661/drugimpact.htm }

Of course, putting a national drug-testing policy into place would be quite an investment in the young people. And it would take time for the existing economic damages to lessen. But, think of the message it would send. Drug abuse is serious. Drug abuse is a symptom. Abusing drugs means that you need help. This leads to another question:

What Message is the National Village Sending its Youth?

Beginning with the widely accepted premise that a nation divided against itself can not stand—what *is* the *united national view* of recreational or illicit drugs?

Government and the school officials broadcast that illicit drug use is harmful and irresponsible. However, a powerful segment of the entertainment industry often disagrees and actually promotes recreational drug use as acceptable, popular, and even glorified. What's a kid to do with two "parents" in his Village influencing or even pushing him in opposite directions? And more importantly, why does America *tolerate* the relentless infusion of pro-drug propaganda through its powerful entertainment industry?

On the flip side, why do people *consume and create a market* for such false and misguided ideas? One answer is gradualism. The children's hit movie Shrek 2 had a very obvious drug reference. Why?

So, in deciding whether to watch the movie or not, parents had to answer a question: Am I going to let this one little message keep my children from watching what is otherwise a great family show? And so, sometimes the consumer can allow a little more, and a little more, until they completely lose sight of their own boundaries.

At some point, *the government*, which enacted drug laws to *protect its citizens*—back in 1914 when all drugs were legal—*may need to act again*. It may need to create guidelines and consequences for harmful pro-drug propaganda *to protect its people.*

And yet, merely changing the national voice will not be enough. Each individual community decides for itself its own attitude about, and tolerance for, illicit drug use in its jurisdiction.

What Can be Learned From One Small Town?

Peering into the future at the community level—Kernersville and its namesake *Cares for Kids* program proves that communities *can* join hands with their youth. A community can *stand up for its youth* and effectively convert destructive peer pressure into constructive peer influence.

It doesn't take an act of Congress. It doesn't take a million dollars. **It simply takes a caring community. When communities** *choose* **to listen to their students—who after all, own the problem and know the best way to reach their peers—then change becomes possible.**

Best of all, when *Cares for Kids*-type programs are created by local people for local students, the whole community—from the town leaders to the least empowered citizens—can be a part of the resulting bonding and embracing that everyone so desperately desires.

And from where does the money, the time, and the workforce for all of this come? It comes from its community! After all, one of the most outstanding qualities of towns like Kernersville—all across the United States—is the exceptional volunteer spirit.

In the end, it all boils down to a personal choice. Do I care? Will I do what I can to help?

2012 Lunch & Listen

Ex-con Fred Moore, keynote

2013 Lunch & Listen

NBA Chris Washburn, keynote

Epilogue

Working in community journalism these past 15 years has turned my world right-side up. I learned that there is no such thing as being number one. Moreover, the pursuit of such a fantasy is at best, distracting, and at worst, divisive and destructive.

In reality, being useful is the highest pursuit. Being useful is sometimes referred to as "showing love"—love of God and love of neighbor—but the word "love" has been so corrupted in recent years that the phrase "being useful" seems easier to grasp.

Making ourselves helpful serves to connect or reconnect us with other people and this leads to a common purpose, healthy relationships, and acceptance. It can even lead to happiness.

My involvement in Kernersville Cares for Kids reaffirmed that there is no flaw in our God-given design. People have the ability to care and to serve others. It is merely a matter of choice.

And it does not matter where we are called to serve. In reality, all members of the body of mankind are necessary and all are best served when we do the jobs we were designed to do and do them to the best of our ability.

> *"Happiness is the net result of making yourself useful."*
> —the late Dot Stone, beloved and extremely useful Kernersville resident.

www.UnderTheInfluence.org

Mini-books

Mini-book I: A Call for Compassion—10 Tips to Help Kids Stay Drug-free......................pg. 319

Please read this Mini-book first. It briefly explains HOW changing family dynamics, sexual abuse, and depression are driving the rise in teenage drug abuse. This is followed by 10 proven tips to help drug-proof young people. Key links give readers quick access to additional online help. Understanding the forces that shape today's young people give readers the power to help and not hurt an already fragile situation.

Mini-book II: Parents' Handbook ....pg. 320

*Misguided wisdom handed down for generations prevent well-intentioned parents from nurturing and protecting their children effectively. Scientific studies in this section reveal the truth, and return to parents their place of authority in the family. Key links give readers quick access to additional online help. **(Please read A Call for Compassion before beginning this Mini-book.)***

Mini-book III: Teens' Handbook……….....………….…pg. 330

*Times have changed and so has the road to adulthood. Read the real life stories and scientific studies to identify the issues confronting youth and forge possible solutions that can work for you and your friends. **(Please read A Call for Compassion before beginning this Mini-book.)***

Mini-book IV: Lessons Learned—Three Recovered Addicts...pg. 340

Three vivid first-person accounts let readers "see for themselves" how and why some teens become addicted to drugs while still in high school. Walk the path of recovery and embrace the healing as these recovered addicts dedicate their lives to helping others. Ask: What if they'd received help earlier—maybe through a random drug testing program in their school?

Mini-book V: Everyone Can Help................................…...pg. 350

Whether you are child, adult, neighbor, single, married, leader, follower, business entity, media, higher or lower education, employer, employee—if you are alive—there is something simple and meaningful that you can do to help keep yourself, your family, your neighborhood, and your community free of drugs and underage drinking.

Online Resources..…...pg. 390

Free videos, brochures, scientific studies and toll-free telephone help lines for teens and adults. Also, go to UnderTheInfluence.org for videos, documents, and resources directly related to this book.

Mini-book I

A Call for Compassion—10 Tips to Drug-proof Kids

What is going on with kids today? Everyone knows that something has changed. Even longtime teachers say that the young people coming into their classrooms today are not the same as the students who came through the doors 20 years ago. So what has changed?

We are going to look at some painful realities, but then we will explore solutions that really work. Though teens do have more challenges, they can thrive.

Teachers in Kernersville joined me in some quick research and found that in one first-grade classroom, 80 percent of the students were living with *only one biological parent.*

In a random sixth-grade classroom, 65 percent of the kids were living with only one biological parent. However, in the "gifted class," 85 percent of the children were living with both biological parents.

Over the course of the past year, as I traveled to other cities and states, educators told me that their communities were experiencing similar changes in family structure.

It is important to note that research indicates that "first families" (living with *both biological parents*) carries the least probability for teens choosing to abuse drugs or alcohol. Step-families — where a child lives with *two parents, but only one is a biological* parent —carries a risk factor similar to single-parent homes. Likely, this is due to the fact that it generally takes four to seven years for a step-family to stabilize — and two out of three second marriages end in divorce.

So what are risk factors? Research indicates that children growing up with only one biological parent in the home account for 63 percent of all youth suicides, 70 percent of all teenage pregnancies, *71 percent of all adolescent drug and alcohol abuse,* 80 percent of all prison inmates, and 90 percent of all homeless and runaway children. (See www.Dads4kids.com for a roadmap to research reports.)

Much of this is due to skyrocketing divorce rates. A 1993 study confirmed the negative impact of *divorce* versus unwed families or losing a parent in death. The researchers reported that when all factors were considered, "only divorce rates were consistently associated with suicide and homicide rates."

No doubt, broken homes are at the root of the "different kind of student." What happened to the "ideal" or "traditional" family in the United States?

"We decided in the 1970s," said Barbara Dafoe Whitehead, "out of a sense of optimism about the future, that we were going to reengineer family relationships in a way that made them more productive for *our own individual satisfactions* and that it was *okay* to give up on an unhappy marriage and move on. That was a big change in our thinking. And the second part was that children would bounce back. That was such a pervasive idea in the literature of the 1970s. Well, who would refuse a deal like that? And then, sadder but wiser, we now stand in the 1990s — and we realize that that optimistic scenario *hasn't* been played out (italics mine)."

Dr. Judith Wallerstein, author of The Unexpected Legacy of Divorce: A 25-Year Landmark Study, stated, "The earlier view of divorce as a *short-lived crisis* understood within the familiar paradigm of crisis theory has given way to a more sober appraisal, accompanied by rising concern that a *significant* number of children suffer from *long-term, perhaps permanent detrimental effects from divorce*, and that others experience submerged effects that may appear years later (italics mine)."

Why? What does divorce feel like? I found a child of divorce and interviewed her.

Katie remembers the day her parents said they were getting a divorce: "It totally turned my world upside down. I'd never known anything different but mom and dad always being together. My brother and I *blamed ourselves*. We asked, 'What did we do?' *We were angry*. It took years for me to learn to *let go of that pain*."

Katie was 28 years old — a grown adult with a fully developed set of coping skills when her parents divorced — and that is how she experienced it.

That is how most children experience divorce. *Pain and self-blame are the automatic response.* So when you look at today's young people, realize that *most of them* are suffering from pain and misplaced guilt.

Now why does that lead to drug and alcohol abuse? On the surface, it may look like teens are abusing substances as a pain killer. But beneath that, what they really have are unresolved problems. In all of my years of research, I've found that most of those problems boil down to one problem. It is a relationship problem — not resolving their relationship with one or both of their biological parents.

Now we are not going to linger too much longer before we begin looking at solutions that work. But we need to look at two more statistics.

- **Sexual Abuse: Nearly one-third of all girls and one out of five boys are sexually abused before their 18th birthday. What does this do to kids? It creates intense feelings of worthlessness and self-blame. Sexually-abused children are *26 times more likely* to use drugs.**

  However, children who get professional help — even years after the incidents — can have their risk factor normalized. For free online help: www.safehorizon.org

- **Adolescent Depression: About 39% of high school students suffer from mild to severe depression. This puts them at increased risk for self-destructive choices, including drug and alcohol abuse.**

Again, children who get professional help can have their risk factor normalized. For free online help: http://www.dbsalliance.org

According to Bert Wood, president and CEO of Partnership for a Drug-Free NC, Inc. and STEP ONE, "Depression and drug use often go hand-in-hand. What has been unclear is whether the person had depression first and then started using drugs or if the person started using drugs and then developed depression. But the April 2004 issue of Counselor magazine cited a study that indicates that in most cases, the depression came first."

The article he referred to, Dually Diagnosed Teens: Challenges for Assessment and Treatment, stated, "In the majority of cases (75 percent) the onset of psychopathology *precedes* the development of SUD (substance use disorders). This is what commonly has been referred to as the "self-medication" model." Here again, professional help and sometimes medication can normalize child's risk factor for substance abuse.

Now the purpose of this disclosure—the problem of broken homes, sexual abuse, and childhood depression—was not to depress the reader. The purpose was to give us a chance to reevaluate our understanding of today's teen. And the overwhelming feeling that comes over me when I meditate on this is a feeling of compassion.

Just to bring these statistics to life, I'd like you to meet Ruth Fair. She embodied all three of these statistics:

"From my earliest memories, I felt that life was not fair. Growing up in a home where each girl had a different father, it was easy to compare the time and attention each dad gave his daughter. The fact was, my dad rarely came to see me.

I started to lie, because I did not like the truth. The truth was, my dad was an alcoholic and he didn't keep his promises and I was jealous of my sisters.

I got my attention by acting out. To compound my pain and frustration, when I was nine years old, a friend of my grandmother's began routinely molesting me.

I couldn't tell anyone because I knew that no one would believe me because I lied so much. By middle school I had earned the reputation of being a bully.

By age 14, I began smoking marijuana to calm the rage. By the age of 16, I was an emancipated teen.

From there I got an apartment and acquired a 19-year-old boyfriend who drank heavily. He moved me to Atlanta, Georgia. I had my first experience with crack cocaine. Mostly to afford this expensive habit I prostituted myself. Eventually, I landed in jail."

Thankfully, Ruth Fair reestablished contact with her mother — whom she had not talked to in 16 years — and the healing began. "At that point, I put my life in God's hands. I chose to help people instead of hurting others," Fair explained.

Instead of judging drug-using or drinking teens as "bad" or selfish" Fair shows us they are in pain and in need of help.

Incidentally, Fair is now living a role model life. She accepted all the help she needed, has a wonderful job at a college and is working on her bachelor's degree in Sociology. (For more success stories of recovered addicts now living dynamic and healthy lives, read Mini-book III.)

TIP 1: Adjust YOUR attitude. See drug-using and drinking youth as people in pain and in need of help. Then begin to build a stronger village to support ALL young people.

TIP 2: Choose to be friendly to ALL kids. Even the ones with purple hair, piercings and angry looks on their faces. Obviously, these kids are asking for attention. Now granted, they are not asking for attention the RIGHT WAY. But if we wait for them to ask the right way, it will be too late. PLEASE give them what they want.

Notice how several people over the course of several years had an impact on this young man's life: Tommy Oliver.

At the age of 16, Tommy Oliver said, "I felt unloved and angry inside." He started smoking, drinking, using marijuana, having sex, and listening to rap and heavy metal music.

"The music always had to do with sex and violence. Shootings were my favorite, and sex. The lyrics to the songs talked about killing people and going to prison."

He grew his hair out, shaved it up underneath into a Mohawk and then twisted it up in knots. He bagged his pants down and left his underwear hanging out. His finishing touch was an earring he self-pierced into his left ear.

"I had this nasty look and I was ugly as sin ...."

He ended up getting into trouble, going to jail, and being sentenced to a youth prison. A few days later, two transport officers came to take Oliver to the high-rise. They let him know right away that they were Christians and they treated him with kindness. They even stopped and bought him a breakfast sandwich.

"I felt like I could not get away from Christians for anything. I had kids at school that talked to me about the Word. A youth pastor had seen me on the streets and tried to witness to me. My attorney, the jail guard, my grandmother, and now these two guys."

He began to think.

TIP 3: See through the mask. Did you notice how several people saw through the mask and talked with him? And though he did not appreciate it at the time, those seeds of kindness and comfort were planted in his heart and in time they grew.

So what ever happened to Tommy Oliver? He turned his life around and became a youth minister in Kernersville, North Carolina. (For Tommy's complete story, read Mini-book III.)

So when we encounter angry or withdrawn teens, it is up to US to say something positive. When you see any young person say to them, "I like your . . ." and then look for something positive. If all else fails, like their shoes!

TIP 4: Make a positive connection. These kids, who are working through this pain that we are NOW aware of — it's not that they really want to disconnect, they just want to connect in a new way. They don't want to be treated as children . . . they want a MUTUALLY RESPECTFUL connection with adults in their community.

But <u>our greatest power</u> lies in what we can do on an individual basis — in our personal sphere of influence: children we see in our everyday routine.

Tip 5: Compassionately EDUCATE others.

Take for instance the BIGGIE—divorce or birth out of wedlock or death of a parent:

- **Educate the child**
    - <u>Tell him or her, "You know, it's not your fault."</u> It's never the child's fault. Help him erase that pain and self-blame.
    - Tell the child something POSITIVE ABOUT THEIR PARENT. Even if their parent is one of those people with purple hair and a nose ring, EVERYONE has something positive about them.

- **Educate the parents: Compassionately & convincingly inform them that**

    1) **Using children as WEAPONS**
    2) **VERBALLY BASHING the child's other biological parent**
    3) **or WITHHOLDING VISITATION**

are behaviors hurt the CHILD. They set the child up for failure. INSTEAD, separated parents should do ALL THEY CAN to nurture a positive relationship between a child and EACH of his parents. IF separated parents have difficulty doing this — and many do — resolve the problem with professional help if needed. In a nutshell: if parents separate or divorce, it is time for the adults to set aside their hurt and negative feelings in order to focus on the emotional well-being of the child. This is challenging, but it can be done. It seems that much of the trauma of divorce is not due to the actual separation, but because of the hurtful stories that parents propagate about the divorce and the other parent. An excellent and free

online resource:
http://www.helpguide.org/mental/coparenting_shared_parenting_divorce.htm

---

Now to understand the next 3 tips, I want to give you a little background.

WHY did I persist in 15 years of research? In my core family of nine children in Michigan, half of my siblings chose to use drugs. Some of them they are still battling with this problem. I, personally never chose to experiment with drugs, not even once. We were raised in a good Christian family with parents that did not smoke; I never once saw either of them drunk; and they never used illicit drugs. So because I could not figure out what my own parents could have done differently, I felt very scared for my own three children.

I wanted to know: *Why would two teens in the same family make opposite choices about illegal drug use?* So I found two families with two children who made opposite choices — and their interviews became Chapter 13 in this book.

In their stories, I found <u>THREE PREDICTORS</u> of a child's choice to use drugs.

THE 3 C's

- **Control**
- **Coping Skills**
- **Connectedness**

www.UnderTheInfluence.org

1) **CONTROL**—how a child relates to the concept of control or authority–specifically do they view control/guidance by parents, teachers, friends, and the law as helpful or harmful?

2) **COPING SKILLS**— WE cannot take away the stress or undo divorces or stop the bullying. So the GREATEST GIFT we can give our child is COPING SKILLS. Now, it turns out that it really doesn't matter HOW MANY UNRESOLVED PROBLEMS the child has thrown at him. What matters is how the child COPES and HOW he solves his problems. AMAZINGLY, the one young man in this mini-book who had THE MOST PROBLEMS, even from birth, chose NOT TO EVER EXPERIMENT with drugs.

3) **CONNECTEDNESS**—research shows that the most important connection teens can have is their relationship with their parents. In fact, the NUMBER

ONE reason young people give for NOT using drugs is that they "don't want to harm the relationship between themselves and the caring adults in their lives."

When you break it down this way, **it takes the FEAR out of parenting**. NOW it is clear that the **parent has three goals**. {*Even if our child is as young as two years old or a grown adult with substance abuse problems—the 3 Cs can help.*}

TIP 6: Help the child APPRECIATE the value of CONTROL—having parents, laws and authority figures. (*Parents have to look at their own views*. Ask: What do I say about my parents? How do I view taxes? Do I obey the traffic laws? What do I say about my boss? Do I disrespect authority?) Rules and control are GOOD. They PROTECT US.

TIP 7: Help the young person develop a WHOLE ARSENAL of COPING SKILLS—which may include some that the teens in Chapter 13 used such as SPORTS, TALKING TO FRIENDS, DOING VOLUNTEER WORK...etc. (*NOTE: If you, as a parent, reach for a glass of wine every time you are stressed, you are modeling substance USE as a coping method. INSTEAD, model coping skills your child can imitate.*) For a longer list of coping skills, see Mini-Book II for teens.

TIP 8: Do all YOU can to help your child experience connectedness. Help them develop a RESOLVED RELATIONSHIP with EACH of their BIOLOGICAL PARENTS. Sometimes, a biological parent makes poor life choices that carry consequences such as divorce, prison, addiction, etc. Sometimes biological parents are abusive or toxic to their children. Even in these instances, a child can have a "resolved" relationship. In time, she can be helped to understand the reality of her parent's behavior without feeling the need to change it. She can be okay with the fact that each person gets to make his own life choices, which of course have consequences. At the very least, she can be thankful that this parent gave her the gift of life. To accomplish this, the child may benefit from professional counseling.

TIP 9: Be a hands-on parent or caregiver. Evaluate your parenting style. Read Mini-book I, "Parent's Handbook." According to a scientific study, *parenting style* has a significant impact on whether or not a given child will choose to use drugs.

326   UNDER THE INFLUENCE

THREE STYLES:

Hands-on parents—parents who adopted 10 simple but effective family rules

Half-hearted parents—parents who adopted six rules

Hands-off parents—parents who adopted five rules or less

Some of these rules include:
   A) Assign your teen regular chores.
   B) Eat dinner or ONE MEAL as a family almost every night.
   C) Monitor what teens do on the Internet.

Unfortunately, 70 % of teens are now being raised in homes with few or no rules. So help parents KNOW there are 12 rules that really work.

TIP 10: *Help children build a life they love. This* **is one of the best drug prevention tips to remember. WHEN teens REALLY love their life, they will make their best progress in learning control, coping skills and connectedness.** {http://www.manifestyourpotential.com/life/make_sense_of_life/life_ages_of_man/4_parents_task_help_childrens_become_meant_to_be.htm }

All of this having been said, the reality is, every teen — regardless of their family life, abuses, or advantages — has a personal choice to make. He or she can choose to abuse drugs and alcohol. Or, the adolescent can choose to stay free of mind-altering substances.

Below is an inspiring true story as told by former Wake Forest Basketball Coach Dino Gaudio.

A sixth grader came home from school one day and found his mom, his older brother, 22, and his older sister 19, who were normally at college, all in the kitchen crying. He asked, "What's the matter?"

They said, "Dad has a terrible disease and he only has one year to live."

The young man denied it and said, "My dad's fine. We just played ball together last week."

They said, "No. He has cancer and only one year to live."

Thirteen or 14 months later, his father passed away. Now he was in 7th grade. Every day he came home to a mom that was incredibly depressed. Every day when he came home, he'd say, "Hey mom, I'm home."

Then he would sit down and do his homework. He'd look out at the basketball court and he wanted to play ball, but first he would do his homework.

One day, he came in the house and said, "Hey mom, I'm home."

No answer.

He changed his clothes and said it again, "Hey mom, I'm home."

No answer.

He pushed open the door. His mom had taken her own life. He had a decision to make. Choice one: He could stay on the path his parents had led him on, the path of homework and school. Choice two: He could run with the wrong crowd.

He had these choices because at 5:00 no one was calling him in to dinner. And at 9:00 there was no one telling him to go to bed.

This kid chose to stay on the right path. He graduated high school in the top 10 of his class. He was part of the school team that won All-State in basketball and he won a basketball scholarship to the University of Tampa. He played ball and earned his degree. Then he moved back to his hometown and he became a role model there.

I know because that kid played basketball for me in high school. No matter what your life is like, you don't have to go down the path of drugs. You can take the other path.

When you are faced with the choice personally, you have a decision to make: Am I going to keep doing what's right or am I going to give up?

When adversity rears its head, can YOU deal with it? The answer to that question will determine your goals, your decisions, and your success.

Obviously, this young man had a lot of support—from his high school, his coach, and his college. The question is: What can your community do help keep its kids on the drug free path?

Let's engage in a little possibility thinking. What if your community instituted a random VOLUNTARY drug testing program—maybe in the schools, because that is where young people hang out.

What if your community found a way to get 80-90% of your 12-18 years old *voluntarily enrolled* in the program? Now here is the best part: If a child has wandered off track and fails the drug test, the child gets:

- Free help
- Nothing is recorded on his permanent school record
- Police are never called
- Classmates never find out because as the student is getting free help he or she continues in sports and extracurricular activities

Best of all, what if this effort is paid for by money confiscated in illegal drug sales? Guess what, this is not wishful thinking. This program had been operating successfully in North Carolina for 15 years. It has changed lives. If you have not already done so, please go back to Chapter One of this book and see how this could work for your community.

Honoring Youth Leaders

Photo by Wendy Freeman Davis, permission by *Kenersville News*

KCK student leaders are invited to speak at Town Hall and the WS/FC School Board Meetings each year. Pictured above: (L-R) Ald. Bob Prescott, Ald. Dana Caudil Jones, KCK Connor Hinds, Mayor Morgan, Ald. Tracey Shifflette, Ald. Kevin Bugg, Ald. Kevin Mason, KCK student Brandon Hall. (2010)

Ciener Botanical Garden hosted a "Community Signing" for this book on November 13th, 2011. This allowed the community to collect the autographs of student leaders and the young people to collect the autographs of their caring community. EVERYONE built their own community "yearbook" to treasure for a lifetime. Above: Reps from 2011-12 KCK students leaders.

Mini-book II

Parent Handbook

The challenge

Adults and 12-17 year olds agree that teenage drug abuse is their number one concern for young people, according to studies. (See the Introduction of this book.) So, why then, do parents and adolescents have such a difficult time *working together* to tackle this problem? One of the biggest obstacles is the lack of easy access to truthful information. This mini-book gives parents the tools to *work with their children* to develop strategies that help young people navigate in the current culture.

What do you expect?

Parents' *expectation* has a huge impact on teen behavior. According to the 2011 National Household Survey on Drug Abuse:

- Of 12-17-year-olds whose parents would *strongly disapprove* if their children used marijuana once or twice, only five percent have used an illicit drug in the past month.
- In contrast, thirty-one percent of teens whose parents would *not* strongly disapprove had used an illicit drug in the past month. (Results are similar for alcohol and tobacco.)
- When parents disagree on their expectation, teens are three times more likely to use marijuana and twice as likely to use alcohol than teens with parents who agree completely.

Don't be fooled! According to the 2003 report by the National Center on Addiction Studies and Substance Abuse (CASA),

- Sixty-three percent of parents "consider the expectation of teen abstinence from drugs to be 'unrealistic.' "
- CASA research states that parents who *believe* that drug-use by their teens is "very likely" to increase their teen's likelihood of becoming substance abusers by 300 percent.

TIP: Ask your children if they are aware that most kids their age (12-17) view teenage drug abuse as their top concern. Explain why *you*, as their parent, want them to stay on the drug-free path and ask how they feel about this. Clearly *state your expectation* regarding experimentation with drugs and alcohol. Assure them that you will *work together* to develop strategies that really work.

The #1 reason *why* kids abstain from drugs and alcohol

The most common reason teens give for abstaining from drugs and alcohol is that *they do not want to "harm the relationship between themselves and the caring adults in their lives,"* according to the free government brochure, Keeping Youth Drug-free (www.drugfree.org).

In their hearts, young people know who really *cares* about them and who is looking out for their best interests. They *value* their relationship with their parents and place it at the top of their list, even as they struggle with it. Compared with *all* other factors, parents' words, expectations, and actions are *the most significant indicators* of their children's decision to use or not use illegal substances.

TIP: Find ways to daily show your children that you *care* about them. When parents listen, ask for their teens' opinions, support their kids' good ideas, give honest commendation, and spend one-on-one time with their children, parents are showing that they care. Help each child to build a life he or she loves.

Am I a hands-on or half-hearted parent?

Many parents are reluctant to set household rules and consequences. It is *not* that the parents don't care. It is that they do not want to *interfere* needlessly in their children's lives.

According to a CASA study, *seven out of 10 adolescents* live in homes where parents set few or no rules. The study indicates that there is a correlation between parenting style and teenage risk for drug abuse.

Parenting Quiz: Am I a hands-on or half-hearted parent?

Hands-on parents = Parents who uphold 10 of the 12 rules listed below.
Half-hearted parents = Parents who establish six of the household rules.
Hands-off parents = Parents who establish five or fewer household rules.

12 Family Rules that really work to drug-proof young people:

1. **monitor what their teens do on the Internet**
2. **put restrictions on music CDs teens buy**
3. **know where their teens are after school and on weekends**
4. **expect to be and are told the truth by their teen about where they *really* are going**
5. **are "very aware" of their teen's academic performance**
6. **impose a curfew**
7. **make clear they would be "extremely upset" if their teen used pot**
8. **eat dinner with their teens most every night**
9. **monitor what their teens watch on TV**

10. turn off the TV during dinner
11. assign the teen regular chores
12. have an adult present when the teen returns from school

Of course, having rules implies that parents establish consequences for broken rules. Instead of getting angry or yelling, many parents create a list of consequences that are put on the refrigerator or in a visible spot. Some parents even let their teens help create the list of consequences.

Aside from common disciplines, such as grounding, restricting cell phone and technology use, or taking away privileges, some parents get creative. Some forms of discipline can actually benefit the whole family, such as requiring erring teens to wash walls or windows, cook dinner for the family, weed the flower bed, or clean the family car.

Of the 12 rules listed above, all of them can be separated into one of two categories. They assist the parents in *nurturing* or *protecting* their children.

Protect your teens

Rules #1, #2, #4, #6, and #9 are *protection rules* that center on parents knowing the people, television, music, video games, and Internet entities with which their children associate. Sometimes adolescents will choose associates who say or do things that parents find unacceptable.

TIP: Before banning unhealthy relationships, observe them and try to discern:
- *Why* is my child choosing that associate?
- What *need* is the undesirable relationship filling?
- How can I help my teen find a *healthy* expression of that need — for comfort, risk-taking, or a strong personal identity — instead of living through another person or association?

Are you tuned in to their music?

A study published in Adolescence said, "Results indicated that adolescents who preferred *heavy metal and rap* had a higher incidence of below-average grades, school behavior problems, sexual activity, *drug and alcohol use*, and arrests."

"If children cannot perform well academically, they end up feeling discouraged and inferior. As adolescence approaches . . . they will grasp at other ways to *fit in* and build their *self-esteem*. One of the things they seem to grasp at is heavy metal and rap music because these types of music offer them several things. They supply them with an *identity*, complete with clothes and hairstyle. They also offer them a *peer group* that has few requirements for entry .... Finally, the *image* of the music gives these adolescents a sense of *power*, something they may not have anywhere else in their lives."

TIP: *Actively help* your children: find a positive place in society (fit in), see the good in themselves (self-esteem), know and accept their gifts and limitations (identity), find nurturing and healthy friends (peer group), and find a way to give to others so that teens *know* they can change the world around them (power).

Home alone can still mean supervised

Rule # 3—*knowing their teens' whereabouts after school* helps parents protect their teens. Many kids have no structured activities or supervision *between the time* when school is out and their parents get home from work.
- Juvenile crime, most first sexual relationships, and *experimentation with drugs and alcohol* peak during the hours of 2:00-7:00 p.m.
- A University of Wisconsin study found that "after-school programs dramatically reduced vandalism, promoted better behavior, and improved academic performance of the participants. The adolescents in structured-activities develop values and skills they need to become good neighbors and better adults."

TIP: If your teen must be home alone, have him call you at a specific time each day. Have a snack-homework-chore routine in place. Ask a trusted neighbor to be aware and available for emergencies. Place protective software on home computers to keep the youth safe and supervised.

Work is a good thing

Rule #5—*"very aware" of their teen's academic performance* and **Rule #11**—*assign the teen regular chores*, are all about *nurturing* work ethic and self-esteem. School is a young person's job. Without micromanaging, many parents hold their students accountable for turning in all work completed and on time.

Regarding regular household chores, here again, parents have a chance to praise a job well done and to retrain as necessary. Regular family chores help a teen feel like a valuable part of their family.

TIP: Teach good work ethic. When children choose to turn in late or incomplete school work, parents can require them to redo the work at home, even if it cannot be turned in for a higher grade. Get tutoring if needed. Hold teens to reasonable standard for household work. Do some chores, such as yard work or mealtime as a family and make it fun. Play after work.

Make it easy for your teen to say "no" to drugs

Rule #7—*make clear they would be "extremely upset" if their teen used pot.* Times have changed. After years of gradual decline, teenage drug-use is now rising. (See Relevance: Young People Need Leadership, prior to Chapter One of this book.)
- Lock up your medicines and alcohol

- Give your teen random drug-tests at home

In 2012, Sherry Koontz, a mother of four, told the *Kernersville News,* "Last year when our oldest child turned 14, we started doing random drug-tests at home."

This wasn't because their son had a drug problem. "Random drug-testing lets him know that we are going to hold him accountable for his choices and his actions."

TIP: Give your teens random home drug-tests. This makes it easy for your teens to say "no" because they can honestly say, "I don't want to fail my parent's drug-test." Wal-Mart and other drug stores sell home drug-testing kits for $12 to $39 — and that includes the cost of a professional lab confirmation for any positive tests.

Make dinnertime fun

Rules #8 and #10 involve meal times. These rules are designed to *nurture* the parent/child relationship. While tasty food is always a plus, the primary benefit of shared meals comes from the opportunity to bond.

The 2011 National Survey of American Attitudes on Substance Abuse XVI: Teens and Parents found that teens who eat dinner with their families five to seven times a week are more than twice as likely to abstain from marijuana or alcohol use than teens who eat as a family less often.

TIP: Come to the dinner table prepared to share a story about your day's experience. When you relate honest and sometimes humorous tales, your children will learn how *you* cope in the adult world. In time, they will likely share stories from their day. Ask questions. Invite friends to dinner.

12 ways to prove you care

Mostly, these 12 rules provide the kind of security, guidance, and mutual trust that convinces a teen that, "My parent cares about me." It is surprising how closely kids link parental rules with *caring*. A young woman told me, that as a teenager, she was let on the loose. She got into all kinds of trouble. One weekend, she did something really "terrible" and her parents took away her car keys. Though angry on the outside, she was *happy* on the inside. She thought, "Finally, I know they really care."

Which is worse—alcohol or drugs?

Some parents believe that *breaking the drinking law* is the lesser of the two evils. After all, it takes the liver only about two hours to process completely and eliminate all the alcohol found in a glass of beer, whereas it takes weeks for the liver to process THC (in marijuana).

The book Drugs and Controlled Substances: Information for Students, stated:
- Alcohol abusers are *six times more likely* to abuse marijuana.
- Teenage drinking *increases the risk* of becoming alcohol-dependent.
- About 10 percent of adults are alcohol and/or drug dependent.
- Alcohol-related accidents are the number one killer of young people.

TIP: Explore websites like www.AboveTheInfluence.com *with your children*. Let *them* guide *you*. Check out the videos, photos, and inspiring true stories.

Is nicotine a gateway drug?

The book, Substance Abuse: The Nation's Number One Health Problem, reported:
- Young people who smoke before the age of 18 are "*10 times more likely* to use illicit drugs than their nonsmoking peers."
- Legal as well as illegal drugs affect an adolescent's mind and body *differently* than that of an adult. This is because *intense growth* — emotional, physical, and mental — takes place during adolescence.

TIP: Parents who choose to use tobacco or alcohol — legal substances — are often speechless when their teens ask, "You do it. Why can't I?" Parents' best response is to tell the truth. Once people reach legal age, they are free to evaluate the risks of legal substances and make their own choices. However, also remember to give them your expectation for them to make healthy choices. Explore www.Teens.DrugAbuse.gov {NIDA for Teens} for free interactive videos, downloads, games and more.

What is the true cost of drug and alcohol abuse?

In 2008, The National Institute on Drug Abuse (NIDA) estimated cost to the U.S. economy for drug and alcohol abuse is as follows:
- Illegal drugs: $181,000,000,000 per year
- Alcohol abuse: $185,000,000,000 per year

(NIDA report Addiction Science: From Molecules to Managed Care)

Findings at Wake Forest University Baptist Medical Center stated:

- In terms of health care one in every four dollars can be related directly to substance abuse.
- Each family in the U.S. is indirectly assessed about $1,000 per person, costing the average family of four about $4,000 per year.

- 40-60 percent of all emergency room visits are drug/alcohol related

Judge Ron Spivey of the 21st Judicial Court in North Carolina said, "Since 1989, we have seen an *explosion* in drug cases .... I have seen nurses, contractors, executives in local corporations, small business owners, bankers, and even a few lawyers get prosecuted and convicted for drug sales and addiction. *These are not losers.* They are working class, tax-paying citizens that have somehow gotten into the drug culture. They have gotten on the slippery slope of drug-use, and, before they know it, they have lost everything."

TIP: Share real life stories of family, friends, neighbors, or community members that *you* have lost due to drug/alcohol abuse. Talk about news and televisions stories that highlight the negative consequences of drug or alcohol abuse.

Peer pressure can be positive or negative.

It always amazes me that after 15 years of working directly with teens, some adolescents make it all the way to high school graduation without ever seeing drugs or being offered drugs. Other students, in the same schools, experience a high degree of negative peer pressure and are offered drugs regularly.

It seems that the main difference between the two groups is the company the young people choose to keep. Choice of friends can be a powerful indicator of a teen's risk for using drugs or alcohol.

Know who your teen's friends are

According to the 2011 National Survey of American Attitudes on Substance Abuse XVI: Teens and Parents, teens were asked if they agreed with the statement: "If a *friend* of mine uses illegal drugs, it's none of my business." Teens who agreed are:
- Almost three times likelier to have used tobacco
- Almost twice as likely to have used alcohol
- Almost three times as likely to have used marijuana

TIP: It is a parent's job to help a teen find two or three friends that share your family values. Make YOUR HOME the hangout place. In addition to providing a safe hangout and plenty of snacks, do some exploring on sites such as www.drugfree.org; www.teens.drugabuse.gov; www.justthinktwice.com

Peer pressure has changed

A KCK prize-winning essay by seventh grader Jason Pruitt stated, "Adults, for the most part, *make light of teens* talking about peer pressure. We *feel the effects* of being called names, belittled in a group, and pointed out as a 'mama's boy,' *more than we fear* "black lung" 20 years from now. We're very well informed, probably more than any generation before us, but *information* doesn't make the choices any easier."

Students are actually feeling *pushed* to take drugs. There is a prevailing *pressure* or *force* bearing on well-intentioned students, and they are finding it more and more difficult to combat. The atmosphere has *changed* since the 1960s and 1970s where people experimented for fun or for freedom. Many students are being *coerced*, and are frustrated by the lack of adult awareness and seemingly adult tolerance for the current culture.

Tip: Role Play. Help your teen create responses that they can say when pressured to use drugs or alcohol. Amazingly, one of the best responses can be, "I don't want to. You can do what you want but it's not for me." For other kids, using humor or turning the question back on the peer — why would I want to do that? — works. Practice this as a family until it feels natural.

Normalize peer pressure

Clearly, students need parental help in responding to negative peer pressure. One thing parents can do is *normalize* the concept of peer pressure. It is not just a teen-thing, it is a life-thing.

TIP: Watch TV commercials together. See if you can spot the "peer pressure" tactics to get people to buy the project. If you buy:
- **Will you feel like part of the group {everyone's doing it}?**
- **Will it make you *smarter, prettier, or more popular?***

Defuse the mystery

Parents can also defuse the mystery of peer pressure. Usually, it has nothing to with benefiting the victim. A teenager who lost his virginity due to negative peer pressure explained how peer pressure self-perpetuates.

"I felt stupid," he said. "I knew that I made a mistake and I was angry. So I went out and tried to pressure other virgins into having sex. When they did, I thought, 'I'm not that stupid. They did it too!' "

TIP: Reason with your teen. Ask him, "Do you really want to be the sacrificial lamb for someone else's guilt? Why would it matter to THEM whether or not you choose to use drugs or drink? Why do they want to influence YOUR choices?"

Am I setting my kid up?

Parents can be too trusting. One woman told me that as a teen, her parents thought that she was "old enough" to stay home alone when they occasionally traveled. She was old enough to care for her needs. But she was not strong enough to resist the peer pressure when her friends found out that she had "the house to herself." This woman swore that she would never put her children in that situation.

TIP: Even if you are going to be gone for a single night, try to have a trusted adult stay in the home. If this is not possible, let trusted neighbors or friends know your plans and let your teen know that they are being observed. Also, be sure to call. Teens can feel abandoned even when they know "why" you left.

There is a place for everyone

For some students, being directly pressured to indulge in drugs, alcohol or sex is not the underlying problem. For them, the pressure comes from an inability to feel accepted by their classmates. Here too, parents can take action.

TIP: Help your child find people who deal with similar issues (obesity, disabilities, shyness, ethnic differences) who are happy with their lives. The fact is: School is NOT fun for everyone. But with a little planning, parents can often make arrangements for their teens to spend plenty of time with people who share their interests and create a positive influence. A GREAT way for teens to meet caring people is by volunteering in their community.

What about God?

Interestingly, the <u>2011 National Survey of American Attitudes on Substance Abuse XVI: Teens and Parents</u> found that,
- Teens who regularly attend (four times a month or more) religious services are at reduced risk for substance abuse.
- Teens who regularly attend are twice as likely to have abstained from alcohol and three times as likely to have abstained from marijuana use than their peers who attend fewer or no religious services.

TIP: Practice your faith. Explore the spiritual principles of staying free of drugs and underage drinking. Compare this to the legal statutes.

ONE FINAL TIP: *Please keep reading!*

- *Read Chapter 13 in this book—"**Four Teens from Two Families**." Read the **Teen Handbook***
- *Read "A Call for Compassion."*
- ***KNOW that your voice has power.*** *Contact the author with your ideas www.UndertheInfluence.org or www.ClassicWritingPR.com.*
- ***Check out the Online Resources at the end of this section.***

Mini-Book III

Teen Handbook

The challenge

Teen time is transition time, and transitions are challenging for everyone. However, the good news is that every adult went through adolescence. There is plenty of rock-solid information to help you successfully navigate the path from adolescence to adulthood.

As you know, you'll also find plenty of useless or even harmful advice. Everyone learns to sort this out — but don't be afraid to ask your parents or trusted adults for help along the way.

This Teen's Handbook cannot address every issue, but it will touch on some of the most common challenges and give you plenty of resources to help you continue your search for solutions that work for you.

Have you ruined your life?

Former Juvenile Probation Officer LuAnn Davis went into a 9th grade public school classroom and asked, "How many of you feel like you have already ruined your life?" A number of hands went up. She then assured them that no matter what their lives have been like up to this point, they can turn their lives around.

In her 50 years of life, LuAnn has witnessed thieves, drug addicts, habitual liars, cheaters of all sorts, haters, and alcoholics — people making hurtful and harmful choices — turn their lives around. She has also seen their victims — sexually abused, robbed, betrayed, humiliated, bullied, degraded, and deceived, people who have been hurt and are still hurting — recover and rebuild their lives.

"Everyone makes mistakes," LuAnn assured them. "You can even make a real mess of your life. But there comes a time when you need to get your train on the right track and start moving in a positive direction. You start that by picking a new destination and making new choices. It's that simple."

LuAnn was not implying that change is easy. But it is also not rocket science. It's like driving a car or a train. First, get honest about where you are. Then, choose a new destination.

Keep it simple. Ask yourself: What is one thing I can do TODAY that will move me one step closer to my goal? Ask yourself that question every day and before you know it you will be there. You can turn your life around. It is your choice. Instead of worrying about your life, work at it.

TIP: Choose one aspect of your life — a habit, a reputation, a personality trait, a relationship — that you would like to change. What is one thing that you can do today to move yourself closer to your new image?

HINT: Keep it simple. Start by focusing on only ONE change. Talk to people who have achieved your goal. You could say, "I'm researching (patience, courage, or time management) and you seem to do well with this. What helped you?" Or, read about your goal. Remember, take one small action a day.

REALITY: In one survey, over 90% of high school seniors did not like themselves. It's normal. The good news is YOU are the only person YOU can change. Today is a good day to start.

Am I working or worrying?

An old proverb says, "Worry is like a rocking chair. It will give you something to do, but it won't get you anywhere." There's nothing wrong with being in a rocking chair if that is really where you want to be for a while. But if that's not where you want to be, then make a change. How can you tell if you are worrying? Are your thoughts going in circles? Likely, that is worry.

One solution to worry and fear is to "make a plan and work it." Unlike circles, planning uses linear thought. Planning moves your mind, step by step, in the direction of your desire. To get started, you only need to ask one question: What is one thing I can do TODAY to move myself closer to my desired outcome?

TIP: Everyone worries — it is part of being human. Pay attention to your thoughts and feelings. Make a list of 5-10 things you tend to worry about. Pick one and make a plan.

WARNING: If you worry about another person, know that you cannot change other people. But you can change yourself and how you choose to relate to the other person. Care about others, but don't try to change them.

HINT: Planning helps, but real power comes when YOU take action in your life. Take one action today.

Angry words leave scars

There once was a little boy who had a bad temper. His father gave him a bag of nails and told him that every time he lost his temper, he must hammer a nail into the back of the fence.

The first day the boy had driven 37 nails into the fence. Over the next few weeks, as he learned to control his anger, the number of nails hammered daily gradually dwindled down. He discovered it was easier to hold his temper than to drive those nails into the fence.

Finally the day came when the boy didn't lose his temper at all. He told his father about it and the father suggested that the boy now pull out one nail for each day that he was able to hold his temper. The days passed and the young boy was finally able to tell his father that all the nails were gone. The father took his son by the hand and led him to the fence. He said, "You have done well, son, but look at the holes in the fence. The fence will never be the same. When you say things in anger, they leave a scar just like this one. You can put a knife in a man and draw it out. It won't matter how many times you say 'I am sorry,' the wound is still there. A verbal wound is as bad as a physical one." (Author unknown)

TIP: When you are feeling angry, take a break. Set a later time to come back and address the person or the problem after you have calmed yourself down. Addressing problems in a calm state of mind increase the odds that we will actually improve the situation, rather than make it worse.

HINT: Go to the section on "coping skills" to find ways to calm down.

Stress

Stress is a part of life. The sooner you learn "stress/management" or "self-management," the more productive your life can be. Most people experience the same basic stressors, just in different orders of personal importance and intensity.

Top 10 Stressors for Young People

1) **Family Problems**—conflict, divorce, death
2) **School**—tests, GPA, teachers, learning style differences
3) **Friends**—fights, betrayal, secrets
4) **Body Image**—obesity, height, hair, ethnicity
5) **Romantic Relationships**—breakups, embarrassment, expectations
6) **Bullying/Cyberbullying**—hurtful/humiliating comments or photos
7) **Depression**—prolonged feelings of sadness and hopelessness
8) **Negative Peer Pressure**—pressure to use drugs, alcohol, sex, risk-taking
9) **Money**—how to buy things you want or "need" to fit in
10) **Change**—moving, birth of sibling, death of a pet

TIP: Make it personal. Most teens feel all of these stressors to some degree. The stressor at the top of your list can change from week to week. List these stressors in the order that they are affecting you TODAY. Do this once a week to track

how your stressors change. Try to become more aware each stressor in your life. Go beyond yourself: While keeping in mind that you cannot change others, try to remember that virtually all of your fellow teens face similar problems.

1. Family Problems

Most teens are growing up in homes with only one biological parent. In some of these homes two adults are present — as in a step family — but only one of the adults is a biological parent. Homes with only one biological parent can cause tremendous stress on the youth. See if you can understand *why* divorce is so stressful for teens. NOTE: Even if *you* are growing up with both biological parents in your home, if you understand the challenges of others, you can be a source of strength and comfort. You can be a real friend.

Lorrie's story

Lorrie was 10 years old when her parents divorced. She felt as if she lost her dad *and* her mom.

"When mom had to go to work full-time," said Lorrie, "I hated that. That was the worst thing. I spent less time with mom. And before the divorce we had nice meals together with meat and potatoes and vegetables. But after the divorce, she was too tired for that."

Finances also changed. Her dad did not pay child support regularly. Most children of divorce have an average drop in their family income of 26%. This drop in their standard of living adds another layer of stress to their lives.

Lorrie and her two siblings moved with their mom several times. This compounded loss upon loss. Now 24, she still cries when she talks about it. "I hated moving. You have to leave all your friends."

Shortly after the divorce, Lorrie's dad remarried. She had to adjust to unwanted and non-traditional relationships.

"When dad remarried," noted Lorrie, "he paid more attention to his new wife than he did to me. And his new wife's daughter hated me."

Questions:
1) *Why* did Lorrie feel that in the divorce she actually lost both her mom and her dad?
2) *Why* do you think that her family had to move several times after the divorce and what pain did this cause to Lorrie?
3) *What new problems* arose when Lorrie had a step-mom?

SKILL: Listen. You can help others simply by caring enough to patiently listen as they talk. You don't have to know the solutions to be a friend.

TIP: Look for classmates and neighboring teens who seem to isolate themselves or who seem lonely. Acts of kindness, a greeting, eating lunch with him/her, or getting to know his/her journey can enrich both of your lives. Be the first to act.

If you were Lorrie and you wanted to talk to your mom about your feelings, how would you phrase your statements? What could you say to your dad?

Communication is like a game of catch

Healthy communication is sometimes likened to a game of "catch the ball." If your intention is to hurt the person, then you will "throw the ball" or your words in ways that are hurtful, blaming, and painful.

For example, you might say, "You tell me not to yell and you are yelling at me. Why don't you practice what you preach!" Ouch! That could hurt.

IF, however the intention is to solve the problem, then you will choose your words carefully and state the problem directly, like aiming for the listener's "glove" in a game of catch.

For instance: "*When* you yell at me, *I feel* disrespected and hurt. *It makes me feel* like I can't come to you with my problems. Can we find a way to talk that doesn't involve yelling?"

***

Not everyone experiences divorce like Lorrie did. But most people react to divorce like Katie. Meet Katie.

Katie's story

Katie remembers the day her parents said they were getting a divorce. "It totally turned my world upside down. I'd never known anything different but mom and dad always being together. My brother and I *blamed ourselves*. We asked, 'What did we do?' *We were angry*. It took years for me to learn to *let go of that pain*."

Katie was 28 years old — a grown adult with a fully developed set of coping skills when her parents divorced — and that is how she experienced it.

Questions: 1) Did you know that most children of divorce *blame themselves* for their parents' divorce? Why do you think that happens?
2) What could Katie have done to prevent her parents' divorce?

EMPATHY: Someone once said, "Empathy is me carrying your pain in my heart." Many young people feel pain at the loss of their "first family" (living with both biological parents.) How can you demonstrate empathy for these peers?

SKILL: *Active listening* **occurs when you repeat to the speaker something that she said to clarify that you heard it correctly. It lets the speaker know that you**

are really listening and that you really care about them and their problem. For example, when Katie said, "My brother and I blamed ourselves," an active listener might say, "You mean you felt like it was your fault?" Active listening does NOT mean trying to solve her problem.

***

Sometimes it is not the actual separation that is so traumatic to the children. Sometimes the pain comes mainly from the way that parents use their children as weapons to hurt each other. Meet Lindsay.

Lindsay's story

Lindsay — another child of divorce — was raised in a "war zone." Her custodial parent (her father) used Lindsay as a weapon to punish her non-custodial parent (her mother). According to experts, this is one of the most devastating and yet *most common mistakes* that divorced parents make.

Her father verbally bashed her mother and he hired a babysitter instead of letting her stay with her mother while he was working.

"My dad tried for years to turn me against my mom. He said that she didn't care about us and that she was selfish for leaving. I was mad at my dad because I knew he was lying, but I was powerless to prove it. I hated both of them for that," said Lindsay.

Lindsay had another problem. Her father treated her like a *miniature adult*. From the time she was in elementary school, he talked to her about his problems, expected her to look after her little sister, and had her cook, clean and do the dishes.

When she went to her mother's house, it was like being demoted.

"At my mom's house," said Lindsay, "I was treated *like a kid*. I didn't have a lot of say in the day-to-day decisions. When I got into trouble she was firm and consistent. I fought with her more because I would actually have to reap consequences for my behavior."

When Lindsay was 16, the overwhelming stress of trying to bridge the gap and synthesize her parents' two worlds finally took its toll. She ran away three times and finally tried to commit suicide.

"I felt *powerless* at both houses because both were extremes. *I couldn't see a way out*. I couldn't see how to get some relief. So I tried to kill myself," said Lindsay.

CHALLENGE: Pretend that you are a family counselor. Go to the attached website and then write a skit or a conversation showing "how" this family could create healthier relationships. Be sure to address the issues of the dad, the mom, and Lindsay.
http://www.helpguide.org/mental/coparenting_shared_parenting_divorce.htm

---

DRUGS: Lindsay tried to commit suicide by taking an overdose of drugs. Did you know that the most common reason teens give for abstaining from drugs and alcohol is that *"they do not want to "harm the relationship between themselves and* *the caring adults in their lives,"* **according to the free government brochure, Keeping Youth Drug-free (www.drugfree.org). On the other hand, teens, like Jill in Chapter 13 of this book, sometimes take drugs to punish their parents, taunt their parents, or to get attention.**

QUESTIONS: 1) Do you think Lindsay's parents cared about her?
                       2) Do you think Lindsay's parents knew how much pain she was in?

SUICIDE: Why is suicide a poor choice of tools for solving problems? What do you think Lindsay wrote in her suicide note? What are better ways that Lindsay could have addressed her problems?

HINT: www.teencentral.net or http://us.reachout.com/wecanhelpus/ or call 1-800-448-3000.

***

Is life easier for children of unwed parents or fatherless students who were not volleyed between homes? Meet Greg and hear his story.

Greg's story

Greg didn't see his dad from age two to seventeen.

"When I was five, I was just happy to have a stepdad. But when I got older I thought, 'I have a man with half my DNA and he would never do anything for me. He wouldn't even call or send a letter.' It cut me deep. He was a person that was supposed to love me and take care of me and he abandoned me," said Greg.

As he progressed through adolescence, Greg began to blame himself. "I would ask myself, 'Am I that *bad* of a person? Was I *that* bad of a mistake that he didn't want anything to do with me?' I thought, 'Man! This person actually did not want me,' " said Greg.

As he got older, typical problems arose between Greg and his stepdad. They disagreed on discipline issues and they developed different interests. Instead of trying to resolve his problems, Greg fanaticized about how much better life would be with his *real* dad.

When he was seventeen, he finally got a chance to meet his larger-than-life biological father.

"When I met him, he said that I should be happy with my life and that he was happy with his. He said, 'It's nice to meet you, but don't expect this to be a constantly recurring thing.' That experience was another blow. I became emotionally detached. I built up an emotional callus. I cared so much for so long that it kind of hardened me," said Greg.

To top it off, Greg's biological father was a role model in the community. "He was the principal of a school molding young minds and what had he done to his own child? Children were looking up to him. He was supposed to be a person you could trust. And he did this to his own child?" asked Greg.

Legal adoption by his stepfather added to Greg's pain. He was 12 at the time and when his biological father signed the papers, he was shocked.

"I felt empty. I felt abandoned. By signing the papers, he said, 'I have no more ties to you.' I thought, 'Could you get any lower?' "

BLAME: Even though feelings aren't always "logical," they can be very powerful and persistent. What do you think? Do you believe that it was Greg's fault that his dad rejected him when he was a baby?

The four most painful human experiences

LOSS: Our brain is "hardwired" to want a healthy connection with each of our biological parents. It is very painful to lose a parent due to death or abandonment. Which loss do you feel was most traumatic for Greg: The loss of his dad as a baby or at the age of 12 or at the age of 17? Why?

REJECTION: Another painful experience for people is rejection. This happens when we want to be attached or connected to someone and they ignore us or refuse us. Why did Greg begin to reject his step-dad?

BETRAYAL: When we trust someone or expect someone to do something for us and they let us down, we can feel betrayed. Why did Greg feel especially betrayed by his biological dad when he realized that his dad was a school principal?

HUMILIATION: We often experience humiliation as a result of an embarrassing or devastating event. Or, we may feel ashamed when one of our mistakes becomes publicly known. Why might Greg's visit with his dad at the age of 17 have been embarrassing or humiliating for him?

***

You will be pleased to know that each of the people in these stories eventually learned healthy coping skills. All of them are now adults, three are married, and some have children of their own. All of them grew up to be healthy, caring adults with a zest for life.

1. Coping Skills

Coping skills have been defined as brain habits — things we do automatically to help ourselves feel better when we are stressed. Coping skills can either be healthy or unhealthy.

UNHEALTHY COPING SKILL: When John feels hurt, or mad, or sad, he hits someone. Hitting someone makes John feel better. But it makes his victim feel worse. This is an unhealthy coping skill.

HEALTHY COPING SKILL: When Lila feels hurt, or mad, or sad, she reads a book. This makes her feel better because it "takes her to another place." Reading a book helps Lila feel calm without making anyone else feel bad.

New coping skills — healthy or unhealthy — can be learned. There are many advantages to having a whole toolbox of healthy coping skills. Sometimes one coping skill will work better than another. When we excel at coping with stress and problems solving, our confidence grows, we spend less time feeling distressed, and we feel more in control of our lives. Stress is not a teen-thing, it is a life-thing.

Beth's story

Beth is a 15-year-old who learned a life-changing lesson from a stranger. Prior to their having met, Beth had mastered caring. Like most teens, she was *very sensitive* to the feelings of those around her and she could *feel* the chaos of a world out of control. Beth kept these feelings bottled up, and, as they fermented and expanded, they caused her severe emotional *pain*.

As her parents, teachers, and employer placed customary demands on her, she felt like she was going to explode. Finally, she decided, "What is the point? Why would I want to live in a world like this anyway?"

Beth attempted a drug-induced suicide and was hospitalized. All through the night, a PCA (volunteer patient care assistant) stayed by her side. This stranger *actively listened* as Beth talked about the problems in and around her life.

The PCA wept with the girl. It was the tears of a stranger that helped this teenager realize how people *actively* care. For the first time, Beth saw clearly that her pain was caused by her own *inability to act* on her feelings. She now knew that even a small action can cause a powerful change.

Beth decided to change her life. She decided to work toward a career that centers on *active caring*. For the first time, this teenager saw clearly how she *fit in* to the adult world. She had discovered her *identity*. Beth now has a reason to live her life fully and to avoid future drug and alcohol abuse.

This volunteer PCA didn't change the world. She helped one person, and changed that teenager's world. That teen is now motivated to change many worlds.

Questions: 1) Why do you think it helped Beth to talk to a caring adult?
2) What did Beth realize that helped her change from a feeling of powerlessness to a feeling of hope?

TIP: When you want to talk with a caring adult any time of day or night, call Girls and Boys Club National Hotline at 1-800-448-3000.

Healthy Coping Skills

1) ASK FOR HELP—talk to a caring adult or supportive friend
2) JOURNAL—get your thoughts out of your head and onto paper
3) MEDITATE/Deep Breathing—focus your mind on your breathing
4) VOLUNTEER/ HELP OTHERS—there is more happiness in giving
5) EXERCISE/SPORTS—this changes your body chemistry
6) READ—you can become engrossed in the story
7) PRAY—faith and hope renew your spirit
8) LAUGH—take your incident to the ridiculous level/make a joke
9) RELAX—progressively tighten and relax the muscles in your body
10) MUSIC—listen to music that helps you relax to "reset" your mood
11) VISUALIZE—picture yourself in a peaceful place
12) PET—pet your pet
13) PHOTO—carry a photo of your pet or friend who comforts you
14) SELF-TALK—talk to yourself like you would comfort a friend
15) REWARD—treat yourself to a movie or other healthy reward
16) SLEEP—rest can "reboot" your mind and refresh your outlook
17) TOLERATE—feel the feeling, pay attention to it, feel it pass
18) RESEARCH—Google the problem and see how others handle it
19) SOLVE THE PROBLEM—speak to the person/apologize/explain
20) RETHINK—what are three different ways to look at your problem
21) http://copingskills4kids.net or http://learningdynamicsinc.org/2012/11/10/coping-with-stress/

TIP: Find 20 more healthy coping skills. Some people have compiled a list of 100 coping techniques or skills. NOTE: Use a coping skill to calm your mind. Then, once you are calm, be sure to address the underlying problem that caused the stress. Remember, we cannot change other people, but we can change the way that we respond to them and their actions.

2. School Stress

School is not fun for everyone and for some students it can be overwhelming. Sometimes better time management, better study habits, or better communication with parents and teachers can help. But other changes — not related to the classroom — can also help.

TIP: Go to http://www.webmd.com/parenting/features/coping-school-stress and see if you can find five ideas that can help you cope with stress at school.

3. Friends

A trusted friend can be one of your greatest stress relievers and at the same time, one of your major stressors. According to the Huffington Post, "A small new study shows that during stressful times, being around a best friend decreases levels of the stress hormone cortisol.... These findings provide a better understanding as to how close relationships might serve as buffers against the adjustment difficulties that result from negative experiences." http://www.huffingtonpost.com/news/best-friend

At the same time, your friends are human and there will be times when they make mistakes, disagree with you, tell one of your secrets, or in some way hurt you. All of these things can greatly add to your stress.

TIP: Resolving conflicts with your friends can make your relationship stronger. It can also give you the tools for solving conflicts with your parents, your workmates, and your future children. For tips on solving conflicts go to http://www.helpguide.org/mental/eq8_conflict_resolution.htm.

CHOICES: In addition to your family, which you didn't get to choose, your friends — whom you DO get to choose — will have a powerful influence on your choices. Pick friends who share your values. IF you want to stay free of drugs and underage drinking, it can be really helpful to choose friends who want this for themselves. Friends can support you and your values.

4. Body Image

Greg, mentioned earlier in section #1 under Family Problems, had another stressor. He felt that he did not fit in at school. Greg was large and students teased him for being "fat."

He said, "School was a lot of negative feedback for me. I had to have positive. My new friends helped me to relax and to see myself in a new way. And when I was around my extended family, I was around people that liked me and cared about me."

Where did Greg get his "new friends?" With his mom's help, he found teens — outside of school — who shared his interests. Also, he spent more time with his extended family — people who looked like him and liked themselves.

TIP: Look for people who share your interests and spend time with them. Surround yourself with mature people who can look past your exterior and see the real you. Seek out others who seem lonely and be a friend.

Ryan, mentioned in Chapter 13 of this book, was predominately black. But he was also white, Asian, Hispanic, and Indian. Sometimes he was the only black student on his bus. He said, "Everyone wants to classify you. Everyone wants to put you in a group. Even at college kids want to know, 'Who are you?' I'm a person. Just a person. When I was young, I thought, 'Maybe if I was white, I would fit in better.'"

By his early teens, Ryan was feeling quite alone and unhappy. It was then that he decided to stop using his shyness and his color as an excuse for his isolation.

"I decided that I have to accept myself for who I am. I am still discovering things about myself, but I like myself. Also, I decided to be more friendly. I decided that I could not be shy and friendly at the same time. So I opened up and made myself talk to more people. The more I did it, the easier it got. And, I made friends with people of all ages."

QUESTIONS:
1) How did Ryan accept personal responsibility for making changes in his life?
2) What evidence is there that body image — his color and ethnicity — were not *really* roadblocks to friendships?

TIP: It is easier for people to accept you if you accept yourself. Everyone has positive and negative attributes. What are five attributes that you like about yourself? Are you kind, friendly, supportive, generous, loyal, joyful, humorous, patient, hard-working, or peaceable? Accept and grow your assets. Then, like Ryan, be honest and make a decision to reach out to people of all ages. Go to http://kidshealth.org/teen/your_mind/body_image/body_image_problem.html

5. Romantic Relationships

Young people seem to be dating at younger and younger ages. This sets the stage for considerable stress. Two people can have vastly different expectations about what is "supposed" to happen on a date.

According to research at www.LoveIsRespect.org :

• Nearly 1.5 million high school students nationwide experience physical abuse from a dating partner in a single year.
• One in three adolescents in the U.S. is a victim of physical, sexual, emotional or verbal abuse from a dating partner, a figure that far exceeds rates of other types of youth violence.
• One in 10 high school students has been purposefully hit, slapped or physically hurt by a boyfriend or girlfriend.
• One quarter of high school girls have been victims of physical or sexual abuse.
• Girls and young women between the ages of 16 and 24 experience the highest rate of intimate partner violence—almost triple the national average.
• Violent behavior typically begins between the ages of 12 and 18.

- The severity of intimate partner violence is often greater in cases where the pattern of abuse was established in adolescence.
- About 72% of eighth and ninth graders are "dating."
- Violent relationships in adolescence can have serious ramifications by putting the victims at higher risk for substance abuse, eating disorders, risky sexual behavior and further domestic violence.
- Being physically or sexually abused makes teen girls 6x more likely to become pregnant and twice as likely to get an STI.
- Half of youth who have been victims of both dating violence and rape attempt suicide, compared to 12.5% of non-abused girls and 5.4% of non-abused boys.

• Another study showed: Nearly one-third of all girls and one out of five boys are sexually abused before their 18th birthday. Sexually-abused children are *26 times more likely* to use drugs. (Getting professional help can normalize the risk factors, even years after the abuse.)

TIP: Be smart. Don't date just because "everyone else is." Wait until you are ready. IF you are in an unhealthy relationship, remember, you cannot change the other person. Take the Healthy Relationship Quiz at
http://www.loveisrespect.org/is-this-abuse/power-and-control-wheel
To chat about a relationship problem: text "loveis" to 77054 or call 1-866-331-9474 or 1-866-331-8553 TTY.

6. Bullying

Meet Ruth Fair, a self-confirmed bully: *"From my earliest memories, I felt that life was not fair. Growing up in a home where each girl had a different father, it was easy to compare the time and attention each dad gave his daughter. The fact was, my dad rarely came to see me.*

"I started to lie, because I did not like the truth. The truth was, my dad was an alcoholic and he didn't keep his promises and I was jealous of my sisters.

"I got my attention by acting out. To compound my pain and frustration, when I was nine years old, a friend of my grandmother's began routinely molesting me.

"I couldn't tell anyone because I knew that no one would believe me because I lied so much. **By middle school I had earned the reputation of being a bully."**

She literally beat kids up if they did not bring her money. This worked until one girl came in with her mother instead of the cash.

"I got called into the office and suspended. My mom whipped and then put me on punishment for two months. After that I calmed down for a while," Fair said. Fair stopped bullying.

But then the envy and anger began to creep back and Fair's life took a nosedive. At age 14, she began smoking marijuana to calm the rage. Soon after that she began running away from home. By the age of 16 she was an emancipated teen with lots of boyfriends, mostly five to ten years older than her. Her life spiraled downhill from there and it would take her another 16 years to recover and rebuild her life.

Ruth now advises: "Stand up to the ill-treatment of others. For instance, if someone is bullying someone else, don't stand and watch it. Go report that person to a higher authority because next time it could be you."

Questions:
1) What factors lead to Ruth choosing to hurt and bully others?
2) How did bullying give Ruth a sense of power in her life?
3) What did one victim do to stop Ruth's bullying?
4) How do you feel about Ruth's advice?
5) What would happen if "everyone" came to the aid of the victim?

Cyberbullying

According to a 2011 scientific study one in five teens reports being cyberbullied: having had mean or embarrassing things posted about them online on a social networking site such as Myspace or Facebook.

"Compared to teens spending no time on a social networking site in a typical day, teens regularly spending time on a social networking site are likelier to experience cyberbullying." See the full report.
http://www.casacolumbia.org/upload/2011/20110824teensurveyreport.pdf

Practical tips to deal with cyberbullying:
- Don't be friends with people that harass and cyberbully others.
- Treat all people the way you want to be treated — kindly & respectfully.
- Limit your use of social networking sites.

TIP: Make the choice NOT to cyberbully others or to laugh at disrespectful or hurtful postings. Go to this website and watch videos of people who have been cyberbullied and what they did to recover.
http://www.stompoutbullying.org/aboutbullying_dont_be_cyberbullied.php
Call for help and support 1-855-790-4357

Gossip

"A person who habitually reveals personal or sensational facts about others ... rumor or report of an intimate nature" http://www.merriam-webster.com/dictionary/gossip

Below is an old proverb (author unknown) about the dangers of gossip:

A man kept spreading hurtful gossip about an older man in a village. One day, he realized the harm he had caused to the older man and he asked for forgiveness. He asked the older man what he could do to make up for the trouble he'd caused.

The older man instructed him to go to the middle of town with a feather pillow, cut it open and let the feathers fly. The man did this and watched as the feathers blew onto roof tops, into the fields, and across town. He went back to the older man to report that he completed his assignment.

The older man said, "Now go and collect the feathers because your gossip has spread as far as those feathers." The older man not only forgave the gossiper, he gave him a gift—the gift of understanding the true consequences of gossip.

Questions:
1) Why do you think that people gossip?
2) Why is it harmful?
3) Why is it so hard to undo the damages?
4) When you hear gossip, how can you stop it from spreading?
5) What gentle reminder could you give to the gossiper?

7. **Depression**

Teen depression is a common problem and it can affect males, females, high achievers, struggling students, rich or poor, and all races of young people. According to research found at http://www.teendepression.org

- About 20 percent of teens will experience teen depression before they reach adulthood.

- Between 10 to 15 percent of teenagers have some symptoms of teen depression at any one time.

- About 5 percent of teens are suffering from major depression at any one time.

- A small percent of teens also suffer from seasonal depression, usually during the winter months in higher latitudes.

- 30 percent of teens with depression also develop a substance abuse problem.

- Depressed teens are more likely to have trouble at school and in jobs, and to struggle with relationships.

- Untreated depression is the number one cause of suicide, the third leading cause of death among teenagers. 90 percent of suicide victims suffer from a mental illness, and suffering from depression can make a teenager as much as 12 times more likely to attempt suicide.

- Less than 33 percent of teens with depression get help, yet 80 percent of teens with depression can be successfully treated if they seek help from a doctor or therapist, and **many local health clinics offer free or discounted treatment for teens with depression.**

Am I depressed?

Read the list below. If you are experiencing these symptoms for more than a few weeks, you may be depressed. Sometimes, getting more sleep, improving diet and exercise, journaling, and talking with family and friends can help. Sometimes therapy, herbal remedies, or medications are beneficial. Sometimes, professional help works best. http://www.teendepression.org

- Difficulty concentrating and/or making decisions
- Trouble sleeping or sleeping excessively
- Feeling down, hopeless, or depressed for the majority of the day
- Feeling worthless or guilty
- Increased anxiety or irritability
- Increased fatigue or loss of energy
- Lacking interest or pleasure in activities you once enjoyed
- Pain anywhere on the body that cannot be explained by illness or injury
- Significant weight loss or weight gain
- Decreased or increased appetite
- Recurrent thoughts of death, suicide or inflicting bodily harm upon yourself

**TIP: Just like there is no shame in developing a physical illness — such as a cold or diabetes — there is no shame in having depression. Like a physical illness, it is good to seek medical attention. In fact, some physical illness can cause depression. Take the depression quiz so that you can be better prepared to help a friend. http://www.webmd.com/depression/rm-quiz-depression
Or call 1-800-273-8255 for a live conversation.**

8. Negative Peer Pressure

Peer pressure is "influence from your peers." That influence can be positive (healthy) or negative (unhealthy). Like stress, negative peer pressure is not a teen thing, it is a life thing. So the sooner you learn to successfully cope with it, the more productive your life can be.

Drew's story

Meet high school soccer player, Drew Craven. Drew went to a party with his friends and at the party, some older teens exerted some negative peer pressure to use drugs.

"We saw a couple of kids go into the woods to use marijuana. We had to decide what we were going to do. (They were invited to join in.) I told my friends that I did not want to do that. They said that they didn't want to do that either. They listened to me," Drew said proudly.

TIP: Sometimes simply stating "I don't want to" is the best response. Most people respect freedom of choice. We don't "owe" people reasons for our choices. Also, we are not responsible for controlling other people's choices.

Questions:
1) What if Drew did not make an "I" statement and instead said that his mom or someone else didn't want him to?
2) How did Drew become a POSITIVE peer influence?
3) What method of negative influence did the older kids use?

CHALLENGE: It is easier to take a stand for your beliefs if you are really convinced of something. In other words, no one could use peer pressure to get you to eat carrots if you really hate carrots! So find out the truth about recreational drug use. Do YOUR OWN research and then you can OWN your decision. http://www.drugfreeworld.org

Theodrick's story

"I was bothered because my father was not there. (He died when Theodrick McCollum was four years old.) When I looked at other people, I just thought that they had perfect homes and mine was just so messed up."

In ninth grade, Theodrick discovered a way to escape these painful feelings. A friend was having a little party. Theodrick's mother, who required him to be in before dark, let him go. She knew the boy's parents and knew the parents would be home.

At this party, like ones in the school gym, McCollum was too scared to ask the girls to dance. That is, until he sneaked outside with another guy and had a couple of drinks. Then he went inside and danced.

"It made me feel like I was okay. I felt like I was as good as the next person. It was amazing! I liked that!"

That same year, after a football game, an upperclassman introduced him to marijuana. In time, Theodrick became addicted to cocaine. Check out Theodrick's full story — his discovery — in the "Three Addicts" mini-book included in this book.

Question: 1) Why do you think Theodrick responded so quickly to the negative peer pressure from a friend who invited him to engage in underage drinking?
2) Theodrick noted that it was an *upperclassman* that introduced him to marijuana. What difference might that make?

CHALLENGE: Theodrick's "quick fix of drugs and alcohol" to cope with painful feelings and his lack of confidence actually set him back in his maturity as months and years passed by. Do your homework. Prove to yourself the true cost of trying to take a short cut to the maturity process. www.TeenCentral.net www.drugfree.org

DID YOU KNOW: Theodrick changed his circle of friends when he decided to change his values and change his life. THEN, he set out to help others who also wanted to make a change. Theodrick led by example and helped others.

Mariah's story

Mariah Scott spent the night with her girlfriends. When their parents went to bed, her friends asked her to join them in sneaking some alcohol from the liquor cabinet.

"I was able to stay strong. I was able to say, 'No thanks. I'm good.' Instead of me being embarrassed, I think they were embarrassed that they asked."

According to Mariah, the whole group decided against drinking alcohol after she declined to participate. Mariah felt respected and stronger after this incident.

Questions: 1) How did Mariah stand up to negative peer influence without making her friends feel bad?
2) Mariah was pleasantly surprised by her friend's reaction. Why do you think her friends respected her and her choice?
CHALLENGE: What is the big deal about underage drinking . . . especially if you are safe and with friends that you trust? Do some research. www.AboveTheInfluence.com

Peer Pressure Responses

You will be tested by negative peer pressure. Knowing that, you can plan in advance what you will say. Below are some responses that have been successful for other teens. Find responses that work well for you. Practice your responses until you get comfortable with them. Practice with friends, family, or in front of the bathroom mirror!

RESPONSES THAT WORK

1) "No thanks. I'm good."
2) "Why would I want to do that?"
3) "I'm not as smart as you. I need to keep all of my brain cells!"
4) "That's not going to get me where I want to go."
5) "Let me think about it. I'll tell you tomorrow."
6) "I don't want to do that."
7) "I haven't got time for that."
8) "I'd rather be me than follow other people."
9) Walk away. You don't OWE them a reason for your choices.
10) "You're kidding, right? You know me better than that!"

TIP: Ask yourself: How will I feel if I stand up for what I believe is right? How will I feel if I cave in to the pressure?

CHALLENGE: A cute comic strip said, "I've got to be me. Everybody else was already taken." (Frank & Ernest 2006) Think about the value of staying true to yourself. Check out http://www.thecoolspot.gov/right_to_resist.asp

BE NOSY: Check out the "Parent Handbook" in this book. The Parent Handbook has different information. Take a peek. See how parents think.

What if my parent is addicted to drugs or alcohol?

About 10 percent of young people are being raised in homes with at least one parent who is addicted to drugs or alcohol. Often this is hidden from neighbors and workers and only the immediate family knows about the problem. What can you do?

Jack's story

Jack grew up in a home where both of his parents were alcoholics. His parents — business people in the community — managed to keep it a secret. But it was no secret to Jack.

"One time, I bought a brand new shirt that I planned to wear to school the next day. I laid it out on a seat in my bedroom. In the middle of the night, my mom stumbled into my room, mistaking it for the bathroom, and urinated all over my shirt," Jack recalled.

Jack was angry. But he didn't stay that way. He solved the problem. He found a different shirt to wear and went ahead to school.

He also solved the problem of laundry in general. He took it upon himself to go to the Laundromat for the whole family. He washed, dried, and ironed the family's clothes. It was his way of making sure that he had clean clothes and that his parents had fresh clothes for work.

In time, Jack came to realize that "getting mad" or trying to "change" his parents was a waste of his energy.

"I came to realize that the only thing my parents needed from me was love. It was a hard lesson to learn. But I learned to genuinely love them," Jack said.

Jack has been happily married for years and he is now a grandfather. Even though being the child of two alcoholic parents made him four times as likely to become an alcoholic, than someone raised without an alcoholic parent, Jack made the choice to stay free of this problem.

Jack is a highly respected business man in his community. He is living proof that our parent's problems do not need to become our problems. Aside from his secular work, Jack has a ministry to help young people growing up in homes with drugs or alcohol trouble. He helps the teens learn how to love their parents. It's hard, but it's the best choice for everyone.

Questions: 1) What coping skills did Jack use to deal with his parents' addiction problems?
2) How did it benefit Jack to focus on "solving the problem instead of "changing his parents?"
3) About how many teens in your school are likely growing up in homes like Jack's? What extra challenges do they face?

Carol's story

Carol Elizabeth Horton never invited friends to her house. That's because she never knew what to expect when she walked in the door.

"My mom was an alcoholic and I never knew if she would be passed out on the sofa, breaking dishes in a rage, or chasing my dad with a butcher knife. She only drank about three days a week, but I never knew which three days that would be," Carol said matter-of-factly.

On the other four days, her mom was fairly typical. She cooked delicious dinners, entertained her family with inspiring stories and listened to them tell about their day.

Carol said that when she arrived home from school, she could tell within five seconds what the night was going to be like. On a bad night, her mom would get up at 2 o'clock in the morning, turn on all the lights, and start screaming. Often, that was on a school night.

Like many children of alcoholics, Carol isolated herself. She never talked about the problem, because while she was ashamed of her family, she also felt compelled to protect it. All of this made Carol feel highly stressed and like a misfit. However, she also became unusually self-reliant.

"I learned to think for myself, to find five other ways to do anything, and to always anticipate the unexpected," Carol explained calmly.

Through it all, Carol refused to harbor negative feelings toward her mother. Instead, Carol listened compassionately to her mom until her moods stabilized and the alcohol wore off.

"My mother was very hurt. It pained her that she did not get a chance to go to college. She was a brilliant woman. She felt as though she was robbed and it caused her deep pain," Carol explained.

At the age of 13, Carol discovered a nearby horse farm. The owners let her "exercise" and care for a horse. "That was my therapy. This horse knew who I was and he loved me. He always treated me like he was glad to see me. It was the closest thing to unconditional love that I had ever felt. He saved me from my isolation," Carol said warmly.

Interestingly, at the tender age of 10, Carol made a promise to herself. She vowed that when she was a mom, she would be the opposite of her mom.

"I knew that I could not change my family, but I didn't have to become it. I could choose my own destiny and I did. My children grew up with two loving parents and all the friends and experiences that I never had," said Carol.

Amazingly, in surviving her childhood chaos Carol developed a unique skill set. Like an expert surfer, Carol can ride the waves of crisis and guide others through it too.

So when it came time to choose a career, emergency room (ER) nursing — constant crisis management — was a perfect match. Carol proved to be that rare mixture of cool-headed problem-solver and compassionate comforter. In short, Carol was a nurse that could bandage the body and mend the soul.

Carol loves her life and still loves and cares for her mom, who is now a recovered alcoholic.

Questions: 1) What did Carol know about her mother that allowed her to develop a feeling of compassion for her?
2) What coping skills did Carol use?
3) What life skills did Carol learn from her trialsome childhood?
4) What evidence do you see that Carol took responsibility for her own life without trying to change her mother?

TIP: It is never the child's fault when a parent has an addiction problem. Decide what aspects of your life you can change and control, without trying to control or change your parents. http://www.alanonla.org/html2/alateen.html

9. Money

If you are like most teens, you want things. You know that it takes money to buy what you want, but you may not be sure how to earn, save, and budget money. It is never too soon for you to take responsibility for earning and learning about money.

TIP: Let family, friends and neighbors know that you are interested in working for money. For teen job ideas and money management ideas go to http://www.money-management-works.com/teens-earn-money.html

10. Change

Change of all sorts can be stressful. For many teens it is stressful to move to a new neighborhood, changes schools, start a new job, welcome a new baby brother or sister, or fit in to a new circle of friends. When people feel the stress of change, they are vulnerable to self-destructive decisions, including the risk of drug and alcohol abuse.

From tadpoles to frogs

As a teen, you are especially vulnerable to drug abuse because you are experiencing intense physical and emotional change. In the midst of this change, you can feel like you don't fit in. Like tadpoles with long tails and short legs, you *know* that you don't belong in the kiddie pond with the pollywogs, but you also know that you are not ready for life on land. This awkward morphing process from adolescence to adulthood makes you easy prey for those marketing drugs as the miracle cure for growing pains.

You can be lured into taking drugs as an *easy* way to *feel* better. Like little mice stealing bacon from a mouse trap, some teens believe that they can increase their *self-esteem* and *sense of purpose* without working for it.

Many teens use drugs for a while and then decide to get back to the work of growing up. For some though, the trap snaps shut. Sometimes it's fatal. The Internet has pages and pages dedicated to the memory of young people who died from drugs. But for most, it is not fatal. It's a trap. Drug abuse becomes a new problem on top of all the other unresolved problems that the teen has been avoiding. Drug use becomes a compulsion, rather than a choice. Drug abuse becomes the disease of addiction.

Once addiction sets in, teens have to break out of that trap, and then face all the unresolved problems they avoided in the first place. The problem is, by the time use escalates to addiction, most teens have bankrupted themselves physically, emotionally, and morally. So they find themselves fighting a bigger battle with lesser resources.

It is likely that all of this could have been avoided if the teen's problems had been solved in the first place. If the teen had received the help he or she needed, even if the teen chose to experiment with drugs, it is unlikely that experimentation would have progressed to abuse or addiction. And in most cases, someone besides the teen knew about the unresolved problem and it continued unchecked.

That brings the responsibility back to the individual. Like the billions of cells that make up a body, if we as individuals nourish and protect those in our sphere of influence—our body will be healthy. In the end, the healthier and more caring the individual, the family, the neighborhood, the state, the country, the hemisphere, and the world; the greater the chances of having a society free from the deception of illicit drug use.

TIP: If there is one guarantee in life, it is this: things are always changing. Try thinking of "change" as an "adventure." Write down what you think will happen and then write down what actually happens. You might be surprised!

Also, stay in touch with friends (phone or text) and let them know how things unfold. Ask others how they coped with the particular "change" you are facing. Remember to use your COPING SKILLS listed earlier in this section. To have a free and real conversation with a caring adult call the Girls and Boys Club National Hotline at 1-800-448-3000.

I have a partner?

Regardless of how your life turns out — wonderfully successfully, ordinary, or a rock-bottom dismal failure — you cannot take all the credit, nor can you accept all the blame.

The relationship between a parent and a child is a *partnership*. Sometimes the parent puts one brick up and the child does the same. Sometimes the parent puts one brick up and the child takes down two. And sometimes the child puts up two bricks and the parent takes down one.

Even for the child who never met his parent, that parent is a partner. Sometimes a parent is only able to give his child the gift of life. But that is still a lot to be thankful for.

In the end, and though the primary craftsmen in the partnership are the child and his parents, other significant influences include adult role models in the child's life, school culture, friends, the laws of the land, and, yes, even a family's belief or lack of belief in God. Prove this to yourself by reading Chapter 13 of this book — Four Teens From Two Families.

I didn't ask to be born!

It may be tempting to disclaim any responsibility for your life by declaring, "I didn't ask to be born." But as my editor, John Staples, explained to me: in the moment of conception, there is only one winner. You swam up stream and beat out all the competition. You chose life. You are a winner! Build a life you love. Help others build a life they love. Continue to be a positive influence.

<u>ONE FINAL TIP:</u> *Please keep reading!*

- **Read Chapter 13 in this book—"Four Teens From Two Families."** Read four first-person accounts of teens. Check out the Three Cs!

- **Read the Parent's Handbook—** It has completely different information—but it is all about parents and teens.

- **Read "A Call for Compassion"**—It will give you the big picture, showing WHY it is challenging to be a teen today.

- **KNOW that your voice has power.** As you make positive choices, take a visible and verbal stand. Encourage others to stand up and speak up. Help give kids a national voice. Contact the author with your ideas: www.UndertheInfluence.org or www.ClassicWritingPR.com.

> *"Free Online Resources"* are listed in the back of this book. Download scientific studies and access free help lines.

General James Gorham's Challenge to YOU

Gen. James Gorham

What kind of influence do I choose to be?

General James R. Gorham (retired National Guard 2012) said that he was willing to die for what he believed in. He challenges all youth, **"Will you sacrifice your *reputation*, your *popularity*, or your *coolness* in order to defend what you know to be right and to help others to stay free of drugs and alcohol?"**

What's YOUR Call?

Mini-book IV

Lessons Learned—Three Recovered Addicts

"One student of ours," said North Forsyth Assistant Principal Sandra Hunter, "went through the drug counseling and it made a difference in his life."

No one at school was supposed to know this. Accepting counseling gave this student—who failed the drug test—immunity from public knowledge. But he told on himself because he knew Hunter *cared*. Her office is filled with students seeking her attention. Even after these kids graduate, Hunter keeps their photographs on display.

"This student was very positive and bright but he got off on the wrong track. I think he was happy for the help—not at first—but after he saw how it changed his life."

This student became a promoter of substance-free living. He kept himself clean and he helped his friends to stay clean. On game nights, he warned them that temptations would abound. He encouraged them to stay away from drugs and alcohol.

"He *voluntarily* stayed in the 'It's My Call' program," said Hunter, "and he got himself into college. This program changed his life."

This was not the only student success story I found. What if the $50,000 annual cost of the drug-testing program saved just one life? Would it be worth it?

*   *   *

Below are stories of three people who lived in Kernersville or attended school there. They went from drug use (voluntary), to drug abuse (voluntary, but excessive and causing problems), to drug addiction (non-voluntary, compulsive, and psychologically dependent), to recovery (not a cure, but abstaining from drug use and rebuilding one's life).

As you read about their lives, ponder these questions: Why did these teens begin using drugs? Was their intention to become addicts? As their lives spun out of control, how did they hurt innocent people around them? Was the high cost of treatment justified? How are they using their lives now?

Theodrick McCollum

Theodrick McCollum graduated from East Forsyth High School in Kernersville in 1974. He didn't get to walk with his class because his daily habit of marijuana and alcohol had cost him one precious class. He had to go to summer school. That September, he got his diploma, became an unwed father, and joined the army. None of these events caused him to "grow up" or "kick" his addiction.

From a young age McCollum was plagued with negative feelings. He felt self-conscious, sad, unloved, and unacceptable. It is not that love wasn't there, he just couldn't *feel* it.

He excelled at Little League, but he didn't remember his homerun hits. He remembered people in the crowd yelling out, "Get that big kid out of there. He's too old. He's too big."

In seventh, eighth, and ninth grades, he played football, baseball, basketball, and ran track.

"I was good at all of them," he said, "but I never *felt* like I measured up."

He was a good student, but high grades didn't bolster his self-worth. Instead, school was an embarrassment. For one thing, back in the 1960s, his teachers did not allow him to use his nickname, Rick. They insisted on calling him Theodrick.

"Every time my name was mispronounced I *felt* very small. People would laugh and I couldn't stand it."

McCollum looked at the other kids and thought they had better families.

"I was bothered because my father was not there. (He died when McCollum was four years old.) When I looked at other people—I just thought that they had perfect homes and mine was just so messed up."

In ninth grade, McCollum discovered a way to escape these painful feelings. A friend was having a little party. McCollum's mother, who required him to be in before dark, let him go. She knew the boy's parents and knew the parents would be home.

At this party, like ones in the school gym, McCollum was too scared to ask the girls to dance. That is, until he sneaked outside with another guy and had a couple of drinks. Then he went inside and danced.

"It made me *feel* like I was okay. I felt like I was as good as the next person. It was amazing! I liked that!"

That same year, after a football game, an upperclassman introduced him to marijuana. He liked it, but in 1971, marijuana was hard to get in the black schools.

Things changed in 1972, when the schools in Winston-Salem were integrated. McCollum was bused to Mt. Tabor High School for 10th grade. He was placed in geometry and other advanced classes.

"My self-esteem really sunk then," said McCollum, "because when the teachers would ask questions, all the white students raised their hands. They had already been through this. I hadn't, and other black students hadn't. We were getting passed down books (at the all-black schools) and got a lesser education. So these white students, it was just like they were taking off. And I remember sitting in class feeling like I didn't know nothing."

McCollum found a couple of white guys at school who smoked marijuana.

"That is when I started smoking marijuana on a regular basis. At my black school, I couldn't get it. At the white school it was plentiful, plentiful. I'm not blaming this on white people. I guess it was just more *available* and I started smoking it more."

Whereas McCollum was able to keep his grades up while drinking, he could not excel while smoking pot.

"With marijuana, what I know from personal experience and from studies is that marijuana interrupts your motivation. You lose the motivation to do the things you once did. It interrupts the transmitters. The tetrahydrocannabinol (THC) collects in fatty tissue. It is fatty tissue that lines our brain cells. So your reaction is slower. Your motivation is lower. I didn't even want to play sports anymore and I loved sports. That was one outlet that I had, but I stopped playing."

In 10th grade, McCollum was smoking marijuana and drinking four to five times per week. That summer he got a job, and with his mother's help he bought a 1963 Rambler. He hid some marijuana in his car and his mother found it. He lied. She didn't believe him.

"She threw it down the commode. I was so mad on the inside. That was $20 of marijuana and it was good," he said with a laugh.

Normally, his mother would have whipped him. But this time she just said, "Look. You stop this. This ain't no good for you.'"

McCollum did make an effort to change. He switched schools to get away from his friends and went to East.

But his plan to start fresh and kick the drugs did not work.

"I got hooked up with that same type of crowd because I still had that same empty feeling inside me. My addiction to marijuana really took off in 11th grade."

By this time, McCollum found an advantage to being big for his age. At 16, he started sneaking into nightclubs to meet older women.

"My mom said I had to be home at 11 o'clock. You know the party started at 11. So I would take the whipping. She would do it. She was doing the best that she could."

Soon, a day did not go by when McCollum was not either smoking pot, drinking, or both.

What were the drugs, alcohol, and sex all about for McCollum?

"Fulfillment. They made me forget everything that I didn't feel. I never *felt* loved. So when I was drinking, I didn't think about not feeling loved. I would forget every negative feeling that I had."

McCollum went to church and sang in the choir throughout his school years. While he did not find peace or love at church, he did find lust. He started dating a girl a year younger than he, and by the time he was 18 years old, he was a father.

"You know why I probably picked her? She wasn't street smart. She just came up in this Christian home and she wasn't worldly. She didn't know things, so I could take advantage of that. I could tell her anything and get by with it."

She had no idea that he was drinking, taking drugs, and being unfaithful to her. She was just one in a long line of innocent girls that he deceived. Days after their baby girl was born, McCollum joined the army.

This was another opportunity for a fresh start. But it failed. McCollum still felt empty inside and in 1974, he found plenty of marijuana and alcohol in the army to fill the void. However, his choice of service—artillery—did not lend itself to the life of an addict. He had to go on week-long training missions in the field and found it impossible to hide enough marijuana and alcohol to last the trip.

"It didn't last but a couple of days. So I'm out here and I think, 'I don't like this. I don't like this.' "

His solution was to stop going to the field. Disobeying orders cost him money, but he didn't care. Then one day, he was given a personal tour of the stockades and a lieutenant offered him a General Discharge under Honorable Conditions.

"I was an addict, but I wasn't stupid," he said. "I knew I was not going to make it in this man's army, so I took the general discharge and they let me out."

McCollum's army career lasted seven months and 28 days. But he wasn't done yet. He returned to Winston-Salem, enrolled in the community college and started collecting about $400 a month from the GI Bill.

Soon, he was failing and stopped attending classes. He continued to cash the free checks, until the army caught on.

Meantime, he found a woman with her own apartment, a nice car, and a job. He moved in. In time, another man and woman joined them. This meant four incomes were coming into one house.

"We smoked weed and drank every night. The other man knew drug dealers who came by the house. That was when (1976) I was introduced to snorting cocaine."

To support his drug habit, McCollum would steal. He never shoplifted as a customer, because his mother had cured him of that as a child.

"When I was 11 years old, I got caught picking up some candy. Now *they* didn't call the police. They called my *mama*. I wish they had called the police. My mama tore my butt up and I would not pick up anything in a store."

But he worked for companies and he would steal from the *inside*.

"When microwaves first came out they were expensive. I found a guy who would buy every microwave that I could come up with. And this place I was working for at this time had plenty of microwaves."

McCollum, as usual, was unfaithful to his girlfriend. Unlike high school girls, she was a grown woman and street smart. She figured him out and kicked him out. He found someone else and entered his first marriage.

It was not about love, it was about lust. The woman refused to move in with him without a marriage license, and so he gave her one. In just a few months, she discovered his other women and left him. Then, his downstairs neighbor, who was selling drugs introduced McCollum to *intravenous* cocaine use.

"We cooked it up and put it in my arm. It felt real good, but I didn't know what was going to be the end result of this."

A couple years later, he met his next wife at a club and was surprised that she was not a drinker or a pot smoker. She was just there to dance. Eventually, they moved in together. He decided to marry her after he got arrested for drunken driving.

"She came and got me out of jail. I said to myself, 'This is the woman for me. This is my wife.'"

He married her, and though he continued drinking and smoking pot, he quit using cocaine. About a year later, he took a job with the sanitation department in Winston-Salem. The other guys on the truck used drugs and he resumed snorting cocaine. Then he got injured on the job and when he returned to work, he was put on a truck with a guy that shot cocaine.

"One Friday, like we always did when we got off work, we went and got some cocaine and marijuana. But this time I had the guy shoot me with some cocaine. My addiction took off and it got worse."

About this time, the credit union made a mistake and gave McCollum access to $10,000 of another man's money. He took it, gave a few hundred dollars to his wife and said he'd be away for a few days. He got a hotel room and bought drugs. In two weeks the money was gone.

"That was the time I almost killed myself doing drugs. I actually seen my shirt pop and I got scared and put down the pipe. (He was smoking crack.) Cocaine can take your heart out. That's how Len Bias died (1986 Boston Celtics' first draft choice). And this is how sick this disease—this addiction—can be. When I heard about Len I said, 'Man, I wish I would have had some of his cocaine. That must have been some good stuff.' "

Just after the Bias tragedy, McCollum had his first encounter with treatment. He was messing up on his job and being unfaithful and irresponsible at home. He was spending all his money on drugs, plus stealing. Still he could not quench his thirst for drugs.

First his mom got tough with him.

"My mom told me, 'I will not do *anything* for you while you are doing what you are doing.'"

Then his wife gave him the ultimatum: "Get treatment or get out!"

McCollum chose treatment and stayed in for 42 days. While there, his first roommate was very serious about staying clean and sober. However, his second roommate was scamming. He had someone bring drugs into the treatment facility. According to McCollum, the roommate asked, "Will you tell?" McCollum replied, "Only if you won't give me any." After he was released he went to a few meetings. Then he resumed his pot habit.

His wife confronted him, but he said to her, "Well, I ain't doing cocaine and that was the problem. I can *maintain* on marijuana."

He did maintain for a while, but then he started smoking crack. His wife had reached her limit and changed the locks on the doors. She didn't leave him in the streets though. She helped him get into a boarding house.

The daily financial demands of his addiction were so heavy that McCollum could not keep up his weekly rent. Then he got a grand idea! He took his Friday paycheck and bought a lot of cocaine. He planned to sell enough to catch up on his bills and save some to get high on.

"I got it all packaged up, but I made one mistake. I had to *try* it. When I tried it, I smoked it all day long until 2 o'clock in the morning and until it was gone."

When McCollum regained his senses, he started to evaluate his life. He was 34 years old and had nothing. His car, a 1988 Isuzu, was wrecked when he lent it to drug dealers in exchange for "rocks" (crack cocaine). He had no car, no money, and only one can of beef stew for food. He had a wife and a five-year-old son, but nothing to give them.

"I was able to sit in that house and *feel* everything. Lonely. Angry at myself. Disgusted at myself. I could not stand to look at myself in the mirror. I had no one to turn to, not my mom, not my wife. I said, 'God *help* me. God this ain't no way to live.' "

Monday morning McCollum went to work and told his supervisor, "I need to go back into treatment. I need some help."

His supervisor said, "You can stop that stuff anytime you want."

McCollum said, "Man I wouldn't want to take a chance with that. (The city of Winston-Salem had started drug-testing employees and McCollum thought he could lose his job if he tested positive.) I wouldn't be taking this chance in telling you if I could just stop."

McCollum got permission to talk to the superintendent.

She said, "Didn't you go to treatment in 1986?"

He said, "Yeah. But then I wanted to go there to fool my wife, my mama, and to fool y'all."

McCollum entered treatment for the second time on March 20, 1990, and has been clean ever since. This time he was serious and he laid down the law for the other patients.

He told them, "Look. If you want to do drugs while you are in here, don't let me see it. Because if I see it, I'm going to tell. Now I am here to save my life. I don't *want* to go back to the way I was living."

This time the 21-day treatment involved the 12-step program of Narcotics Anonymous (NA). While at an NA meeting, McCollum met a recovered drug-user he'd known on the streets. The guy had been clean for about a year and McCollum asked him to be his sponsor.

After he was released from treatment, McCollum returned home to his wife and now, two children. The city held his job for him, but the guys on his truck used drugs. He found it hard to stay clean.

"But I had found God and I kept praying to God to *help me* not to use. And I didn't."

Then McCollum changed his prayers. He prayed for God to *remove* him from the situation.

"They say you have to watch what you pray for. Shortly after that prayer, I ruptured my Achilles tendon on my left leg and had to be out of work for about a year."

This made it possible for McCollum to attend NA and AA(Alcoholics Anonymous) meeting every day. Meetings were his new addiction. He was moved by the love of total strangers who picked him up for meetings. The honesty and the love of the group touched him.

"They taught me how to *love* another human being without conditions. I was loving another man, my sponsor. I was loving women without having a lustful feeling—because at NA we hug and these women were just like sisters to me. I loved these people more than I loved my biological family, because I never *knew* how to love before."

The 12-step program taught McCollum a *better way* to feel good. He learned to face himself, accept himself, and to take responsibility for his actions. After he learned how to love himself, he found it easier to love others.

He discovered what he'd been doing wrong as a teenager. He was trying to earn self-esteem and love by being better, faster, smarter, and stronger than other people in school and in sports. But healthy self-esteem does not come from comparing ourselves to others. It comes from embracing ourselves and embracing others. It comes from sharing, caring, giving, helping, forgiving, and loving.

At times McCollum still feels self-conscious, sad, and unacceptable. But now he knows what to do. He *expresses* his feelings by praying, talking to someone who cares, making a list of things he is grateful for, and helping others in need. This process is slower than a quick fix of drugs or alcohol, but it solves the problem instead of avoiding it.

"Had I known this as a young person," McCollum said, "I would have had a whole different life."

By working the 12-steps to reclaim his life and by listening to hundreds of stories from addicts, McCollum has come up with a theory about substance abuse:

"I believe drugs and alcohol are spirits. When we feel low self-esteem, unloved, or like we don't measure up—one choice is to take in a spirit like drugs or alcohol. This spirit will lift us up quickly and fill that void. It feels like a good friend, but then it turns against us and destroys our lives. Eventually, we have to use more and more drugs and alcohol to fill the ever-growing void. In time, we become emotionally and spiritually bankrupt. Our other choice is to learn to feed and grow our inner spirit. This is a much slower process and it takes a lot more work. We do this by accepting God's love, praying, reading the Bible, doing what it says, and learning to wait on God. And, as they say, you have to give away what you want to keep. We must give love and help other people to keep the love that God gives us. Giving to others grows our spirit. It can grow so big that it overflows."

McCollum's loving spirit has been overflowing for years now. When he sees an addict, he does not feel disgust or contempt.

"When I see addicts, I feel love for them. I look at them as a piece of coal and I know that there is a diamond in there. God has put this person in my life—so I can help him find that diamond."

According to McCollum, addicts don't need to be pushed away, ignored, and avoided. They are already *feeling* depleted, unworthy, and unloved.

"I hug them. I don't shake hands. I hug them. And then I tell them that the same God that helped me can help them too. Then I show them that I love them. I offer to *drive* them to a meeting. I *talk* to them. More importantly, I take time to *listen* to them."

Addicts and people with other problems are attracted to McCollum like iron to a magnet. Shortly after he got out of treatment, people from many walks of life kept suggesting that he become a drug counselor. They said he had the experience and the understanding. But most importantly, he *cared.* So in 1992-94, McCollum attended community college and received his certification.

Since that time, he has worked as a substance abuse counselor in the private sector, and in the prison system in North Carolina. Today, he is working for the mass transit system in Winston-Salem, as this allows him to provide better for his wife and two children. However, he is still busy helping others get on and stay on the path to recovery.

Weekly, he attends NA meetings and shares his success story with new arrivals. As assistant minister at his church, he facilitates Friday night meetings where people learn the 12-steps through the scriptures. This group evangelizes once a month, door-to-door, to search for people who need help. Twice a month, McCollum visits the homeless shelters in the city. And in day-to-day life, he is always on the look-out for people in pain.

"Helping others makes me feel like my life is worthwhile. Now I know why God let me live through what I went through—to help other people."

> *"I believe drugs and alcohol are spirits. When we feel low self-esteem, unloved, or like we don't measure up—one choice is to take in a spirit like drugs or alcohol. This spirit will lift us up quickly and fill that void. It feels like a good friend, but then it turns against us and destroys our lives. Eventually, we have to use more and more drugs and alcohol to fill the ever-growing void. In time, we become emotionally and spiritually bankrupt. Our other choice is to learn to feed and grow our inner spirit".*
>
> —Theodrick McCollum, former drug addict

Sheila DeFoor

In August 2002, Sheila DeFoor opened Peacegoods Mission Inc. in Kernersville. She sheltered over 60 homeless women and children during the first 18 months of operation. She gives the women a place to live and a job in the mission thrift shop.

Most of the women are broken—depleted physically, mentally, emotionally, and spiritually. Often they are addicted to drugs and/or alcohol. Sheila understands them because she used to be one of them.

When women are asked to leave the mission because they steal or refuse to get treatment, or they come home under the influence of drugs—DeFoor doesn't count it as failure. She knows that a seed was planted—a seed of hope. For some, it may take many times in treatment, intervention, and accepting a helping hand—before they choose to stay on the path to recovery.

"God is the one that deserves the credit for Peacegoods," said DeFoor. "I could not have done this on my own. God is the one that made this happen and He is the one that keeps it going."

God wasn't always a part of DeFoor's life. DeFoor first became intimately associated with God when she tried suicide.

"I was looking at my daughter (sleeping on the couch during a weekend visitation). I knew that I could not quit using drugs because I had already tried so many times. And I knew that I could not go on using drugs. I did not want my addiction to ruin my children's lives. I would die before I would do this to my kids (she also has a son)."

DeFoor thought back to her childhood. On the outside, her life was a dream come true. Her family had horses, a cook, a maid, a gardener, and a governess. They belonged to two country clubs and their house was built on the Palma Ciea golf course in Tampa, Florida. Materially, DeFoor had everything she wanted.

Emotionally, the family was bankrupt and out of control. Her mother was addicted to prescription painkillers, alcohol, and later, marijuana. She screamed at her children and demeaned them with name-calling. She set no boundaries and let the children swear, smoke cigarettes, and run wild. These were the kids that other children were told not to play with.

DeFoor also lived in fear. She feared for her mother's life and her own when her mother passed out or was carted off to mental institutions. On the inside, DeFoor's life was a nightmare.

Her father abandoned the chaos when DeFoor was six or seven years old. She was stuck there—in the pain, confusion, and anger—until age 11 or 12 when she began using drugs to escape.

Now, as a mother, DeFoor wanted to spare her children this pain. So, with her daughter asleep in the next room, she decided to kill herself. She imagined a glamorous exit—like Marilyn Monroe. She donned a beautiful nightgown, wrote a suicide note, and took three bottles of sleeping pills.

Lying on the bed, she recalled something she had always heard. She had heard that people who kill themselves go to Hell. So she began crying and praying for God to forgive her.

It was soon apparent that suicide by sleeping pills is not glamorous. Her body began grotesquely writhing as her back arched way up off the bed and then fell heavily. Her full body spasms were so intense and so bizarre that it finally woke her husband.

DeFoor's heart stopped and her husband hesitated to call 911. He was afraid that the police would detect that he was high on drugs and that he had drugs in the house. Finally, he decided to make the call that saved DeFoor's life.

She was revived and spent almost two weeks in intensive care.

"Somehow God touched me with that experience. I knew that I would not be doing drugs any more."

DeFoor entered the AA and NA programs. She was a few steps ahead of most new arrivals.

Step One: *"Admitted we were powerless over alcohol (and drugs)—that our lives had become unmanageable."*

Step Two: *"Came to believe that a Power greater than ourselves could restore us to sanity."*

Step Three: *"Made a decision to turn our will and our lives over to the care of God <u>as we understood Him.</u>"*

Step Four: *"Made a searching and fearless moral inventory of ourselves."* This is where the 12-steps started to get tough for Defoor. When she took an honest look at herself, she did not like what she saw. She stole cars, drove drunk and drugged, caused accidents, lied, cheated, shoplifted, stole merchandise on the job, abandoned her two children, had several abortions, divorced four times, slept with her friends' husbands, and deliberately sabotaged her friend's recovery.

DeFoor knew why she lived like this for 25 years. She was trying to numb the pain caused by those who were supposed to love her. Aside from the trauma in her family, two so-called friends raped DeFoor while she was passed out from drugs at age 17. The final blow came a few months later.

She was madly in love with a boy two years her senior. His father owned a pharmacy and he stole enough drugs to keep them perpetually high. A blissful six months went by. One day, without warning, he said goodbye and left town.

"I remember consciously thinking, 'No one will ever hurt me again.' My motto: 'Don't trust, don't feel, and hurt them before they hurt you.'"

> *"I remember consciously thinking, 'No one will ever hurt me again.' My motto: 'Don't trust, don't feel, and hurt them before they hurt you.'"* —Sheila DeFoor, recovered addict

Now, instead of just numbing the pain, she began to inflict pain on others.

"I would look for a guy who thought he was really something and I would try to reduce him to nothing. It was a challenge. I would become whatever he wanted me to become until he fell in love with me and then I would leave him. My heart was stone."

DeFoor's behavior hit rock bottom when she became addicted to cocaine. Cocaine addiction was different than alcoholism. As an alcoholic, she lost her "brains" or her ability to use sound judgement. But with cocaine, she lost her heart and soul. She began to act like an animal.

"The addiction was so bad that I would be crawling around on the carpet looking for pieces of cocaine that may have fallen out of my nose. Sex became almost brutal. I had such a deadened conscience that I could rationalize that anything I did was okay."

Step Five: *"Admitted to God, to ourselves, and to another human being the exact nature of our wrongs."* This step was fairly easy for DeFoor because she was well-practiced at confessing. When she was drunk, she confessed to whoever would listen. It was a little more difficult to confess when both she and the listener were sober, but she humbly complied.

Step Six: *"Were entirely ready to have God remove all these defects of character."* DeFoor realized that many of her problems resulted from pride, covetousness, selfishness, and other negative personality traits. In this step, she prepared herself to let go of negative coping methods and to become vulnerable while learning a new way of living.

Step Seven: *"Humbly asked Him to remove our shortcomings."*

Step Eight: *"Made a list of all persons we had harmed, and became willing to make amends to them all."* Making the list was easy for DeFoor. She knew everyone she had hurt. It was the next step that proved to be the hardest.

Step Nine: *"Make direct amends to such people wherever possible, except when doing so would injure them or others."* Amazingly, most people forgave DeFoor. Three of her four ex-husbands are now friends. However, the father of her daughter and his parents refuse to forgive the havoc DeFoor wreaked on their child.

Business associates, friends, and acquaintances, by and large, were happy she was owning up to her mistakes and moving ahead with recovery. However, some people were difficult to locate. When DeFoor was 17, she was driving drunk and hit a man on a motorcycle. He was seriously injured and may have lost a leg. She has yet to find him.

"Step nine is the hardest step, but also the most freeing step. I was in a perpetual state of fear because I had hurt many people. But once I faced them, once I faced my past, it wasn't there to bite me anymore."

Step Ten: *"Continued to take personal inventory and when we were wrong promptly admitted it."*

Step Eleven: *"Sought through prayer and meditation to improve our conscious contact with God <u>as we understood Him,</u> praying only for knowledge of His will for us and the power to carry that out."* In this step, DeFoor stopped asking God to give her things and instead asked God what he wanted her to give to Him.

Step Twelve: *"Having had a spiritual awakening as the result of these steps, we tried to carry this message to alcoholics (drug addicts), and to practice these principals in all our affairs."* DeFoor likes her life now. Creating and growing Peacegoods has been challenging, but it gives her a chance to teach people the two most important lessons she has learned in life.

"Addiction is a disease. People with addictions are not bad people trying to get good, but sick people trying to get better. And being clean and sober is not enough. We need Jesus too."

Tom Robert Oliver, Jr.

On December 8, 1974, Tom Robert Oliver, Jr. was born amid heartbreak and tragedy. A car accident took his father's life, left his mother permanently disabled, and hastened his entrance into the world.

He lived with his grandparents and was well cared for until he was five years old. Then his mother sued for custody and won. His world was again turned upside down when he was forced to join his family in a small mining town in West Virginia.

"It broke my heart. Every day I missed my grandma and granddaddy. I was sad and angry and felt like I didn't fit in with my stepfather or my mom."

Things Oliver took for granted—food, clothing, and love—became a source of constant anxiety. He couldn't fit in with his family. It was abusive and dysfunctional, as later proven by the courts.

"There were no cookies and milk when I came home (from school), but instead, there were many nights when I went to bed with nothing to eat. If there were no apples on the trees or beans in the field, there was nothing to eat."

School offered little reprieve from home life. Oliver's classmates called him stupid and he was labeled as learning disabled. He was teased about his clothes and was beaten up because he was so small and easy to abuse.

"I felt unloved and angry inside. I felt that if my daddy had been there, things would have been different. And yet, I felt safer at school than I did at home."

> *"I felt unloved and angry inside."* —Tommy, recovered addict

The family got a break when the mining town began to close down and Oliver's grandparents moved the family to Virginia Beach. Oliver's stepfather got a job at the shipyard and suddenly there was plenty of food to eat. His mother's abuse lightened.

Oliver shined at the new elementary school. He was still in a learning disabled class, but he was learning and doing the work.

"This time, instead of getting 'sad faces', I was getting all 'happy faces'. In the mining town they said I could not read, and I was reading. They said I could not spell and I was spelling. And that did away with the 'dumb kid' thing."

When Oliver was 11, his mother divorced and her abuse toward Oliver resumed. The family moved again.

"At (the new) school, it was not uncommon for the other kids to stick me in the dumpster. Even though I was a year or two older than them, I was the shortest and the lightest. I thought, 'If only I had cool clothes, then I would have friends.'"

When he was in junior high, the family moved again. Oliver's grandparents bought them a new trailer and moved it into an old trailer park. It was like having a mansion in the middle of the slums. Oliver was as out-of-place as his house. He was a rare white boy in a predominately black neighborhood.

On the bright side, the house smelled good, the water worked, there was plenty of food, and Oliver didn't have to scrounge for firewood. However, he was planted in the middle of someone else's turf. The boys ended up dividing up the neighborhood and pretending they were in gangs. It was fairly harmless, but it gave Oliver an appetite for violence and control.

When Oliver was in seventh grade, his mother's abuse escalated. The courts ordered him to be returned to his grandparents. He was elated. His grandparents loved him and gave him all the food he wanted. They bought him nice clothes—clothes that were in fashion. They lived in a beautiful house and the neighbors treated Oliver with the same kindness and regard that they had for his grandparents.

"My confidence went sky high. I was wearing Nike sneakers and no one could tell me that I didn't have these. I started fitting in better and making friends. When my confidence went up it was obvious to everyone."

Oliver's grandmother thought that he needed something to boost his self-esteem. She enrolled him in karate classes. He worked very hard and in a few years advanced in belt colors through white, yellow, orange, purple, blue, and finally green. When he hit green, he said he felt like, "I was the man!"

Though life was good, as Oliver advanced in his teenage years, his earlier pain and anger began to boil up inside him. In high school, he decided that *no one* was going to pick on him. He had the means and he was going to defend himself.

Once he got a reputation as a fighter, it seemed as if everyone wanted to test him. Though skilled, Oliver was still small. He built himself up physically as well as he could and then searched for mind control. He had read in magazines that people can create force fields and that mind control can make you twice as strong. He thought if he combined his physical strength with supernatural mind control he would finally be somebody.

"I didn't realize it, but I was getting into the occult. I believed the spirits would give me the power to control anything. I believed it because I wanted it so bad. I wanted control because I never had it."

In a quest for popularity and power, one day Oliver turned on a friend at school.

"He was a rough kid and was trying to fit in too. And I thought that if I beat him up in front of everyone, that would make me the top dog. I wanted to impress everyone, especially the girls."

The fight ended in a tie, but it was a turning point for Oliver's relationship with the school authorities.

"Prior to this, I would play the innocent little thing. The school knew that I had a history of being picked on. I was so little and had a baby face and they never believed that I was starting the fights until this one."

Oliver's lust for violence continued to grow. When he 16, he spotted a tough Vietnamese student at school and marked him for a fight. It was a mistake. Oliver's imagined victory proved to be a devastating defeat. The other guy pummeled Oliver and then humiliated him in front of his friends. At the end of the fight, the guy dropped his shoe and forced Oliver to pick it up.

Oliver's anger festered for an entire year, as he secretly prepared for a rematch. On his chosen day, Oliver picked a fight after school. The other boy met him at a store parking lot. By the time the fight started, Oliver had already worked himself into a rage. He would not stop beating the kid until a store manager came out and threatened to call the police.

The next day the boy came to school and showed Oliver his eye. Cockily, Oliver admired his handiwork and made sure all the other kids knew who made a mess of the boy's face. The boy got angry and called for another fight after school.

Oliver found a metal pipe and began to beat the boy. All the anger and all the hatred he felt deep inside himself was focused on this one student. He couldn't stop himself and probably would have killed the kid had the other students not intervened.

"The kids said I was crazy and pulled me off and broke the fight up."

At age 16, Oliver was arrested and charged with first-degree assault. It took one year for the court date to arrive and Oliver's life spiraled out of control in a hurry.

He started smoking, drinking, using marijuana, having sex, and listening to rap and heavy metal music.

"The music always had to do with sex and violence. Shootings were my favorite and sex. The lyrics to the songs talked about killing people and going to prison."

Oliver found his grandparents' house rules too restrictive, so he got a part-time job and moved out. He grew his hair out, shaved it up underneath into a Mohawk and then twisted it up in knots. He bagged his pants down and left his underwear hanging out. His finishing touch was an earring he self-pierced into his left ear.

"I had this nasty look and I was ugly as sin, but I got more girls like this than I did when I looked innocent."

In the height of his rebellion, Oliver's court date arrived. He was just 17 years old and he felt pretty powerful. His grandparents hired a top-notch attorney and he felt he could beat the rap.

His attorney, whom he called a "Christian lawyer", recommended that Oliver cut his hair, take out the earring, pull up his pants, and tuck in his shirt. Oliver refused.

"He said, 'Son, if you continue down the track you are going on and don't let the Lord take control of your life—I'll see you in here for something twice as bad. Tommy, you have the heart of a murderer.' He was right. I did have the heart of a murderer."

Oliver decided to play the game. He cleaned himself up and did everything in his power to convince the court that he was a nice guy. He even told them about his part-time job and the fact that he was still attending school though not living at home. His attorney told the judge that Oliver had a tough childhood.

"I thought the judge had gone for it. Then he said, 'Son, I sentence you to three years in Western Youth Institute in North Carolina for youthful offenders.' I felt like they could not do that to me. I had all these powers. I saw that I could not control other people. At that point I realized that maybe I wasn't in control."

Before going to the high-rise, as the institute was called, Oliver spent a few days in jail.

"I was the smallest and the youngest. They picked on me, whistled at me, and said they were going to get me. When it came time to eat, the littlest guy doesn't do too good. I gave up my food. If they didn't want the peas or carrots I could eat that, but my Twinkie was always gone."

A few days later, two transport officers came to take Oliver to the high-rise. They let him know right away that they were Christians and they treated him with kindness. They even stopped and bought him a breakfast sandwich.

"I felt like I could not get away from Christians for anything. I had kids at school that talked to me about the Word. A youth pastor had seen me on the streets and tried to witness to me. My attorney, the jail guard, my grandmother, and now these two guys."

He began to think that maybe there was something to Christianity and the Bible.

When he arrived at the high-rise, he was given a room instead of a cell. The rule was, he had to stay in his room for a week while he was being processed. The only reason he could come out of his room was to go to the Chapel.

He went to Chapel, but he went his way. He went smoking a cigar. He knew that it was against the rules, but he wasn't into following rules.

The old preacher asked him to put the cigar out and Oliver refused. They quibbled over this a couple of minutes and then the pastor switched tracks. He turned his Bible to John 3:16 and asked Oliver to read it.

"I realized that Jesus had went to the cross for me. I started shaking and crying. The Holy Spirit convicted me of my sin. And I knew that I needed to change. The pastor led me in the sinner's prayer and at that point, I knew I was saved."

After that, Oliver started reading his Bible daily. In about three months, he was able to give up his addiction to alcohol, drugs, and cigarettes. He joined Prison Fellowship, a group started by ex-con Chuck Colson. Oliver began telling his story to visitors to the facility as part of STOPP (Street Teens Organizing Progressive Progress).

He completed his G.E.D. and went on to take Bible correspondence courses. When he was released from the facility, a group of 10 church members needing a pastor financed his classes at Word of Life Bible School in New York. Though on probation, an exception was made and he was allowed to leave the state.

Oliver carried a 3.4 G.P.A. and was recognized as 'Counselor of the Summer' for excelling in his work with young people in New York.

At age 20, he received a certificate in Rescue Ministry. Then he was off to Moody Bible Institute. In all, he attended four years of Bible college and made the honor roll every semester.

While he was preaching at the Trinity Baptist Fellowship back in Elizabeth City, a Kernersville resident heard him and recommended him as the new Youth Minister at Main Street Baptist Church. In May of 1998, he accepted the job and moved to Kernersville.

"This is something I really believed the Lord wanted me to do. My purpose is to reach out to young people who are hurting—who need a message of hope. I want others to experience what I have experienced. I'm living consistent with The Word—no alcohol, no drugs, no violence."

* * *

Clearly, these lives were worth salvaging. After being successfully treated, each recovered addict has vowed to a lifetime of giving. Each has already helped hundreds of people. As DeFoor noted, "Addicts are not bad people trying to get good, we are sick people trying to get better."

McCollum, DeFoor, and Oliver were all hurt as children. As teenagers, they did not solve their childhood problems. Instead, they attempted to escape emotional pain by using drugs and alcohol. At some point, the repeated voluntary use became excessive and then *compulsive*. While still in high school, each of them was overcome by the insidious *disease of addiction*.

This chronic disease is similar to hypertension and adult onset diabetes. Once someone has the disease, treatment for addiction has the same relapse patterns as other chronic illnesses. Unlike the other two diseases, *addiction is preventable* (but not curable).

McCollum and DeFoor were typical in that they attended treatment two or more times before they decided to practice abstinence and adhere to the treatment regime. By this time they were over 30 years old and had caused considerable harm to themselves, their children, and their community.

Oliver and the North Forsyth student who was caught in the drug test, responded to *early* intervention. Though it is not known how deeply involved the North Forsyth student was in drug abuse, it is known that intervention changed his life. Research indicates that *earlier intervention* has more impact and a higher retention rate.

Early intervention, resolving hidden problems, and getting students' lives back on a positive track—that is what drug policy in the WS/FC Schools is all about.

www.UnderTheInfluence.org

Mini-book V

EVERYONE Can Help

Students

One person can make a difference. That person does not even have to be an adult. A sixth-grade student Amber Bowman made a difference in her class, her school, and her community.

She motivated 16 classmates to raise money for *Kernersville Cares for Kids* during a two-week fundraiser at Southeast Middle School.

"We started off with just $1.50," said Bowman, "and so I got in my piggy bank and took part of my allowance, and collected money from the cheerleaders. *Then,* the whole class got involved."

> In the newspaper story, her teacher Sharman Lakey, said that Bowman was "the little flame that lit the whole class on fire."

That same year, sixth-grade student, Andrea Torres, became the leader in her class at the other middle school in Kernersville.

"In Mexico," said Torres, "I would see people that needed money for food or for clothes and I would give them *my money* instead of buying something for myself. I felt proud to give money to *Kernersville Cares for Kids* because I like to help other people and someday I will need someone to help me."

When her classmates heard her testimony and followed her lead, they too felt the power that comes from giving.

> *"This lets us save lives, kind of like being a hero. It was great because we got to help people we didn't even know."*
> —Jennifer Holmes, 6th grade

These 10 and 11 year olds raised money to buy KCK incentives for *high school* students.

On the other end of the spectrum, Kernersville Mayor Larry Brown (a non-parent) put "Kernersville" into *Kernersville Cares for Kids*. After attending the 2001 Special Leadership Meeting, he helped the KCK board attain an annual Town grant of $4,000. Mayor Brown wanted to help kids because he had received help from the community when he was in his crucial teenage years.

Principal Adolphus Coplin became an excellent case study for the power of *one*. During the first six years of student drug testing, there was the same principal (Coplin) at the same school (Glenn High School) with the same students (approximately 25 percent left each year at graduation and were replaced by incoming freshmen).

In 2001, at the peak of his leadership, 98% of his students joined the random drug/alcohol-testing program. In 2003 and 2004, Coplin let the "It's My Call/It's Our

Call" pledging program "slip off his radar screen." When he stopped leading, his students stopped following and participation nose-dived below 60%.

While Coplin faltered, Principal Dan Piggott rallied Carver to claim the KCK trophy for the first time in 2003 with 92% participation. East Forsyth, under the new leadership of Principal Trish Gainey, came in for a strong second place at 83%. That same year, Southeast Middle School Principal Debbie Blanton-Warren had 89% participation, while Principal Debbie Brooks had 80% voluntary participation at Kernersville Middle School.

These examples demonstrate that *one person*—young or old—can make a difference in the choices that other people make. The key to each person's success was that he or she *cared* and *shared* with the people in his or her *sphere of influence*. It is this pattern of caring and sharing that allows *everyone* to help reduce substance abuse.

It is just that easy. Actually, it's easier. You don't have to join an organization, wear a name badge, or even mention the word "drugs" or "alcohol" to help reduce substance abuse.

Neighbors

When teens are helped to find a *connection in their neighborhood,* substance abuse is reduced. When neighbors see adolescents who are highly stressed, frequently bored, or performing poorly in school, they are seeing teens that have about twice the average risk of using drugs and alcohol. If neighbors can help teens *solve the problems* that are causing the stress, find work or hobbies to reduce the boredom, or help them with their homework, these neighbors are greatly decreasing the odds that these teens will use drugs. It starts by caring enough to make a connection.

Corporate Partnerships

The WS/FC Schools—in partnership with the local Chamber of Commerce and a local bank—found that the *earlier* children receive help, the more effective the help is. In 1999, this partnership recruited about 800 corporate volunteers. Employers paid employees to work one hour a week with developmentally delayed kindergartners. By working one-on-one with their assigned students, these corporate volunteers helped at-risk kindergartners attain about 18 months of development by the end of the school year.

"Sometimes," said Jennifer Propst, from the Winston-Salem Chamber of Commerce, "a single mom is working two jobs and the teacher has 18 students who all need her attention. This volunteer program gives students *individual* time. The kids feel like, 'I'm important. Someone is coming to help *me* every week.' "

Unlike HeadStart or SmartStart, this one-on-one personal mentor program could easily be coined *Heart*Start. Children want to learn and do learn better once they *feel* valued. They feel valued when they receive *personal attention* from a caring adult.

Employers

Employers can do much to help their employees prevent family substance abuse. Just as schools have a captive audience of children, the workplace is often the *best place* to reach parents. At the web site www.theantidrug.com/atwork/ "ready-made resources" such as newsletter articles, parenting brochures, and multilingual literature are available *at no charge*. Aside from assisting employees to help their children, there are direct benefits to the employer. The web site states, "Distribution of these resources can help reduce absenteeism and health care costs while increasing productivity."

Better yet, why not reverse the flow of the corporate partnerships? Just as Chuck Chambers talked to the *students* at Carver High School about goals, attitude, and substance prevention—school personnel can visit the workplace and talk to *parents* about the importance of family rules and consequences, myths that don't work, and problem-solving strategies.

Also, companies interested in becoming drug-free workplaces can visit the U.S. Department of Labor web site at www.dol.gov. The site has statistics, answers to commonly-asked questions, and the tools needed to create a customized drug-free workplace program.

On a micro level, businesses can make a difference one person at a time. In Kernersville, Rex Idol owns Farmer's Feed & Seed store. He created a *teaching moment* when two teenage boys came in to ask for a donation. They wanted free railroad ties to restore a sandbox in their neighborhood park. Idol told the boys he would help them if they would help themselves. He instructed them to collect half the cost of the ties from their neighbors and then he would donate the other half. First, though, the teens would have to promise him that they would stay free of drugs, alcohol, and cigarettes. The boys made the promise and Idol made an impression. The boys told their friends and family about "their promise to the hardware man."

Retired People

Matching retired people with the young seems to create a symbiotic solution. Both groups are at increased risk of feeling disconnected. By working together, the young and the aged can create a fresh connection with a powerful sense of purpose.

Esther was 81 years old before she began to volunteer at school. She got the idea from her younger friend, Cynthia. Cynthia was in her mid-sixties at the time. Cynthia thought that working with children would take Esther's mind off the recent loss of her husband. She was right.

> *"If you are helping other people you have to put your own problem into perspective. You have to put your problem on the shelf so you can work with their problem. You are forced to think about them and not yourself."*
> —Esther, an 81-year-old volunteer

Most children like having a "grandma" or "grandpa" help them with their reading, spelling, and math. And they especially like a warm and listening ear.

"Kids will talk to their mentors about things that they will sometimes not talk to their parents or teachers about. I help them *accept and cope* with their problems. I help them put things *in perspective* so that their problems do not interfere with the rest of their lives. That is the most fun part of mentoring—helping the kids solve their problems," said Esther.

Over the last six years, Esther has worked with over a dozen children. All but one has been happy to work with her. The exception was a fifth-grade boy who previously had only male mentors. Probably none of them were as old as Esther. When she was assigned to him, he told her bluntly, "I don't want you."

Esther was not deterred. She assured him, "If you will give me a chance, I'll try really hard."

She won him over and by Christmas he sent her a card that said, "You are a really cool mentor."

Unfortunately, at the time when students most desperately need mentors—ages 12 to 18—adult volunteers are usually scarce at school. And yet, there's reason to believe that students would genuinely welcome adult mentoring.

Once I took a mini-poll of several high school students and asked them what one change would most improve their high school experience. Some noted longer lunch hours or more time with teachers before or after class. But several noted that if they could talk to a caring adult once a week about their goals and how to meet them—that would be most helpful. They didn't feel that it would need to take an hour, maybe only five minutes a week. The point is, these teens want to be heard, helped, and enabled to help others.

Retired people can also help young and old alike put problems into historical perspective. My neighbor Junius Idol (now deceased) was born in 1923. His family has farmed the same land since 1770. This original land grant farm was authorized by King Charles II via the Earl of Granville.

Idol said, "When I was grubbing (clearing trees off the land) as a kid, I learned *time frame*. You got on a job and you stayed on it for hours and hours. Removing one tree could take hours or days and you didn't give up. You learned perseverance, patience, and you overcame obstacles. *That* laid the foundation for the rest of my life."

That is how long-term challenges, such as growing to adulthood or changing a community, are solved, one root system at a time. It is hard work, but it can be done and has been done.

Retired people are a growing and largely untapped resource—a veritable *silver mine*. Perhaps it is time to *elevate the elderly* to a higher role in the community.

Higher Education

Every year, Wake Forest University (WFU) invites 40 middle and high school students from Kernersville to come to campus to learn about drug addiction. While there, students work with real scientists and examine real rat and human brains. The students absolutely love the experience and they share their stories with hundreds of friends and relatives.

The conception of this program gives remarkable insight into how great ideas come into existence. Though it didn't happen by accident, it didn't happen by design. It happened, quite simply, because WFU was caring and sharing within its realm of influence.

It all began in March of 2001, when the *Downtown Winston-Salem News* editor asked me to write a story on Dr. James E. Smith. Smith was the chairman of the Physiology and Pharmacology departments at WFU. As the interview proceeded, Smith mentioned that his department focuses on addiction studies—big studies—and WFU runs two of the biggest NIH (National Institute of Health) funded studies in the country.

I couldn't hold back from telling him of my special interest in drugs and addiction—especially when adolescents are involved. He listened attentively and at the end of the interview Smith invited me to attend the upcoming "Wake Forest University Addiction Studies Program for Journalists." The program was being held in Scottsdale, Arizona and included an invitation to attend the annual NIDA convention. It was a dream come true—my best chance to find the best answers to my remaining questions—but I did not have a dream budget. Smith encouraged me to apply for a scholarship and it was granted.

When introductions were made at the onset of the program, I realized what an honor it was to receive an invitation. Most of the journalists seated around the table had large regional, if not national, audiences. All my readers lived in little, tiny Kernersville.

As one might expect, the program was fascinating. Real scientists—the ones who actually do the studies—presented their findings. For instance, we learned that when a group of monkeys has unlimited access to alcohol, some will become alcoholics and some will not. Scientists can actually produce monkeys that are genetically predisposed to alcoholism. But if a group of monkeys has unlimited access to cocaine, *all* of them will become addicted. Cocaine is one of the most addictive substances known to man.

We had slide shows, hand-outs, books, and plenty of question and answer sessions. To be perfectly honest—though it was a red carpet affair—we were expected to work.

For those of us who came there looking for answers, that's exactly what we did. We worked! And yet, I wasn't sure what I was going to do with this newfound mountain of knowledge. The big "Drugs in Schools" investigation had ended five years earlier. I was still writing about drug issues, but mostly I reported on the successes of local students in their campaign to keep their student body free of drugs and alcohol.

And then it happened. As I was wandering around the NIDA exhibits, I saw a woman wearing a large button that read: I Dissected a Rat's Brain. The pin did exactly what it was supposed to do. It made me ask questions. It turned out that, in an unforgettable learning encounter, this woman was invited to a university to dissect the brain of a drug-addicted rat. The idea fascinated me. That would be a lesson that no one—no teen—would ever forget. I asked WFU Professors David Friedman and Kent Vrana if we could let students from Kernersville dissect a rat's brain.

While this was not possible, the professors arranged for other addiction studies lessons that would have a similar learning impact. For instance, while students could not dissect brains, the professors let them hold and examine real brains—even a human brain. Graduate students helped the teens observe live rats, some sober and some under the influence of drugs. Professor Kent Vrana presented a question and answer slide show with the latest scientific findings on the causes of addiction and brain changes associated with prolonged drug use. WFU graduate students helped the teens operate equipment that simulated reflex and response time changes while driving impaired.

While WFU hosted the event, *Kernersville Cares for Kids* arranged for transportation, sponsored an onsite pizza party, and provided supervision. At the end of the event, all 60 students went back to school with a conversation starter—a large white button. In the middle of the disk was a cute little pink mouse with a surprised look on his face. Above him it read: I Saw a Rat's Brain.

For most students, the climax of the event is holding that grey wrinkly mass—the human brain. It really brings it all home. It's all about the brain. It's real. It's fragile. We need to be careful with it.

This extremely fruitful teen learning experience grew from the fertile soils of *caring*. Wake Forest University *cared* enough about drug addiction research to create a way to bring together *caring* journalists with the *caring* scientists. The criteria for *caring* was evidenced in that the person was already actively involved in writing or researching drug and health issues. Journalists were under no obligation except to keep doing what they were already doing—but hopefully with better resources and more accuracy. In this way, WFU *hoped* the public would be better served.

In my case, my *caring* about drugs in the schools was with me all the time. Even when I didn't know I was thinking about it, it was always there in the back of my mind. Wherever I went—even to the WFU program—I was constantly looking for ways to help the students. So even though neither WFU nor I had any premonition of this exact outcome, the *caring* environment established by two *caring* entities created the best chance of conception. Eureka! The new idea of the "I Saw a Rat's Brain" field trip was hatched and the results were better than anyone could have imagined.

Other universities across the nation could create equally impelling programs.

The Media

The media industry differs from all other community resources. The media's sphere of influence transcends the limits of individual, business, or school boundaries and can move a community as a whole. As demonstrated in this book, a newspaper's ability to amplify *local voices* led to *local* school board policy change, which led to a *local* community partnership.

Kernersville News owner John Owensby knew this was possible. What he did not foresee is the way that he would be personally touched by the process. Though he was reluctant to co-found KCK, once he did, he never let go. As the years passed and I stepped off the KCK board, it was Owensby that watched over the program like a mother hen.

Why? Because he cared. He knew what it was like to lose a beloved brother to alcohol addiction. He knew what substance abuse of any kind can do to a family. In his neighborhood, he saw "good kids" from "good families" sacrifice promising futures on the altar of drugs. And he saw evidence of drug dealing at his children's high school. Owensby always *felt* concerned and when he found a way to *act* on that feeling he made a difference in himself and in his community.

> Newspapers across the nation can give their students a voice. Students *want* to tell adults what they think and how they feel. Subsequently, caring local adults can join with caring local students to help the community cope with the local drug problem.

Putting It All Together

After 15 years of wrestling, I finally figured out that drug abuse is not a scary monster that is too powerful to confront. Stripped of its mask and myths, drug abuse stands exposed as nothing more than a *symptom*. Like an elevated temperature—which signals an infection or problem in our physical body—drug abuse is a symptom of a life that is not working due to unresolved problems. Period!

Much of the solution to the drug and alcohol abuse problem comes down to the individual. Like billions of cells that make up a body, if we as individuals nourish and protect those in our sphere of influence, our body will be healthier. In the end, the healthier and more caring the individual, the family, the neighborhood, the state, the country, the hemisphere, and the world; the greater the chances of having a society free from the deception of illicit drug use.

www.UnderTheInfluence.org

About the Author

Patty Jo Sawvel learned to listen by first being listened to as a child. A sober, sickly, and stubborn child, PJ always had much to say. From her earliest memories, her father, Forrest Ray Bailey, always encouraged her to speak. By granting PJ the gift of a listening ear, he brought comfort, perspective, and wisdom into her life.

Patty Jo was the youngest girl in a family of nine children, but somehow her older brother, Roger M. Bailey, always guided the way. Not quite as patient a listener as their father, Roger nonetheless always helped Patty Jo reach things beyond her grasp. Over the years, Roger became a mentor, friend, and soul mate. Only 364 days older than PJ, he still shows her the way.

Dorothy Baker is the only school principal's name that Patty Jo remembers from her childhood. Mrs. Baker truly wanted to know what her students thought about the school, the teachers, and life itself. The way she treated and cared for *all the kids* in her school, her sense of justice and genuine love of children created in Patty Jo the desire to help all children feel like Mrs. Baker made her feel. Valuable. Listened to. Appreciated.

John Ed Staples made a dream come true for Patty Jo. Taking a chance on an unschooled and untried journalist, John gave Patty Jo a chance. A gentle teacher with a laugh as soothing as a warm cup of tea, John made learning an adventure and mistakes became nothing more than a predictable part of life. Staples continues to be a friend, a mentor, and a genuine source of encouragement.

Ed Friedenberg was *The Horse Whisperer* for writers, or at least for Patty Jo. Always careful to reflect her work back to her without any distortion from his own personal feelings, Ed was expert at asking just the right questions. His gentleness, his genuine intrigue with the story, and his determination to stay useful despite the toll of time still inspires Patty Jo.

Carl Clarke gladly took over when his friend Ed passed away in 2006. Carl added a whole new level of energy, enthusiasm, and drama to the writing process. Carl stopped talking and literally started acting as he clearly demonstrated effective public speaking at the Saturday "Students Only" Leaders Meetings. Carl continues to mentor, edit, and inspire the work of author and journalist Patty Jo Sawvel.

The Book Team

First and third photos by Amanda Weiss · Last Photo : Gilford A. Goodrow/ (Michigan)

Jim King · Amanda Weiss · Deborah Jarrett · Clif Sawvel

The transformation of this manuscript into a genuine printed book is again a testament to how things can happen in a caring community.

On April 28, 2011, I joined the Kernersville Chamber of Commerce and attended my very first Business After Hours Event. On that occasion, I met Jim King, a newcomer to Kernersville, with a background in national marketing and business. Jim also volunteered at the Chamber. When he found out I'd written a book, he offered to help me publish it.

In short, I was having a difficult time transitioning from writer to publisher. Jim gently facilitated the process each step of the way. First, he introduced me to Amanda Weiss. She was also new to town since 2010 and Jim had met her at the Kernersville Job Fair. Amanda, a gifted graphic design student at Guilford Technical Community College–who plans to transfer to Savannah College of Art and Design–was more than willing to help.

She had recently designed a book cover as a classroom project and like Jim, she wanted to see this book happen for the good of the community.

Next, Jim found Deborah Jarrett in a chance meeting downtown. In true Jim-style, he asked her who she was and what she did. When he found out Deborah had intense knowledge of word processing and proofing and that she was temporarily unemployed, he invited her to join the team.

Deborah was thrilled to help out. As she said, "I've lived in Kernersville my whole life and I know about KCK. I feel so honored to be a part of this."

Next, my son Clif, joined the team. He found a program to convert my manuscript into book format. Then Clif patiently taught me, step-by-step, to put all the text and pictures into one cohesive PDF file for printing.

And finally, there was CreateSpace and *Dan Poynter's Self-publishing Manual*–two entities looking out for the little guy or gal who is trying to publish a book on a shoestring budget. Once again, this entire process was proof that virtually anything is possible in a community where people care enough to help each other.

Thank you, Book Team, for a job well done.

"If we didn't have Kernersville Cares for Kids, we'd have to create it, because this community doesn't want a drug problem." –Bruce Boyer

www.kernersvillenc.com

KCK youth leader, Carter Maffett, who designed the 4'x 8' mural for the Town, is pictured with Bruce Boyer, president of Kernersville Chamber of Commerce and long-time friend of KCK.

"At our school, there really is a drug-free environment. People that use drugs or drink alcohol actually become unpopular."

–Carter Maffett, 8th grader at East Forsyth Middle School where 99.4% of students voluntarily signed up for drug-testing (2010).

http://www.wsfcs.k12.nc.us

A Reading Group Guide to *Under the Influence*

1. *Under the Influence* is a work of narrative non-fiction. How did the newspaper's mission to win the Community Service Award assist journalist Patty Jo Sawvel in finding answers to her own personal questions? Why did Sawvel choose to investigate "drugs in the schools?" What do you think would have happened if the journalist did not have a choice, but was assigned a topic? Do you think she would have moved the community?

2. Read Chapter 13, *Four Teens from Two Families* to become familiar with the Three Cs—a person's relationship to *control, coping skills,* and *connectedness.* Then read Mini-book IV, Lessons from Three Recovered Addicts. Discuss how each recovered addict related to each of the Three Cs.

3. Why did the survey prove to be a valuable tool to create a community conversation about drugs in the schools? Create a simple survey for your class or grade. Be sure that people do not put their names on their surveys. You might create a 3 question survey similar to the drug survey Sawvel used. Or, you might create a survey to check attitudes. For instance, you can ask: On a typical day, how often do you visit social networking sites such as Facebook? How many times have you seen photos or videos of teens drunk or using drugs or passed out on these sites? How many times a month do you attend religious services? Then, access a copy of the 2011 National Survey of American Attitudes on Substance Abuse XVI: Teens and Parents.
http://www.casacolumbia.org/upload/2011/20110824teensurveyreport.pdf
Compare your local survey responses to the findings of these same questions in the 2011 National Survey. Use this to estimate the risk factor for drug, tobacco, and alcohol abuse for students at your school.

4. Carver High School instituted the "It's My Call" voluntary random drug testing program to provide a means for students to earn respect. How did this help the students earn the community's respect? When the "It's My Call" program was promoted at Glenn High School and East Forsyth High School in Kernersville, respect was not the issue. What motivated these students to join the drug-testing program? Do you think a program like this could work in all schools?

5. Schools in the WS/FC District with 90 percent or more of their students enrolled in the drug-testing program typically had incentives. Incentives included free T-shirts, candy, and parties for students who signed up for drug testing. How do you feel about the use of incentives to influence the decisions of teens?

6. In the prologue the author asserts: ***Profound change often hangs by the thread of one committed person. Though different people fill that role as time marches on, that person is always someone who cares deeply, connects with others, and is convinced that change is imminent.*** List five people who were instrumental in the growth and continued development of *Kernersville Cares for Kids (KCK)*. From the student's point of view, how does KCK prove to its youth that the adult community cares about the teens?

7. KCK students defined leaders: Leaders breathe life into ideas and move people to action. What tools for leadership did the KCK students receive at their monthly leadership meetings? When did the KCK students actually begin to feel like leaders? Why is it empowering for students to do "real" work in their "real" community as volunteers in promoting the Lunch and Listen? Why do adults enjoy supporting teen leadership?

8. In Mini-book I: A Call for Compassion—10 Tips to Help Kids, several suggestions are given so that adults can support young people more effectively. Do you agree or disagree with these tips? If YOU were asked for an 11th tip, what would you want adults to know?

9. For years the author grappled with the concept of "who is my community" and "who is my neighbor?" Ultimately, she discovered that the real definitions transcend the dictionary and relate closely to the concept of choice. Based on Sawvel's findings: WHO is *your* community in your town? WHO is *your* neighbor? {Hint: See page 162}

10. Mini-book II: Parent Handbook cites a study which lists 12 family rules that have been proven to reduce the risk of self-destructive decisions by youth. Do you feel that these rules are fair? What consequences do you feel would be appropriate when a youth breaks each of the family rules?

*Please visit **UnderTheInfluence.ORG***

Free Online Resources

Truth shatters the shackles of myth. It works for adults and it works for young people. Below is a list of free resources to help you get started.

- www.UndertheInfluence.org A website for teens and adults based on this book. Activities and information are linked directly to this story. Videos, family explorations, and teacher resources.
- Growing Up Drug-free: A Parent's Guide to Prevention. (Google the title) Download at www.ed.gov/offices/OESE/SDFS   (Free 46-page PDF)
- Dynamic Teen Resource with TELEPHONE HOTLINE, videos, & more
    Go to www.TeenCentral.net
- Online videos, booklets, parent's telephone help-line 1-855-378-4373.   Visit www.drugfree.org.   Topics include:
    13. Cheering your child up when a friend lets her down.
    14. Does your teen have a toxic friend? 20 questions to find out.
    15. Helping your child through life's major transitions.
    Site also includes a "Time to Act" and "Time to Get Help" section.
- Questions Young People Ask: Answers That Work Vol. I & II. Visit www.jw.org/books   Select publications. Select Young People Ask Vol. I or Vol. II. (Free PDF) Topics include: Drinking, Drugs, Peer Pressure
    NOTE: This site has books and videos in over 400 languages, and a read aloud feature. Vol. I Appendix: Questions Parent's Ask—Communication, Rules, Independence, Sex and Dating, Emotional Issues, Spirituality.
- Suicide, Bullying, Self-harm, Drugs, Alcohol—See how other teens have overcome their obstacles **http://us.reachout.com/wecanhelpus/**
- Visit www.NationalParentHelpline.org for downloads or call
    1-855-4A-PARENT (1-855-427-2736) for a one-on-one conversation.
    1. Your Child May Be Stressed
    2. Many Kids Who Drink May Get Liquor at Home
    3. Tips For Kids to Stop Cyberbullying
- For a complete PDF of the 2011 National Study cited many times in this book http://www.casacolumbia.org/upload/2011/20110824teensurveyreport.pdf
- www.parentingisprevention.org
- www.prevention.org
- www.safeyouth.org
- www.madd.org
- www.saddonline.com
- www.JustThinkTwice.com
- www.NHTSA.gov
- www.samhsa.gov
- http://www.greatschools.org/parenting/4503-dangerous-teen-trends.gs

Photographer Gil Goodrow

Patty Jo Sawvel is a two-time North Carolina Press Association award-winning journalist. *Under the Influence: The Town That Listened to its Kids* is based on her stories that originally received first place for investigative reporting.

A member of the National Speakers Association, she continues to enlighten and enliven thousands of listeners as she "gives kids a national voice" on television, radio, and before live audiences of all ages. For more information, a downloadable media kit, video clips, or other resources visit her online at UnderTheInfluence.Org or write to

Patty Jo Sawvel
931-B South Main Street #215
Kernersville, NC 27284

www.UnderTheInfluence.org

Index

alcohol, iii, abuse, 321, cost, 334, friends, 348, **Mariah story, 355,** risk, 334, **Theodrick story 354-55,**

bully, **cyberbully, 340, 351,**Ruth Fair Story 281-84, **322, 351**

choice, 32, 60, 77, opposite,**99,** 115, drug use,**117-21,** 162, 178, 187, 212, **LaRue Story, 215-16, Gaudio story, 255-6,** power of **270,** 285, 287, 316, 317, predictors of, **324-327,** 334-5, friends, **348,** cyberbully, **351,** peer pressure, **354,** alcohol, 357, challenge, 361, Twelve Steps,**368-9.**

community, care, 127, choices, 316, church, 61, connectedness, **159-62,** 226-7, **definition, 162,** 1-3, drug testing, 327, how to involvement, 57-60, leaders, 37-43, meeting, 53,**73-5,** move,7, 16-19, police, **133-5,** 156, questions, 388-9 resources, 47, role, **381-4,** Service Award, **87-98,** students vs. adults, 27-9, support, 307, thankfulness, 253, volunteers, **264-5,**

connectedness, (dis)connect, preface, 204, 380, 345, community, 66, 73, 229, drug, 159, family, 5, 75, **324-26, John Hopkins study of, 117-23,** loss of, 166,Lunch & Listen, 265, **parental, 324-6** school, 25, **226-8,** teen, 139,

control, anger, **107, anger story, 340,** Beth **story, 346, Carol story, 358, Drew story, 354,** drugs, 106, 116, **187, 198,** 362, government, **314,** loss of, 9, 40, 76, 105, 362, 370, Office of Nat'l Drug Con. Pol. 213, parental, 83,relationship to, **324-26, self, 109, 122, 314, study of, 118, Tommy story, 373**

coping skills, **Carol story, 357-8,** change, 359-60, **defined, 345-6,** Jack story, **356, Katie story,** 320, **list of 20, 347, study of, 118-21, three Cs, 324-6,**

divorce, **Katie story, 342, Lindsey story, 343, Lorrie story, 342, Greg (abandon) 344,** study of, 319-20, verbal bashing/withhold visitation, 323,

Drug, addicts, 362-77, definitions, 187, 276, 362, disease, 54, **laws, 209-14,** 315 teen, 38, 209-10, 315, use, 13, 33, 46

drug testing, **Carver H.S., 62, 64-69**, at work, 42, **community choice, 78-9, deterrent,** 85, **146-7, 159**, enrollment %, 312, excuse to say "no", **60,**Glenn H.S., 89-92, **home testing, 208, 333**, implement, 209-14 incentives, 201, KCK, 231, **national view, 171-3**, privacy violation, 50, **64**, proof of care, 207, **punitive/non punitive, 130, 211-13, 211,** school brd. Policy, 125-30, school safety,185,**study of, 225-28**, **test 10-13 yr. olds, 177-8**

influence, community, 162, **Drew story, 354,** drug testing, 222, drugs, 118, 184, 189, 196, **family, 121, 329-30,** friends,**348,** 357, gang, 77,general, 360, 384, media, 383, **Mariah story, 355,** peer, 75, 83, 117, 336, personal, 323, 337, 359, 379, **positive leaders, 271, 273,** 316, **Sheila story, 369**

Kernersville Cares for Kids (KCK),community involvement, 264-65, **history, 136**-37, 149, 152, 161-64, 179, **217-19, mission statement, 230,** update 2013, **307-8**

Kernersville News, **community journalism, 1-3, 15-17,** 75, **Community Service Award, 3, 86-87, 93-94,** forum, preface, **John Owensby,** 143, 157, 383, **John Staples,** 2-4, 29, 57, 126, 160, reporter, prologue, epilogue, **survey, 30-35,** vox populi, 321,

Leadership, **Chuck Chambers, 70,** community, 95, 156-58, define, 271, education, 68, KCK, 163-4, 192, 194, 201, 304, **307-8,** lack of, 140, 172, 292, lead by example, 132, **m**eeting, 57, newspaper, 94, school, 174, 179, 199, **201, 223, 378-9, youth leadership,** 137, 162, 178, 229, 232, 234, 238, 263, 267, **270-75, 280-81, 285, 293-94,**

peer pressure, **Drew story, 354, Fred/Jill story 118-20, 275,**investigate/normalize 335-37, **Jason story, 40, Mariah story, 355,** negative, 105, 109, positive, 60, 61, 75, 77, 78, 307, 326, **responses that work, 356, Theodrick story, 354,**

stress, **Bobby story, 107-8,**coping, 119-20, 340-50, list to cope, 347,**romance, 349, Ryan story, 112-13, top 10 stressors, 340,**

tobacco, **CASA study pdf link, 388**, disease, 54, farming, 151, friends, 335, pledge, 205, risk, 83, promote tobacco free, 307